More Praise for Steve Kemper's

A Labyrinth of Kingdoms

"H   ich Barth belongs in the ranks of the greatest explorers of Africa.
     like most of the others, he was less interested in imperial con-
     ind self-promotion than in the cultures, the peoples, the lan-
     ;, and the ancient manuscripts that he found there. It's a pleasure
     a lively, readable biography of him in English at last."

—Adam Hochschild, author of
King Leopold's Ghost and *To End All Wars*

times a book grabs you by the throat and won't let you put it
I recently experienced that with *A Labyrinth of Kingdoms*."

—Pamela Toler, History in the Margins blog

s hope Steve Kemper's fine study of an extraordinary person-
ives Barth the wider, albeit posthumous, audience he so widely
es."   —Justin Marozzi, *Literary Review* (London)

per ably resurrects the unsung and unappreciated accomplish-
; of this intrepid explorer and clearly shows that his high level of
arship and attention to detail are relevant and useful today."

—Ben Moise, *Post and Courier*

"Barth's story comes alive in Kemper's capable hands; *A Labyrinth of Kingdoms* is erudite but never stuffy—at its core, the book is an excellent adventure story." —Biblioklept

"An enticing read of history and anthropology, very much recommended reading." —*Midwest Book Review*

"Steve [Kemper's] book brings home what an extraordinary feat a 19th-century expedition really was. . . . The story is an insight into what really lay in those blank bits on European maps of the time. . . . [T]hese areas, far from being blank, teemed with life." —Nicholas Walton, New Books in African Studies

"Stories in the vein of explorer Heinrich Barth's are seldom told outside of the summer blockbuster. . . . [Kemper] documents the remarkable journey of one man in the darkest territories of unknown Islamic Africa." —Louisville.com

"Kemper has created a vivid celebration of determination and curiosity while exploring a hostile and still little-known region." —*Richmond Times Dispatch*

"A fascinating new account of a much-overlooked explorer and his incredible journey." —Newport Library blog

"A nicely rounded literary study of an intrepid explorer undone by the cultural biases of the time." —*Kirkus Reviews*

"[Barth's] story has been known primarily to scholars, so this is an important corrective." —*Library Journal*

"*A Labyrinth of Kingdoms* is a fascinating account both of one man's journey and of African cultures on the eve of European expansion. . . . Barth's story is equal parts adventure and scholarship. Kemper treats both with a sure hand."   —Shelf Awareness

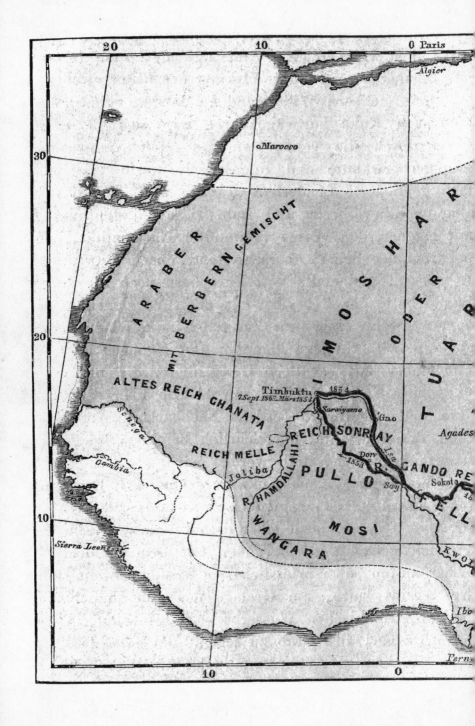

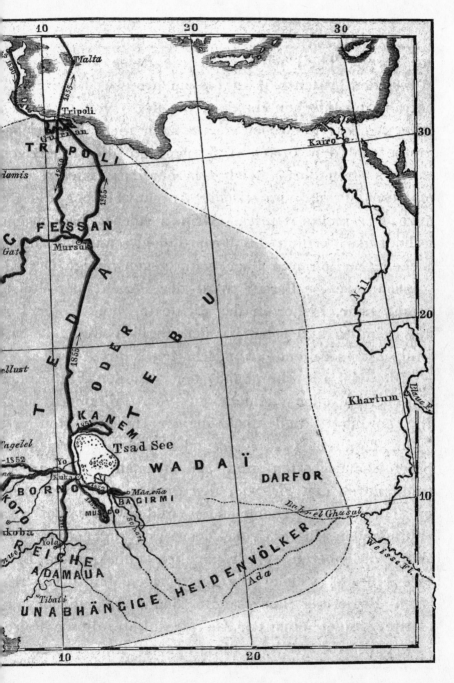

A Labyrinth of Kingdoms

A
Labyrinth
of
Kingdoms

10,000 Miles
through
Islamic Africa

STEVE KEMPER

W. W. NORTON & COMPANY | New York   London

Copyright © 2012 by Steve Kemper

Map courtesy of the Watkinson Library, Trinity College, Hartford, Connecticut.

For information about permission to reproduce selections from this book, write to
Permissions, W. W. Norton & Company, Inc., 500 Fifth Avenue, New York, NY 10110

For information about special discounts for bulk purchases, please contact
W. W. Norton Special Sales at specialsales@wwnorton.com or 800-233-4830

Manufacturing by RR Donnelley, Harrisonburg
Book design by Helene Berinsky
Production manager: Devon Zahn

Library of Congress Cataloging-in-Publication Data

Kemper, Steve.
A labyrinth of kingdoms : 10,000 miles through Islamic Africa / Steve Kemper. — 1st ed.
p. cm.
Includes bibliographical references and index.
ISBN 978-0-393-07966-1 (hardcover)
1. Barth, Heinrich, 1821–1865—Travel—Africa. 2. Africa, Central—Discovery and
exploration—German. 3. Africa, Central—Discovery and exploration—British.
4. Africa, Central—Description and travel. 5. Africa, North—Discovery and
exploration—German. 6. Africa, North—Discovery and exploration—British.
7. Africa, North—Description and travel. 8. Explorers—Africa, Central—Biography.
9. Explorers—Africa, North—Biography. 10. Explorers—Germany—Biography. I. Title.
DT351.B277K46 2012
916.70423—dc23
2012002562

ISBN 978-0-393-34623-7 pbk.

W. W. Norton & Company, Inc., 500 Fifth Avenue, New York, N.Y. 10110
www.wwnorton.com

W. W. Norton & Company Ltd., Castle House, 75/76 Wells Street, London W1T 3QT

1 2 3 4 5 6 7 8 9 0

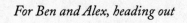

For Ben and Alex, heading out

Contents

Prologue

THE YOUNG SCIENTIST KNEW HE WOULD SOON DIE OF THIRST. LAST night, far across the desert plain, he had seen bonfires built by his companions to guide him back to the caravan. But he was too weak and feverish to move, with no strength to gather wood for an answering fire. He shot his pistol twice, but the Saharan night absorbed the sound. No reply came.

Behind him rose the peak called the Palace of the Demons. His Tuareg guides had warned him not to antagonize the powerful desert spirits by trespassing on their sacred mountain. He scoffed at their superstitions. He was a scientist, trained by the greatest scholars in Europe, and he was fit and strong. He suspected that this verboten home of demons might be some ancient place of worship where he might find inscriptions or carvings that added to the world's store of knowledge. Nothing could keep him from exploring such a place. "At any cost," he said, a phrase he didn't yet fully understand. The expedition's leader asked him not to go alone. The young scientist shrugged him off as overcautious, but persuaded a younger colleague to come along. He agreed to meet the expedition at the next well, as he often did, impatient with the caravan's slow pace.

Now his self-confidence looked like fatal arrogance. First he underestimated the distance to the mountain. He also hadn't expected the extensive plain of black pebbles, so tiring to traverse, and scorching from the radiant heat. Nor had he foreseen the deep ravine that protected the mountain like a moat, adding more distance. His companion, exhausted, had turned back there, but he refused to retreat.

When he finally reached the mountaintop, he found nothing but wild jumbled boulders, as if titans had been at war. He began the descent. By noon he was out of water. His exertions under the summer Saharan sun drained him. He kept moving, though he now had no idea where the caravan was, or his position in relationship to it. In midafternoon he saw some huts and hobbled toward them, desperate for water. They were abandoned. He dragged himself beneath a slender leafless tree that stood alone on the arid plain. He watched for rescuers. Near sunset a string of camels in the distance sparked some hope, but it dissolved, a mirage.

Fever kept him from sleeping that night. Dawn cheered him until he realized that this day's sun would finish him. He changed position as it rose, crawling after the shadow cast by the tree's slim trunk. As he began dying, his body pulled moisture from wherever it could find any, to keep his heart pumping. His joints stiffened, his lips cracked, his tongue swelled from lack of saliva. Around noon, when there was only enough shade for his head, thirst drove him mad. He cut his arm and sucked blood from the wound. The effort threw him into delirium.

As the sun set, he flickered in and out of consciousness, his mind drifting. His dreams and ambitions had burned to cinders on this flat wasteland. He would not make spectacular scholarly discoveries that changed Europe's perception of Africa. He would not visit the ancient kingdom of Bornu on Lake Chad or the Fulani empire of Sokoto. He would not explore the mysteries of Timbuktu. His contract with the British Foreign Office would die with him. Instead of fame, his reward would be a footnote in the history of African exploration, another futile death among so many others. He would not end his days among the scholars of Europe, but here, a husk in the shadow of a gaunt tree. He commended himself to God and closed his eyes.

After a time, from a distance, he heard the bawl of a camel. "It was the most delightful music I ever heard in my life," he later wrote. Like Lazarus, he had been given a second chance, and he promised himself to make the most of it.

HIS NAME was Heinrich Barth. In 1849 he joined a small British expedition to Islamic North and Central Africa. His five-and-a-half-year, 10,000-mile adventure ranks among the greatest journeys in the annals of exploration. His feats rival, if not surpass, those of the most famous names in nineteenth-century African travel: Park, Burton, Speke, Livingstone, Stanley, Baker, Cameron. In terms of knowledge collected and ongoing relevance, none of these famous men compare with Barth, whose discoveries and written work are considered indispensable by modern historians, geographers, linguists, and ethnographers.

Yet because of shifting politics, European preconceptions about Africa, and his own thorny personality, Barth has been almost forgotten. The general public has never heard of him or his epic journey or his still-pertinent observations about Africa and Islam. His monumental five-volume *Travels and Discoveries in North and Central Africa*, written first in English, is rare even in libraries. Though he made his journey for the British government, he has never had a biography in English. Barth fell through a crack in history.

This is a forgotten story of survival, adventure, and scientific discovery by a remarkable man.

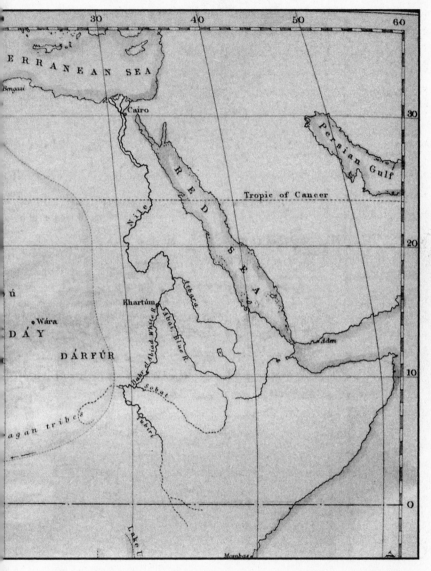

Map of the Expedition's Routes, 1850–55
(from *Travels and Discoveries,* drawn by August Petermann)

A Labyrinth of Kingdoms

1

Preparations

THE AUGURIES FOR AFRICAN EXPLORATION MUST HAVE BEEN STRONG in 1821. Both Richard Burton and Samuel Baker, famous for their discoveries in East Africa, were born that year, and the British explorers Walter Oudney, Hugh Clapperton, and Dixon Denham left for their pioneering journey to Lake Chad and the kingdom of Bornu. Heinrich Barth, the next European to see Bornu, was born February 16, 1821 in Hamburg, Germany.

He was the third of four children born to Johann and Charlotte Barth. Johann came from austere beginnings. His parents, Thuringian peasants, both died when he was a boy. This calamity had a silver lining, since the orphan was taken in by a relative in Hamburg, a cosmopolitan port in northern Germany. The city offered ample opportunities to the sharp and energetic. At first Johann worked as a butcher, but he soon found his way into Hamburg's mercantile class, and married into a respectable Hamburg family. By the time Heinrich was born, Johann was a trader doing thriving business with Hanseatic cities along the coast of northern Europe. He and Charlotte were strict Lutherans, and they raised their children according to exacting notions of morality, duty, industry, and discipline.

Though uneducated, Johann respected learning and gave his children the best possible schooling. In Hamburg that meant the Johanneum, the city's oldest and most rigorous academy, founded in 1529. Barth was accepted in 1832 at age eleven. From his first days there he was a misfit. He was already exhibiting many of his marked characteristics: a gift for art and languages, severe self-discipline, omnivorous intellectual energy, and a devotion to scholarship that sometimes looked like conceit. All these set him far apart from his classmates, socially as well as academically.

"It is true that Barth was no ordinary schoolboy," recalled one of his schoolmates from those years. "He interacted very little with the majority of the class. . . . During the breaks he mostly stood alone at the end of the bench, displaying an aristocratic aloofness towards his classmates and only exchanging a few words with his closer acquaintances. He rarely smiled and I never heard him laugh heartily. . . . He also studied things that were not even part of the curriculum. People said that he was teaching himself Arabic, which to us brainless schoolboys certainly seemed the pinnacle of insanity."

The Arabic rumor was true. Barth was also teaching himself English, which he could read and speak fluently by age thirteen, a crucial skill in coming years. Despite the Johanneum's reputation for academic rigor, Barth later wrote that he felt understimulated there. In addition to his independent language studies, he set himself the extracurricular task of absorbing the classic histories, geographies, and scientific works of the Greeks and Romans, in the original languages. An avid book collector, he amassed a large library—another hobby that baffled his classmates.

He was weak and sickly in his early teens, until he focused his considerable self-discipline on his body. During recesses at school, instead of playing or lounging with the other boys, he did gymnastics and arm exercises. To toughen himself he took cold baths, even in winter. His classmates noted that he did these things with grim intensity rather than gusto. By his late teens Barth was a strapping young man well over 6 feet tall.

It's tempting to see his mental and physical regimens as signs of an explorer-in-training, to imagine him daydreaming about distant lands while gazing over the masts hung with foreign flags in Hamburg's crowded harbor. More likely he was in thrall to his beloved Greeks and their ideal of physical and intellectual excellence.

His quirks amused and mystified his schoolmates and ensured that he had few friends. No doubt he endured the mockery of conventional teenaged boys for eccentric, introverted bookworms. He must have been lonely and felt his oddity keenly. He longed for release from the stifling atmosphere of the Johanneum into the wider horizons of university and adulthood.

"Mostly left to his own devices, the boy early on developed a strong will and a large ego," wrote Gustav von Schubert, Barth's brother-in-law, close friend, and biographer. "He occasionally seemed to believe that he was unique and deserved special treatment. This characteristic helped him a great deal on his later expeditions, which covered great distances and were usually undertaken alone. In day-to-day life, however, it made him come across as gruff and awkward. On top of this his strict, acerbic character was attuned only to a sense of duty. Neither humor nor happy enjoyment of life made any impression on him."

In October 1839, two weeks after graduating from the Johanneum, Barth enrolled in the University of Berlin. This was arguably the most dynamic university in Europe, especially in the sciences. It was the world's first research-intensive institution, a ground-breaking model of higher education that came to dominate Western universities. Berlin's brilliant professors were revolutionizing the fields of history, geography, and philology, and were leading the way in the evolving fields of archeology, biology, botany, geology, and ethnology. The intellectual foment there attracted exceptional students, including, during Barth's years, Karl Marx, Friedrich Engels, Mikhail Bakunin, Jacob Burckhardt, and Søren Kierkegaard.

Though the University of Berlin was the pinnacle of higher education in Germany, colleges throughout the country were offering progressive instruction in the sciences, with facilities that included well-equipped research laboratories. By contrast, Oxford and Cambridge were snubbing science at the time, and research labs were almost unheard of in British schools. Science was considered the province of enthusiastic amateurs (Charles Darwin comes to mind).

Consequently, by the mid nineteenth century German universities were graduating thousands of students in scientific disciplines every year, while Britain turned out only a handful. When the British government decided to mount an expedition to the Sudan in 1849, it looked to Germany for scientists to accompany it. (By the end of the century British universities had started to catch up, but even then the science faculties tended to be German or to have doctorates from German universities, and the students learned from textbooks written in German or translated from it. This eventually led to xenophobic fears that Oxford and Cambridge were being "Prussianized"—a backlash whose early phase would sting Barth.)

At the University of Berlin, Barth met three dazzling professors who shaped his intellectual development and professional future: Alexander von Humboldt, the great botanist who pioneered the field of biogeography after spending five years exploring South America; Carl Ritter, who with von Humboldt is credited with transforming geographical study to include what are now commonly called "earth sciences"—geology, geophysics, soil science, geodesy, and comparative geography; and Philipp August Böckh, who expanded the field of philology beyond linguistics and literary arts to encompass all the cultural expressions of the ancient world—history, philosophy, science, religion, law and government, and daily life.

For Barth the university offered almost too much stimulation, too many choices. He was unsure where to concentrate his energies. This unfamiliar problem made him unhappy and restless. During his second semester he decided to drop academics for action—a trip to Italy to study ruins and perhaps to clarify his life's direction. The trip was no lark. He prepared for it thoroughly, first by learning Italian. With his father's blessing and funding, he spent nearly a year traveling alone to classical sites throughout Italy—Venice, Florence, Rome, Naples, Sicily. He was nineteen.

The trip exhilarated him, though not because of Italian cuisine, women, or other delights of *la dolce vita* that might distract a young man far from home. Fun was never among Barth's goals. No, the trip elated him because he felt independent and self-confident, intellectually stimulated and physically robust. Traveling alone, he immersed himself in the solitary world of scholarship. He took copious detailed notes, a lifelong habit. "I am working terribly hard," he wrote home from Rome in November 1840. "I go everywhere on foot. It has become no problem for me to walk around for nine hours without eating anything apart from a few chestnuts or some grapes."

The trip confirmed his fascination with ancient Mediterranean cultures and activated his lifelong wanderlust. But it didn't clarify his educational path. Back in Berlin he bounced between classes in archeology, law, geography, and philology. His lack of a firm direction frustrated him. He considered the academic year almost wasted, despite spending all his time studying. Socially he remained inept and aloof. "His disciplined personality meant that true enjoyment of the Berlin social scene was out of the question for him," noted his brother-in-law von Schubert. "He was only interested in his academic pursuits."

In May 1842, Hamburg's "Great Fire" destroyed nearly a quarter of the inner city, including half of Johann Barth's business and Heinrich's entire precious library. Barth's letter to his father about these losses was characteristically mature and dispassionate: "One's only secure possessions are those which he carries within him. Wealth? Can be gone in a second. Outward joy? Breaks as easily as glass. But inner strength and refinement can never be taken away—they only disappear when one ceases to exist, making them superfluous." He was twenty-one.

Despite the financial blow, Johann funded another trip for Barth during that year's summer break, along the Rhine to Switzerland. Over the next two semesters Barth took classes from some of the university's most renowned professors: classical antiquity with Böckh, geography with Ritter, philosophy with Friedrich Schelling, and history with Leopold von Ranke.

Several letters written home during this period provide glimpses of Barth's ambitions, idealism, and loneliness, his gravity and devotion to learning. "My only interest," he wrote, "is my own education, my own intellectual competence, so that I may be as useful to humanity as possible—for which I would gladly earn recognition and possibly even a bit of fame." On March 20, 1843, he wrote:

To see how, from hour to hour, day to day, one delves into science more deeply, more vividly, and more precisely—how one works ever more thoroughly as part of a small, specialized field and sees more clearly the relationship between this one small part and all of science, to all of mankind's intellectual progression—is an endless, deep, quiet joy. Of course this can result in monstrous egotism—that one cares about nothing but one's own work. When one finds complete satisfaction in one's own thoughts, one learns to do without, or even scorn, other people. But the more one's inner spirit is filled with scientific thought, the more it drives outward as well—it drives one to share this intellectual life with other people and thus give them strength to keep fighting against their other, sensual sides. This is the victory of true science.

Perhaps most revealing in its psychological nakedness is this letter:

I have a great drive, an absolutely selfless drive, to find the great, the true, and the beautiful. To be useful to humanity, to encourage them towards common enlightenment, to feed their spirits and give them strength—this is my only goal. And I see that very few people really know me, that most people misunderstand me, and others slander me terribly. But I am too proud to defend myself before these often pathetic people, to share thoughts and feelings with them that they would only laugh at anyway. I'm not so full of myself that I believe I have found the truth, but I do think that I am not a pathetic person and that I can be useful in the grand scheme of things.

"A scientific nature like this one," commented von Schubert, "is destined for bitter experiences."

BARTH BUCKLED DOWN to work on his doctoral dissertation. His esoteric subject was trade relations in ancient Corinth, a busy port like Hamburg. After receiving his degree in June 1844, he returned to the family home, with the understanding that he could spend the next six months working undisturbed for ten hours per day. His goal was a university appointment, which would require several years of postdoctoral research. Meanwhile he looked for work as a private tutor, without success. Probably just as well, since his introverted and sometimes abrasive manner wasn't suited for young students.

After six months at home, with no job prospects, Barth asked his father to fund a grand research trip. He wanted to travel the shores of the Mediterranean along the three continents that bordered it. A scholarly book about such a trip, he told his father, might help secure a university position. Johann, ever supportive, agreed to the plan.

Barth threw himself into the preparation. In late January 1845 he left Hamburg for London, where he perfected his spoken and written Arabic through intensive tutoring. He also roamed the British Museum to study its collection of antiquities. He paid attention to practical matters as well, securing letters of protection from the British consulates on the Barbary coast. And he sought useful contacts, such as Chevalier Christian Charles Josias Bunsen, the shrewd, urbane Prussian ambassador to the Court of St. James's, who would play a crucial role in Barth's future.

On August 7, 1845, he touched Africa for the first time at Tangiers.

Next came Algeria, Malta, Tunisia, Tripoli, and Cyrenaica. He started across the northern desert to Egypt. One night as he lay in his tent, he was attacked by eight Bedouin bandits. He fought back with his sword but was shot in both legs and knocked unconscious. One slug passed through his right leg; the other lodged in his left thigh. The bandits evidently assumed that Barth's fancy red chest held gold, and must have been irate to find a worthless machine inside—a new invention for recording images called a daguerreotype. Barth also lost most of his papers, sketches, and photographs—a lesson he never forgot. He was lucky to survive the attack, the first of many scrapes with rapacious desert nomads.

After a brief convalescence he took a detour up the Nile to Wadi Halfa, then across the desert to the ruins of Berenice on the Red Sea, and finally back north to Cairo. He crossed the desert again to Gaza, where he learned Turkish and the Syrian-Arabic dialect before continuing through Palestine to Damascus. He returned to the sea at Beirut and went north through the ancient Phoenician cities along the Syrian coast. Then Cyprus, Rhodes, and the rock tombs of Lycia in Turkey. By September 1847 he was en route to Constantinople. From there he headed west through Smyrna, Mykonos, and Athens, and finally on toward home. He reached his parents' house on December 27, 1847. He had been traveling for nearly three years and was almost twenty-seven.

The trip changed him. He had been tested by the myriad difficulties of foreign travel through dozens of cultures, many of them Islamic. He had, as he later wrote, "familiarized myself with that state of human society where the camel is man's daily companion, and the culture of the date-tree his chief occupation." He had learned how to travel leanly and alone for long periods. He had coped with fever, illness, and an attack by murderous thieves. He had greatly deepened his knowledge of history and languages. The trip sharpened his ability to detect the connective tissues between countries, cultures, and eras, links that he would later find in Central Africa.

The trip also intensified certain personality traits. Von Schubert met him for the first time six months after Barth's return, when the young soldier came to ask for the hand of Barth's beloved younger sister, Mathilde. "He had become the very model of the imperious, the closed-off, and the ascetic," remembered von Schubert. "His behavior at that time was still very much under the influence of this trip: he was silent and withdrawn. Later we became close friends, but it took a long time before I was able to thaw the ice around his heart and experience the depths of his character. In his first letter to me, he wrote, 'If you make my sister unhappy, I will shoot you dead,' which was clear enough."

Immediately after his return, Barth renewed his search for an academic position, but two months later France's revolution of 1848 triggered a wave of turbulence across Europe. In Germany, republicans agitated for reform and nationalists urged unification. (The German Confederation comprised thirty-nine independent German-speaking states.) Prussia took advantage of the chaos to invade Denmark's German-speaking duchies, Schleswig and Holstein, next door to Hamburg.

Colleagues urged Barth to jump into the ferment, but he declined. His long absence in Africa and the Middle East had left him aloof from national politics. Besides, history had taught him that patriotic fervor was often the enemy of truth and knowledge, his guiding values. A decade later when chauvinism in both Britain and Germany lashed him, he was shocked that honorable people could put narrow national interests above science and the pursuit of knowledge.

He may have paid more attention to another piece of stunning news in 1848: a German missionary in East Africa named Johann Rebmann reported that he had visited the interior near the Equator and seen a mountain called Kilimanjaro, whose summit was covered with snow— news that a prominent British geographer named William Desborough Cooley, who later became important to Barth, mocked as absurd, since logic dictated that snow at the Equator was impossible.

Barth also might have read in 1848 about the departure of two British naturalists, Henry Walter Bates and Alfred Russel Wallace, for the Amazon. It's even possible that he noticed the publication that same year of *Travels in the Great Desert of Sahara, in the Years of 1845 and 1846* by a British abolitionist named James Richardson, who would soon change Barth's life.

What's certain is that Barth avoided the brushfires of German politics and stayed focused on his professional and personal future. Full of self-confidence from his travels, he began writing an account of his Mediterranean journey. He also decided to get married. Neither venture ended well. Barth's utter lack of social skills, particularly with women, and his unease in parlors doomed him as a suitor. One can only imagine his awkward facsimile of courtship, his attempts to charm his chosen damsel with scientific and historic data, his frequent lapses into moody impatience with small talk and perfumed niceties.

She rejected him. "The experience was a great blow to Barth's self-esteem," wrote von Schubert. "His bitter fear of romantic relationships lasted for a long time after that, and even in later years he could not bring himself to enter into marriage."

Barth assuaged himself with his professional prospects, which looked brighter by early 1849. Through the efforts of Ritter and Böckh he was offered a part-time job for the spring semester as a lecturer in the university's archeology department. Best of all, the first volume of his *Wanderings Along the Shores of the Mediterranean* was coming out in June.

But again he reaped bitterness, first in the classroom. His lecture topic was soil composition, principally in Africa. This subject somehow failed to captivate his few students. His droning lecture style snuffed any possible sparks of interest. The students quickly stopped attending. Stunned by his failure to enthrall young minds by reciting scientific data, Barth canceled the class.

His book fared marginally better. Reviewers praised his energy and stamina, as well as his wide-ranging and meticulous scholarship. But like the students, reviewers were bored by the book's numbing welter of undifferentiated detail and its tedious pace. The general public yawned. The publisher dropped plans to print the second volume.

In the space of a year, all of Barth's glowing ambitions had turned to ash. He had failed as a teacher, a writer, and a wooer. Still, the trip around the Mediterranean had demonstrated his strengths, to himself and others. He also had discovered his twin passions—deep scholarship and rigorous travel—but hadn't figured out how to combine them into a living. He began daydreaming about a long trip into Asia. He was twenty-eight.

In early October 1849, Carl Ritter asked him a question that changed everything.

2

Invitation to Africa

AFTER EIGHTEEN MONTHS OF SILENCE FROM THE BRITISH FOREIGN Office, James Richardson's patience was running thin. He had been pushing the British government to fund an expedition into the Sudan but couldn't get a response.

(At the time, "the Sudan" referred to the vast area south of the Sahara and ten degrees or so north of the Equator, from the Atlantic coast to the mountains of Ethiopia, which encompasses most of today's Senegal, Gambia, Guinea, Mali, Burkina Faso, Niger, Chad, and Sudan, as well as northern Nigeria and northern Cameroon.)

Born in 1809, Richardson had trained as an evangelical minister. His two great drives were to spread Christianity and to abolish slavery, "the most gigantic system of wickedness the world ever saw." He put himself on the line for his principles, spending several years in northern Africa to gather information about the slave trade for Britain's Anti-Slavery Society. His time in Africa also gave him a more nuanced perspective on the continent and on Islam than was typical in Victorian Britain, where the public's perceptions rarely went beyond harems, slavers, and naked dark skin. Richardson, by contrast, credited the strengths and benefits of Islam to Africans. He was also commendably blunt about how Britain's love of money led it to overlook horrible policies and practices among its own merchants and allies abroad. Europe's effect on

Africa, he wrote, was "to plunge her into deeper misery and profounder degradation."

Like most proselytizers, he could be tactless and grating. In the introduction to his two-volume account of his fact-finding trip to northern Africa, *Travels in the Great Desert of Sahara, in the Years of 1845 and 1846* (1848), he comes across as peevish, thin-skinned, self-congratulatory, and holier-than-thou. He had the evangelist's knack for being irritating even when he was right.

Still, his commitment to abolition went beyond finger-pointing and grandstanding. He wanted to be on the front lines. His firsthand look at slavery had convinced him that prayers and protests in London wouldn't reform slavers in Africa. The best way to do God's work against this abomination was not religious missions that encouraged piety, but new consulates that encouraged trade. Open the gates of commerce between Africa and Europe, ran the argument, and Africans would give up the depraved traffic in flesh for an exchange of products with fewer moral and financial risks. Prosperity would make virtue possible, virtue would lead naturally to Christianity, and together this trinity would replace barbarism with civilization. Merchants on both continents would profit. Oppressed tribes would no longer suffer the depredations of slave-raiders. And since Africa was an unplucked market, Britain could extend its influence far into the future by getting there first, in particular before the French.

The notion of using commerce as the flying wedge of Christianity and civilization was common by the mid nineteenth century. Richardson hoped it would convince the British government to fund an expedition. He knew that Lord Palmerston, the secretary of state for foreign affairs, opposed slavery but also disliked political entanglements in foreign lands. Yet Palmerston did believe wholeheartedly in the blessings of commerce. "It is the business of government," Palmerston wrote in 1841, "to open and to secure the roads for the merchant."

But before the blessings of British commerce, Christianity, and civilization could rectify African barbarism, there was groundwork to do.

First, prospective avenues of trade had to be discovered and mapped. True, Mungo Park had probed inland from the west coast before being killed somewhere on the Niger River in 1806. True, the Lander brothers had solved a major geographic question in 1830 by proving that the Niger didn't flow east across the continent to the Nile, as many geographers had assumed, but turned sharply south at Gao and emptied into the Gulf of Guinea. In the early 1820s, Oudney, Clapperton, and Denham had traveled south through the Sahara to the kingdom of Bornu in Central Africa, on the west side of Lake Chad. But they hadn't determined whether the lake was connected by navigable waters to the Niger's river system in the west, or to the Nile's system in the east, and their crude maps were untrustworthy.

Most European expeditions had tried to penetrate Africa by traveling from the continent's west coast through the Gambia, or south from the Barbary Coast. Europeans knew there were three ancient trade routes through the Sahara—Taghaza to Timbuktu in the western Sahara; Ghadames to Hausaland in the central Sahara; and Tripoli to Bornu in the east. But the Arab traders who profited from these routes didn't want Europeans horning in on their business and impeded them whenever possible. Consequently, despite many European expeditions over several decades, maps of the interior were sketchy at best and often dead wrong. Distances were mere estimates, as were the locations of important cities such as Kano, Kukawa, and Timbuktu.

But opening trade between Europe and Africa required far more than better maps. Most of the explorers who ventured into the interior on Britain's behalf left their bones there. The continent was rife with hazards—hostile natives, strange diseases, harsh terrain and temperatures, frightening animals. Mungo Park and his entire party of three dozen were wiped out by sickness and violence on the Niger. John Ledyard died after reaching Cairo in 1788. Daniel Houghton vanished in the desert in 1791, en route to Timbuktu. Dysentery killed Friedrich Hornemann in the Sahara in 1799. Henry Nicholls perished in 1805 on the Guinea coast and never saw the interior. Dysentery killed Johann

Burckhardt in 1817 before he could leave for the Fezzan, and felled Clapperton in 1827. Fever got Joseph Ritchie in 1819 and Oudney in 1824. Alexander Gordon Laing was shot, stabbed, and left for dead by desert pirates, but recovered and reached Timbuktu in 1826, only to be expelled and murdered not far from its precincts. Shortly after John Davidson left Morocco for Timbuktu in 1836, robbers slaughtered him. The list of fatalities goes on.

European commerce couldn't flourish in Africa if Europeans couldn't survive there. The continent's rulers and warlords had to be courted. Agreements that protected European traders had to be signed. The anarchy caused by bandits and freebooters along the trade routes had to be squelched. European merchants also needed to know which European products the Africans craved, and which African products might be profitably imported. Much needed to be done before commerce and Christianity had any chance of civilizing Africa by exploiting its resources.

This had been Richardson's appeal to Lord Palmerston at the Foreign Office eighteen months earlier, and he repeated it in a letter in September 1848. This time Palmerston responded. On September 30 he asked Richardson to submit a proposal with routes, a timetable, and an estimated budget.

Richardson was ready. Five days later he sent back ten pages in his chicken-scratch handwriting with the heading, "Projected Journey of Discovery and Philanthropy to Central Africa via the Great Desert of Sahara." Richardson noted that expeditions attempting to enter Africa through the Gambia, "the White Man's Grave," had been miserable failures, mostly because of the malevolent tropical climate. For Europeans, he wrote, the old north-south caravan routes through the desert were far healthier, aside from the problem of attacks by bandits. He proposed a route from Tripoli through the Fezzan to Murzuk, Ghat, and the Aïr Mountains, which had never been visited by Europeans. From there, south to Katsina and Hausaland, then east to the kingdom of Bornu before turning due north back to Tripoli.

The expedition's purposes, he continued, would be to persuade Africans to replace the slave trade with legitimate commerce, to sign trade agreements, and to collect information about the continent's peoples and places: "and so promote the sciences and geography, language, ethnology, and general knowledge."

He estimated the trip would take one to two years and cost at most £500, including the expense of gifts "to conciliate the princes and personages" along the route. In a bow toward Palmerston's reputation for frugality, he added that the mission's success would not depend on a lavish budget or presents, "but on the tact, prudence, and experience of the Traveller. . . . In the Desert, the poverty of the Traveller is oftentimes his greatest security."

Richardson also proposed establishing a British consulate in the northern Sahara at Ghat, a popular stopover for merchants traveling to and from Bornu and Timbuktu. Such a consulate would become "a centre of influence . . . from which could radiate the light of British Christian civilisation." If the government would fund an expedition to Central Africa, he concluded, "We could, undoubtedly, by perseverance and pacific policy, materially benefit and morally enlighten the African tribes and peoples, raising up degraded Africans to the standard of civilised Europe—and so expect, in humility, the favour and blessings of Almighty God upon us as a nation and the world at large."

Palmerston finally answered in August 1849: Richardson could make the necessary arrangements and leave whenever he was ready.

To MEET HIS pledge to collect scientific information, Richardson needed a scientist. "When a man has no science in him," he wrote apologetically in his book about the Sahara, "or no education in science, he can give you none."

Chevalier Bunsen, the Prussian ambassador, got wind of Richardson's expedition. Always alert for ways to promote Germans and German interests, Bunsen offered to use his contacts among his country's eminent scholars to find Richardson the best available German scientist—that is, the best in Europe. Richardson happily accepted the offer. Bunsen asked his friend Carl Ritter to recommend someone. After conferring with von Humboldt, Ritter replied, "The only person known to Professors Ritter and Baron Alexander von Humboldt on the Continent, who would unite the necessary qualities, experience, and scientific knowledge to undertake such an expedition as that proposed, the scientific and philological functions, is *Dr. Barth.*"

The famous geographer's recommendation was good enough for Richardson. Bunsen asked Ritter to sound out Barth. On October 5, 1849, exactly one year after Richardson sent his proposal to Palmerston, Ritter called Barth to his office and asked if he would be interested in accompanying a British expedition to Africa. To a man with no prospects and many recent setbacks, the offer was a godsend. The invitation came with one stipulation: Barth must contribute £200 to cover his own expenses. He was sure his father would fund him once again.

But as Barth's acceptance was making its way to England, his father nixed the plan. Johann's objections weren't financial, but parental and professional. He pointed to the appalling death rate among African explorers. He had almost lost his son to Saharan bandits once, and he forbade Heinrich to give the continent another whack at him. Further, he worried that another long absence from Germany might jeopardize his son's goal of landing a professorship. Crushed but obedient, Barth told Ritter he had to back out.

Ritter quickly enlisted another promising German scholar, a geologist and astronomer named Adolf Overweg. Though born just a year after Barth, Overweg seemed much younger because of his boyish enthusiasm and his lack of travel experience. Overweg eagerly agreed to go.

But Palmerston refused to let Barth withdraw. If the great von Humboldt and Ritter considered him the best man for the job, then Britain would have him, regardless of a father's fears. Palmerston sent word through Chevalier Bunsen that Britain considered Barth under verbal contract.

Barth, delighted, probably appealed to his father's strict sense of honor. Johann relented, on one condition: the Prussian government must promise to give Heinrich a professorship at a good salary upon his return. Von Humboldt used his influence at court to secure this future commitment, which turned out to be as trustworthy as most political promises. Next, Bunsen convinced Palmerston that the expedition should retain Overweg as well, since his skills complemented Barth's. Further, he persuaded the Foreign Office to repay Barth's and Overweg's £200 contributions during the course of the expedition, and to reimburse them for the expense of traveling to and from Tripoli. In return, the Germans would send periodic scientific dispatches, and upon their homecoming they would submit a scientific report to the Foreign Office. Bunsen emphasized that Barth and Overweg would be independent scientists, not agents of Her Majesty's Government. This independence would cause Barth much trouble, both during and after the journey.

Now that he was back on board, Barth began laying down conditions. He scolded Bunsen for asking the British government to pay him £200, since he could not accept any money from a foreign government that might restrict his independent pursuit of scientific truth. Bunsen, amused by Barth's touchy rectitude, wrote to a correspondent that he had no intention of informing Palmerston of Barth's stance, since the foreign secretary "might think Dr. Barth was mad, for refusing what probably he might get, in the shape of money, which in this country always is considered a good thing, of which you cannot have too much." Bunsen eventually persuaded Barth to curb his foolish virtue and accept the fee against unforeseen expenses in Africa. The Geographical Society of Berlin, founded by von Humboldt and Ritter, also contributed £150 toward the Germans' expenses.

Barth wrote a long letter to Richardson under the heading "Reflections on the projected exploring expedition into the interior of Africa." It prickled with his strong opinions. First, he insisted that they must be in Tripoli by mid-December 1849 and leave no later than early January 1850 with the last caravan heading for Bornu and Lake Chad; otherwise they wouldn't get through the Sahara before the hot season began and wouldn't reach Bornu before the start of the region's unhealthy hot and rainy summer. Second, once the Germans had explored Lake Chad, Barth wanted to be released from his obligations to the British government so that he could proceed eastward, as Ritter and von Humboldt had urged, to search for connections between Lake Chad and the Nile, as well as the sources of the Nile. Above all, Barth insisted that the expedition's chief goal must be changed from commercial relations to exploration and science.

Whether Richardson was offended or amused by this cheeky letter isn't clear, but he recognized its borderline insubordination. He wrote to a correspondent that he had replied to Barth that the mission's main purpose was to open North and Central Africa for trade and commerce, "and that on no account could I deviate from the necessities of this course of my mission for any *merely scientific* object, however important it might be for science, and that it was necessary that he and Dr. Overweg absolutely must submit to this."

"Merely scientific" must have struck Barth as sacrilegious, and submission was against his nature. A gulf separated their perspectives.

Richardson, Barth, and Overweg met for the first time on November 30, 1849, in London. They signed a contract with the Foreign Office that specified roles, money matters, and a long list of terms. Richardson, the director, would decide the expedition's route and pace. The main mission was commercial. Richardson was authorized to make treaties with African potentates. If the group decided to split up for any reason, the medical chest would be divided into thirds. After reaching Lake Chad, if Barth and Overweg wanted to continue eastward, Richardson was authorized to draw money on the Crown for their expenses.

Palmerston also wrote a letter of final instructions to Richardson:

> The countries you are about to visit are as yet so little known to the Nations of Europe, that every information of every kind respecting them which you may be able to collect will be interesting and useful;

but besides those Political and Scientific subjects of investigation to which your attention will of course be directed, it is the wish of H. M. Government that you should especially endeavour to ascertain by what means the commercial intercourse between Great Britain and Africa might be extended and developed; what are the Districts and what the lines of communication in that country which offer the greatest facilities for commerce; what are the European commodities which are most sought after by the natives; and what are the main articles of African produce which could best be obtained in payment for the productions of Europe.

Palmerston also directed Richardson "to act with entire unreserve and in the most cordial union with the Prussian gentlemen with whom you are to be associated; and you will of course give all due attention to their wishes and suggestions with regard to the course of your common proceeding." He noted that the Foreign Office had fronted Richardson £394.19 thus far, and added, "You will however be careful to keep your expenditure within the narrowest limits consistent with an efficient attainment of the objects of your expedition."

Richardson responded to Palmerston on December 5. "Our enthusiastic German friends," he wrote, "unable, it would appear, to restrain their ardour to get into Africa, left me yesterday morning before I could receive your Lordship's instruction. They will wait for me at Tunis."

Indeed they would, and at Tripoli, Murzuk, Ghat, and other places along the route. The expedition hadn't really begun, and Barth was already impatient with Richardson's tendency to dawdle. But the great point was that the mission was underway toward the unknown.

BARTH AND OVERWEG sailed from Marseilles on December 12, reached Algeria the following day, and were in Tunis by the 15th. They waited in vain for Richardson until the 30th, then left overland for Tripoli, the expedition's staging point, arriving on January 18. They expected

Richardson to be waiting there after taking a boat from Malta but found no sign of him or their supplies, and no word about either. The Germans had expected to depart immediately. "A great deal of patience was required," noted Barth.

Richardson had reached Tunis the day after Barth and Overweg left. The British vice-consul there, Lewis Ferriere, thought Richardson would leave immediately to catch up with his colleagues, but instead he dallied in the city for several weeks. "The Germans and our Englishman do not appear to pull very well together," wrote Ferriere in a confidential memo to the Foreign Office, "and there seems to me a degree of jealousy between them. It strikes me also that the Germans are the scientific men and Mr. Richardson the Bookmaker only. . . ."

Ferriere added that Richardson was already dissatisfied with a British sailor named William Croft who was traveling with him. The expedition needed a sailor to assemble and operate the boat that Richardson intended to haul across the Sahara to Lake Chad. The notion sounds harebrained, but one of the expedition's goals was to explore and survey Lake Chad, which had never been done. The explorers hoped to determine whether the lake drained the Niger River system or was connected to the Nile's. Based on Denham and Clapperton's twenty-five-year-old account of Bornu, Richardson had concluded that the native vessels available at Lake Chad were unsuitable for this task. Hence the sailor and the boat. It's unclear why Richardson was unhappy with Croft, except for the clue that he hoped to replace him with someone "steady." It must have doubly exasperated Richardson that he had handpicked Croft, who also happened to be his nephew.

So as 1850 began, several points of friction were chafing the group. Surely things would get sorted out in Tripoli.

3

At the Edge of the Desert

THE MEDITERRANEAN SPLASHES ONE SIDE OF TRIPOLI, THE SAHARA rubs the other. The Phoenicians, with their keen eye for commercial real estate, founded the town in the seventh century B.C. It quickly became a trade hub. By 1850 it had absorbed twenty-five centuries of war, commerce, political intrigue, and forced occupation. Greeks were followed by Romans, Carthaginians, various Muslim regimes, Spaniards, the Christian Knights of St. John, and, most recently, the Ottoman Turks, who took control in the sixteenth century.

When Barth and Overweg arrived, the city's population of about 15,000 was a stew of Berbers, Moors, Arabs, Jews, Turks, Maltese, Italians, and black Africans from various kingdoms and tribes in the south. Tripoli was a swinging door that connected the Mediterranean countries with the interior of Africa. Merchandise from Europe entered through the city's busy port. Goods from Africa's interior—ivory, gold, indigo, cotton cloth, animal skins, ostrich feathers, leather goods, kola nuts— left the city for Europe and the Ottoman countries. But the main export moving through Tripoli was slaves.

The amount of human flesh that passed through the slave markets of Barbary was a trickle compared to the torrent from Africa's west coast. That torrent, directed at the New World, was industrial in scope and purpose, and favored strong young males. In the trans-Saharan trade, the majority of slaves were females—the younger and prettier, the higher the value. Most of them were bound for domestic duties in the houses and seraglios of Barbary, Egypt, Anatolia, and the Levant. Slave raiders in the Sudan often killed males because they were less docile on the slog to market and less profitable once there.

Some of the captured slaves were retained by the nobles of Islamic kingdoms in the south, but most were sold to Arab traders who took them north to the big markets on the Mediterranean. Many European travelers commented that slaves in Islamic lands were treated relatively well compared to slaves in the West. They had certain rights and privileges. For instance, though the Qur'an permitted masters to enjoy their female slaves sexually, children from such unions were born free and their mothers could not be sold. Once a female slave married, her master lost sexual privileges. The Qur'an encouraged masters to marry their slaves and free them, and forbade the separation of slave mothers from their children before age seven. Some slaves became wealthy landowners and high government officials with slaves of their own. In a few cases the children of royal slaves became kings.

Slaves bound for the markets of Barbary first had to survive the horror of being torn from their villages and marched in coffles across the desert to the sea. Crossing the Sahara on foot, even in the best circumstances, was brutal—choking sandstorms, extreme temperatures, awful thirst. But these conditions were infinitely more taxing for youths recently wrenched from their homes, fettered together, and terrified about their unknown fate. They were often whipped and deprived of sufficient food and water. Those who couldn't keep up were abandoned. The caravan route between Bornu and Fezzan, in what is now southwestern Libya, was littered with their skeletons. Mortality rates are inexact but historians estimate at least 20 percent and often much higher. In 1849 the British vice-consul in Murzuk, an oasis town on the route between Bornu and Tripoli, reported to the Foreign Office that 1,600 slaves traveling from Bornu had died of thirst after attempting to survive by killing camels to drink their blood and the putrid water in their stomachs. Five months later the vice-consul sent a similar report: en route from Bornu, 795 of 1,770 slaves had perished of thirst.

Britain had established a consulate in Tripoli in 1780. A number of British expeditions launched from there. Captain G. F. Lyon, in his account of the ill-fated Ritchie mission of 1818–20, portrayed Tripoli to British readers as crowded with drunkards, prostitutes, slave-traders, and religious fanatics. He wrote that the cruel, whimsical pasha who ruled the city amputated the limbs of lawbreakers and festooned the city's gates with hanging corpses. Lyon described frenzied scenes of marabouts (Muslim holy men) whirling crazily, biting their tongues, piercing their cheeks with nails, sniffing out the houses of foul Christians. Yet he also admired the exotic beauty of young Arab women, despite the tattoos on their chins and noses, and between their eyebrows: "Nothing, in fact, can exceed in prettiness an Arab girl." And he luxuriated in the city's hot baths, where attendants provided vigorous body rubs and languorous shampoos, followed by pipes, coffee, and incense to perfume beards.

Other visitors to Tripoli also noted the way fanaticism rubbed shoulders with dissipation. The German explorer and doctor Gustav Nachtigal, who began an expedition from Tripoli about twenty years after Barth, wrote that because of the city's large number of "dissolute slave girls," many residents had syphilis, yet Tripolitans deftly conflated religious belief and wantonness by turning the malady into a mark of distinction, referring to it as "the Great" or "the queen of diseases," on the theory that even saints in Paradise had it.

Richardson found Tripoli disgusting. On his previous visit he had called it "the most miserable of all the towns I have seen in North Africa." He curled his lip at "the squalor and filth of Tripoli, with its miserable beggars choking up all the thoroughfares." For Richardson the filth included moral and political corruption, which in his view stemmed directly from the slave trade. His opinion of the Europeans in the city was not much higher: ". . . in truth, the greater part of the Europeans of Tripoli, and in all Barbary towns, are a degraded unenthusiastic race, wholly occupied with their petty quarrels and intrigues."

He returned there on January 31, 1850, two weeks behind Barth and Overweg. The expedition's supplies still hadn't arrived. Richardson estimated that departure would be delayed at least another month. To Barth and Overweg, already impatient to leave, the idea of sitting around for that long sounded intolerable. They left immediately for a three-week exploration of Tripolitania.

Richardson stayed in the city and set about organizing the caravan. No easy matter, considering Tripoli's crooked merchants and the demands of the bureaucracies, local and British. Add the heavy syrup of the enervating climate, and delays became inevitable. African travelers were often left stranded, as Richardson put it, "in ludicrous suspense between indignation and surprise."

He gradually bought camels and hired camel drivers, servants, and guides. He procured several months of provisions, including rice and dry biscuit in ten large iron cases, which Tuareg bandits would later assume were filled with gold. He bargained for cooking dishes and waterskins. From the British arsenal in Malta he ordered "half a dozen muskets, half a dozen pairs of pistols, and half a dozen short swords; some powder and shot." He bought lots of "articles of manufacture, as cheap watches, etc. for presents and barter."

"All these preparations," he wrote, "cost me prodigious anxiety, as I was obliged to study at the same time efficiency and economy." Arranging these complicated logistics was new to Richardson, and, it turned out, beyond his fiscal and managerial abilities.

Richardson's fretting and incompetence annoyed British officials in the city. The consul, G. W. Crowe, already disliked him from his earlier visit. At that time, Lord Palmerston had suggested appointing Richardson vice-consul at Ghadames, an oasis town about 350 miles southwest of Tripoli. But Crowe vehemently objected, citing the abolitionist's tactlessness and impolitic fervor. Richardson had caused diplomatic problems for Crowe by loudly criticizing the Ottomans' oppressive taxes, which led the Turks to request that Richardson be sent home.

Now Richardson was back in Tripoli, accompanied by his wife, living in Crowe's house, at Crowe's expense, and once again burrowing under Crowe's skin. Crowe was astonished that Palmerston had entrusted Richardson with such a difficult mission. He was still seething a year after the expedition's departure. "I cannot express to you how much I am disgusted by the ingratitude of Richardson," he wrote in a letter to the Foreign Office's undersecretary marked "Private." "I fear his wretched mismanagement will lower the reputation hitherto enjoyed by the English nation in Central Africa."

For instance, everyone knew that travelers in Africa must pay for their security by offering gifts to chiefs and rulers along the way. Mediocre gifts endangered their givers. But Richardson, complained Crowe, had not bought any "decent gifts, nothing that the chiefs [in the interior] can't find in their local market. When Mr. Richardson arrived from England, he had not a penny left of the sum he had received from you—and yet he had not purchased a single article of British manufacture to take with him, except a secondhand brass-hilted sword about five feet long, apparently a stage property, such as are carried in Corporation processions before the Mayor."

Richardson, by the way, was rather pleased with this sword, because it was so large and shiny, which he felt sure would please some desert chief.

The supplies finally arrived in mid-March—guns, medicines, several tents, "desert spectacles," the boat, and other important equipment such as scientific instruments. These included sextants, compasses, telescopes, chronometers, azimuths, a barometer, two dozen thermometers of various types, a psychrometer for measuring humidity, and chains for measuring distance.

The medicine chest contained:

Sulphate of quinine (for fever)	1 ounce
Compound of chalk powder with opium (for dysentery)	1 pound
Powdered ipecacuanha (an emetic)	8 ounces

Dr. Dover's powder (a mixture of ipecacuanha,
   opium, saltpeter, tartar, and licorice, used to
     induce sweating and head off colds and fevers)   8 ounces
Calomel (a laxative)   8 ounces
Lunar caustic (a disinfectant)   8 ounces
Powdered opium (a sedative, also for dysentery)   1 ounce
Sulphate of zinc (a powerful emetic, also taken
   for dysentery and night sweats)   1 ½ ounces
Tartar emetic   1 ½ ounces
Tincture of catechu (for dysentery)   24 ounces
Aromatic spirit of ammonia   2 pints
Liquor cinchonae pallidae (for fever)   5 ounces
Basilicon ointment (a mixture of hog lard, resin,
   and wax, for ulcers and burns)   4 pounds
Blistering paste (also called "Spanish fly," made
   from crushed "blister beetles" and used to raise
   blisters for relief of fever and other ailments)   2 pounds
Lint (dressing)   2 pounds
Diachylon plaster (a sticky mixture of oil and
   lead monoxide, for closing wounds)   1 tin

The chest also held two iron spatulas, two lancets, two glass measures, scales and weights, and a Wedgwood mortar and pestle.

A British doctor in Tripoli named Edward Dickson examined the chest and judged it inadequate for a long journey to the interior. At Dickson's suggestion, Richardson added another ounce of sulphate of quinine and 21 ounces of powdered Peruvian bark, both for fever. (Quinine was known to reduce fever, though the reasons, like the causes of fever, weren't understood. At that time the drug was taken after the onset of illness, not preventively.) Richardson also followed Dickson's advice about adding more laxatives—six pint bottles of castor oil and five pounds of Epsom salts.

This list makes two things clear: Richardson's main medical worries were fever, dysentery, and better health through purgatives; and second, since these scanty amounts of medicine were supposed to last three people and their servants for up to two years, and also to cover the inevitable requests for medicines from Africans along the way, he didn't worry nearly enough.

Barth was immediately dismayed at some of the equipment and its condition. The minimum and maximum thermometers arrived "so deranged" (phrasing that underlines Barth's foreign relationship with English) that they couldn't be repaired. The expedition's sole barometer, entrusted to Overweg, somehow got broken before the caravan ever left Tripoli. To Barth such carelessness was nearly unforgivable in a scientist; now they would have to boil water to determine elevations, a less precise method. "For the use of future travelers," Barth wrote, "I always wore not only my azimuth, but even my chronometer in my belt, and found this an excellent precaution against accidents of any kind."

He also judged the tents supplied by the British as "quite unfit for the country whither we were going"—too high, too lightweight, and lacking top ropes to keep them anchored in desert winds. Barth bought his own tent in Tripoli, heavily lined to keep out the sun, low-ceilinged, with top ropes. When traveling, he wrapped his pack, guns, and the planks for his bed and writing desk inside this tent. He also carried a double-barreled gun and a revolver, though unlike Overweg, who was an enthusiastic hunter and an excellent shot, Barth was neither.

His small travel library included two well-worn books taken on earlier journeys: the Qur'an and Herodotus. In the second book he later wrote, "This Herodotus was my steadfast companion on both my great journeys, round the Mediterranean in 1845–47, when he joined up with me in Alexandria, and in 1848–55 through Central Africa. Thus he is immortally dear to me, despite being so soiled."

The stories in Herodotus sometimes mirrored what Barth saw in

Africa: factional conflicts between cities and small kingdoms, raids to capture women and slaves, power-mad rulers, love of ceremony and rich tribute, fierce punishments and superstitious beliefs, distinctions drawn with absolute certainty between the civilized and the barbaric.

Barth also took a large supply of notebooks. Paper was scarce in Africa. On the inner front cover of the first notebook, he wrote, in Arabic, " 'Abd el Karim Barth el Inglisi." 'Abd el Karim, "Servant of the Merciful," was the name Barth used throughout his journey. As the notebook's epigraph, he wrote:

> *Knowledge is power.*
> *Because science is*
> *the confidante in the wilderness,*
> *the companion in a foreign land,*
> *the storyteller in solitude,*
> *the guide in joy and sorrow,*
> *the weapon against the enemy,*
> *and the ornament for friends.*

This poetic tribute to science is striking for several reasons, starting with its source. Aside from the first sentence, the passage comes from an obscure hadith attributed to the Islamic scholar Al-Suyuti (c. 1445–1505 A. D.), an Egyptian who wrote roughly five hundred works in Arabic on law, theology, and science. Barth elsewhere describes Al-Suyuti as "that living encyclopedia and keystone . . . of Mohammedan learning." That Barth knew this work speaks to his deep scholarship. He surely nodded at what came before and after the passage in the epigraph: Al-Suyuti declares that Muhammed championed science and urged believers to pursue knowledge "even to China." The Prophet also said, according to Al-Suyuti, "On the day of resurrection, the ink of scholars will be equal to the blood of martyrs." Science, said Muhammed, is "the light tower of the Path to Paradise." And scientists, he added, are touched by the wings of angels. Such sentiments spoke to Barth's most deeply held convictions. He must have been delighted to find them expressed by an early African Islamic scholar.

Richardson packed Bibles in Hebrew and Greek. He also took *Comus*, Milton's tale about black magic, virtue besieged by temptation, tribulations in a strange land, and eventual escape and homecoming—a parable that probably spoke to Richardson's anxieties about the journey.

With the supplies finally at hand, Barth wondered why the mission was lingering in Tripoli. To nudge Richardson along, the Germans left the city on March 24 and camped nine miles to the south. Richardson was delayed partly by the logistics of transporting the boat, a wherry with long oars and poles. It arrived in two pieces instead of the expected four, which posed difficulties for loading. Richardson eventually cut it up. The boat alone required eight camels.

The other delay was personal. Unlike Barth and Overweg, Richardson had a wife, who was with him in Tripoli. In the days before he left, he wrote a letter asking Palmerston to approve a payment of £60 to her if he didn't return—a modest price for his life. "Hope and the spirit of adventure sustained my courage," he wrote on March 30, the day he finally left the city, "but it is always sad to part with those we love, even at the call of duty. However, I at length mustered strength to bid adieu to my wife—the almost silent adieu of affection. How many things that were thought were left unsaid on either side!"

4

First Steps

R ICHARDSON REACHED THE GERMANS' CAMP ON MARCH 31. ON
April 2, 1850, the expedition finally set off into the desert. Most
caravans left Barbary in September or October to make the crossing
during the desert winter. This one would reach the heart of the Sahara
at the height of summer.

In addition to the four Europeans (including the sailor Croft), the
expedition included an assortment of helpers and hangers-on, whose
number ebbed and swelled as the caravan progressed. Richardson's dragoman (fixer and interpreter), Yusuf Moknee, dark and handsome, was
the son of a wealthy former governor of Fezzan, and hence arrogantly
self-important even though he had long since drunk away his father's
estate. Richardson hired him because he couldn't find anyone better in
Tripoli. As bodyguards, Richardson hired two quarrelsome Arab janis-
saries. Several servants and camel drivers rounded out the payroll.

Like all caravans, this one attracted tagalongs: a marabout from Fezzan, a couple of Arabs "going with camels to somewhere," and about a
dozen free blacks hoping for protection while traveling through the violent territories separating them from their homes in Sudan and Bornu.
They carried a folded document in their turbans or neck pouches that
proved their emancipation.

The caravan also attracted two lunatics. One, a Neapolitan in rags, insisted that he was Richardson's servant. He trailed the Englishman around Tripoli for weeks and finally into the desert. At the camp Richardson popped this delusion by giving him two loaves of bread, a Tunisian coin, and a polite bow, followed by a firm order to go home. The other madman, wrote Richardson, was a Muslim with "an unpleasant habit of threatening to cut everybody's throat." He lugged around a bunch of old metal, including a large knife, which he often pulled from beneath his robe and flourished while ranting about slit throats. He was eventually disarmed and forced back toward Tripoli.

The caravan set off with sixty-two camels. Barth and Overweg accounted for ten of them, including the two they were riding. About half the camels carried luggage, supplies, equipment, trade goods, and guns. The trade goods and guns were as essential to the expedition as the camels. The 1,300 miles between the Mediterranean and the Sahel—the semiarid lands south of the Sahara where Muslim Africa met pagan black Africa—were seething with raiders, freebooters, war parties, and thieves. Muslim slavers prowled the Sahel and kept the black tribes boiling with fear and anger. Old rivalries between kingdoms, tribes, and ethnic groups flared up constantly. Travelers crossed these turbulent lands at their own peril.

And yet the desert was also alive, as it had been for centuries, with an extensive web of long-distance commerce, from salt caravans of several thousand camels to smaller groups of traveling merchants who offered everything from indigo and cotton cloth to foodstuffs and swords. Travelers tried to protect themselves by banding together to discourage pirates, and by buying safe passage with tributes paid to every local chief whose territory they entered. Though the countryside was ostensibly governed by several large kingdoms, the force of law came in a distant second to force of arms.

For Christians these dangers increased exponentially. Many Muslims considered Christians evil infidels. Black tribes associated them with the lighter-skinned slavers who killed and stole their people. Consequently hundreds of Europeans had died attempting to trace the Niger

River or reach the fabled city of Timbuktu. If the natives didn't kill these explorers, something else usually did—thirst, starvation, disease, poisonous snakes, or large carnivores.

Little was known about these lands, especially when approached from the north through the Sahara. No accurate maps existed. Distances were unknown, as were the precise locations of major towns in the interior such as Timbuktu and Kano. The region was thought to be relatively flat, but in fact was rumpled with mountain ranges. Some of Central Africa's great kingdoms—Bornu, Kanem, Sokoto— were little more than rumors in Europe, and little or nothing was known about their rulers, populations, cultures, products, politics, or trade relations.

Richardson expected the mission to be gone for two years at most, if things went according to plan. The expedition's goal was the kingdom of Bornu on Lake Chad, where present-day Niger, Nigeria, Chad, and Cameroon meet. Twenty-five years earlier, Oudney, Clapperton, and Denham had proven that Europeans could reach it. They had taken the ancient route that ran directly south from Tripoli. But now the depredations of Tuareg bandits and Arab raiders had almost shut down that corridor, and caravans weren't risking the trip.

The current expedition had different plans. The first stage of a journey between Tripoli and Bornu ended at Murzuk, 500 miles to the south. Two tracks connected Tripoli to Murzuk. Most travelers, including the Oudney expedition, took the easterly one because it was easier and better-watered. The westerly track, developed by the Romans in the first century A.D., cut ten days from the journey but was rarely used because it crossed the arid plateau called the Hammada, a harsh landscape of scorched rubble. No modern European had traversed it. To Barth this scientifically unexplored route that also saved time must have seemed ideal.

From Murzuk the shortest route to Bornu plunged directly south through the Sahara by way of Bilma for about 1,000 miles. But Richardson planned to take a detour west for 250 miles to Ghat, then go southwest for another 400 miles to the mountains of Aïr, a Tuareg stronghold never conquered by Romans, Arabs, or Turks. No European had ever seen it.

THE FIRST TWO WEEKS of travel passed pleasantly. These northerly regions of the Sahara were relatively moderate. Contrary to the stereotypical image, the Great Desert is not a barren tract of rolling dunes. Rock and gravel are as common as sand. The topography varies tremendously: stony plains and plateaus, steep ravines, wide channels carved by ancient watercourses (wadis), shallow basins left by ancient lakes, isolated mountains and jagged massifs. Trees and bushes manage to grow; a camel can often find something to munch. Wells stipple the arid emptiness, if you know where to find them. And of course people have lived throughout the Sahara for centuries in oases and nomadic camps, farming or raising livestock. The Tuareg call the Sahara "Tinariwen"— "the deserts"—because it is many deserts, not one.

The caravan moved in the straggling Arab style, the camels widely separated, grazing as they ambled. The richer the vegetation, the slower the caravan's progress. Barth preferred the Tuareg method of tying the camels one behind the other, to keep them moving. Stymied by the leisurely pace, he channeled his frustration into data, repeatedly and laboriously measuring the mileage with a watch and a chain. Result: the caravan's rate was 2 to 2½ miles per hour.

He soon began leaving camp early in the morning to spend the day exploring on his own, rejoining the caravan in the evening. He found much to see, sketch, climb, measure. His journal entries are clotted with precise details about every geographic feature along the route, every ruin (Roman, Arabic, Turkish), every form of vegetation and crop (corn, figs, dates, olives, almonds, pomegranates). He describes every village and its people, often accompanied by pertinent scholarly references.

His observations about a small oasis 100 miles south of Tripoli are typical: "Mizda, most probably identical with the eastern 'Musti kome'

of Ptolemy, appears to have been an ancient settlement of the indig-
enous inhabitants of North Africa, the Berbers, and more particularly
of a family or tribe of them called 'Kuntarar'. . . ." He details Mizda's
geophysical characteristics and soil composition (gypsum). He notes the
depths of its wells and its use of oxen to draw water, plus the number
of oxen in the village (three). He sketches the oasis and remarks that it
is actually two distinct villages with two chiefs, one who stays in tents
some distance away and another who lives inside the village's crumbling
walls. He describes the architecture and counts the number of trees in
Mizda's palm grove (about 200), which is also dotted with onions. He
notices an unusual abundance of lizards and chameleons, and measures
the oasis's circumference (2,260 paces). The people suffer from eye problems, he wrote, and the barley is ripening.

Barth noticed everything and recorded it all scrupulously, almost
compulsively. His note-taking reflected his faith in the power of scientific observation to discover and crack open the secrets of nature. To
Barth the parallels between scientific and geographic exploration were
clear. Both were journeys into the unknown. His mentor, Alexander von
Humboldt, had spent five years exploring South America and returned
with 60,000 botanical samples and zoological specimens. Von Humboldt's multivolume narrative extolled the excitement of scientific exploration and was a trumpet call to younger scientists.

Barth surely knew John Herschel's influential *A Preliminary Discourse on the Study of Natural Philosophy* (1831), which confidently
proclaimed that once one adopted a scientific outlook, "Everything in
nature became interesting and significant, nothing was beneath notice.
The most 'trifling natural objects,' such as a soap bubble, an apple or a
pebble, could reveal a scientific law (respectively, the laws of aerostatics,
gravitation or geology). . . . To the natural philosopher there is no natural
object unimportant or trifling. . . . A mind that has once imbibed a taste
for scientific enquiry has within itself an inexhaustible source of pure and
exciting contemplations. . . . Where the uninformed and unenquiring eye
perceives neither novelty nor beauty, *he* walks in the midst of wonders."

Mundane details were not minutiae, but grains of gold that could accumulate into a treasure. Barth considered it his scientific duty to observe and record everything, and then to find correlations between cultures and eras, between a place's geography and its history, between environment and ethnography. He did this partly for science, partly to aid future travelers, and partly because he couldn't help himself.

Most earlier travelers to Africa were soldiers or adventurers, and if they survived, they wrote books more personal than scientific. (Richard Burton, the other great explorer-scholar of Africa, would soon combine the two.) Barth's model was not Mungo Park or Dixon Denham, though he admired those brave men and their books, but von Humboldt.

Barth was a new breed, an explorer who was also a trained linguist, scientist, and historian. Personal anecdotes could be charming, he believed, but were an unnecessary distraction from the high calling of scientific research. He drew this contrast clearly in his preface to *Travels and Discoveries*, noting that Richardson's journals were "full of minute incidents of traveling life, so very instructive to the general reader. But, from my point of view, I had to look very differently at the objects which presented themselves; and Mr. Richardson, if he had lived to work out his memoranda himself, would not have failed to give to his journal a more lasting interest." Barth's goal was posterity, not popularity, yet it wounded him when the public granted his wish.

THE EXPEDITION moved in fits and starts, some days traveling for four hours, some days for ten. A camel driver's greyhound ran down a hare one day, a gazelle the next, adding fresh meat to their meals of rice and grain. They met a slave caravan of thirty young girls headed to Tripoli from Ghat.

In his solitary excursions Barth frequently came across signs of ancient Rome, including milestones used to mark this rarely used route. Barth admired the Romans' fearless penetration into the desert and their attempt to impose order upon wild nomads and emptiness. He discovered a crumbling arched gate, covered with Berber graffiti, that once marked the outpost of a Roman horse squadron in the third century A.D. He came across two elaborate Roman sepulchers, one 48 feet tall, the other 25, both in the middle of nowhere. "Like a solitary beacon of civilization," he wrote, "this monument rises over this sea-like level of desolation, which, stretching out to an immense distance south and west, appears not to have appalled the conquerors of the ancient world."

Everything he was seeing would be news in Europe. He measured and sketched, and sent a packet back to Tripoli, still only days away. His report quickly reached Europe, where it caused a small stir and raised hopes among scholars about future discoveries by this energetic and thorough young man. Overweg, meanwhile, discovered fossil oyster shells left behind after warm seas retreated from the Sahara. The genus was new to science, and was eventually named *Exogyra overwegi*.

On April 12 the desert abruptly changed moods. A fierce south wind—called sirocco in Europe, ghibli in Libya—filled the air with dust and sand, blinding and choking both humans and animals. The caravan stalled. "Here was a foretaste of the desert, its hardships and terrors!" wrote Richardson with characteristic drama. Barth, apparently unable to extract data from the storm, didn't even mention it. At least the wind had given them momentary peace from the flies that had plagued them since leaving Tripoli.

"Nothing can be more overpowering," wrote Captain Lyon about such a storm. "In addition to the excessive heat and dryness of these winds, they are so impregnated with sand, that the air is darkened by it, the sky appears of a dusky yellow, and the sun is barely perceptible. The eyes become red, swelled, and inflamed; the lips and skin parched and chapped; while severe pain in the chest is very generally felt, in consequence of the quantities of sand unavoidably inhaled."

Soon after the storm, the caravan reached the shelf leading up to the dreaded Hammada, "uninhabited and without wells." This stony tableland guarded the northern Fezzan like a fortress. It marked their plunge into the real unknown; they would be the first modern Europeans known to cross it. "It is difficult to convey an idea of the solemn impressions with which one enters upon such a journey," wrote Richardson. "Everything ahead is unknown and invested with perhaps exaggerated terrors by imagination and report." He wanted to pause for a day and travel at night to avoid the sun, but Barth and Overweg needed light to gather information. The group agreed to separate once again and reunite somewhere on the plateau.

The expedition was also being delayed by a violent quarrel among the camel drivers. Richardson blamed a young Tuareg named Ali, but Barth, always more perceptive and fair than his leader, noticed that Ali was justly fed up; the Fezzanee drivers had been taking advantage of him by burdening his camels with the heaviest loads. The real fault, Barth knew, lay with Richardson for not maintaining discipline.

The next morning as the camel drivers renewed their threats to kill each other, Barth and Overweg started up toward the plateau. The baggage creaked as the camels strained, occasionally bending to tear off a mouthful of vegetation. At the top, Barth added a stone to the heap left by travelers coming from the north.

At first the wasteland didn't live up to its dire reputation. The camels could find bits of herbage. A small green bird entertained the travelers by picking vermin from the feet of passing camels. After "a moderate march of ten and a half hours," they camped in a green hollow.

That night a strong cold wind kicked up, bringing rain. Their tent, one of the light, high British ones, blew down. Richardson's group stumbled into camp at five that morning, drenched and miserable after marching in the dark for eleven hours. Dawn lit up a flat wasteland of hard red dirt strewn with flints and stony rubble.

Barth and Overweg broke camp and plodded south. En route they were delighted to find truffles, and that evening made a delicious soup, spiced for Barth by the knowledge that Ibn Battuta, "the greatest of Mohammedan travelers," had enjoyed a similar meal during his journey across Africa in the fourteenth century. The night sky was hazy with windblown dust, refracting the moonlight into a spectacular halo.

They slept on the ground and suffered from the cold. In the morning light, frost—frost in the desert!—glinted on the dreary plain.

On the third day they came to a pile of stones that marked the plateau's highest point, which they measured at 1,568 feet. Another storm blew up, so ferocious that the swallows that had been following them tried to take shelter inside the heaving tent. But the wind tore it down again, leaving the winged and the wingless miserable in the gale.

On the fourth day they got to El Hamra, "the very dreariest part of the Hammada." It was not only uninhabited and waterless, but barren of plants and animals. Richardson passed them during the night; they caught up with him the next day. Two days later they finally reached the southern edge of the plateau. The descent ran between cliffs completely blackened as if by fire, a constricted gloomy passageway that led to a valley heaped with massive black boulders shadowed by black cliffs. But there was also a good well, so they stopped. The drivers, too exhausted to unload the camels, shouted, "Farewell to the Hammada!" and collapsed into sleep.

It had taken six days to travel 156 miles, by Barth's measurement. Richardson wrote in his journal that in North Africa "there is no traverse of six days comparable in difficulty to that which we have just accomplished"—except, he added, a horrible desert between Ghat and Aïr—the route they would be taking.

Despite the dreary setting and the ceaseless wind, and the complete absence of shade, fatigue kept them there the next day. "Scarcely any of our places of encampment on the whole journey seemed to me so bad and cheerless as this," wrote Barth. He looked longingly at a cluster of date palms several miles away, imagining their shade. But getting there was impossible: "Our camels were too much distressed."

WHEN THE CARAVAN continued south, the terrain turned to sand, making travel more difficult, but at least there was a well every day. No markers indicated the route. "The road is not in the sand," said the camel drivers, "but in our heads." The days were long. On May 1 they walked for fourteen hours across heavy sand, scorched by a relentless hot wind that blew grit into eyes, mouths, clothing. Aside from the listless cries of the camel drivers, no one spoke, stupefied by heat and the rocking motion of the camels. Richardson wore a lady's veil to shield his eyes from flies, grit, and hot wind. In the evening, crickets rasped in the burning sand.

The mountains ahead seemed to retreat before them. As the light and the winds shifted, the color of the sand flickered between red, yellow, and blinding white. Mirages shimmered and vanished. One day a thermometer stuck into the sand at noon shot up to 122 degrees; a few days later, to more than 130 degrees.

The next day Barth was excited to reach the oasis of Germa, a name that he suspected—correctly—had evolved from Garama, capital of an ancient Berber empire. Barth knew about Garama from his beloved old historians—Herodotus, Strabo, Lucan, Tacitus, Pliny the Elder. The Garamantes were famous in the ancient world as fierce warriors who ran down prey, whether four-legged or two-legged, in chariots drawn by four horses. By the third century B.C. they controlled the caravan routes through the central Sahara.

Their isolated capital city boasted temples, baths, markets, and towers, all surrounded by a lofty wall. They irrigated their farms of wheat, olives, and dates with water from reservoirs shunted through underground channels. They alternately raided the cities on the Mediterranean and traded with them. After the Romans finally won the Punic Wars in the middle of the second century B.C., the new conquerors eagerly traded with the desert kingdom for gold, horses, slaves, ivory, and wild animals to use in gladiatorial games. But the Garamantes' chronic depredations eventually galled the Romans into mounting an expedition that defeated them in 19 B.C. To keep tabs on them the Romans established an outpost at Garama.

Barth was moved by the monument he found there, adorned with

Corinthian pilasters, "an object of special interest as the southernmost relic of Roman dominion." It had been defaced long ago with Berber graffiti.

The caravan plodded toward Murzuk. The pace of travel had irritated Barth from the first, and his frustration had worsened. In the mornings the caravan often started late because the drivers took so long to round up the camels, which roamed at night while grazing. Once underway, the drivers sometimes insisted on stopping after just a few miles or a few hours, citing good forage or water. On the frequent occasions when the caravan started late or ended early, Barth worked off his exasperation by dashing off on little excursions to climb a peak or explore a wadi. He wondered why Richardson put up with the drivers' transparent rationales for laziness. He shook his head when Richardson didn't object to their obvious ploy of taking a long detour, which cost days of delay, simply because it took the caravan past their home village in the Fezzan. Richardson had estimated the 500-mile journey from Tripoli to Murzuk at twenty-five days. It would take thirty-nine, even with the shortcut over the Hammada. Such things added to Barth's doubts about Richardson's ability to lead the expedition.

Some of his criticisms were unfair. Barth was accustomed to traveling alone, at his own energetic pace, and had a hard time adjusting to the rhythms of caravan travel. Large caravans tended to move slowly and stop frequently, regardless of who led them. Pausing to take advantage of good water and forage could be prudent in harsh places where those essentials were scarce. Nor could Richardson be blamed for the ingrained Arab customs of letting camels graze as they walked and leaving them unfettered at night.

On the other hand, Richardson was too acquiescent to his drivers' demands, too easily persuaded to halt and rest. He also misread situations, made poor decisions, and failed to keep order and discipline among the caravaneers. Perhaps worst, he was too convinced of his own wisdom to consider adjustments.

5

Stalled in Murzuk

THEY ARRIVED AT MURZUK ON MAY 6, 1850, A HOT BLUSTERY DAY, murky with blowing sand. The town's clay walls glittered with saline crust from the nearby salt flats. Murzuk was an oasis and entrepôt of about 2,800 people who came from all over North and Central Africa. "The people vary greatly in colour," noted Richardson. Traders from other places kept homes in Murzuk because it was a minor hub of commerce with spokes radiating to Bornu in the southeast, Tripoli in the north, Ghat and Ghadames in the southwest. The major goods passing through its bazaar from the interior were slaves, ivory, senna, animal skins, cotton cloth, and ostrich feathers. Goods heading into the interior included swords, knives, guns, paper, and other manufactured goods. The pasha of Murzuk maintained his palace by taxing the oasis's gardens and cultivated fields, and by collecting levies on passing caravans.

Murzuk was a long way from anywhere, hemmed in by desert, and in summer was doubly isolated by intense heat that deterred caravan travel. Its people entertained themselves with the usual vices of lonely places. Richardson, Hornemann, and Lyon all noted that the men tended to be genial drunkards (their beverage was fermented date juice). Murzuk's women were infamous for their dancing, singing, and licentiousness. Venereal disease was prevalent. So were hemorrhoids, which Hornemann attributed to "the immoderate use of red pepper." Murzuk was also notorious for a virulent strain of fever, which the natives treated by putting slips of paper inscribed with Qur'anic verses into amulets worn around the neck. The fever was especially deadly to foreigners. It had killed Dr. Ritchie, Lyon's colleague, and had damaged the health of the current British vice-consul. Barth, Overweg, and the sailor Croft suffered bouts of it in Murzuk.

The day after their arrival, the three explorers put on their best European clothes and paid a call on the pasha. He served them coffee, pipes, and orange sherbet. After the rigors of the journey Richardson seemed content to rest for a while in Murzuk's relative comfort and Christian company. Despite the oasis's isolation and unhealthy climate, a few Europeans lived there. On Richardson's first visit in 1846, he wrote about a sumptuous dinner with a Greek doctor, an Albanian gunpowder-maker, and the British vice-consul of Murzuk, a native of Trieste. They ate roasted lamb and dried salmon and sardines, washed down with rum, bottled stout, and several kinds of wine. Richardson looked forward to more of the same while planning the next phase of the current journey.

On his second day in Murzuk, the first sentence in his journal reads, "We are already busy with preparations for our start to the interior." Barth's entry on the same day begins, "Unfortunately, our stay in Murzuk seemed likely to become a very long one. . . ."

This difference in perspective had several layers. Barth knew that Richardson intended to hire Tuaregs from the oasis of Ghat to escort the expedition across the 250 miles of desert between that place and Murzuk, followed by another 400 miles southwest into the mountains of Aïr. Barth agreed that the expedition would need strong protection to travel safely through Aïr, but he doubted that the Ghat Tuaregs could provide it. He said so to Richardson, without effect. "Though it might have been clear, to every one well acquainted with the state of things in the interior," wrote Barth, "that their protection could not be the least guarantee for our favorable reception and success in the country of Aïr or Asben, inhabited and governed by an entirely different tribe."

He also considered it a strategic mistake to ask the Ghat Tuaregs to come all the way to Murzuk. The invitation would inflate their self-importance and their fee. As the news traveled through the desert grapevine, other tribes would be encouraged to charge exorbitant rates for protection. Richardson's plan was also a political mistake, in Barth's view, because it had insulted and enraged Muhammed Boro, a wealthy merchant with homes and contacts in Aïr and Sokoto, whose protection could be crucial. These misjudgments, wrote Barth, caused "some very bad consequences for us."

And lastly, Barth was dumbfounded that the letters summoning the Ghat Tuaregs to Murzuk had not gone out until that very morning. Worse, Richardson intended to stay in Murzuk until the Tuaregs arrived. That meant weeks of idleness while the letters made their way to Ghat and then onward to the chiefs in the desert.

The explorers waited in Murzuk for six weeks—mired there, in Barth's view, resting comfortably, in Richardson's. In *Travels and Discoveries*, Barth never said anything directly harsh about Richardson, but the depth of his exasperation in Murzuk was clear in his crisp critique of Richardson's plans and in his cursory treatment of Murzuk. He gave the place not quite six pages. Richardson devoted seventy, which are pleasantly diverting.

He described his visits to the pasha, who served coffee and lemonade. He detailed another banquet at the home of the Greek doctor: "Besides two whole lambs, fowls, pigeons, there were at least twenty made dishes, with every variety of rich sweetmeat. Amongst the early fruits of the season we had figs and apples." On May 24 the explorers celebrated Queen Victoria's birthday at the vice-consul's house by raising the Union Jack, firing fifty-one guns at noon, and eating a dinner of thirty or forty dishes with the pasha and his officers as guests. "The healths of her Majesty, the Sultan, and the King of Prussia, were drunk in champagne with enthusiasm," wrote Richardson. The decorations included "a small portrait of her Majesty; an Ottoman blood-red flag, with its crescent and star; and a white flag with the Prussian black eagle.

The effect was excellent, and quite astonished the natives. The Turks ate and drank famously, and for the most part got 'elevated.' " Barth didn't mention any of this. To him, it all must have seemed beside the point.

Not all of Richardson's time in Murzuk was spent on entrées and lemonade. He also tended to some business. His nephew, the sailor Croft, was debilitated with Murzuk fever. Richardson wrote to Palmerston that Croft was also "terrified with the vastness of the desert and the uncertain dangers of the way." He had to be sent back to Tripoli. Richardson asked Palmerston to consider sending two or three English shipbuilders from Malta to meet the expedition in Bornu. Their boats could be used to clear Lake Chad of pirates and to establish commerce with neighboring countries. This would create a "nucleus of British influence which striking downwards and spreading round, could not fail to establish firmly a paramount interest in favour of Great Britain in the heart of Africa." Palmerston instructed his deputy to look into the idea.

IN MURZUK, Richardson, Barth, and Overweg stayed in the spacious house of the British vice-consul, G. B. Gagliuffi. About fifty-five years old, Gagliuffi was one of those enigmatic expatriates who always pop up in chronicles of foreign adventure. Born in Trieste, he spent the 1830s and early 1840s as a trader in Tripoli. He spoke excellent English as well as Arabic, Turkish, Greek, and Italian. The British consul in Tripoli during those years, Hanmer Warrington, recommended Gagliuffi for the new post of vice-consul at Murzuk.

He started in 1843. He built himself a large house and set about his business: looking after British interests without neglecting his own. For the British he monitored the slave trade, established good relations with the local authorities and desert chiefs, and kept tabs on the various conflicts and alliances in Central Africa. For himself he developed trading partnerships with merchants in several towns throughout the Sudan. One such partner was the vizier of Bornu, Beshir ben Tirab. The two wheeler-dealers met and hit it off in January 1844 when the vizier was on his way back from a haj to Mecca. The vizier would soon become vital to Barth and the expedition.

Gagliuffi was an operator who knew the territory and all the main players. He somehow maintained good relations with everyone—a considerable skill in the volatile, ever-shifting politics of Central Africa. Certainly he was flawed. No one ever described him as incorruptible. No doubt he lined his pockets under the aegis of the British flag. But he also took his position seriously. He worked hard, and successfully, to advance British influence through diplomacy, which earned him the respect of Africans and colleagues in the Foreign Office.

His conduct toward the Richardson expedition was typical. He sent letters to all the regional desert chiefs, whom he knew, asking them to aid and protect the explorers. He arranged for a line of credit for them in Bornu through his friend the vizier. He offered Richardson much good advice about the peoples and territories ahead. Yet he also took a sharp markup on the goods Richardson purchased in Murzuk, and charged high interest on the credit Richardson drew there.

"Mr. Gagliuffi has been hospitable," wrote Richardson in his journal. "Justice, however, compels me to say, that the British Consul sometimes remembered too vividly that he was also a merchant, and a Levantine merchant to boot. I am afraid he is not quite satisfied even with the profits he has already made out of the expedition."

In several letters to the Foreign Office, Richardson accused Gagliuffi of profiteering and deceit. The FO, ever fastidious, began an investigation. It progressed glacially through the sporadic mails between London, Tripoli, and the Sudan. The accusations wounded Gagliuffi. He wrote the FO that he had hosted the explorers for weeks, without recompense, and had done all in his power to promote their safety. All this was true. He added that the expedition obviously was "badly managed, and in miserable condition," with inadequate equipment—observations Barth would second. Richardson seemed to be blaming others, wrote Gagliuffi, for additional expenses that were his own fault.

From Tripoli, Consul Crowe also responded angrily to Richardson's charges. "I am very unwilling to say anything, which may appear harsh, of a person engaged in a hazardous expedition, from which he may never return," Crowe wrote to Palmerston. "But Mr. Richardson's deep ingratitude merits with indulgence—he seems to have undertaken the direction of the mission, without any thought or care for the responsibilities attached to it, and now finding the difficulties of his position to be greater than he anticipated, and that there is not the slightest hope of affecting the principal object of his mission, he seems to attribute to other causes the natural consequences of his own incapacity and presumption."

Richardson worried constantly about money and grumbled about the gougers surrounding him, complaints that had some merit. Yet he also mismanaged the expedition's finances, and his gripes often sounded like whining self-justifications. He had told Palmerston that the expedition would cost no more than £500 and would last one year, maybe two. Then he spent nearly £400 before the expedition ever left Tripoli. In June 1850, two months into the journey, he wrote to Palmerston that he now believed the expedition would not return to Tripoli until spring of 1852 at the earliest, six months beyond his maximum estimate. Therefore he needed another £600 for provisions, presents, and other expenses. When Palmerston received this letter weeks later, he wrote at the bottom, "This may be allowed."

But just three days after asking for an extra £600, Richardson wrote Palmerston again. The prices in Murzuk, he complained, were higher than expected. He had just given Gagliuffi a letter of credit drawn on the Foreign Office for £600—the amount supposed to last another two years. Obviously, he said, he would be needing more money. On this letter Palmerston wrote, "We must not grudge a small addition to the originally contemplated expense."

To Barth, Richardson's fiscal incompetence was as alarming as his plan to hire the Ghat Tuaregs. Both endangered the explorers and the mission. Barth also had money worries of his own. The three-months' delay in Tripoli had been an unforeseen expense. Now it appeared that the expedition would continue much longer than expected. Because of these changed circumstances, he sent a letter from Murzuk asking Palmerston to grant him and Overweg another £100 pounds each. He also wrote to Chevalier Bunsen, urging him to press their case on Palmerston because of "the immense procrastination which our journey has undergone."

While waiting in Murzuk, Barth studied the local languages, especially Berber, which gave him the "immense advantage" of being able to gather information directly from the camel drivers and the local people. From Gagliuffi he learned that the vizier of Bornu was a learned man who loved books. To create goodwill Barth suggested that the British government send to Bornu "some good *Arab books*, principally the Thousand and One Nights . . . together with some treatises on geography, astronomy, etc., as no present would become more to the scientific character of the Mission and as none—besides firearms and shot—would be more acceptable, there being a great interest for books in Bornu and only a very few ones being brought in to the country from Egypt." The Foreign Office may have been surprised to hear that a black official in deep Africa would be interested in such scholarly books, but they were duly sent.

Barth also worked on his journal, and sent off dispatches and sketches about what he had seen and learned. But instead of sending them directly to the Foreign Office, as Richardson suggested, he sent them to Chevalier Bunsen with instructions to forward them to the FO. Bunsen also circulated them among Barth's colleagues in Berlin. Based on his contract, Barth considered himself an independent scientist, not a government employee. He also naïvely regarded scientific information as a universal possession beyond national claims. For both these reasons he felt comfortable sending his reports through Bunsen and sharing them with German colleagues.

After receiving Barth's packet of information and plea for money, Bunsen wrote to Palmerston about the £100 (which was granted). He also mentioned that von Humboldt, Ritter, and the Berlin Royal Academy were very pleased with the papers sent by Barth. Bunsen would send them along, he added, once the German scholars released them.

That nettled Palmerston. He had also gotten a letter from Richardson saying that there was some confusion about who should get the Germans' reports first. In a note attached to this letter, Palmerston wrote tersely, "as they are all employed by the British Government they should address their communications to F. O. direct." Because of slow communications, this misunderstanding festered. It later led to some ugliness with Britain's Royal Geographical Society, which accused Barth of using British money to finance German science.

By EARLY JUNE, after baking in Murzuk for a month, Barth and Overweg had had enough. The daytime temperatures were above 100 degrees in the shade, up to 130 in the sun. They told Richardson that they wanted to move toward Ghat. Richardson, ever cautious, asked them to wait for the Tuareg escort. They declined. The explorers agreed to reunite somewhere west. Barth and Overweg left on June 12.

The Ghat Tuaregs reached Murzuk on June 21. Barth was with them. He had met the party in the desert and decided it would be wise to be in Murzuk to monitor Richardson's negotiations with these desert sharks. The Tuaregs included two sons of the sultan of Ghat, and an older minor sheikh named Hatita who had known Lyon, Oudney, and Clapperton in the 1820s. Richardson also knew the old man from his earlier trip to Ghat. Lyon described Hatita as "the only Tuarick I ever saw, who was not an impudent beggar, or who made presents without expecting a return." This utterly contradicted the experience of every other European who met him. Hatita was a tireless wheedler. Around Europeans he spent much of his energy begging for presents and scheming how to shut out his fellow tribesmen.

Richardson began the grueling process of bargaining with Tuaregs who smell an easy mark. He was buying in a seller's market. "Our escort is to cost us dear," Richardson wrote afterward in his journal, "but it will ensure our safety." He was right about the expense—200 Spanish dollars (about £40), a small fortune—but terribly wrong about buying safety, even if the Tuaregs had actually honored the agreement.

As Richardson fretted in his journal about the dangers and expenses ahead, Barth felt reenergized by the prospect of movement. "[We] roused our spirits for the contemplation of novelties and the encountering of difficulties; for the latter could certainly not be wanting where the former were at hand."

On June 25 the main caravan finally headed out of Murzuk. "The Greek doctor came to see us off," wrote Richardson, "but we started in a little confusion, for Mr. Yusuf Moknee was drunk, as he was nearly all the time of our stay in Mourzuk."

Gagliuffi, who didn't yet know about Richardson's accusatory letters to the Foreign Office, was worried about the expedition. A few days after it left, he wrote to Consul Crowe in Tripoli that he wished Richardson had hired people with real power to protect them. He was also uneasy about Richardson's inadequate stock of goods for winning over rulers in the interior. "He thinks to travel far, and spend little," wrote Gagliuffi, "and that is impossible in these countries: he is too confident in himself and listens to little advice. May God protect them!"

6

The Palace of the Demons

THE TUAREGS BROKE THEIR AGREEMENT FOR THE FIRST TIME WITHIN days of leaving Murzuk. Hatita mournfully informed Richardson that instead of taking the direct route to Aïr, as contracted, they needed to stop in Ghat for at least a month of preparations. It was an obvious ploy to milk the expedition at leisure. Richardson objected, sighed, acquiesced. Barth, incredulous, stepped in and told Hatita that the caravan would stay in Ghat no more than seven days. Hatita was already peeved at Barth for traveling ahead of the caravan, out of reach of his demands for presents. Richardson often griped about Hatita's daily nagging ("I cannot fill this craving abyss to the brim"); Barth just shrugged him off.

They were traveling through a desert of stony rubble and dark sand. As they went west, the country grew more hot, arid, and desolate. Vegetation was so scarce that they carried forage for the camels. There were days without wells. They found fossilized starfish and plants. Occasionally they passed low stone walls forming a square or a circle—makeshift mosques where passing travelers could pray to Mecca. Temperatures in the shade rose above 100 degrees. Richardson felt the heat intensely and tried to make the Tuaregs travel at night, but they refused. In the late afternoons, for extra protection from the sun, he lay on the floor of his thin-ceilinged tent with his head shaded beneath his bed and table, which he piled with blankets.

At a place called Wadi Telisaghe, Barth discovered some remarkably skilled bas-reliefs cut into the blocks of sandstone that littered the valley. The most striking depicted two godlike figures with human torsos, one with the head of a long-horned bull, the other with the head of a bird, perhaps an ibis, which reminded Barth of Egyptian motifs. The figures carried bows and were fighting over a bullock standing between them. Other carvings also portrayed bullocks and ostriches. None showed camels. All demonstrated flair and expertise far beyond what Europeans, including Barth, expected to find in remote Saharan Africa. Barth's classical sources didn't mention anything like them, nor did the Arab historians who came later. The carvings suggested that skilled unknown cultures had existed in the desert even before the introduction of camels around the first century B.C. The historical implications electrified Barth. The carvings showed him how much still awaited discovery in the heart of Africa.

ON JULY 13 they traveled through a pass lined with huge boulders. Some of the boulders rocked on pivots in the hot gusty wind, others were neatly cleaved as if by a divine sword. Ahead, the crenellated peak of Mount Idinen towered out of the plain. Its massive walls and turrets looked hand-hewn. Desert winds had sculpted the mountain's massive jumbled rocks into strange ribs and battlements that resembled a ruined castle or a blasted cathedral. Nature had painted it all in striking colors—cream, black, purple, russet, lavender. The effect was eerie.

The Tuaregs had been talking about the mountain all day. They said that jinns—spirits—from all over the desert gathered there to confer and pray. Caverns in the mountain were filled with the jinns' treasure—gold, silver, jewels. No Tuareg would dare set foot there. They called it the Palace of the Demons.

The caravan traveled toward the mountain until seven o'clock, then camped. A strong wind kicked up, preventing men and animals from sleeping. When they started again at sunrise, the wind was still blowing hard and hot. They walked straight toward the looming mountain all day before making camp.

Barth wanted to climb it. This blasphemous idea alarmed Hatita and the other Tuaregs. It also distressed Richardson. He had passed by the mountain on his previous journey, and had tried to disprove the Tuaregs' superstitions by climbing partway up it alone. He got lost and spent a terrifying night, afraid he was going to die.

Despite these warnings—in fact, partly because of them—Barth was determined to explore Idinen for inscriptions or carvings by ancient worshipers. He owed it to science. Hatita angrily refused to find him a guide. Yusuf Moknee told Barth that the mountain was farther than it appeared and advised taking a camel. Barth brushed them both off. Early the next morning he and Overweg set off on foot, carrying a few dates, some dry biscuit, and one small waterskin.

Overweg reappeared in camp at five that afternoon, thirsty and exhausted. He had given up within a few hours. Sharp black rocks made walking difficult, and a deep ravine greatly lengthened the approach to the mountain. Overweg thought it was foolish to continue, but Barth refused to turn back.

As the sun went down with no sign of their colleague, Overweg and Richardson became alarmed. They built big signal fires and hung a lantern in the tallest nearby tree. Overweg and several Tuaregs went out to look for Barth. They returned at midnight, having seen no sign of him.

At daybreak two search parties mounted up and left camp. They returned at noon. Overweg's party found nothing. The other came across footprints to the north, but lost them in the stony sand. Now fully alarmed, Richardson offered a reward of 50 Spanish dollars for finding Barth, which inspired most of the Tuaregs to saddle their camels and join the search.

It was the height of the Saharan summer. Barth had no water. Such conditions, the Tuaregs told Richardson, usually killed people within twelve hours. Barth had been gone for more than twenty-four. The Tuaregs expected to find a corpse. "I confess, that as the afternoon wore on," Richardson confided to his journal, "I had given up nearly all hope, and continued the search merely as a matter of duty."

The sun was setting when a servant ran into camp shouting. A Tuareg had tracked Barth's footprints and found him eight miles away. He was alive but unable to move. Blood oozed from his cracked mouth, the residue of an attempt to drink his own blood. His throat was so dry and swollen that at first he couldn't swallow the water he desperately needed. The Tuareg rescuer bathed and sprinkled Barth's head as the explorer hoarsely whispered over and over, "El hamdu lillahi," a Qur'anic verse recited by Muslims many times per day: Praise be to Allah. He had been gone for twenty-eight hours. The Tuaregs were astonished at his survival. They were equally surprised by his toughness and quick recovery. Though he could hardly speak or eat for the next three days, on the day after his rescue he mounted his camel and rode with the caravan for seven hours.

Barth felt grateful, sorry, embarrassed. His impetuous curiosity had nearly killed him and crippled the expedition. He had let down his colleagues and caused them tremendous anxiety as well as expense. He had been headstrong, ill prepared, and overconfident both in his judgments and in his physical strength. He had disregarded good advice and flouted the thin line between life and death in Africa. He had almost thrown away his ambitions and dreams, had almost let down science just as the expedition was on the verge of territories never explored by Europeans. To bring his discoveries home, he must survive. He would not forget the hard lessons taught at the Palace of the Demons.

7

To Aïr

ON JULY 18 THEY REACHED THE SMALL CARAVAN TOWN OF GHAT, a huddle of 250 houses. For nearly 1,000 miles to the south, the territory was unknown to Europeans. Barth felt sure discoveries awaited there.

But first they had to escape the conniving spongers of Ghat. Hatita, an expert on the species and an exemplar of it, advised the Europeans to keep their doors shut and to answer all knocks with "Babo!"—"No one's here!" The one exception to this rule, of course, was Hatita, whose begging remained shameless and insatiable.

The Europeans further infuriated the town's spongers by refusing to pause there for weeks so they could be cadged into penury. In retaliation, their Tuareg escort reneged on their pledge to accompany the expedition to Aïr, brushing aside the mere detail that they had already been paid to do so. In fact, they demanded additional money for protecting the freed slaves who had accompanied the expedition to Ghat, a fee they had already collected once. For their finale, they insisted on a bonus.

This was the atmosphere in which Richardson attempted to negotiate a commercial treaty between Her Majesty's Government and the chiefs of Ghat. These worthies quickly grasped that such an agreement could benefit them. They were poised to sign when Richardson pulled out another document requiring them to end the slave trade. Richardson's tactlessness stunned Barth. The chiefs broke off negotiations.

"It is a serious undertaking," noted Barth, "to enter into direct negotiation with these [Tuareg] chiefs, the absolute masters of several of the most important routes to Central Africa. It required great skill, entire confidence, and no inconsiderable amount of means, of which we were extremely deficient." That last clause referred not just to their merchandise but to Richardson.

A caravan of Tuaregs from the Kel Owi clan, whose territory extended into Aïr, happened to be in Ghat. The expedition hired them as their new escorts through the mountains of Aïr and on to Zinder, a Hausa city in central Sudan. The fee was relatively low—about £15— but turned out to be merely a down payment.

On July 26, after only eight days in Ghat, the expedition moved on. Richardson captured this pivotal moment well:

. . . we were about to enter upon a region totally unknown, of which no authentic accounts from eye-witnesses—unless we count the vague reports of natives—had ever reached us; valleys unexplored; deserts unaffronted; countries which no European had ever surveyed. Before us, somewhere in the heart of the Sahara, raised into magnificence perhaps by the mirage of report, was the unknown kingdom of Aheer [Aïr], of which Leo Africanus hints something, but the names of whose great cities are scattered as if at haphazard over the maps, possibly hundreds of miles out of their right position. What reception shall we meet with in that untried land? In what light will its untravelled natives—fierce from ignorance and bigotry— regard this mission of infidels, coming from latitudes of which they have never dreamed, with objects unappreciable and perhaps hostile? Will nature itself be hospitable? Are there no enemies in the climate, no perils peculiar to the seasons? These questions occupied my mind as the caravan wound between the last palm-groves of Ghat; and my camel, resuming its swinging march, went away with its neck advanced like a bowsprit over this desert sea, which might be scattered with hidden dangers at every step.

That evening he fretted to his journal, in barely concealed irritation, "Dr. Barth was again lost this evening, having pushed on in his usual eager way for about half an hour. We were filled with alarm." Barth, traveling ahead of the caravan as always, had reached a fork and stayed on the main path; the expedition took the other way. Barth was mounted, with plenty of water, and he caught up with the caravan before dark. It was a nonevent, but Richardson was still shaken from the scare at the Palace of the Demons ten days earlier, and irritated that Barth persisted in his impatient ways.

The next day they passed through a beautiful desert valley that ran between high rocky hills. Quail flitted in the bushes. Vultures, crows, and white eagles crisscrossed the sky. In a pleasant ending to the day, they camped among the rocks at a pool, wide and deep, where the slaves of the Kel Owis merrily swam and splashed.

In the following days the caravan climbed and descended through fantastical rock formations that resembled castles, forests, and human tableaux. Water and pasturage were plentiful. Five days out of Ghat, this idyll ended.

Word arrived that a Tuareg chieftain from farther south was en route to annihilate the expedition. Richardson was aflutter. Barth, always the scientist, considered the rumor an untested hypothesis.

Less at ease, they moved on. The terrain flattened into bumpy gravel. They occasionally passed small pyramids of mounded stones left by travelers to mark the route. Smaller heaps marked the graves of slave children who had died on the march. On August 2 the expedition sighted a steep ridge called Mariaw, harbinger of the Ténéré, a desolate plain of sand and gravel that stretches across 150,000 square miles in the central Sudan. "Entirely destitute of herbage," wrote Barth, "and without the smallest fragment of wood for fuel." Wells were rare. The temperature was 111 degrees.

For several days, traveling for twelve hours at a stretch, they pushed across this bleakness toward a destination equally bleak called Falesselez. This barren place offered not a stick of shade, but for the first time in two days there was a well. After drinking, Barth measured its mouth: one-and-a-half feet across. The water was "very dirty and discolored," he wrote, "but it gradually became clearer, and had but little after-taste." On the Ténéré such a spot passed for luxurious. In other places the water tasted salty or sulfurous. At one well the murky water tasted like ink, "and when boiled with tea became entirely black."

Falesselez revealed two sides of the Saharan character. The expedition's camel drivers, traveling several days ahead, had left a stash of dates at the well, marked by a stick in the sand. Though everyone traveling through this part of the Ténéré stopped at Falesselez, and though desert tribes were rapacious by habit, the dates had not been touched. The Saharan code dictated that no one would steal provisions left for someone else's survival, in the same way that someone in great need was never denied water. The code was practical, not compassionate. No desert traveler knew when he might be the one desperate for help. If not for the stashed dates at Falesselez, some of the expedition's camels would have been unable to continue.

On the other hand, the Kel Owis began to extort the expedition here. Capitalizing on Richardson's fears about being attacked, they demanded twice the fee they had agreed to, for half the work. They now intended to leave the expedition in the middle of Aïr, about 300 miles short of Zinder. Richardson felt trapped by circumstances. He also half-suspected the Kel Owis of being in cahoots with the rumored attackers. He agreed to the new terms. He also agreed with Barth's comparison of the Kel Owis to snakes.

The caravan continued south. Some Tuareg hunters entered camp and bartered two carcasses of Barbary sheep (aoudad) for a length of gray calico. Ravenous for meat, Richardson ate so much that "it threatened to produce injurious effects."

As they exited the Ténéré, the gravel plain gave way to rugged mountains, ravines, and sharp cliffs, with patches of grass and trees. All of this contradicted European assumptions about the Sahara as a vast stretch of sand. Just ahead, in the district of Aïr, lay even greater surprises. About 300 miles long and 200 miles wide, Aïr was filled with steep disconnected massifs and volcanic cones, some of them rising more than 6,000 feet from the desert floor. The region was notorious as an isolated redoubt haunted by gangs of Tuareg brigands who had never been subdued by an outside power.

ON AUGUST 10 a man appeared in camp with the news that a nearby caravan of Merabetin Tuaregs had heard about the Christian expedition and were threatening to stop the infidels from entering Aïr. The Kel Owis immediately started a fresh round of extortion. At the same time, Richardson was besieged for gifts by a Ghat Tuareg whom Hatita had sent with the expedition, with instructions to milk it. Richardson eventually offered this persistent man, who was providing no services, a small burnoose and a fez. He rejected them angrily. "Money, money, money!" he shouted. His threats grew so violent that Richardson loaded his pistols. This had the intended calming effect. The man also tried squeezing Barth to pay him "taxes" for visiting the Palace of the Demons and for drinking at various wells. These demands, wrote Richardson, merely amused the German.

The landscape changed again, becoming more desolate. Fog hid the mountaintops, a precursor of tropical latitude. The Kel Owis had gotten word that a large group of Tuaregs from the desert mountains of Hoggar, to the west, were in pursuit of the Christian caravan. That brought the number of rumored hostile gangs to three. These threats triggered grumbles within the expedition's Muslim employees, most of whom were unwilling to die protecting infidels. Richardson didn't seem to notice. "To any one who paid due attention to the character and disposition of the people," wrote Barth, "serious indications of a storm, which was gathering over us, became visible."

In response to the threat from pursuers, the Kel Owis pushed the caravan to travel for twelve to fourteen hours each day, covering more than 30 miles at a stretch. On August 16 they ran into a violent sandstorm followed by a drenching rain, with winds that threatened to knock them from their saddles—another tropical greeting. They marched for fourteen hours that day, rested for four, then remounted at eleven o'clock to trudge through the night, rocking in a half-doze on their camels. After nine more hours they reached another bleak place with several wells called Asiu. When Ibn Battuta stopped here in 1353–54, it was already an important way station on the caravan route. Asiu also marked the northern boundary of Aïr, home of the Kel Owis.

Richardson, relieved, thought they were now safe. Barth wasn't so sure. He reminded Richardson that nomads ignored territorial frontiers. Absurd, insisted Richardson, adding that desert tribes respected boundaries even more scrupulously than Austrians. "But he was soon to be undeceived on all the points of his desert diplomacy," wrote Barth, "at his own expense and that of us all."

8

Plundered

A FTER A DAY OF REST THEY CONTINUED SOUTH. TWO HOURS LATER, a cry advanced up the caravan: the Hoggar Tuaregs are coming! The expedition, already tense, was thrown into turmoil. Richardson, hard of hearing, at first didn't know what was happening, but jumped off his camel and cocked his pistols. The Germans loaded their guns. Any man with a firearm was given powder and shot. The slaves grabbed their bows and arrows.

The warning came from a member of the caravan who had lingered at the well that morning after the expedition left. Three Tuaregs had ridden up on mehara camels, the fast slender breed favored by desert raiders. The man asked the Tuaregs if they were traveling with others. The terse reply—yes—sent him scurrying in panic toward the expedition.

They rode all day with their weapons in hand, scanning the hills above them for silhouettes. They camped in late afternoon and propped up the boat sections as barricades. Near sunset three Tuaregs on mehara ambled into camp. They dismounted and strolled with haughty nonchalance through the caravan, enjoying the jittery silent stares. Under their dark blue flowing robes and headdresses, only their predatory eyes were visible. They cast appraising looks at the caravan's mass of baggage and its 107 camels. The Kel Owis were swiveling their heads, looking for the rest of the raiding party. Their alarm was contagious.

After their stroll, the strangers sat down and asked for supper, claiming they hadn't eaten for fifteen days. The Kel Owis confirmed that the men were carrying no supplies except a single waterskin. The strangers were given hamsa (hot rice pudding) and zummita, a dish made of parched ground corn. They pretended to be surprised that the caravan contained infidels, and maintained that they were en route to visit relatives in Aïr. No one believed them. Nevertheless, Richardson hoped that hospitality would soften their intentions toward the caravan.

Barth scoffed at this naïveté. He recognized the classic tactics of desert freebooters: "They will cling artfully to a caravan, and first introduce themselves in a tranquil and peaceable way, till they have succeeded in disturbing the little unity which exists in such a troop, composed as it is of the most different elements; they then gradually throw off the mask, and in general attain their object." The strangers' disingenuous conduct, added Barth, "was mere farce and mockery, and the only way of insuring our safety would have been to prevent these scouts from approaching us at all."

Barth had learned that the three strangers were not from the Hoggar, but were Kel Fadey Tuaregs. Their home was in northern Aïr near Mount Ighalgawan—"eyrie of vultures." Still, there were sixty armed men in the caravan. But most were Muslims, and their loyalty to infidels might quickly evaporate when threatened by a Tuareg raiding party. Even Richardson noticed that the servants were becoming troublesome. The three strangers bedded down on the camp's perimeter. The caravan posted watchmen throughout the night. It was August 18.

Early the next morning the three strangers disappeared over a ridge. Some members of the caravan, cutting herbage there later, found the tracks of nine camels. The caravan was being shadowed. Despite the danger, they didn't break camp that day because the Kel Owis wanted to rest and feed the camels. They also suggested that, for safekeeping, the Europeans give them everything of value, a self-contradictory proposition that amused Barth.

That evening three Tuaregs rode into camp, different men from the night before. Barth learned that they were Hadanara, a division of the Hoggar Tuaregs and infamous as "migratory freebooters." Richardson evidently didn't notice the new men's dissimilarity, perhaps because both groups of nomads were covered head to toe in blue robes. But the differences were immediately apparent to a discerning eye. Like their companions on the other side of the ridge, these new strangers requested and received supper. They promised to go their own way tomorrow and not to ask for hospitality again.

The next day, wrote Barth, "we started with an uneasy feeling." For once he didn't range ahead. No one straggled. The three strangers, despite their promise, followed on the caravan's flank. They occasionally cantered with their spears held in battle position, their long shields of bullock hide clasped at their sides.

Four men materialized on a hill ahead. The Kel Owis instantly sent a small troop of archers to investigate. The rest of the caravan moved forward tensely. Barth, anticipating trouble, dismounted to give himself more secure footing. As the caravan neared the ridge, two of the four strangers and several of the Kel Owis suddenly started "a wild sort of armed dance" while the others sat quietly. When Barth reached this perplexing scene, the two strange dancers, whom he could now see were black, rushed at him and grabbed the rope of his camel while vigorously demanding a gift. Barth, already nervous, pulled his pistol and was about to fire when someone hurriedly began explaining this weird encounter.

Long ago the Kel Owis, a Berber people, had taken possession of Aïr from the Goberawa, part of the black Hausa nation. In a peacemaking pact, the two groups agreed that from then on, the head chief of the Kel Owis could only marry a Gober woman. To commemorate the event, which had occurred on the little hill where Barth now stood, the black "slaves" were licensed to make merry while levying a small tribute from any passing caravan. One of the dancers who had rushed Barth was the chief of the slave-acolytes who lived there. They collected their levy. As the caravan marched on, "these poor merry creatures" were still dancing at their good fortune.

The incident would have been even more fascinating, noted Barth, if the caravan's members had not been "vexed with sad forebodings of mishap." The shadow riders with their spears still haunted the flank. One of the camel drivers insisted that Barth stay in the middle of the group as a precaution against a sudden lancing.

They camped that afternoon on a gravelly plain but didn't pitch their tents, in case of attack. Though the caravan had been on the march for fourteen hours, that night the slaves of the Kel Owis ran through the encampment, dancing and singing as they exercised their privilege of collecting tribute from every free person in the caravan—a few dates, a piece of cloth, a shirt. Richardson was baffled by their joyful antics and didn't know what was going on. It's telling that Barth didn't bother explaining the old custom to him, and that Richardson didn't bother to find out what was happening. One man saw only incomprehensible native conduct; the other explored its origins and meaning.

The three shadow riders entered camp again. As they ate another meal of the expedition's food, they told the camel drivers that when reinforcements arrived they intended to kill the infidels. Richardson seemed oblivious. "God knows they may be honest men," he wrote, "in reality poor devils obliged to beg their way to [Aïr]." Barth entertained no such delusions. Despite marching for fourteen hours, he and Overweg took turns watching all night.

The next day, August 21, a Tuareg rode into camp and demanded that the Kel Owis give up the Christians. This was refused. That afternoon, while Barth was exploring another group of rock sculptures near camp, a member of the Kel Owi escort attempted to throw him down and steal his pistols. The big explorer easily repelled the attack, but such bald treachery by an alleged protector was a bad sign about the caravan's changing stance toward the Christians. That night Barth took the first watch and used "the splendid moonlight to address a few lines in pencil to my friends at home."

As the caravan continued south, the landscape grew more wet and green. Valleys with sandy wadis ran between jagged mountains. Waterfalls, verdure, and wildflowers abounded.

On the evening of August 22, two mounted men entered camp and demanded the surrender of the Christians. Again, they were refused.

On August 23 the caravan reached the first inhabited place in the long-imagined region of Aïr. It was an unimpressive introduction. The village looked shabby and defeated. It didn't have a single sheep or goat to sell the expedition, nor any of the famous Aïr cheese that Barth had been craving. The people were Kel Fadey Tuaregs, part of the Kel Owis. Without explaining what he meant, Barth described the village's women as disappointingly wanton, which surprised him in such a small remote place, until he remembered that "we have ample testimony in ancient Arabian writers that licentious manners have always prevailed among the Berber tribes on the frontier of the desert."

Tuareg men preferred corpulent women, and Barth noticed that several of these beauties possessed the desirable callipygian immensity called *tebulloden*, a Tuareg word whose definition Barth quotes from Leo Africanus in the original Italian, to soften its impact: "the parts behind exceedingly rich and succulent." (Richardson expressed his delicacy in French, noting that some Tuareg women "attain to an enormous degree of *embon-point*.")

The men looked scruffy and degraded, especially when compared to the "noble and manly appearance" of "our martial pursuers"—the three freebooters, who were once again in the camp. "Though I knew the latter could and would do us much more harm than the former," wrote Barth, "I liked them much better."

Barth's reaction was typical of Westerners who dealt with Tuaregs. The men personified mystery in their flowing robes and turban-veils, dyed a deep indigo that rubbed off on the skin. The slender "blue men" of the desert carried themselves with haughty grace, like vain kings. They esteemed courage, endurance, and elegance of movement. They were proud, warlike, and ascetic, indifferent to hardship, merciless to enemies.

The Tuaregs' origins were shadowy but emerged from the Berber tribes of North Africa. They were already a distinct people by the second century A.D., when Ptolemy mentions them. The Arabic armies of Islam that swept across northern Africa in the seventh and eighth centuries gave these desert nomads the name Tuareg, "the Abandoned of God," perhaps because they resisted so ferociously, both militarily and religiously. Barth and others suggested that the religion they had abandoned was Christianity, pointing to clues such as their word for God, Mesí (Messiah), their fondness for the decorative motif of a cross, which Islam forbids, and their custom of monogamy in contrast to Muslim polygamy. In any case, the Tuaregs adopted Islam much later than the rest of northern Africa. Their names for themselves were Imoshag or Imajughen, meaning either "the free people" or "the noble people," or Kel Tagelmoust, "the people of the veil," or Kel Tamasheq, "speakers of Tamasheq," their Berber-related language.

Conflict with the Arabs drove some Tuareg tribes south into the western Sahara and the desert mountains of Hoggar and Aïr. There they collided and commingled with the dark-skinned Hausa and Fulani peoples of the Sahel.

The Tuaregs partitioned themselves into bewildering divisions of confederations, tribes, subtribes, clans, and factions. Barth's brief descriptions of the branches just within Aïr runs for a dozen pages. Every Tuareg, male and female, belonged to one of three overarching feudal categories: nobles, vassals, or slaves. Nobles disdained ordinary labor. Male nobles raided, waged war, and protected their vassals and slaves. Female nobles focused on artistic activities such as music, poetry, jewelry-making, and other decorative crafts. Vassals handled livestock and crops, from which they supported nobles. Male vassals often accompanied nobles on raids. Slaves—blacks captured in raids, and their descendants—did the domestic and outdoor labor.

Tuareg men, then as now, were distinctive because of their *tagelmoust*, or turban-veil. They wrapped this 10-foot cloth around their head, leaving a slit for their eyes. Once donned in early manhood, the tagelmoust was not taken off even for eating, drinking, or sleeping. It's unclear when and why Tuareg men adopted the veil. Speculation varies from the practical—to protect against sun and blowing sand—to the superstitious—to keep out evil spirits. But since Tuareg women do not wear the veil, no explanation is entirely satisfactory.

A Tuareg warrior carried a spear, a double-edged cross-hilted sword about 3 feet long, and a shield of tanned animal hide 4 or 5 feet long. On his inner left forearm he stored a sheathed dagger with a 6-inch blade, the tip pointing to the elbow, the hilt at the wrist for instant access. Above his right elbow he typically wore a ring carved from soft stone, to protect his sword arm. During Barth's time a few Tuaregs started carrying muskets and other firearms, but most scorned such weapons as unmanly. A Tuareg man adorned his austere robes with silver ornaments and decorative leather charms and amulets to ward off the evil eye. He wore wide sandals for support on sand. Though his feet were as tough as thick leather, the dry heat sometimes cracked them badly, in which case he sewed them up with a needle and thread.

As raiders Tuaregs were rapacious and ruthless. Everyone, including Tuaregs from other factions, was fair game, though raiders did not steal or molest Tuareg women. Plunder taken on raids or extorted from caravans wasn't considered theft, but the well-deserved spoils of daring and force. An anthropologist once noted that for the Tuaregs, "the idea that man is free and a brigand is so inseparable that the same verb (Iohagh) means 'he is free' and 'he pillages.'"

The Tuaregs built their way of life around the camel. Camels represented wealth and sustenance. They made possible the long-range desert mobility that Tuaregs needed for trade and pillage. They supplied milk. If their owner was dying of thirst, their blood and the water in their stomachs provided emergency fluids. When age, sickness, or exhaustion claimed camels, they became meat. Their hides became tents, ropes, saddles, bags, waterskins, and gear.

The triad celebrated in Tuareg song and poetry was women, daring deeds, and—essential for success with both of the former—camels. Men and women judged a man not only by the number of his camels but by his style while mounted, which included his ornate saddle and other camel trappings. Camels attracted and bought brides. They were also given as payment to settle disputes.

Camels also pervaded the Tuaregs' language, Tamasheq. Terms covered every aspect of camelness, starting with types, their uses, and every inch of their exteriors. Glossaries were necessary to describe a camel's age, health, defects, distinguishing features, and colors (white, whitish, whitish yellow, dirty white, and on through the spectrum). There were terms for special qualities, such as a camel that neighed with joy or one that bellowed when lonely. There were terms for camels that roared in complaint when being loaded or unloaded. There were words to describe the length of a camel's step and the many possible gaits. The Tuaregs had words for small groups of camels and large groups, for camels in caravans and camels at pasture, for a camel forced to go grazing while its calf remained tethered in camp.

Camel maladies required another set of terminology, as well as veterinary skills. The most common problem, saddle sores, was treated with a lotion made of urine from a female camel. If infected, the sores were cut or burned. Sometimes the clouds of flies that followed caravans laid eggs in these open wounds, attracting birds that pecked at the maggots and irritated the camel. This could be stopped by tying a pair of crow's wings to the camel's hump. Tuaregs treated other camel ailments with salt, tobacco, and heated butter. Other remedies—enemas, bleeding, cauterizing with a hot iron—were used on humans (in Europe, too) as well as on camels.

The animals were watered every three days or so, but before a long dry journey this was gradually lengthened so that before the trip began, the camels would drink nearly to bursting.

Every Westerner noticed that Tuareg culture upended certain practices of Islam. This was especially noticeable in the position of women in Tuareg society, whether noble, vassal, or slave. Most of Islamic North Africa espoused the Arabic attitude that a respectable female should go out only three times in her life: once when she left the womb, once when she left her father's house for marriage, and once when she died. By contrast, Tuareg women enjoyed a wide degree of autonomy. As Barth noted, "the women appear to have the superiority over the male sex in the country of [Aïr], at least to a certain extent."

Tuareg women did not wear veils or hide their sexuality. They adorned themselves to be alluring, with henna on their nails, kohl around their eyes, and, for special occasions, red or yellow ochres daubed on cheeks and foreheads. They were not restricted to the indoors or to certain areas of the dwelling. They usually ate with the men and with guests, not separately. They were heard as well as seen—the men sought and respected their opinions.

The women were often better educated than the men, since they had the task of teaching their children to read and write Tamasheq, a strange language that can be written left to right, right to left, up and down, in a spiral, or boustrophedon style (alternating lines in opposite directions). Noble Tuareg women also learned to sing, play music, and recite poetry. Westerners universally commented on the easy respect between Tuareg men and women, and on their tenderness for their children. Though Islam allowed a man four wives, monogamy was typical among the Tuaregs.

The culture was matrilineal. When a Tuareg woman married, her husband left his village for hers. The camels, livestock, and jewelry that he was obliged to give her became her property. If she used these to increase her wealth, it belonged solely to her. If the marriage didn't work out, a woman could get a divorce simply by decreeing it. Whatever property she had accumulated stayed with her. So did the couple's children, since, the Tuaregs reasoned, she had carried them before birth. If a married couple had children and the mother died, the children stayed with the mother's clan. If the clans of the mother and father went to war, the children fought for the mother's side. Similarly, when slaves belonging to different masters married, their children were considered the property of the female's master. In some tribes, slaves had a degree of self-determination—a slave who felt mistreated could change masters.

Relations between the sexes also differed markedly between Tuaregs and their Islamic neighbors. Tuaregs did not fetishize virginity and female purity. Charles de Foucauld, a French monk who lived among the Tuaregs for a dozen years in the early twentieth century and compiled a four-volume dictionary of Tamasheq, found no word in the language for virginity. Young Tuareg males and females mixed frequently at nighttime social events called *ahal*, filled with music, dancing, and flirting. Couples often wandered off into the desert night. This time of courtship and experimentation before marriage was called *asri*, "to gallop with free reins." Both sexes did so without penalty. After marriage, a woman wasn't put into seclusion but could visit her friends at will, including male friends.

Much of this ran counter to Islamic practice everywhere else, which added to the Tuaregs' fascination for Westerners, who often made the error of mythologizing them. But the Tuaregs' independence included acute hardship, especially for their slaves. These desert people were tough beyond belief, but existed on the edge of survival. They often subsisted for months on milk and coarse grain. Everyone except the small minority of nobles survived through backbreaking labor, much of it done by the women.

As THE CARAVAN rested in the village, the alarm sounded again: the Tuaregs are coming! Rumor flashed the number of warriors at fifty to sixty. Richardson again ordered the distribution of powder and shot, including, to Barth's amazement, to the three strangers. Richardson justified the action in his journal by noting that these men had vowed to defend the Christians to the death. Barth called this "imprudence and absurdity," since the three men "made no other use of the present than to supply their band with this material, which alone gave us a degree of superiority, and constituted our security."

Around ten o'clock that night, as the caravan's forces stood in nervous battle lines, a small troop of mounted men advanced toward them. A volley fired over the riders' heads persuaded them to retreat. Shooting and shouting continued for the rest of the night. Barth somehow stepped outside of this alarming situation and observed it as an enjoyable spectacle: "The scene which followed in the bright moonlight evening, and lasted throughout the night, was animating and interesting in the extreme."

The next day the expedition stayed put. The leaders of the shadow troop sent word that they would not molest the caravan if the Christians were handed over. This was rejected. It seemed clear to Barth that their foes were motivated less by faith than by avarice, and wouldn't attack until they had reinforcements. Tensions and divided loyalties roiled the caravan. Barth called the situation "tedious" because it kept him in camp. That afternoon, "not being able to refrain wholly from excursions," he spent several hours exploring a nearby valley, despite the obvious danger.

The following morning, August 24, they moved on without incident. That evening five mounted men leading six camels camped within a pistol shot of the caravan. They were joined by the three strangers who had vowed to die for the Christians. The group's "wild, ferocious laughter" put the caravan on edge. Then all the strangers sauntered into camp and asked for supper. Richardson, still swerving between panic and willful naïveté, didn't like the looks of these new strangers but nevertheless convinced himself that they "gave a tolerable account of themselves," an opinion that almost made Barth snort.

The new strangers slipped away during the night. At dawn the Kel Owis discovered that most of their camels had disappeared as well. At six o'clock that morning the strangers from the night before rode down from a rocky ridge and ordered the Kel Owis to turn over the Christians and all their baggage. When the Kel Owis again refused, a troop of forty men, mounted on mehara and carrying spears, swords, and shields, boiled over the ridge and charged with wild cries. The caravan's armed men were ready and marched forward, shouting defiance. When they

aimed their muskets, the charging line scattered and retreated without a
shot being fired. Richardson was shocked to see, among the raiders, the
three strangers who had sworn undying loyalty while eating his food
and accepting his powder and shot.

A party of the raiders soon approached to parley. They didn't want to
fight other Muslims, they told the Kel Owis, they just wanted to kill the
infidels. From the ridge angry men on camels shouted that more raiders
would soon arrive to help take the Christians.

The caravaneers' loyalty to the Europeans was eroding. The camel
drivers, who passed this way often, were reluctant to endanger their live-
lihood by affronting the local tribes. The Kel Owis, if given no alternative, would certainly trade the Christians for the return of their camels.
In this dire situation Richardson told the Kel Owis to open negotiations
with the raiders.

The bargaining began. We want to kill the infidels, repeated the
raiders. Unacceptable, replied the Kel Owis. In that case, said the raiders,
the caravan must turn around and leave Aïr. Unfeasible, said the Kel
Owis. Then if the infidels want to proceed, they must convert to Islam.
Impossible, replied the Kel Owis. Which brought the raiders to their real
goal: the infidels could buy their lives by giving up half their goods and
baggage. After further haggling, the raiders settled for goods worth £50
(about a quarter of the expedition's cargo), plus an enormous celebratory
meal of hamsa for everybody.

The raiders' leader pledged that the Christians were now safe, but
they remained unconvinced that he could control his wild companions.
After all, he also told them that while he had been bowed in prayer, asking for the strength to defeat the infidels, one of his own Tuaregs had
crept up and stolen his burnoose, carpet, and fez.

That evening other Tuaregs from the vicinity entered camp. Angry
at missing the fleecing of the Christians, they were bent on further
shearing. Richardson handed over another £5-worth of goods. All this
gift-giving to foes aroused resentment among the camel drivers, who
also had to be placated with presents.

On August 26 as the caravan approached the high mountains of Aïr, at about 19 degrees of latitude, the Kel Owis announced that they were crossing another invisible boundary into a new region—the Sudan. The word, shortened from the Arabic *Beled e' sudan,* meant "land of the blacks," or Negroland. To the Tuaregs it was simply the South.

They broke camp so early on the 27th that Barth made his first notes of the day by moonlight. The landscape blossomed and grew various. Veins of beautiful white marble patterned the granite hills. Sometimes the rocks were pink or red, or varnished to gleaming black by blowing sand. The valleys were luxuriant with tall acacia trees draped with hanging vines. They passed green gorges and mountainsides indented with glens.

But there were less welcome sights as well. Three men on mehara rode parallel to them, and the caravan came across a spot recently trampled by the footprints of many camels and men. "There was not the least doubt that another host was gathering against us," wrote Barth. They rode with their weapons in hand.

The day's destination was the village of Selufiet. Eight miles before it, the guide led the caravan off the path to a campsite. Barth's suspicions were quickly confirmed: Another plot was afoot. Fifty armed men rode into camp, followed after dark by fifty more. They were Merabetin Tuaregs from deep within Aïr. The Kel Owi escort warned the Europeans to stay together in one tent. All remained quiet until after the sunset prayers. And then, wrote Barth, "the calm was at an end, and the scene which followed was awful."

From inside their tent, the Europeans could hear angry debate. The Merabetins and the Kel Owis had begun a long night of intense conference. The Europeans' servants occasionally brought reports. One of the Kel Owi leaders had thrown down his sword in front of his tribesmen, shouting, "Let us all die with the Christians!" But the reports were otherwise alarming and unchanging: The Merabetins swore that no infidels had ever passed through their country, and none ever would. The ones in the tent must either convert to Islam or die.

Barth judged the threat to be real this time, not a bargaining ploy. The Kel Owis and the Europeans' servants begged the Christians to convert, at least for a few days. "My colleagues," wrote Richardson, "and particularly Dr. Barth, indignantly and passionately resisted." Their servants, planning ahead, asked for letters that cleared them of blame for the coming slaughter. Richardson sent word that conversion was impossible, but they would pay the tribute required of infidels. If that was unacceptable, "we would wait patiently for death." In that case, the Kel Owis told them, your deaths are certain.

The next half-hour, as the Merabetins and Kel Owis continued to argue, was excruciating. The Europeans sat in the tent without speaking. Every sound outside seemed to signal an attack. Finally, according to Barth, Richardson broke the silence. "Let us talk a little," he said. "We must die; what is the use of sitting so mute?" It was Richardson's finest moment as the expedition's leader—calm and strong, like his faith.

They heard voices approaching and tensed. One of their servants rushed into the tent: "You are not to die!" The Merabetins would accept a heavy tribute after all, equal to the payment given to the Kel Owis. "For some minutes death seemed really to hover over our heads," wrote Barth, "but the awful moment passed by."

The next morning they forked over goods worth £35, as agreed. But a large hostile crowd had gathered and wanted more. Most of the expedition's cargo, noted Barth, consisted of "worthless bulky objects" which gave the false impression of great wealth. As the caravan prepared to move out, the crowd seemed about to attack, drawn to the huge iron cases that promised gold coins. One of the caravaneers had the wit to smash open one of the cases. Instead of gold, dry biscuit spilled out. The disappointed crowd turned back to the original mound of plunder. As the caravan departed, the Merabetin were "swearing, and griping [sic] one another by the throat, and fighting over the booty."

That afternoon they reached Selufiet, a village of sixty or seventy huts made of grass—a sign of the Sudan. Despite the Merabetins' promise of protection, fresh troubles arose. The caravan was besieged that night by a mob "howling like hungry jackals." The remaining goods were saved by firing warning shots throughout the night.

Perhaps more seriously, the camel drivers had been hired only to this point, and weren't interested in prolonging the nightmare of working for infidels. Their departure left the caravan short of baggage animals, a plight worsened by the theft during the night of most of the camels belonging to the Kel Owis and the expedition. The Kel Owis recovered some of them the next morning, but fifteen remained missing.

That day, on the way to the main village of the Merabetins, they saw their first field of millet, "a delicious sight to travelers from the desert." Barth admired the teenaged boys in the village, who were tall and light-skinned, and wore only a leather apron. Their light hair was shaved on the sides, with a crest in the middle. When they matured, all this would be covered by the robes and veil worn by adult Tuareg men.

After the torments and deprivations of the past month, the Europeans hoped to comfort themselves here with fresh meat, cheese, and butter, but the villagers would only sell them a bit of millet at an exorbitant price. Yet compared to their recent bivouacs, the village offered relative safety, and the expedition rested.

As was his habit, Barth expanded his rough notes, made while riding, into the comprehensive entries of his journal. Working at his portable desk, he also wrote a letter to Europe and entrusted it to a man leaving for Ghat. This letter, later found in the desert and brought to the British vice-consul in Ghadames, would cause much grief.

Nineteenth-century correspondence is often difficult to read because of sloppiness, tiny script, pale ink, or eccentric penmanship. Barth's handwriting, by contrast, reflected his personality—clear and meticulous, with a firm thick stroke in dark ink. He wanted to eliminate any possibility of misreading or illegibility, in case he didn't survive his correspondence and journals.

His journals eventually would hold about 12,000 dated entries in English, German, and Arabic. In addition, he sent hundreds of pages to Europe about itineraries, vocabularies, tribal divisions, cultural reports, and so on, all of it easy to read. Paper was scarce in Africa, so he typically crowded 40 to 45 lines on sheets 12 inches long by 8 inches wide, for about 500 words per page. His dispatches often ran more than ten pages, sometimes much more.

Richardson also used this respite to work on his journal. He tallied up the expenses since Ghat, most of it for extortion, and was aghast at the total: £150. He fretted about how Her Majesty's Government would react, even though the expenditures had saved their lives. He also joked that, to offset this £150, the expedition had just received its first gift in Aïr: two melons, some onions, and a bit of wheat. "The fact must be recorded as something wonderful," he noted dryly.

He also indulged in some of his characteristic self-pitying self-aggrandizement: "The being chief of an expedition of this kind is certainly no sinecure; but I am sure that no one who has not occupied a similar post can conceive the anxieties and disquietudes under which I have laboured during all these difficult days. Almost ever since our departure from Ghat," he went on, "we have been in fear, either for our lives or our property. Danger has ever hung hovering over us, sometimes averted, sometimes seeming to be turned into smoke; but within this week the strokes of ill fortune have fallen upon us with increasing fury. We try to persuade ourselves that there is now nothing more to fear, and every one joins in nursing what may be a delusion."

It was. They had noticed storm clouds over the mountains to the south, without giving them much thought. On the afternoon of August 31 a cry spread through the camp: the wadi is coming! Richardson came out of his tent and saw a torrent roaring down the valley toward them. Within minutes the camp was an island. Sheep, cattle, and uprooted trees rushed by.

It rained in hard gusts through the night. Everything was damp, including spirits. "We have hitherto had to struggle against mental anxieties," wrote Richardson, "against fatigues, heat, drought, and thirst: we have now to contend with rain and with floods."

The next morning they rose to see that their little island was shrinking. After several more violent downpours the cry again went up: the wadi is coming! This time the white waves overflowed the camp. Richardson's servants quickly moved as much of his goods as possible to slightly higher ground. Barth, Overweg, and the Kel Owis moved as well, leaving fragments of the caravan scattered on small hummocks. Trees, houses, animals, and rafts of debris shot past them in the torrent.

Sitting on their sodden islands, wondering what they would do if the water kept rising, they saw a troop of men on camels ride up to the western edge of the river. They were from Tintellust, home of Sultan Annur, chief of the Kel Owis. Annur had sent them to escort the caravan to him. Throughout the day another large group of mounted men had been milling on the other side of the river. They were Merabetins who wanted to rob the caravan one last time before it entered Annur's protection but had been thwarted by the flood. When they saw Annur's men, they dispersed.

When the rain stopped, the river ebbed as fast as it had risen. Everything was soaked. Barth's tent and baggage lay at the bottom of the wadi in the mud. While retrieving it, his camel slipped and sent him into the muck, where he lost his shoes. The caravan spent the next morning recovering from this misery and drying out baggage.

They left for Tintellust with their new escort of thirty-one men, who immediately began demanding payment for their services on the two-day ride. They scorned Richardson's first offer of about £12 of goods, so he added another burnoose and several small things. The leaders agreed to this, but their men reacted with disgusted shouts and threats, and seized some bales of goods. By this point the Europeans were blasé about such antics. "There was more turmoil and disturbance than real harm in it," noted Barth.

They traveled through rugged granite mountains and deep ravines. This "labyrinth of valleys" led Barth to call Aïr "the Switzerland of the desert." On September 4 they reached the Valley of Tintellust in the heart of Aïr. The Kel Owis had described their capital in glowing terms, so the Europeans expected a city. They found a large village of about

250 houses and huts in the Sudanese style, clustered in a pleasant valley beneath peaks. Many trees shaded the sandy ground.

The Christians were directed to a beautiful camping spot 800 yards from the village on some sand hills. Barth relished the expansive views looking over the valley, scattered with acacia and mimosa trees and marbled with white sandy wadis, all set against a backdrop of craggy multicolored mountains. But he also noted that the site might be a bit too far from their protector, Sultan Annur, since they were still "in a country of lawless people, not yet accustomed to see among them men of another creed, of another complexion, and of totally different usages and manners."

The Europeans sent their compliments to Annur, who replied that his rheumatism kept him from greeting them. He added that they should now consider themselves safe, and that he or his sons would escort them onward. These were welcome words after nearly two months of physical and mental duress.

They hoped Annur would follow his words with some supper, as etiquette dictated, but only darkness arrived. They tried to buy a chicken or eggs or cheese in the village, without success. Richardson fell back on his supply of olive oil and pasta. Barth and Overweg made their supper from the only provisions they had left, couscous and onions.

But their spirits were high. They had survived the northern Aïr and felt relatively safe. Surely the worst of the journey was behind them. To the south lay the heart of the Sudan and its famous cities—Zinder, Katsina, and Kano—which promised new peoples, discoveries, and adventures.

Overweg chose this moment to break out a bottle of port wine he had been saving. The three Europeans drank it down and felt merry. "Let us raise our hearts in thankfulness to Almighty Providence," wrote Richardson in his journal that night, "who still watches over us, preserves our health, and saves us from destruction."

9

Days and Nights in Tintellust

THE NEXT MORNING THEY CALLED ON ANNUR. THE OLD CHIEF WAS seventy-six, with black skin and European features. "He received us in a straightforward and kindly manner," wrote Barth, "observing very simply that even if, as Christians, we had come to his country stained with guilt, the many dangers and difficulties we had gone through would have sufficed to wash us clean, and that we had nothing now to fear but the climate and the thieves."

He offered neither hospitality nor protection. This severe reception was to be expected, wrote Barth, since they had "come into the country as hated intruders pursued by all classes of people." Richardson, however, was irate. In his journal he mocked Annur for his age, infirmities, and mud "palace."

It was a gross underestimation that Barth didn't share. Annur was old but retained the hard-nosed acuity and ruthlessness that had made him rich and kept him powerful in a tumultuous region. Richardson asked Annur to protect them during the onward journey to Zinder, more than 300 miles to the south. A week went by in which Annur accepted Richardson's lavish gifts (most of which the sultan publicly gave away) but didn't return the strangers a single morsel. Then he stated his terms: If the Christians wanted to travel through Sudan at their own risk, he would neither stop nor harm them. But since everyone in the region was eager to plunder or kill them, and since the roads of Aïr were at present infested with robbers, the price for his protection to Zinder would be steep—700 Spanish dollars (about £140). Take it or leave it.

Richardson, still furious about the extortions along the route, was incensed. This was just another shakedown, on a grander scale. Barth disagreed. The fee was heavy, but so were the risks for Annur. And unlike the expedition's previous escorts, Annur actually had the power to protect them. Barth urged Richardson to hire the old gold-digger.

Richardson fumed. His mood wasn't improved the next day when Annur sent word not to darken his door again unless they took the deal. Richardson offered 500 Spanish dollars. Annur eventually agreed to 600. He also warned the Christians not to tell anyone about this fee because he didn't want to be badgered for gifts by his subjects.

As was his habit, Richardson blamed others—in this case Barth and Overweg—for this unexpected expense. "Possibly, had I been alone, I might have been able to hold out long and more successfully," he wrote in his journal, "but it is somewhat embarrassing to act with persons who share in your councils without sharing in your responsibility, and who naturally seek the shortest and easiest method of getting over difficulties."

Two nights later, thieves snuck into Richardson's tent as he slept and stole some tin boxes. They expected to find money. Instead they got 9 pounds of tea and, even more worthless, some Bibles in Arabic. Annur considered the theft an affront to his authority and sent a posse after the robbers—thirteen of them, judging by the camel tracks. The thieves dumped the Bibles on the road with some of the tea, which Richardson's servant recovered. "I grieved very much for the loss of my tea," wrote Richardson, "and employed six or seven hours in picking the stones out of what Amankee recovered." He hoped to get back more after Amankee had the brainstorm to offer a reward, with the warning that only Christians could drink tea because it was poison for Muslims. Richardson's journal is silent on whether this ploy worked.

After the night attack, Annur insisted that the Europeans move closer to town for better protection. He also asked the qadi, or Sharia judge, whether it was lawful "to rob and murder Christians by night." The qadi answered no, and added that Christians could kill Muslim robbers. Annur circulated this ruling throughout the region. He also sent men to repossess the camels previously stolen from the Christians, by force if necessary. He decreed that if the camels couldn't be found, then camels owned by the thieves, who were widely known, would be confiscated.

Annur was clearly an ally worth paying for. This was further under-lined when news arrived that 400 Tuaregs from Hoggar had pursued the Christians into Aïr. Every brigand within 300 miles had been roused by Richardson's tactical mistake of sending to Ghat for an escort. As Barth predicted, this triggered a rumor that spread through the desert, swell-ing as it moved. By the time it rolled into Hoggar, it bulged with rich Christians and dozens of camels staggering beneath burdens of gold, silver, and sumptuous cargo. The real Christians, who still couldn't find enough to eat and whose cargo had been reduced by half, didn't doubt that leaving Tintellust without Annur's protection would be dangerous if not fatal.

Annur was in no hurry. He wanted to wait until the salt caravan returned from Bilma, 200 miles due east into the Sahara. But the salt caravan hadn't even gathered yet, and once it left Tintellust, it wouldn't get back for nearly two months. Richardson complained, but Annur refused to budge.

Barth started planning a way to fill the delay. He wanted to visit Aga-dez, an oasis famous in old chronicles, about a week's journey south of Tintellust. Richardson had decided not to take the caravan there. Barth began negotiating in secret with Annur, whose permission he needed.

Meanwhile, Barth and Richardson worked on their journals, letters, and dispatches to the Foreign Office. Richardson added to his list of use-ful Tamasheq phrases. Some of them were a map of his mind:

I want it cheap.

It is very dear.

That is false.

Can you cook European dishes?

I like strong coffee.

I want a strong camel.

Do you love Christ?

Did you ever read the Gospel?

Do you believe in purgatory?

I hope you will teach your daughters to read.

Ask him the name of this place.

Is there any danger in the road?

This man has robbed me.

That man is a thief.

They sent off their packets of correspondence with a caravan headed to Murzuk, a journey of two-and-a-half months. If the packets made it to Murzuk, they would wait there, perhaps for months, until a caravan left for Tripoli. (Several of Barth's letters, including a long report on the topography of Aïr, never arrived. Another sent to Ghadames lingered there for several months because the English vice-consul was away in Tripoli.) A month or two after leaving Murzuk, if the packets reached Tripoli, they would be placed on a ship bound for England or, more likely, for Malta or Italy. Whether by land or sea, the final transit to London took another month. The reply, of course, spent just as long returning, with the additional complication that the recipient was on the move somewhere in Africa. For routine matters this snail's pace was inconsequential. But when a letter contained an urgent request for help, as Barth's one day would, the delay became agonizing.

Barth noticed several differences between the Kel Owis and the Tuaregs of the true desert to the north. The Kel Owis were darker and shorter, with rounder faces and more cheerful dispositions. Instead of the somber blue-black robes worn by the desert Tuaregs, the Kel Owis veered into color and gaiety, such as light blue tobes, their long, loose cotton outer garments. This made historical sense. As some Tuareg tribes swept south into the old black kingdoms of Sudan such as Goberawa, the groups had intermarried, "blending the severe and austere manners and the fine figure of the Berber," wrote Barth, "with the cheerful and playful character and the darker color of the African."

ON SEPTEMBER 27, Richardson complained that he had been bothered all night by crickets, a screech owl, and beating drums. When he left his tent, he saw that the village was filling up. Men on camels draped with jingling bells were riding slow circles around groups of squatting women. Other mounted men charged the women at a gallop. A few men and women were dancing within the circles. Many women were ululating and everyone else seemed to be shouting.

One of Annur's daughters was getting married. The celebration continued for the next two days and nights, to the ceaseless throbbing of drums and the screeching of owls, driving Richardson half-crazy.

Barth doesn't mention the wedding, perhaps because he was busy preparing to depart. In the midst of the celebration, Annur had given Barth permission to visit Agadez, despite Richardson's decision to bypass it. To Barth, Agadez was irresistible. "For what can be more interesting," he wrote, "than a considerable town, said to have been once as large as Tunis, situated in the midst of lawless tribes, on the border of the desert and of the fertile tracts of an almost unknown continent, established there from ancient times, and protected as a place of rendezvous and commerce between nations of the most different character, and having the most various wants? It is by mere accident that this town has not attracted as much interest in Europe as her sister town Timbuktu."

He left Tintellust on October 4, invigorated by a fresh breeze and the prospect of adventure.

IDLING IN TINTELLUST, Richardson did some bookkeeping. He was shocked by the mission's expenses to date: £600 pounds, more than his original estimate for the entire journey. The expedition was still 700 miles short of its destination, Lake Chad, not to mention the costs of the return trip. Fees, gifts, and extortions had nearly exhausted their store of goods for trade and safe passage. Richardson didn't know how or when he could get more financing. His money worries kept him in a state of low-grade panic, with frequent flare-ups caused by the latest outrages. For instance, people occasionally offered to sell him goods previously stolen from the mission. The merchants charged him double the usual price. "An infidel traveller, who is known to be in possession of any property," he wrote in his journal, "is sure in these countries to be looked upon as a milch-cow."

Annur's parsimony continued to give Richardson heartburn. The old chief had become friendly after securing the lucrative deal to escort the expedition to Zinder, but he never sent the Europeans the customary gifts of food. Nevertheless he relished Richardson's tea and coffee two or three times every day, preferably with English pickles and marmalade.

Annur also coveted Richardson's loaves of sugar. Since Richardson needed money, he offered to sell Annur a loaf at the Murzuk price, plus a few cents for the freight to Tintellust. Annur insisted on the Murzuk price, no freight. No, said Richardson. Then no deal, said Annur. Richardson gritted his teeth and poured his fellow skinflint more tea.

He did persuade Annur to sign the commercial treaty by tempting him with a sword, gaudy with polished brass and gilding. Annur asked Richardson to read the treaty in English, to hear the sound of the language. Richardson celebrated this first diplomatic success by raising the Union Jack and firing off 100 musket caps. Soon afterward a Tuareg arrived from Ghat and told Richardson that the treaty left there had been read aloud, including the alarming news that the Queen of England was in Tripoli, with plans to buy half of Ghat and settle there. "Such is the nature of Saharan reports," wrote Richardson.

There was music and dancing almost every night in Tintellust. The din irritated Richardson and disturbed his sleep. He detested "the usual singing business, with Moorish hammering on tambourines." The dancing he deplored: "of the usual inelegant and indelicate description," with "gross imitations of natural acts." He mused that such suggestive gyrations must be an ancient human instinct. "The performances at European Operas," he noted, "are often nearly as indelicate."

Richardson had a wide streak of prudery befitting a Victorian evangelical. He reported, in a prim tone, his dragoman's comment that none of the cultures they were traveling through had a word for chaste, since "all the women are alike, and equally accessible when danger is absent." Richardson censured the traders' practice of having a "wife" in every town along their route, and referred reflexively to "African lewdness."

Yet he could also be good-humored on the subject of women. He observed that all of them, from shepherdesses to princesses, "are as fond of the bustle as European dames; but the important difference is, it is the natural bustle which they here delight to exhibit to the admiring male population. If a woman be called to, going off to the well for water, she does not turn round to see who is calling, but immediately draws her frock tight round her form, and imparts to it a most agitated and unnatural swinging motion, to the great satisfaction of the admiring lookers-on. Thus we see how the coquettes of London and Paris meet at opposite poles with these of the Sahara and Central Africa."

He also noted, half-insulted, that in contrast to Barth and Overweg, no women had offered themselves to him. He observed that the natives were baffled that these white men who could afford concubines were traveling alone. "The people begin to pester me to marry another wife in Soudan," wrote Richardson, amused, "—one very young and with large breasts is the kind of article they recommend."

He showed strong sympathy for women treated poorly, especially slaves, though his pity was often marbled with condescension and sentimentality. It also tended to disappear if the woman tried to escape victimhood in ways he didn't approve. A woman whose husband divorced her during the caravan had Richardson's sympathy until her desire to survive led her to hop from tent to tent. Worse, she was cheerful about it. When she eventually married one of Richardson's servants, Richardson was disgusted, and was scandalized that Overweg accepted some food from the wedding supper. Similarly, when a young woman traveled from a distant village to ask Overweg for medicine to induce an abortion because she was afraid her mother would beat her for getting pregnant, Richardson commented, "Young ladies often think of their mothers a little too late under these circumstances," without seeing any contradiction in his attitudes.

All of his contradictions were visible after Annur grabbed a burning stick from the fire and severely beat his wife with it, splitting open the space between her nose and upper lip. Annur immediately repented and sent for Overweg, known as Tabib, or Doctor, to tend to her for several days. The old man's brutality appalled Richardson. "Beating a wife is so common in these countries," he wrote, "that, only when the fact is attended with features of unusual ferocity, as in this case of [Annur], does it excite any attention." Rumor said the beating was caused by the wife's "eternal loquacity," but Richardson suspected infidelity. The assumption revealed more about him than about Annur's wife, and led him to ruminate on "what can reasonably be expected from these African women":

> They are not allowed scarcely to believe themselves to possess souls; they have no moral motives to be chaste, and certainly none of family and honour, being mostly slaves. Then the greater part of the young girls of consequence are married to old men, who are worn out by their sensual habits and indulgence with innumerable concubines. These young women are thus left, though married, like so many widows, and with all their passions alive, to the first opportunity which presents itself. We know what they do, and we cannot expect anything else from them.

This muddle of attitudes reflects his reactions to Africa: sympathy, moral outrage, condescension, misinterpretation, and prudery. He eventually learned the real cause of the beating. Against Annur's orders, his wife had been sneaking out at night to watch "the beastly dances of the north coast . . . these filthy exhibitions." "Many Europeans, it must be confessed," concluded Richardson, "would beat their wives for less cause."

OCTOBER IN TINTELLUST had its attractions. Birds were plentiful—linnets, woodpeckers, beautiful doves. There were also gazelles, ostriches, boars, jackals, wolves, hyenas, and lions. The temperatures were pleasant. The night sky glittered with thick constellations and the Milky Way, which the Fezzanees called "the road of the dates" because it appeared at harvest time. Autumn was also the season of meteors—they flamed across the sky at the rate of one per minute. One night the entire camp watched breathlessly as a huge blue-headed meteor burned for two minutes from east to west.

Such phenomena stirred up the superstitious. The village's charm-writer stayed busy, jotting verses of the Qur'an on tiny slips of paper, which people bought and carried in amulets to ward off swords, the evil eye, and other maladies. Sometimes the charm-writer dissolved the words with water so his customer could drink the verse.

On October 24, Annur's massive gong notified the village's men to prepare for departure to the salt fields of Bilma. This arduous trip into the middle of the Sahara took about two weeks each way, plus time spent there to recuperate and trade for the salt. To Richardson the gong signaled the expedition's eventual release from Tintellust, because Annur had promised to accompany the expedition to Zinder once the caravan returned. Richardson celebrated by cracking open one of his two bottles of champagne, pouring it around for Overweg and the servants. He saved the second bottle for the launching of the boat on Lake Chad.

The salt caravan left Tintellust on October 28. For safety it would merge with caravans from throughout Aïr, because other Tuaregs were sure to stalk the group in hopes of pillage. In some years the caravan swelled to 20,000 camels. (The largest ever reported claimed 30,000.) Barth later estimated that this year's caravan numbered about 4,000 camels, low because of political unrest in the region. The route to Bilma was bleak, so the camels carried their own forage, as well as bundles to be left behind for the return trip.

At Bilma the Tebus were waiting. The short rainy season had turned Bilma's salt flats into shallow ponds. The Tebus scooped out salty slurry and poured it into wooden molds in the shape of cakes or cones, which dried in the desert air. These coarse brownish loaves contained as much sand and dirt as salt, and tasted bitter. But some of the salt was of finer quality, pinkish and loose-grained. This was highly desired and brought three times the normal price.

It was said that the Tebus knew two days in advance when a caravan was coming, because a nearby peak would begin "singing." It was also said—"It is a notorious fact," stated Richardson—that when the caravans arrived, the Tebu men vanished into the nearby hills, leaving their women to trade the salt and, in Richardson's words, to "make a good mercantile speculation with their charms."

For the Tebus and the Tuaregs of Aïr, the salt caravan was the central economic event of the year. Salt was money. The Tuaregs carried it to the principal cities of central Sudan—Kano, Katsina, Zinder, and Sokoto—and used it to buy cloth, swords, and other essential supplies. Salt was one of the few things that could unite the fractious Tuaregs of Aïr. In early 1850, as Barth's expedition prepared to leave Tripoli, an army of 7,000 Tuareg warriors joined together to hunt down and massacre the Welad Sliman, a rapacious Arabic tribe that had been attacking the salt caravans heading to Bilma. (Barth and Overweg would later travel with the Welad Sliman.)

Salt was the lifeblood of Aïr. Annur, the region's principal chief, couldn't turn his attention to the infidels until the caravan came home safely from Bilma. Five days after it departed, the rest of the village—

women, children, the aged, the livestock, the Europeans and their servants—left Tintellust, led by Annur. They bivouacked about fifteen miles southeast to await the salt caravan's return.

Richardson was in good spirits. "Never was there a more picturesque caravan," he wrote. "Ladies on bullocks, children and women on donkeys, warriors on maharees, merchants on camels, the Sultan's horse harnessed going alone, and following steadily; goats and their kids, sheep, foals of camels, &c. running or straggling along!" The next day, November 3, was his birthday, which passed "almost unthought of." He was forty-one.

Barth, as usual, was still off on his own and would have to catch up to them when he could.

10

Desert Port

BARTH'S GUIDE TO AGADEZ WAS ANNUR'S SON-IN-LAW. THEY TRAV-
eled with 2 servants, 6 camels, 35 asses, and 2 bullocks. To avoid
attracting attention, they took no tents. Barth always felt rejuvenated
when embarking for an unknown place. Escaping Richardson's restric-
tive eye probably added to his elation. So did the landscape of jagged
mountains and grassy valleys densely shaded by tall trees. "This delicious spectacle filled my heart with delight," he wrote, "and having sat
down a little while quietly to enjoy it, I made a sketch of the beautiful
forms of the mountain peaks."

They came across "two droll and jovial-looking musicians." Each
carried a large drum and wore short blue shirts and small straw hats.
They had been playing at a wedding and were en route to another. On
a narrow path through thick vegetation Barth's group passed a caravan
of 40 camels and 60 slaves, the slaves singing as they walked. Barth recognized one of the slavers, a camel driver who had worked for the expedition. Barth grimly noted that the man had evidently used his wages
from the anti-slavery trade mission to enter the slave trade.

The country changed again, turning gloomy in the Valley of Taghist,
where the ground was littered "with basaltic stones mostly of the size
of a child's head." The place was considered holy because Muhammed
al-Maghili, an Islamic scholar and fundamentalist, had stopped here to

pray while en route to Katsina and Kano. Barth found a spot where stones formed a narrow rectangle, a traveler's mosque where every passing Muslim stopped to pray.

Al-Maghili was venerated, wrote Barth, for bringing Islam to Central Negroland. He had ventured into the south around 1490 after being pushed out of North Africa for instigating a massacre of the Jews in Tuat in central Algeria. Al-Maghili preached a harsh version of Islam—he called it a purer version—that endorsed the killing of male Jews and the enslavement of their women and children. According to al-Maghili, all infidels were enemies of God and subject to jihad, and any Muslim who helped an infidel was himself an infidel. But al-Maghili also denounced Muslim rulers who levied unfair taxes or confiscated property. He condemned Muslims who practiced Islam with half-measures, including mallams (teachers) with a shallow knowledge of Islamic law. He became an important advisor to the emir of Kano and then to Askia, king of Songhai (1493–1529), rulers of the era's two greatest kingdoms in central Sudan. Eventually neither ruler could stomach al-Maghili's extremism. Nevertheless his writings, which Barth knew, remained deeply influential within Islam.

Near this shrine Barth saw three slaves yoked to a plow and "driven like oxen by their master." Ever the scientist, he noted that this was "probably the most southern place in Central Africa where the plow is used; for all over Sudan the hoe, or fertaña, is the only instrument used for preparing the ground." He saw many lion tracks and heard the call of the guinea fowl for the first time.

On the morning of October 10, Barth's group shared the road with more and more travelers. And then his companions pointed proudly to the horizon, where a tall tapering minaret with four sides rose from the plain. It belonged to Agadez's great mosque, built in 1844, and was nearly ninety feet tall. To Barth's surprise, instead of proceeding, they made camp. His companions explained that it would be safer for him to enter the town at night in native dress. (From this point on, Barth wore native clothing, consisting of a black Sudan tobe over a white one, with a white burnoose). He was about to become the first European to see the famous desert entrepôt of Agadez.

In the fourteenth century the restless Moroccan traveler Ibn Battuta called Agadez "the largest, handsomest, and strongest of all the cities in Negroland." In Battuta's day 30,000 people lived there. It flourished as a caravan crossroads, where the Sahara met the Sahel, a band of semiarid land 300 to 600 miles wide that stretches for 2,600 miles along the Sahara's southern edge and buffers the desert from green Africa. "Sahel" came from an Arabic word for shore or coastline. The sea was the Sahara. When travelers from the north reached the Sahel after crossing the desert, they felt the relief of stepping ashore after a long sea passage. Travelers heading north from the Sahel felt that they were casting off. Agadez, like Timbuktu, was a desert port town.

By the time Barth got there, the population had shrunk to about 7,000, but Agadez still fascinated him. The new sultan, who was about to be officially installed, received him hospitably. They conversed in Hausa, which Barth had learned during the traverse of Aïr. The sultan had never heard of the English nation, but was pleased to learn how the famous "English" gunpowder had gotten its name. That evening, he sent Barth a dish called finkaso, a thick pancake made of wheat flour, covered with butter. After the deprivations of Aïr, it tasted like "the greatest luxury in the world." Thanks to the sultan, who sent Barth two meals every day, the explorer ate very well during his three-week stay—lamb, dates, melons, cucumbers, grains. The sultan sidestepped Barth's invitation to sign a commercial treaty with Britain, but did write letters of passage for him to the governors of Kano and Katsina, "in rather incorrect Arabic," sniffed the German pedant.

Barth saw slave caravans, and a salt caravan headed east to Bilma that was said to have 10,000 camels. The men of Agadez carried bows and arrows instead of spears, and rode horses instead of camels—signs of the Sahel. The busy market offered further signs: meat, millet, wheat, dates, wine, melons, and other vegetables. Women sold beads, necklaces, and finely-worked leather boxes for tobacco and perfume.

Like most port towns, Agadez had a mongrel population that reflected all the peoples who passed through it, beginning with the Berber tribes that had founded it. There were Tuaregs, Hausas, Fulanis, Tebus, Kanuris, and Arabs. And also, Barth was puzzled to find, Songhais, a black ethnic group based 600 harsh miles to the west. All this diversity made Agadez a polyglot town where interpreters did good business.

But Agadez also had its own unique language, Emgedesi, spoken nowhere else in the region. To a linguist such as Barth, this was a mystery to pursue. He detected the influences of Hausa, Tamasheq, and Songhai in Emgedesi, but remained puzzled about the dialect's origins and exclusivity to Agadez. Then came the clue that connected the dots: several Tuaregs who had been to Timbuktu told him that Emgedesi was also spoken there, 800 miles west. Barth was surprised, then thrilled as he realized the implications.

Songhai had been the most extensive empire in Central Africa's history, greater than Mali or Ghana. It had covered portions of present-day Mali, Burkina Faso, Guinea, Senegal, and Niger. Songhai had conquered Timbuktu, another Sahelian port city of Tuaregs and Arabs. The language of the conquerors mixed with Timbuktu's other tongues, creating a distinctive language unique to the town.

Then early in the sixteenth century, Askia, Songhai's king, decided to extend his realm to the east, into central Sudan and Hausaland, and to curb the pesky Tuaregs to the north. He conquered Agadez in 1515 and left an occupying force there before proceeding on a haj through Egypt to Mecca, scattering legendary amounts of gold in his wake.

By the end of the sixteenth century the empire of Songhai had disintegrated. But in Agadez the descendants of the occupying army had melded with the local population. So had their language, and the resulting hybrid dialect evolved along similar linguistic lines as the hybrid language of Timbuktu, like related bird species on separate islands. This link, wrote Barth, "throws a new light over the history and ethnography of this part of the world," and is "of the highest importance for the whole ethnography of North Africa." It also gave him his first whiff of the fabled city of Timbuktu, a place he never expected to see.

BARTH'S CURIOSITY took him all over Agadez. He visited the Sharia court to observe Islamic justice and found it just as tedious as courts everywhere. He connived to get inside the mosque, and took its measurements. He noticed that the finest house in Agadez was ornamented with ostrich eggs, perhaps a talisman of fertility. (Nachtigal noticed the same thing in Kukawa twenty years later). Walking the streets, Barth heard the high voices of young boys reciting verses from the Qur'an, written in chalk on wooden tablets. By the end of his stay Barth had established that 250 to 300 boys were enrolled in five or six religious schools in Agadez.

He watched the formal extravaganza of the sultan's inauguration, and noted with satisfaction that the sultan was wearing the fine blue burnoose presented by himself—a sign of open-mindedness toward Christians that would be broadcast throughout the Sudan. Hamma, Annur's son-in-law, took him to visit his Agadez mistress, whom Barth described as "very comely," with a fair Arabic complexion. She was married, but her husband lived 300 miles away in Katsina, "and she did not seem to await his return in the Penelopean style."

Many of Barth's visitors were traders who had traveled throughout the Sudan. He questioned them closely. "All these I found to be intelligent men," he wrote, "having been brought up in the centre of intercourse between a variety of tribes and nations of the most different organization, and, through the web of routes which join here, receiving information of distant regions."

Another frequent visitor was a learned mallam. After several conversations about religion with the infidel Barth, the mallam wondered why Christians and Muslims were such enemies, since their essential beliefs were so similar. Because, answered Barth, most people in both religions paid less attention to beliefs than to matters unrelated to religion. Both Christianity and Islam, he added, had lost their purity. The mallam asked for a copy of the Gospels in Arabic. "Mutually pleased with our conversation," wrote Barth, "we parted from each other with regret."

Barth was always willing to engage Africans about anything, including the volatile subject of religion. His learning and familiarity with the Qur'an earned him respect and friends throughout his journey, and probably saved his life more than once. He also had studied African historians. He knew the names of famous African places, kings, and kingdoms. Unlike most African explorers, who couldn't speak to the people they met and hence learned little about the cultures they were passing through, Barth was a gifted linguist who got his information firsthand. He spoke seven African languages and compiled vocabularies for twenty-four, which allowed him to talk to everyone from kings and viziers to merchants, imams, thieves, and slaves.

No other African explorer collected the voices of so many African individuals from so many walks of life, including their names, histories, and personal details. He did not assume that Africans were barbarians or primitives, nor did he judge them strictly by appearances. A raggedy camel driver or an itinerant mallam could be sources of information, even scholarship. He questioned, listened, tried to understand. In his chapters on Agadez, he pointed out that someone who can talk to the local people and knows something about their culture can ask the right questions and get far better information than "that which is picked up incidentally by one who scarcely knows what he asks." Without his combination of curiosity and linguistic skills, he wouldn't have discovered the link between Agadez and Timbuktu, wouldn't have been able to find common ground with the mallam, wouldn't have understood what he was seeing and hearing in Agadez.

In the evenings, as he lay on his mat, Barth often listened to music and singing that filled the night. In addition to many kinds of drums and tambourines, he most likely heard the imzad, a one-stringed fiddle played by Tuareg women, and the molo, a three-stringed lute with a calabash body, favored by the Hausa, Fulani, and Songhai peoples. One evening he traded a piece of lamb's meat for an extemporaneous song on his favorite instrument, the molo.

Barth heard music almost everywhere he went, despite Islam's divided attitude toward it. Musicians had low status yet were treasured. All Muslims acknowledged music's power. Some condemned it as pagan, sensual, and apt to be accompanied by alcohol—instruments of the devil and distractions from the teachings of the Prophet. Others, especially Sufis, believed that music, especially chanting, could connect people to God. Most simply enjoyed it as pleasurable entertainment.

One night Barth's interest in these subjects turned dangerous. At the suggestion of a mischievous servant, he went alone to see a crowded dance celebration. His curiosity pushed him closer and closer until he scared himself and backed out. Too late. Someone shouted the war cry of Islam. The men drew their swords and chased him through the dark streets. He reached his house but the servant, laughing, chained the door. Barth turned to face the mob with his cutlass. Luckily they settled for insults instead of blood.

The authorities heard about this and asked Barth the next day whether he had a complaint against the townspeople. No, he said, the fault was his own imprudence. "In fact, the people behaved remarkably well," he wrote, "considering that I was the first Christian that ever visited the town; and the little explosions of fanaticism into which the women and children sometimes broke out when they saw me on our terrace, rather amused me."

Barth's comprehensive curiosity was sometimes comical. He noticed that the houses of Agadez lacked indoor privies and that the natives relieved themselves outdoors. "As in many Italian towns," he wrote, "the principle of the 'da per tutto' [everywhere], which astonished

Goethe so much at Rivoli on the Lago di Garda, is in full force, being greatly assisted by the many ruined houses which are to be found in every quarter of the town."

Not content to rest on these investigative laurels, he further noticed that the Tuaregs disliked this custom, preferring the open desert. But since the countryside was so dangerous, security obliged them to go en masse. "When they reach some conspicuous tree," wrote Barth, "the spears are all stuck into the ground, and the party separates behind the bushes; after which they again meet together under the tree, and return in solemn procession into the town."

(Barth is often accused of having no sense of humor, but that's not quite true. He doesn't rollick or crack jokes, he's never whimsical, and no one reads him for his wit. But he does see the comical side of things and responds to it with understated humor, usually as dry as chalk and sometimes dusted with scholarship. It's easy to miss amid the general earnestness. Examples: the wife who did not wait for her husband's return "in the Penelopean style"; his description of certain reactions to him in Agadez as "little explosions of fanaticism"; the reference to Goethe in the context above; the description of dignified Tuaregs returning "in solemn procession" from their collaborative defecation. Not hilarious, not humorless.)

Barth paid close attention to the females in Agadez, and they returned his interest. The day after the sultan left town, five or six young women visited, "and with much simplicity invited me to make merry with them, there being now, as they said, no longer reason for reserve, 'as the sultan was gone.'" Two of them, he observed, were "tolerably pretty and well formed." But he declined a dalliance with "these wantons" as a bad idea for a European traveling through a Muslim country, because it was "best to maintain the greatest austerity of manners with regard to the other sex, though he may thereby expose himself to a good deal of derision from some of the lighter-hearted natives."

Barth was often mocked for being a bachelor who turned down

female offers and traveled without a concubine. With African women he was direct and unblinking as an observer, but resolutely prim as a man. He considered it his anthropological duty to record frank physical descriptions of the tribes and peoples he met. But unlike his fellow explorer and friend Richard Burton, he evidently didn't do hands-on research into the natives' sexual practices, despite frequent offers and temptations. Still, he was a young man, and his eye for women wasn't strictly scientific. It became less so as his celibacy lengthened into years and his primness softened enough that he felt comfortable flirting.

AGADEZ THRILLED BARTH. To someone of his cast of mind, constantly searching for connections—historical, linguistic, geographic—the city was a gold mine. It linked the old Berber tribes of North Africa, the Songhai empire of West Africa, and the Hausa empire of central Sudan. As an entrepôt, it connected much of the geography of north-central Africa. Pull a thread in Agadez and the map of Africa puckered from the Atlantic to the Mediterranean to Lake Chad.

Agadez was a turning point for Barth. He was on his own and free to go wherever his curiosity took him. He seemed to expand and to relax into his powers, and also into his personality, which becomes more apparent in his journal from Agadez onward.

After three weeks in the city it was time to end his sabbatical. On October 30 he left for Tintellust. He arrived on the evening of November 5 to find the village empty. Exhausted, his party rode through the night and reached the caravan that morning.

Richardson and Overweg gave Barth a cool reception. His companions "apparently felt some jealousy," wrote Barth, "on account of the success which had attended my proceedings." Richardson was also peeved that Barth hadn't persuaded the sultan to sign the treaty.

Barth shrugged and began his extensive report about Agadez. He felt he was writing to save the expedition. If his discoveries could spark

enthusiasm within Europe's scientific community, the British government might approve more funding. Otherwise, he noted, "after our
heavy losses, we should be obliged to return directly, leaving the chief
objects of the expedition unattained."

Seven months after leaving Tripoli, those objects were almost within
reach. And just ahead lay Kano, the greatest city in central Sudan.

11

Separate Ways

THE EXPEDITION WAS STALLED, AWAITING THE RETURN OF THE SALT caravan. After sending off his long report about Agadez on November 14, Barth filled the time by intensifying his study of Emgedesi, the town's distinctive language. His tutor was Zummuzuk, "a reprobate of the worst description." A servant of Annur's, Zummuzuk had been severely beaten in Agadez by Barth's guide, first for using the guide's name to buy goods, and again for selling the caravan's donkeys without permission. Barth hired the scoundrel under strict conditions: "... during his presence in my tent, he was not to move from the place assigned him, the limits of which were very accurately defined—of course, at a respectable distance from my luggage; and if he touched any thing, I was officially permitted by A'nnur to shoot him on the spot." Barth progressed quickly. When he was visited by Amagay, "the chief eunuch and confidential servant of the Sultan of A'gades," the two conversed in Emgedesi. (Zummuzuk later fled the caravan after filching a caftan from Richardson.)

Richardson's reaction to Barth's report about Agadez illustrates their different personalities and focuses. "The worthy Doctor," Richardson wrote in his journal, "seems to have been too much occupied in collecting geographical data to preserve many picturesque facts by the way." This criticism did not, however, keep Richardson from cribbing large chunks of the report for his own journal.

Richardson had adopted a new tactic to avoid the constant requests for gifts: he rarely spoke to anyone in the caravan. But he couldn't avoid Annur, who continued to expect daily infusions of tea and coffee. In exchange, the old chief began sending milk to Richardson every morning. The Englishman used it in his tea and coffee in place of precious sugar. Annur seemed to develop a genuine liking for Richardson, visiting often and sometimes napping in his tent. Richardson didn't return the warmth. He resented Annur for his parsimony and for the high fee he was charging to escort the expedition to Zinder.

Annur also liked to visit Barth. The explorer's avid interest in Aïr delighted the chief, and he enjoyed studying Barth's sketches. This set Annur apart from many of the people along the route. Islam frowned upon two-dimensional images, including drawings. Some Africans, principally those with too little education and too much religion, were also deeply suspicious of Barth's constant note-taking. They called these activities "writing down the country" and, in the enduring alliance of ignorance and paranoia, assumed these pursuits were Christian espionage done in preparation for an invasion.

Many Africans were understandably wary of European travelers, who were alien, white, Christian, and well armed. These strangers obviously had money but evidently wanted something more. Why else would they come all the way to Africa? Yet when asked why they were there, they answered with absurdities about wanting to see plants, animals, rivers, peoples. To leave one's family and country, to endure hardships and risk death for the sole purpose of seeing new places, struck many Africans as preposterous. People who said otherwise were either lying or mad and couldn't be trusted.

"The notion of traveling for curiosity was new to him," wrote Mungo Park about a wary ruler. "He thought it impossible, he said, that any man in his senses would undertake so dangerous a journey merely to look at the country and its inhabitants. . . . it was evident that his suspicion had arisen from a belief that every white man must of necessity be a trader."

Yet other Africans were fascinated by these white men who had traveled so far. Denham once told a chief near Lake Chad that he and his companions had come to see the country and its people, and had been traveling for a long time. The chief said, "Are not your eyes dimmed with straining to the north, where all your thoughts must ever be? Oh! you are men, men, indeed! Why, if my eyes do not see the wife and children of my heart for ten days, when they should be closed in sleep they are flowing with tears. . . . My heart says you are my friend. May you die at your own tents, in the arms of your wives and family."

"Wonderful!" exclaimed a regional governor of Sudan in 1824 when Clapperton refused his gifts and explained why he had come. "You do not want slaves, you do not want horses, you do not want money, but wish only to see the world? You must go to Sultan Bello [ruler of the empire of Sokoto], who is a learned and pious man, and will be glad to see men who have seen so much."

"Everything is wonderful," Bello said after accepting Clapperton's gifts, "but you are the greatest curiosity of all!" Bello was a warrior-king, an Islamic fundamentalist, the skillful governor of a turbulent empire, and a scholar who had read widely and written a number of books. He questioned Clapperton closely about Britain, Greece, India, and the Moorish kingdom of Spain. Clapperton was embarrassed that Bello knew more about the distinctions between various Christian sects than did the visiting Christian. The explorer brought home a copy of Bello's history of the Sokoto regime, the first such document to reach Europe. In his account of the expedition to Bornu and Sokoto, Clapperton wrote that the people of England "erroneously regarded the inhabitants [of Africa] as naked savages, devoid of religion, and not far removed from the condition of wild beasts: whereas I found them, from my personal observation, to be civilized, learned, humane, and pious."

On the other hand, Clapperton also reported that four years earlier Bello had ordered the mass beheadings of 2,000 Tuaregs captured during war. "I may here add," the explorer continued, "that the capi-

tal punishments inflicted in Soudan are beheading, impaling, and cru-
cifixion; the first being reserved for Mahometans, and the other two
practised on Pagans. I was told, as a matter of curiosity, that wretches
on the cross generally linger three days, before death puts an end to
their suffering." The executioner of Sokoto, who visited Clapperton to
ask for a gift, said that he had auditioned for the job by cutting off the
head of his brother.

European history was filled with the same vicious punishments
meted out by equally merciless kings and clerics. But Europeans found
it nearly impossible to overcome their preconceptions about Africa and
see such parallels—to see Bello's scholarly curiosity as well as his brutality, his cosmopolitan interests as well as his religious severity. It was
far simpler to focus on Africa's exoticism, fanaticism, and barbarism, all
of which were easily found but only part of the story. It was also simpler
to ignore Islam's centuries-long respect for education and learning, and
to reduce it to a religion of violent polygamous slaveholding fanatics.

Early African explorers often found the tables turned: *they* were
the ones considered ugly, barbaric, pitiable. People stared at them as if
they were circus freaks because of their whiteness. African women were
especially curious. Mungo Park was compelled to display his pale skin
several times for inquisitive women. (A group of them also requested
visual proof of his circumcision.) Clapperton mentioned a governor's
three wives "who, after examining my skin with much attention,
remarked, compassionately, it was a thousand pities I was not black, for
I had then been tolerably good-looking." Clapperton, sometimes a mischievous flirt, asked one of them if she would marry him. "She immediately began to whimper; and on urging her to explain the cause, she
frankly avowed she did not know how to dispose of my white legs."
Annur urged Richardson to spend more time in the sun so his skin
would get darker, like Barth's and Overweg's, instead of being so dis-
gustingly white. He also shook his head at the barbarity of European
warfare, in which big guns slaughtered multitudes, as opposed to civilized Tuareg warfare with spears and swords.

———

ON DECEMBER 5 the first camels from the returning salt caravan wobbled into camp. The rest trickled in over the next few days and bivouacked throughout the area. On December 14 all the groups began moving south to converge into one big caravan. They traveled together so that no one got the advantage of reaching the markets first.

Everyone felt rich and ready for a binge in Sudan's big markets. That night, and every night as the caravan moved south, the camp pulsed with music and dancing, propelled by the throbbing rhythms of competing drummers. Each morning, to hurry everyone along, drummers pounded while the camels were loaded. The caravan traveled all day to the monotonous beating of drums, punctuated by the jingling bells on the Tuaregs' horses.

Barth celebrated, too, by climbing a mountain. But months of inactivity and poor diet had weakened him, and the steep descent on crumbling rock exhausted him. For the next four-and-a-half years he never again felt strong enough to climb a moderate peak. The mountain goat who had bounded up every elevation in the expedition's first months had been chastened by Africa.

They ran into a caravan that had left Tripoli three months earlier. "Without bringing us a single line, or even as much as a greeting," complained Barth. On Christmas Eve the Europeans ate a dismal supper of the "eternal bitter 'tuwo,'" a coarse paste made of millet. On Christmas morning they were cheered when a drummer and a flutist came to their tent and played, not for the holiday but for a gift. Richardson gave them three cheap rings and some sugar. Each of the expedition's seven servants received a cotton handkerchief and a ring. Richardson prayed to see another Christmas Day.

Though they were moving south, the nighttime temperatures were dropping, from the fifties in November to near-freezing. The Tuaregs hated the cold. So did the Christians, after acclimatizing for months in the desert. The idea of ice in such latitudes had seemed preposterous to Europeans until Denham sent a dispatch dated late December that described waterskins "frozen as hard as a board."

The cold killed off the butterflies but didn't reduce the mobs of flies that always followed the caravan. The terrain became more verdant, dominated by the slender doum palm and the ubiquitous thorny acacia, whose amber sap (gum Arabic) provided a sweetish treat. They passed patches of wild melons, eaten by the natives but too bitter for the Europeans. Everyone was made miserable by "karengia," a prickly burr whose myriad tiny barbs infiltrated clothing and stung like packs of hornets. Every native carried pincers to remove the barbs immediately. And yet karengia was also useful; people collected and pounded its seeds to make a nutritious drink.

They saw tracks of antelopes, gazelles, warthogs, wild oxen, and lions. By late December they often glimpsed giraffes and ostriches. Someone ran down a newly hatched ostrich to keep as a pet. On the last day of 1850, Annur sent the Europeans two ostrich eggs, a luscious treat. Meat also reentered their diet. Barth bought a hunk of wild ox. Richardson sampled giraffe, which he likened to beef. It came from the Tagama people, who hunted giraffe from horseback with spears.

The Tagama women offered themselves to the explorers, with the encouragement of their brothers and husbands. Barth, appalled, noted that the women were pretty and fair, though some were "immensely fat, particularly in the hinder regions," another illustration, he pointed out, of tebulloden. The next day one of these bulgy women rode up on a tottering white bullock and asked for medicine from Overweg, whose reputation for doctoring always preceded him. Barth dryly noted that Overweg's doctoring "was rather of a remarkable kind." Since Overweg usually didn't have the time or knowledge to make a diagnosis, he didn't treat his patients according to their complaints, but according to the day of the week. One day everybody got Epsom salts, the next day Dover's powder, and so on. No one complained. To the Africans it was all white man's magic.

As THEY PENETRATED farther into Sudan, the landscape and architecture changed. The huts were made of hides, branches, and the stalks of Indian corn, exactly as described by Leo Africanus two centuries earlier.

A week into January 1851 they began traveling past extensive corn-fields, the first they had seen. They were in Damergu, which Barth called "the granary of Aïr." The neat landscape reminded Richardson of the undulating fields of Essex. They also saw many herds of cattle and horses. Overweg hunted ducks in a lagoon, a sign that the desert was behind them. Food was plentiful. The population mixed Kel Owi Tuaregs, Hausas, Fulanis, and Kanuris from Bornu. There were slaves, runaway slaves, and free people, both Muslim and pagan. These settled folks were more cheerful than the desert nomads, less hostile and suspicious. Damergu impressed Barth as orderly, peaceful, and prosperous, a welcome change.

Richardson had estimated that the expedition would get from Tripoli to Damergu in less than four months. It had taken nine. Gifts, extortions, and depredations had eaten up more than half of the expedition's goods, and the budget was long since blown.

This was their situation when they stopped in early January at a village called Tagalel, about seventy-five miles northwest of Zinder. For reasons left vague by both Barth and Richardson, the three Europeans decided to split up here. They planned to reunite two months later in Kukawa, the capital of Bornu near Lake Chad, where they hoped to be resupplied. Barth explained that by traveling alone they could cover more ground, and do it more cheaply and inconspicuously. This was no doubt true for him, and also preferable to being under Richardson's clumsy authority.

Richardson gave no reason for splitting up his command and didn't take responsibility for it. "It has been agreed," he wrote in the passive voice, "that I and my colleagues should here part for a time." Perhaps he was weary of Barth or yielded to pressure from him. Neither man acknowledged that separating also increased the risks to themselves and hence to the expedition.

In any case, on January 10, 1851, Barth and Overweg departed with the salt caravan headed to Kano. Three days later Overweg would break off westward toward Tessaoua and Maradi. Richardson, traveling with Annur, continued toward Zinder. Richardson expected to be the first to reach Kukawa, but Barth had a foreboding. At the last moment he decided not to give Richardson an important package of documents to send to Europe from Kukawa.

"We took leave one of the other with some emotion," wrote Richardson, "for in Central Africa, those travellers who part and take divergent routes can scarcely count on all meeting together again."

12

"The Celebrated Emporium
of Negroland"

THE TWO GERMANS PARTED ON JANUARY 13, 1851. THAT LEFT
Barth in his favorite circumstance—independent and self-reliant.
"I now went on alone," he wrote, "but felt not at all depressed by solitude, as I had been accustomed from my youth to wander about by
myself among strange people."

The pastoral landscape added to his expansive mood. He passed comfortable villages where cattle grazed alongside fields of corn and millet.
Women sold delicacies—sour milk (thin yogurt), butter, sweet pota-
toes, roasted peanuts, savory fried cakes made from the bean pods of
the dorowa tree, a paste of pounded guinea corn and pepper, sweetmeats
made of pounded rice, butter, and honey. On his second evening without
European company, he feasted on chicken while a musician played the
three-stringed molo and sang an extemporaneous song in his honor. "I
might have fancied myself a prince," wrote Barth. After the austerities
of the desert, this was literally the land of milk and honey.

Threats had diminished. Nighttime sneak thieves, though plentiful,
were mere pests compared to marauders, highwaymen, and religious
fanatics. Barth usually fired several shots after camping, to warn potential thieves that he was armed.

Tessaoua, the first large town he had seen in Sudan, with about
15,000 inhabitants, exemplified this brief interlude between troubles:

". . . it made the most cheerful impression upon me," wrote Barth, "as manifesting every where the unmistakable marks of the comfortable, pleasant sort of life led by the natives." Their airy houses made of clay, wicker, and reeds offered both privacy and shade. In contrast to the severe Tuaregs, Tessaoua's people were sunny and easygoing, "bent upon enjoying life, rather given to women, dance, and song, but without any disgusting excess. . . . Drinking fermented liquor can not be strictly reckoned a sin in a place where a great many of the inhabitants are pagans; but a drunken person, nevertheless, is scarcely seen. . . ."

In the market he ate small kebabs of meat roasted over open fires, the kebabs leaning against each other vertically so that the fat from the top pieces basted the lower ones. He was amused to see some red cloth for sale that had been stolen from him in Aïr. There were also calabashes filled with roasted locusts. Barth called their flavor "agreeable," partly because revenge against these ravagers tasted so sweet. Hornemann had been more enthusiastic, likening roasted locusts to "red herrings, but more delicious." Livingstone found them distasteful when boiled, but when roasted preferred them to shrimp, "though I would avoid both if possible." Nachtigal relished them roasted, but made distinctions: the tastiest were the voracious light brown ones, followed by the green ones, then the speckled green-and-white ones. The type called "princess's finger," slender with white cross stripes on its throat, was avoided as bitter. He mentioned nine others.

Tessaoua's systems of government and justice were as well organized as the surrounding fields. Each village had a mayor who decided minor matters and collected taxes and fees payable to the king in Tessaoua. Every household in the territory paid a poll tax. Tessaoua, in turn, paid tribute to the pagan Hausa king of Maradi, seventy miles to the west. Fines were levied for offenses such as assault or illicit paternity. A murderer forfeited all his property to the government, and perhaps his life, depending on the king's ruling. The king decided all matters of consequence, after first consulting with his privy council and vizier, or prime minister. All of this contradicted the common

European assumption that Africans were unable to organize and govern themselves.

The unit of currency had changed to the cowrie shell. Cowries had reached Africa through Persia and the Maldives. Though heavy and inconvenient to lug around, the shells had been used as money for centuries throughout Central Africa, as far west as Timbuktu. They were also worn as ornamentation, like expensive jewelry. Small purchases—a needle, an onion, the small kebab that Barth enjoyed—cost a cowrie or two. Barth noted that a poor man could eat for five days on twenty-five or thirty shells, and a family could live for a year on 50,000 to 60,000, the equivalent of about £5. Larger items, such as a sword, cost 1,000 shells. A bull could run 7,000, a healthy young slave more than 30,000. In Tessaoua, Barth witnessed a major transaction in which half a dozen people did "the really heroic work of counting 500,000 shells." He estimated that the current year's rather scanty salt caravan from Aïr, consisting of 4,000 camel loads, would bring about 100 million cowries, or £8,000.

BARTH AND THE CARAVAN continued south toward Katsina. The idyll of Tessaoua soon faded. The fifty-mile stretch between Gazaoua and Katsina was turbulent with overlapping hostile factions—Hausas, Fulanis, Tuaregs. Troops of horsemen and archers kicked up dust as they hurried by. Barth also saw the tracks of elephants for the first time, and surmised that this must be their northernmost range.

On January 21 the caravan came to a wide ditch dug across the path. It was the first fortification protecting Katsina. In the seventeenth and eighteenth centuries the city had been the greatest in Central Africa, with about 100,000 inhabitants. But forty-five years before Barth's visit it was ravaged by the jihadi armies of the fanatical Fulani reformer Usman dan Fodio. The city's population had plunged to between 7,000 and 8,000.

In the early nineteenth century several reformist movements detonated in Central Africa. The most important ignited in Hausaland from a fuse lit by Usman dan Fodio. Islam had reached the Sudan in the 1500s, but for centuries afterward it coexisted alongside paganism. The region's rulers often converted to Islam for reasons of politics or profit. They built mosques and Islamic schools as emblems of prestige as much as faith. Most rulers were casual at best about the religion and did little to hinder pagan practices, not to mention other behavior that appalled strict Muslims. The ruling class naturally preferred the status quo to radical change.

For these reasons devout Muslims sometimes chose to live in rural areas apart from the sinful towns. Dan Fodio was one of these. In some ways he fit the familiar mold of a religious fanatic. He had visions and believed that the Prophet had commanded him to wield the Sword of Truth against unbelievers. Yet he also came from a family of scholars. He was a learned man and a poet who wrote many works in Arabic on law, theology, and government.

Nor was he a fiery young revolutionary. He spent nearly twenty years urging the leaders of Hausaland to reform, though with increasing fervor. He accused them of corruption and tyranny, and deplored their semipagan ways. He chided them for injustices, including onerous taxes on rural people, most of whom were Fulanis like himself. He attacked the poorly educated mallams who debased Islam with their pretensions and misinterpretations of the Qur'an. Dan Fodio preached for a return to a purer form of Islam, with strict adherence to Sharia—laws derived from the Qur'an. The Hausa nobles tolerated dan Fodio until his followers, many of whom were Fulani herdsmen and peasants, grew dangerously numerous. By the time the nobles decided to exterminate him, it was too late.

Pushed to act, dan Fodio called for a jihad in 1804. Thousands responded. His revolutionary armies eventually overran Hausaland, including the major towns of Katsina and Kano. The Hausa nobles fled and established strongholds in their old domain of Gober. While dan Fodio's son Muhammed Bello and his brother Abdullahi conquered territories throughout Central Africa, dan Fodio focused on governance. A fundamentalist but also a reformer, he moderated taxes and established a coherent system of justice based on Islamic law. He wrote about his reforms in classical Arabic, the traditional language of Islamic scholarship, but also in the vernacular languages of Hausa and Fulfulde (the Fulani language). In this way his writings were recited, circulated, and absorbed by the masses throughout Central Africa.

Dan Fodio established his empire's new capital at Sokoto, 160 miles west of Katsina, and divided his kingdom into thirty emirates. After he died in 1817, his son Muhammed Bello, who so impressed Clapperton, succeeded him as sultan of the Sokoto Caliphate, the larger eastern portion of the new Fulani empire. Dan Fodio's brother Abdullahi was given the smaller western emirates, and the title emir of Gwandu.

(Most of the current emirs are direct descendants of dan Fodio's original appointees. Likewise, the current sultan of Sokoto, who is still considered the spiritual leader of Islamic northern Nigeria, is a direct descendant of dan Fodio.)

Dan Fodio's revolution transformed Central Africa, but like all revolutions, it fell far short of its ideals and had unintended consequences. For instance, in keeping with the Qur'an, dan Fodio outlawed the killing and enslavement of Muslims, as well as the theft or destruction of their property. But most of dan Fodio's soldiers were angry peasants, not Islamic scholars. They slaughtered and pillaged their way across the region.

Nor could the population of pagans supply all the slaves needed for agricultural labor and for export to pay the costs of running a vast kingdom. Dan Fodio's successors and the Fulani emirs soon began justifying their razzias, or slave raids, on the grounds that even if their victims were Muslims, they weren't devout enough, and hence could be enslaved in the name of the Prophet. When Clapperton visited Kano in the early 1820s, the emir told him that the city contained thirty slaves for every free man. In the next decades things worsened. The incessant razzias kept the Sudan in fear and chaos. Since the raids usually crossed territo-

rial boundaries, the entire region stayed in a constant state of warfare—
Muslims against pagans, emirates against emirates, the empire of Sokoto
against the Hausa states of Gober and Maradi, Sokoto against the empire
of Bornu, Tuaregs against whoever happened along.

WHEN BARTH REACHED Katsina, it was greatly reduced from its former
glory. The jihadists had sacked the city and destroyed most of its books
in an attempt to erase the former regime from history.

(Muhammed al-Kanemi, the ruler of Bornu, chided Muhammed
Bello for the way the jihadists destroyed Islamic books: "We see among
you a thing which every Malam rejects. You are destroying books; you
are scattering them in the roads; you are throwing them in the dirt. But
the name of God is on these books and you know that he who throws
the name of God in the dirt is heathen." This insulted Bello as both a
Muslim and a lover of learning. He replied:

> . . . let me inform you, el-Kanemi, I went out on an expedition and
> captured one of the Katsina towns. . . . I saw papers being blown
> about by wind. They were falling into the dirt. I endeavoured to pick
> them up, till I was weary for they were so many. . . . Then I gathered
> the people together . . . they said the cause of what had been done
> was a quarrel that arose over the spoils of war. They further said
> that if anyone had intentionally thrown these papers away, he could
> only be one of the lowest of our people and if we had seen him we
> would have . . . punished him severely.

Many of Katsina's inhabitants had fled to Kano, 65 miles to the southeast, which soon supplanted Katsina as the most populous and commer-
cially important city in Central Africa, a position it retains.

Barth camped outside of town. To honor the visiting Christian, the
emir sent a ram and two large calabashes of honey. The gifts conster-
nated Barth. He couldn't reciprocate with anything of value because his

luggage had gone ahead to Kano. He was so destitute that when some royal musicians performed for him that day on drums, flutes, horns, and tambourine, he had little to offer them except a few cloves. He had learned that in Africa gifts were crucial to progress. He suspected that his lack of merchandise might stall him in Katsina.

THE NEXT DAY he was summoned to an audience outside the town walls with the emir, Muhammed Bello Yerima. Wearing a simple white shirt and a black shawl, the emir sat beneath a magnificent tamarind tree, one of the botanical glories in that part of the world. Barth immediately pegged him for a ham who lived for the grand gesture. Barth explained that he and his companions had lost most of their goods to robbers in Aïr. The rest were en route to Kano. Therefore he could offer only a modest gift, which he then produced: two red caps, a piece of printed calico, an English razor and scissors, a pound each of cloves and frankincense, a piece of soap, and some English needles.

As Barth feared, it wasn't enough. But instead of showing irritation, the emir dramatically welcomed Barth under his protection, the way a kidnapper offers protection to a hostage. Barth overheard him add, to the people sitting nearby, that since his enemies in Maradi possessed one of Barth's companions (Overweg), and the ruler of Bornu had the other in Zinder (Richardson), he would be a fool to let this one pass out of his hands.

Meanwhile horsemen from Bornu had arrived with orders from Sheikh Umar to take the Christian directly to Zinder. Barth had other plans and told them to go away. The protective emir also had other plans for the explorer. Barth, having no choice, resigned himself "to wait patiently for the end of the comedy."

The next day he was summoned into town. The clay walls were thirty feet high and many feet thick. Once inside, he passed through stubble fields and outlying houses for a mile and a half before reaching the town center. The emir was receiving people under the shade of a towering fig tree. Barth expressed his wish to leave quickly for Kano. The emir, however, insisted that he move into a nearby house as his guest. Barth had barely settled in when the emir sent another ram and two oxloads of corn. The gifts horrified Barth. They put him even more deeply into the emir's debt and clutches.

The next day the emir made his opening move: he would be pleased to accept Barth's pistols. Barth refused: "I was convinced that the whole success of further proceedings depended on our fire-arms." The emir's next move: he would settle for 100,000 cowries. "A sum certainly small, according to European modes of thinking, barely exceeding £8," wrote Barth, "but which I was quite unable to raise at the time."

To pass the days he strolled around town. He admired the big limes and papayas in the market, and talked with a man who had accompanied Clapperton on his second journey from Kano to Sokoto. He also dressed down a tormentor who called him a kaffir, an insulting term for an infidel. This led, as it often did with Barth, to a theological discussion that ended in religious détente. He never backed off from a debate about religion, and his Muslim opponents invariably ended by admiring his knowledge not only of his religion but of theirs. In this instance Barth acknowledged that Islam was "somewhat purer than the creeds of most of the Christian sects." His opponent conceded that Barth and the English were not kaffirs, but insisted on keeping Russians in that category.

After idling in Katsina for a week, Barth was anxious to go. He asked Muslim friends in the caravan for a loan to buy more gifts for the emir. They obliged with 31,000 cowries. They also suggested that he use the money to buy quantity, not quality, and offered to shop for him. They bought a velvet caftan, a carpet, a waistcoat, and a shawl. Barth, "to give the whole a more unpremeditated, honorary, and professional appearance," added a pencil, a bit of frankincense, and two doses of Epsom salts.

The emir surprised them all by replying that he no longer expected any gifts. Nevertheless he would honor Barth by keeping the caftan and the carpet. And on second thought he wouldn't refuse a generous gift of medicines, with a tutorial by Barth on their uses. In return, he would send the explorer a horse and saddle. Barth put together a small package of powdered quinine, tartar-emetic, and acetate of lead (for diarrhea, fever, inflammation, and conjunctivitis), plus a small bottle with a few drops of laudanum. He presented the package the next morning and spent two hours explaining the medicines. Almost satisfied, the emir requested something "to increase his conjugal vigor." Oh, and some fireworks. Barth regretted that he could supply neither.

Despite these disappointments, the emir kept his word, in his fashion. The next morning he sent Barth an unsightly nag with a matching saddle. "I exulted in my good fortune," wrote Barth. That nag was his ticket away from Katsina and its avid emir. On January 30, Barth passed through the city's southeastern gate, in the direction of Kano. He would have been astonished to hear that in two years he would be back. At the moment, his future lay to the east. "It was as if I had just escaped from a prison," he wrote, "and I drew my breath deeply as I inhaled the fresh air outside the wall."

BARTH CALLED THE country between Katsina and Kano "one of the finest landscapes I ever saw in my life." The undulating terrain was adorned with stately trees—figs, tamarinds, shea-butters, doum palms, the stupendous cotton-silk, or kapok, tree. Singing birds filled them. These groves alternated with fields of cotton and grain, indigo and tobacco. Herds of white lyre-horned cattle grazed in pastures. Bees made honey in hollow logs affixed to giant baobab trees. Barth marveled at women carrying their produce to local markets in half a dozen enormous calabashes stacked on their heads.

The pastoral calm was sometimes broken by troops of armed cavalry and infantry, hurrying past on their way to join the newest war against the pagans of Maradi. In the evenings Barth's small camp was swarmed, as always, by "hucksters and retailers" who pestered him even into his tent. The area teemed with thieves, so Barth posted watchmen at night. But such inconveniences couldn't dampen his mood.

He was now traveling separately from the salt caravan. His little group consisted of three servants, a camel, a mare, a pack-ox, the emir's nag, and "one half-barbarized European." Everyone was excited by the prospect of Kano, "the celebrated emporium of Negroland." The road grew increasingly crowded with travelers heading to and from the city. On the evening of February 2, after three days of travel, they saw Kano's famous two hills, Dala and Goron Dutse, rising from the plain.

By the time they passed through one of the city's fourteen gates, set into a clay wall 30 feet high, darkness had fallen. They had some difficulty finding their quarters. But Barth's spirits were unsinkable: "Kano had been sounding in my ears now for more than a year; it had been one of the great objects of our journey as the central point of commerce, as a great store-house of information, and as the point whence more distant regions might be most successfully attempted. At length, after nearly a year's exertions, I had reached it."

THIS BUBBLE POPPED the following day. Barth learned that his stock of goods was worth far less than expected in Kano's markets, which put his future in jeopardy. The present wasn't rosy either. The agent in charge of his goods in Kano, a man recommended by Gagliuffi, turned out to be a blatant chiseler who refused to advance him any money against the sale of his goods. Barth didn't have "a single farthing in cash." He had to borrow money to eat and live. Meanwhile he was hounded every day by creditors for expenses incurred on the road and in Katsina.

Kano's emir, like Katsina's, considered Barth a prize to be squeezed. He wouldn't hear of departure. To meet the emir's expectations would wipe out his goods, so Barth played for time. This put him in poor graces with the emir. Richardson inadvertently worsened Barth's circumstances by sending the emir a letter from Zinder, promising to visit with a gift once he was resupplied. But the letter didn't even mention Barth, which made the emir wonder whether this visiting Christian was a loner without the means to make generous presents—a dangerous status for an infidel stranger in the Sudan.

Adding to his misery, Barth's lodgings were dim and dreary, and his roommates were lively throngs of mice and vermin. Then fever knocked him down. Characteristically he decided to cure himself through willed exertion. He roused himself and ventured into Kano on horseback. The city's vitality revived him.

He estimated its population at 30,000, perhaps double that during the busy trading season, plus 4,000 domestic slaves. The city bustled and lazed, delighted and appalled. He glimpsed naked slaves, gaudy Arabs, lovely women, luxury, poverty, pleasure, distress. "So different in external form from all that is seen in European towns," wrote Barth, "yet so similar in its internal principles." London, he pointed out, had more in common with Kano than it suspected.

Barth knew that comparing Africa's way of life to Europe's would surprise his readers, so he illustrated the similarities at length in one of his best passages. Unlike the European racialists and nationalists whose views would soon devastate Africa, Barth was interested in connections and world history. His description goes beyond exotic details, reaching across cultures and continents to find a common humanity:

> Here a row of shops, filled with articles of native and foreign produce, with buyers and sellers in every variety of figure, complexion, and dress, yet all intent upon their little gain, endeavoring to cheat each other; there a large shed, like a hurdle, full of half-naked, half-starved slaves torn from their native homes, from their wives or husbands, from their children or parents, arranged in rows like cattle, and staring desperately upon the buyers, anxiously watching into whose hands it should be their destiny to fall. In another part were to be seen all the necessaries of life: the wealthy buying the most palatable things for his table; the poor stopping and looking greedily upon a handful of grain: here a rich governor, dressed in silk and gaudy clothes, mounted upon a spirited and richly

caparisoned horse, and followed by a host of idle, insolent slaves; there a poor blind man groping his way through the multitude, and fearing at every step to be trodden down; here a yard neatly fenced with mats of reed, and provided with all the comforts which the country affords—a clean, snug-looking cottage, the clay walls nicely polished, a shutter of reeds placed against the low, well-rounded door, and forbidding intrusion on the privacy of life, a cool shed for the daily household work—a fine spreading alleluba-tree, affording a pleasant shade during the hottest hours of the day, or a beautiful gonda or papaya unfolding its large, feather-like leaves above a slender, smooth, and undivided stem, or the tall date-tree, waving over the whole scene; the matron, in a clean black cotton gown wound round her waist, her hair neatly dressed in "chokoli" or bejaji, busy preparing the meal for her absent husband, or spinning cotton, and, at the same time, urging her female slaves to pound the corn; the children, naked and merry, playing about in the sand . . . or chasing a straggling, stubborn goat; earthenware pots and wooden bowls, all cleanly washed, standing in order. Farther on, a dashing Cyprian, homeless, comfortless, and childless, but affecting merriment or forcing a wanton laugh, gaudily ornamented with numerous strings of beads around her neck, her hair fancifully dressed, and bound with a diadem, her gown of various colors loosely fastened under her luxuriant breast, and trailing behind in the sand; near her a diseased wretch covered with ulcers or with elephantiasis.

Now a busy "marina," an open terrace of clay, with a number of dyeing pots, and people busily employed in various processes of their handicraft: here a man stirring the juice, and mixing with the indigo some coloring wood in order to give it the desired tint; there another, drawing a shirt from the dye-pot, or hanging it up on a rope fastened to the trees; there two men beating a well-dyed shirt, singing the while, and keeping good time; farther on, a blacksmith busy with his rude tools in making a dagger . . . or the more estimable and useful instruments of husbandry; . . . close by, a group of indolent loiterers lying in the sun and idling away their hours.

Here a caravan from Gonja arriving with the desired kola-nut, chewed by all who have "ten kurdi" [cowries] to spare from their necessary wants, or a caravan laden with natron, starting for Nupe, or a troop of A'sbenawa going off with their salt for the neighboring towns, or some Arabs leading their camels, heavily laden with the luxuries of the north and east . . . ; there, a troop of gaudy, warlike-looking horsemen galloping toward the palace of the governor to bring him the news of a new inroad of Serki Ibram. Every where human life in its varied forms, the most cheerful and the most gloomy, seemed closely mixed together; every variety of national form and complexion—the olive-colored Arab, the dark Kanuri with his wide nostrils, the small-featured, light, and slender Ba-Fellanchi, the broad-faced Ba-Wangara (Mandingo), the stout, large-boned, and masculine-looking Nupe female, the well-proportioned and comely Ba-Haushe woman.

Kano's vast market, the largest in Central Africa, astonished Barth, as it had Clapperton. Then as now, the market sprawled in the center of town near the filthy elongated pond called the Jakara. Rows of stalls and sheds lined a labyrinth of narrow alleys. Everything under the sun could be found there, organized in sectors like a department store: every local fruit, grain, and vegetable; livestock of all varieties; slaughter-houses and butcher shops, with the meat temptingly displayed, some-times with a dab of sheep's wool stuck to a goat's leg to trick the gullible into buying it for mutton; stacks of animal fodder; calabashes, spoons, baskets, and other domestic utensils; cakes and breads; savory dishes; refreshing drinks and fresh water; scissors, knives, and swords; beads of glass, coral, and amber; jewelry and amulets; kohl and antimony; gold, silver, copper, zinc, and iron; frankincense, cloves, and other spices; kola nuts, a mild stimulant "as necessary as coffee or tea to us"; herbal medicines and charms. Some merchants hired musicians to attract buyers to their stalls.

Many of the shops sold Kano's most famous product: fine cotton cloth, beautifully dyed in many shades of indigo, in solids and patterns. Kano cloth and the garments made from it were in demand as far north as Tripoli, as far west as Timbuktu, and as far east as Lake Chad—essentially everywhere in north-central Africa where people wore clothes. As soon as he could afford it, Barth bought a Kano "guinea-fowl" shirt with a speckled pattern of small blue and white squares for about £1.50.

The city was also renowned for its leather goods, especially sandals. Other important items included salt, slaves, and natron (sodium carbonate, found in saline deposits, and used as a cleaning agent, preservative, and bleach). Barth estimated that 5,000 people were sold for the coastal slave markets every year, plus a greater number for domestic slavery.

He was especially struck by the abundance of European goods in the market. He found calicoes from Manchester, silks and sugar from France, red cloth from Saxony, beads from Venice and Trieste, mirrors and needles from Nuremberg, razors from Austria. Sword blades for sale came from Solingen, Germany, famous for its steel. He estimated that 50,000 such blades reached Kano every year, where blacksmiths set them into hilts. Barth saw Solingen blades, sometimes at uncomfortably close range, everywhere he went in Africa, from the Sahara to Lake Chad to Timbuktu.

The Kano market also sold paper with the *tre lune* watermark, made in Italy; it was ubiquitous in north-central Africa. (Paper was precious in the Sudan, and profitable in the markets. Barth wrote several letters and dispatches from Kano on the backs of printed stationery from the Bordeaux & Cette Railway Office in London that informed the recipient about an upcoming board meeting: in short, scrap paper.)

The oldest part of Kano, inhabited since the sixth century, was Dala, a steep flat-topped hill of hard red earth, about 1,700 feet high. Barth climbed it and sketched the city below. To the north the sky was hazy with windblown sand from the Sahara. To the south lay the emir's palace, a walled thirty-acre compound within the city's walls. Built in the fifteenth century, the compound contained (and still does) living quarters for the emir and his wives, concubines, children, and royal slaves, as well as reception halls, courts, forests, and grazing lands. The emir's army consisted of 7,000 cavalry and more than 20,000 infantry.

To pay for all this he levied heavy taxes, starting with a per capita tax. He also taxed every hoe, dye pot, and palm tree. He collected a tax on everything sold in the market, from vegetables to slaves. And of course every caravan and merchant that passed through the city or did business there was required to honor the emir with extravagant gifts. No doubt Barth's European readers noticed these similarities to their lives as well.

BARTH HAD BEEN stuck in Kano for a month. He needed to leave for Kukawa, the capital of Bornu, to meet Richardson and Overweg. His Muslim friends had been interceding for him with the emir, a stout, handsome man of thirty-eight whom Barth found intelligent but lazy. Eventually, as always, a bargain was struck. The emir agreed to honor his Christian visitor by accepting a load of presents: an elaborate black burnoose with silk and gold lace worth 60,000 cowries, a red cap, a white shawl bordered with red, a length of white muslin, cloves, rose oil, a razor and scissors, an English clasp-knife, and a large German mirror. In return the emir granted Barth permission to leave.

Unfortunately he had sold everything else he owned to buy gifts and pay debts, and couldn't afford the expense of getting to Kukawa. One of his Muslim friends shamed the emir into sending Barth a gift of 60,000 cowries. Of this, 6,000 went to the friend, 6,000 to the officer who delivered the shells, and 8,000 to clear the last of Barth's debts. With the remainder he bought two camels and some provisions. He couldn't find a guide. Everyone was afraid of the territory between Kano and Kukawa. On March 9, he finally left the city, accompanied by three teenaged servants.

"There was no caravan," he wrote, "the road was infested by robbers; and I had only one servant upon whom I could rely, . . . while I had
been so unwell the preceding day as to be unable to rise from my couch.
However, I was full of confidence; and with the same delight with which
a bird springs forth from its cage, I hastened to escape from these narrow, dirty mud-walls into the boundless creation."

He sprang forth, he added, on his "unsightly black four-dollar nag."
In this bedraggled yet cheerful fashion he started for Kukawa and the
empire of Bornu, the expedition's goal. There he expected to reunite
with his European companions and be resupplied with money and
merchandise.

13

An Ending

Soon after leaving Kano, Barth's group joined the small family caravan of a wealthy Arab trader. They traveled together for a few days. The trader was accompanied by his veiled concubine, her three female slaves, six natives, and six pack-oxen. One of the Arab's servants, a black African, surprised Barth by speaking to him in modern Greek—the man had spent twenty years in Istanbul. The trader, refined and educated, entertained Barth with fine pastries and coffee. Barth, nearly destitute, could contribute only a couple of onions in return.

The contrast deeply embarrassed him. It inspired one of his occasional peevish outbursts about his constant lack of means, outbursts that shrink him to normal human dimensions: "The barbarian and the civilized European seemed to have changed places," he wrote. "Really it is incredible what a European traveler in these countries has to endure; for while he must bear infinitely more fatigue, anxiety, and mental exertion than any native traveler, he is deprived of even the little comfort which the country affords, has no one to cook his supper and to take care of him when he falls sick, or to shampoo him."

On March 12 a passing caravan from Kukawa told Barth that no Christian had arrived in that city or been heard of. This puzzled him. Richardson had expected to reach Kukawa by late February.

Four days and 85 miles after leaving Kano, Barth came to Gumel, on the western frontier of Bornu. It was a flourishing town with narrow streets and a busy market with 300 stalls. Barth's habitual questions led him to a man who had been Clapperton's servant on the first expedition.

But Gumel delighted Barth most for another reason. March 15, he wrote, was "a most fortunate and lucky day for me": he received his first mail in ten months. Nothing lifted an explorer's spirits as much as correspondence from home, or depressed him more than feeling forgotten. Barth luxuriated in letters from England, Germany, and Tripoli. Their praise and encouragement reinvigorated him. Equally important, one of them, from Gagliuffi, contained 2 Spanish dollars, the refund from an accounting error. "It was the only current money I had at that time," wrote Barth, "and they were certainly more valuable to me than so many hundreds of pounds at other times."

As he moved east, the language and culture changed from Hausa/Fulani to Kanuri. "It is remarkable what a difference there is between the character of the ba-Haushe and the Kanuri," wrote Barth, "the former lively, spirited, and cheerful, the latter melancholic, dejected, and brutal; and the same difference is visible in their physiognomies—the former having in general very pleasant and regular features and more graceful forms, while the Kanuri, with his broad face, his wide nostrils, and his large bones, makes a far less agreeable impression, especially the women, who are very plain, and certainly among the ugliest in all Negroland, notwithstanding their coquetry, in which they do not yield at all to the Hausa women."

The day after leaving Gumel he heard distant drums of war. They belonged to Buhari, the former emir of nearby Hadejia. Buhari had been deposed by the sultan of Sokoto in favor of Buhari's brother. Now the ex-emir had turned rebel to recover his throne. The vizier of Bornu, who seized every opportunity to torment Sokoto's ruler, was secretly supporting Buhari with arms and men. The region's people suffered the consequences.

Barth witnessed the revolt's first spasms. He began passing empty devastated villages. When he returned this way a year and a half later, en route to Timbuktu, many more villages and towns had disappeared, wiped from the landscape by war, their inhabitants killed or seized as slaves. Rapacity typified the region's rulers, noted Barth. Whenever they needed money, they descended on nearby districts to take slaves, sometimes even snatching their own subjects.

The region also swarmed with thieves. On most evenings Barth fired his gun to warn them away.

Wars, thieves, and razzias kept the area between Kano and Kukawa in upheaval. Traffic on the road dwindled because people were afraid of being robbed or captured and sold as slaves. The roadside markets where lively women sold their goods disappeared. The landscape changed as well, turning monotonous—flat, sandy, uncultivated, with little vegetation except occasional doum palms and baobabs (also called kuka trees and monkey-bread trees). The road splintered into many tracks, which also splintered.

Barth needed a guide through this maze, but finding one was nearly impossible. Everyone was scared of being seized as a slave. He did manage to hire several guides, but they all deserted within a day or two. He had higher hopes for two short muscular Manga warriors who seemed tough enough for the perils of the road, with their leather aprons, bows and arrows, small battle axes, leather provision bags, and small water gourds. But they quickly developed jitters and quit before the end of their first day.

Disgusted, Barth plowed ahead with his young servants. "I could only rely upon Providence and my own courage."

WHILE BARTH WAS trapped in Katsina, Richardson was in Zinder, a city of 20,000. He reached its outskirts on January 14 with Annur, and was so eager to ditch the old chief that he galloped into town ahead of his party and immediately placed himself under the hospitality of Zinder's sultan. When Annur chastised him for this, Richardson exulted at being released from Annur's custody, thus adding insult to bad manners. But

Richardson was fed up with larcenous, wheedling Tuaregs, and he still carried a grudge against Annur for the steep price of his protection. When Barth learned of Richardson's conduct, he called it "not only impolitic, but unfair," since the old chief, though pricey and stingy, had at least kept his word, unlike almost everyone else in Aïr.

Richardson's delight at escaping the Tuaregs gave Zinder a rosy hue, at first. The sultan and his chief advisor, a Moroccan sherif, plied Richardson with so much food that he nearly took ill. "Really the world seems turned upside down when the conduct of the people here is compared with the hospitality which we received from [Annur]," wrote Richardson. He praised the sultan, Ibrahim, as an intelligent fifty-year-old with a sparkling sense of humor. Ibrahim also had 300 concubines, 100 sons, and 50 daughters. The concubines weren't shut in, but were free to roam the streets and even to take other lovers.

In partial return for the sultan's generosity, Richardson satisfied his host's "ardent desire" to become acquainted with the strong spirits of Christians—alcoholic, not religious. Richardson gave the sultan half a bottle of mastic, an anise-flavored liqueur. The sultan, accompanied by his son-in-law, retired to his inner chambers and "made himself very merry." The next day he didn't appear in public.

Richardson sometimes spent evenings in the garden of the urbane sherif. They talked about political developments in Algeria, which France had invaded in 1830. The sherif had fought the French for fourteen years and been their prisoner for seven months. Now 2,000 miles from Algiers, he was the sheikh of Bornu's eyes and ears in Zinder, as well as the sultan's advisor. All this easy living and political sophistication impressed Richardson.

He was less pleased to see Zinder's lower classes greet grandees by kneeling and tossing dust onto their heads. The greater the discrepancy in rank, the bigger the cloud of dust. Social equals greeted each other with a gesture that would become familiar in the New World: they slapped hands with open vertical palms. Zinder's fashionable women stained their teeth yellow and their skins indigo, and wore their hair in large knots, one hanging above each ear, one in back. Above the waist they were bare. Every night there was dancing to drums.

The sultan lost some of his sparkle when Richardson learned about his methods of capital punishment. In some cases the offender's chest was sliced open and his heart torn out. For a slower doom, the offender was hung by the heels. Richardson visited the place of executions and its Tree of Death, a vestige of paganism. Fifty vultures killed time in the branches. The ground was a horror show of bones and hyena feces. "Never in my life did I feel so sick at heart—so revolted at man's crimes and cruelties."

He noticed that every household in Zinder chained its slaves tightly at the ankles so that they couldn't run away, forcing them to move "in little jumps." He was shocked when his cultured friend the sherif casually gave away a freshly caught slave—a frightened little boy, scarred on only one cheek, a sign that his mother had lost all her children before him. Such were the scenes of everyday life in Zinder.

Then Richardson heard the royal drum call together the sultan's forces to "eat up the country" in a razzia, or slave raid. Whenever the sultan needed money, whether small change for kola nuts or large sums to settle heavy debts, he paid in human flesh. He raised this capital through razzias. "As the largest fish eat the little fish," Richardson was told, "so the great people eat the small people." (In a few years, Europe's rulers would justify the same practice in Africa under the fancier aegis of social Darwinism.)

The Qur'an prohibited the enslavement of Muslims. For that reason, said the imam of Zinder to Richardson, it was not in the economic interest of the sultan or the merchants to convert pagans. But in practice it mattered little to the sultan and his fellow lords whether the seized flesh was Muslim or pagan, because it all could be sold. For Africa's rulers, greed and power trumped religion, as they soon would for Europe's Christian rulers. Richardson astutely remarked that these indiscriminate raids would hinder the progress of Islam in Africa as the blacks realized that conversion did not protect them.

(Power operates similarly in every age, on every continent. Shortly after dan Fodio was succeeded by his son, Muhammed Bello, Bello invaded Bornu. Bornu's ruler, al-Kanemi, wrote to him, "We profess the same religion, and it is not fitting that our subjects should make war on each other. Between our two kingdoms are the pagan Bedde tribes, on whom it is permissible to levy contribution: let us respect this limit: what lies to the east of their country shall be ours: what lies to the west shall be yours." This finds its European echo in the Berlin Conference of 1884, where the European powers began the partition of Africa among themselves.)

Nor did it matter if vassal lords stole subjects from provinces belonging to their liege, the sheikh of Bornu. The sheikh looked the other way as long as he got 20 percent of the take. "Really it is difficult to compare the condition of this extraordinary region to anything but a forest," wrote Richardson, "through which lions and tigers range to devour the weaker and more timid beasts—to which they grant intervals of repose during the digestion of their meals."

Richardson described the razzia and its effects unflinchingly. His convictions burn on the page, in emotional but controlled prose that Barth was incapable of, as in this description of the return from the razzia:

There cannot be in the world—there cannot be in the whole world—a more appalling spectacle than this. My head swam as I gazed. A single horseman rode first, showing the way, and the wretched captives followed him as if they had been used to this condition all their lives. Here were naked little boys running alone, perhaps thinking themselves upon a holiday; near at hand dragged mothers with babes at their breasts; girls of various ages, some almost ripened into womanhood, others still infantine in form and appearance; old men bent two-double with age, their trembling chins verging towards the ground, their poor old heads covered with white wool; aged women tottering along, leaning upon long staffs, mere living skeletons;—such was the miscellaneous crowd that came first; and then followed the stout young men, ironed neck to neck! This was the first installment of the black bullion of Central Africa; and as the wretched procession huddled through the gateways into the town the creditors of the [sultan] looked gloatingly on through their lazy eyes, and calculated on speedy payment. . . . It was exceedingly horrifying to hear the people of Zinder salute the troops of the razzia on their return with the beautiful Arabic word, *Alberka,* 'blessing!' Thus is it that human beings sometimes ask God for a blessing on transactions which must ever be stamped with his curse.

Richardson's close look at the ugliness of the razzia altered some of his views. He abandoned the idea that slavery would disappear if white people—Arab slavers and their customers outside of Africa—abandoned it. "The blacks are, in truth, the real active men-stealers," he wrote. "It must be confessed, that if there were no white men from the north or south to purchase the supply of slaves required out of Africa, slavery would still flourish. . . . Africa is bled from all pores by her own children, seconded by the cupidity of strangers." The rich black men of Central Africa, he noted, owned thousands of slaves who worked their plantations.

This led him to another change. He had begun the expedition with the firm belief that strong commercial relations between Europe and Africa would lead to the end of slavery. The brutalities he witnessed in Zinder smashed that idea. Near the end of his stay there he recorded several variations of his new conviction: "only foreign conquest by a power like Great Britain or France can really extirpate slavery from Africa."

By the time Richardson said goodbye to the sultan on February 8, Ibrahim had lost his sparkle. Richardson seemed psychologically exhausted. "His highness had nothing to say, and we as little to him," he wrote. "We just shook hands, and that was all."

ZINDER MARKED a turning point for Richardson. Ever since Aïr he had been slowly distancing himself from all but a few Africans. In the salt caravan he stopped speaking to people to avoid beggars. For the same reason, he left Zinder's market after a quick visit. After leaving the city he traveled a route parallel to Barth's, but recorded markedly different reactions to what he saw: "I am afraid I shall soon get tired of this negro population and these towns, all built and all peopled in the same manner," he wrote. "They seem remarkably curious at first, but curiosity soon palls." It's impossible to imagine Barth writing such a sentence.

Several factors cooled Richardson's interest in Africa. The heat of the Sudan sapped his energy and slowly undermined his health. As those things waned, so did his intellectual curiosity. Zinder also forced him to acknowledge that his life's goal of contributing to the end of slavery was a pipe dream. The psychological shock seemed to rock him.

These losses of energy and purpose fed his growing impatience with, and despair about, black-on-black violence. All this perhaps contributed to his more frequent refuge in racial clichés and stereotypes. In Zinder, for instance, he bemoaned Central Africa's lack of any written history. This was a standard European trope, and an ignorant one. Richardson compounded this arrogant assumption by adding that even if there *were* written histories, posterity would ignore them as accounts of nothing more than "barbarism and slave-hunting."

In another sign of Richardson's fading interest in actual Africans, he resorted to generalities about "the negro character." When his kaleidoscope and peep shows delighted the sultan of Zinder, he wrote, "These barbarians are nothing but great willful children." His visit to the Tree of Death inspired more racial boilerplate: "Here, then, we have a specimen of the negro character, with all its contradictions; soft and effeminate in its ordinary moods; cheerful, and pleasant, and simple, to appearance; but capable of acting, as it were without transition, the most terrible deeds of atrocity." Was this intended to contrast, one wonders, with specimens of white character displayed throughout European and American history?

Richardson's mental and imaginative exhaustion was especially apparent during his stay in Gouré, a town of 7,000 about 100 miles east of Zinder. Gouré's ruler, Koso, was handsome, educated, affable, and full of questions. He quizzed Richardson about his health, his European clothes, his impressions of the Tuaregs. He wanted to know if any wars roiled Europe at present, and asked for details about Britain's political relations with the Ottoman Empire. He was politely but intensely curious about his visitor and the world he came from.

"It was really a scene of African state, but without deformities," wrote Richardson. "There was no blood, no slaying of victims, no abject ceremonies; nothing," he added in a telling phrase, "to offend the eye of the European." That had become his measure.

That evening Richardson trotted out all the marvels he used to amuse African rulers—compass, telescope, kaleidoscope, peep shows. He expected the usual "childish" response. Naturally these wonders did entertain Koso, but during the entire time he was examining them, he was also questioning Richardson about his life, his country, his beliefs. Was it true that the ruler of England was a woman? Would Richardson read something in English? Richardson obliged with a passage from Milton's *Comus*. The questions turned to religion. Did Richardson pray? Did he know the Gospels and the Psalms? Richardson showed Koso a copy of these in Arabic, to demonstrate that the English were not pagans. But Richardson was careful not to let the conversation go any further, since that might lead to religious debate, which "a prudent man . . . will evade." The next day Koso, ever inquisitive, "began by asking me all manner of questions, the subjects ranging from the affairs of kings and princes down to the handkerchief round my neck."

Richardson didn't try to square his racial stereotyping with his own description of Koso; he simply made Koso an exception who was tolerable to Europeans. (Barth later wrote that Koso "by his personal dignity had more the appearance of a prince than almost any other chief whom I saw in Negroland.")

In Gouré's court, when Richardson took off his boot to show it to Koso, the people "burst out into an involuntary exclamation of astonishment" at the whiteness of his leg. As he traveled into remoter regions east of Gouré, hundreds of people sometimes followed him or came to his tent, eager to glimpse this pale Christian freak of nature, and perhaps to cadge some of his white medicine.

Richardson disliked being treated as an ugly oddity. He also bitterly resented the offensive label of kaffir (unbeliever). Yet his sense of superiority kept him from noticing his similar derogatory assumptions about Africans. This condescension also added distance between him and the people around him.

In essential ways Richardson was Barth's opposite. Africa seemed to wear Richardson out, psychologically as well as physically. By contrast, the deeper Barth immersed himself in Africa, the more fascinating, not frightening, he found it. Avoiding Africans was against his nature. Rather, he sought them out, because they had what he wanted—information, knowledge, understanding. When he talked to Africans, he didn't strive for prudence, but for frank engagement, whether the subject was women, politics, or religion.

Though Barth shared some of the racial assumptions of his era, the Africans in his writings were distinct people with idiosyncratic qualities, not stereotypes. He granted them their individuality by taking them seriously—he was sincerely interested in them, their lives, their cultures. Barth engaged with them as individuals and hunted for whatever nuggets of information they could provide. He explored Africans as well as Africa. Consequently his account contains more individually limned Africans than that of any other African explorer. And unlike Richardson's journal, Barth's was full of warm feelings about many of the people he met. The simple truth was that he liked Africans and considered many of them friends, and they reciprocated.

RICHARDSON LEFT GOURÉ on February 19. That evening he drank the last half of a bottle of port wine and wished he had a bottle to drink every day for his health. On February 21 he complained about the ferocity of the sun. After setting up camp he was bothered, as usual, by people wanting to see him and to beg medicine for various ailments. "I had numbers of other patients all day; my Epsom is fast going," he wrote. "Thermometer at sunset, 82°; weather very troublesome to-day, blowing hot and cold with the same breath."

Those were his last lines. Eleven days later he was dead, in a decaying village called Ngurutuwa. Whatever happened in between remained a mystery. He left no instructions about the mission, no orders transferring authority, no letters to the sheikh of Bornu about his European companions. Perhaps he died too suddenly to do so, though that doesn't explain the eleven-day gap. Or perhaps he did leave instructions and his servants destroyed them, thinking to improve their chances of profit by leaving matters in confusion. What's certain is that Richardson faded away, overwhelmed by Africa.

BARTH WAS LOST in one of his esoteric daydreams, wondering how a small grove of out-of-place date trees had reached this region. "I was leaning carelessly on my little nag," he wrote on March 24, "musing on the original homes of all the plants which now adorn different countries." His reverie was broken by four armed men riding toward him. Barth spurred his horse to meet them. Their leader, a regal and richly dressed Moroccan, stared at Barth, then asked if he was the Christian traveling from Kano. Yes, said the explorer. The rider bluntly told him that his fellow Christian had died before reaching Kukawa. His property had been seized and taken to the city.

The news stunned Barth. The expedition's leader, his companion, was dead. The mission's future was thrown into confusion.

Barth hurried east toward the place where Richardson had died.

Swarms of hawks began shadowing his small group. The birds were preying on clouds of locusts, disturbed from the trees by the passing caravan. The hawks swooped down on Barth's group, beating each other with their wings and agitating the caravan's animals.

After three days Barth reached Ngurutuwa. A spreading fig tree sheltered Richardson's grave. Thorn bushes protected it from hyenas and other scavengers. Barth was relieved to see that it hadn't been molested. The villagers told him that the white man had arrived one evening looking ill, and died quietly the next morning. Barth gave a small present to a man who promised to care for the grave. Later, in Kukawa, he convinced the vizier to protect it with a stronger fence.

"My way of looking at things was not quite the same as that of my late companion," wrote Barth, "and we had therefore often had little differences; but I esteemed him highly for the deep sympathy he felt for the sufferings of the native African, and deeply lamented his death."

Yet he began the next sentence, "Full of confidence, I stretched myself upon my mat, and indulged in my simple supper. . . ."

Barth had rushed to Richardson's grave, paid for its maintenance, and praised his companion's virtues. His conduct was honorable. Yet in the next moment he was savoring his self-confidence and enjoying a meal.

Perhaps some part of him was pleased that Richardson was out of the way. Barth had always been a loner. He had long ago devoted himself to science and learning with the expectation of making a contribution to knowledge. Such a person was not cut out to play second fiddle behind a man of limited intellect and ability such as Richardson. Yet Barth's egotism was kept in check by his stern sense of duty and honor. Though he sometimes complained bitterly about his treatment by the British government, his loyalty to the expedition and its goals never wavered.

Perhaps his reaction to Richardson's death also reflected a distrust of emotion. Emotion could impede progress and interfere with the work at hand. Barth's intense focus and indestructible will sometimes made him rather chilly.

Richardson was dead. Nothing would change that. Barth's business was with the present and the future. How would the British government react? Would it continue to support the expedition? Would it allow a German to be in charge, or send a British replacement? Had Her Majesty's Government sent supplies to Kukawa, as promised, or would he and Overweg be stuck there without means to continue? And where was Overweg? There had been no word from him or about him for nearly two months. Was he healthy and safe, or buried in some forsaken place like Richardson?

Barth hoped to find some answers in Kukawa.

14

The Kingdom of Bornu

As Barth continued through Bornu toward its capital, Kukawa, he passed dozens of villages abandoned because of pillage and fear. This farmland, the finest in Bornu, was being reclaimed by forest and scrub, elephant and lion. Barth called the waste and devastation disgraceful. He blamed the greed and apathy of Bornu's leaders. "Even the best of these mighty men," he wrote, "cares more for the silver ornaments of his numerous wives than for the welfare of his people."

On April 2, 1851, he reached the white clay walls of Kukawa—the mission's objective. It was a year to the day since the expedition's real start. Barth had ridden ahead of his servants, and he hesitated outside the massive wood-and-metal gate. His situation was unpromising. His director was dead, his remaining colleague unaccounted for. He was entering Kukawa alone, with no resources and no standing. Yet the mission's fate depended heavily on his reception here.

He rode through the gate and asked some surprised people for directions to the sheikh's palace. Barth was surprised as well. Kukawa was actually two towns separated by an open area about half a mile long. "I was equally astonished," he added, "at the number of gorgeously-dressed horsemen whom I met on the way."

He came first to the house of the vizier, Haj Beshir ben Ahmed

Tirab. The vizier was about to leave with 200 horsemen for his daily visit to Sheikh Umar, Bornu's ruler. Haj Beshir greeted Barth with delight. He told a servant to show the Christian to his quarters, a spacious two-story house.

Barth had barely crossed the threshold before creditors besieged him. First came two Arab ship's carpenters from Tripoli. Richardson had requested them to replace his naval nephew, who had come unglued in Murzuk and been invalided home. These replacements had been idling in Kukawa for months, waiting for the boat. Now they demanded five months' salary—110 Spanish dollars. Weary of Kukawa, they intended to leave as soon as they were paid.

Next came, in Barth's description, the thirstiest bloodsucker of them all—Richardson's arrogant sot of a dragoman, Yusuf Moknee. Richardson had fired him in Zinder but owed him wages. Nor had Richardson paid Moknee's replacement or any of his other servants. Most of them had given up hope and left town a day earlier, but would return when they heard about Barth's arrival. These wages came to another 300 dollars.

Richardson owed most to an agent of Gagliuffi's, a merchant named Sfaski who had accompanied the mission into Aïr from Murzuk and was now in Kukawa. Richardson evidently had agreed to pay 100 percent interest on a debt of 636 dollars, plus other onerous terms that brought the bill to nearly 3,000 dollars. Sfaksi presented an invoice for 1,270 dollars. Richardson had expected to be resupplied here with money and goods from the British government. Nothing had arrived.

Barth, freshly aghast at Richardson's mismanagement and ashamed of the mission's debts, promised to pay everyone. He gave his word, since that's all he had. "I did not possess a single dollar, a single bernus, nor any thing of value." The mission's few remaining goods had been confiscated by the vizier upon Richardson's death.

Barth's anxiety and his resentment of Richardson and the British government boiled over in a letter he wrote a few days later to Charles Beke, an English geographer and African traveler:

. . . we poor Germans, who, in order to go on with *the scanty means* . . . with which we have been supplied by government— sacrifice our own property (not to mention our lives), have not been regarded as members of the mission or as gentlemen, but almost as servants. The consequence is that Mr. Richardson's death has not only stopped the proceedings of the expedition for a short time, but has threatened even to put an end to it altogether. . . . Instead of finding preparations made for our journey around Lake Tshad, I found the whole expedition in despair and everybody about to return. . . . Instead of meeting with fresh supplies for myself, I found debts of over 300 dollars; and in order to maintain the honour of the government in whose service we are traveling, I have felt it my duty to exhaust my own private credit to pay off a part of the debts incurred by the mission, from which I myself have to demand 91 dollars.

He also wrote to the Foreign Office, informing them of Richardson's death and requesting funds and instructions. A month would pass before a caravan left Kukawa with the letters.

Meanwhile the sheikh and the vizier were expecting rich presents. On his second morning in Kukawa, Barth visited Sheikh Umar, who received him with cheerful warmth. Umar wore a simple tobe and a burnoose around his shoulders. His skin was a deep glossy black, inherited from his mother, a Bagirmi princess captured in war who became a concubine of Umar's father, Muhammed al-Kanemi, the architect of modern Bornu.

Barth reminded Umar of the old friendship between the English and his father, begun in the 1820s by the expedition of Denham, Clapperton, and Oudney. The members of the new mission, added Barth, "had come without reserve, to live a while among them, and under their protection, and with their assistance, to obtain an insight into this part of the world, which appeared so strange in our eyes." After explaining his inability to offer anything worthy, Barth gave Umar his personal Qur'an, purchased in Egypt during his trip around the Mediterranean. Barth noted that some English readers would disapprove, but that Umar was open-minded enough to accept it from the hands of an infidel.

(Oudney made a similar, though grammatically deformed, comparison between the British and the Bornuese: "I have nothing to complain of all classes of people have been amazingly kind, and not viewed us with that horror which Mohametans in some places view Christians, we have had, indeed, a toleration shewn us much greater than is to be found among a great many of our Sectarians." Nevertheless al-Kanemi drew gasps from his court when he touched the British infidels by shaking their hands.)

Barth was determined to reclaim Richardson's possessions. It was a matter of both honor and financial necessity. He requested an inventory of the seized property and was relieved to see Richardson's journals on it. But when he asked for everything to be returned, he was instead shown several boxes and told to choose a few things. He refused. The vizier and the sheikh, he said, had been generous and hospitable, but if their habit was to confiscate other people's property, he was leaving. This was pure brass, but for Barth it was simply the honorable course.

The vizier sent for him that evening to discuss the issue. Barth said that once the goods were returned, he would give most of them as presents to the vizier and the sheikh, as Richardson intended. He also emphasized the urgency of getting letters to Tripoli about Richardson's death and his own safe arrival. And he shrewdly asked for help in starting his scientific work right away, because the resulting dispatches could help persuade the British government to continue funding the mission, which would include more gifts. The amiable vizier, who soon became Barth's close though not completely trustworthy friend, agreed to everything. Barth left after midnight, encouraged about the future.

"Having in this way vindicated the honorable character of the mission and my own," he wrote, "I applied myself with more cheerfulness to my studies and inquiries, for which I found ample opportunities; for many distinguished personages from distant countries were staying here at the time, partly on their journey to and from Mekka, partly only attracted by the fame of the vizier's hospitable and bounteous character."

BORNU HAD BEEN a magnet for travelers, scholars, and merchants for many centuries. Barth was shown documents about its history dating to the first half of the sixteenth century. Using various histories and accounts, including oral ones, he traced the origins of Bornu's Saifawa dynasty to "a little before the year 900." The historical record became more clear from the twelfth century onward.

(Barth saw an extract of a long written history of Bornu, but the main volumes were kept hidden because some members of the current regime were intent on destroying documents from the previous dynasty. The vizier showed Barth the extract but wouldn't let him touch it, and required him to read it from over his shoulder. Entitled *The Kanem War of Idris Alooma*, the chronicle dated to the late 1500s. Barth made a copy and sent it to Europe.)

By the sixteenth century Bornu's immense territory encompassed Tibesti and Bilma to the north, Kanem and Bagirmi to the east, and most of Aïr and Hausaland to the west. Its kings made the haj to Mecca. In the late seventeenth and eighteenth centuries Bornu became a center of Islamic learning, attracting scholars from throughout North Africa and even the Middle East. Educated men and their families established "mallam villages" where they farmed and studied together, exempt from taxes because of their religious scholarship.

Barth noticed that the kings of Bornu took their mother's name, and that the royal mother retained considerable influence. He surmised that this represented an ancient peacemaking gesture between Berber invaders and the local tribes they blended into—an arrangement similar to that between the Kel Owis and the Goberawas, commemorated by the strange dancers Barth had seen in Aïr. He added, in one of his wide-ranging connections, that such arrangements recalled the one made between ancient Greek conquerors and the people of Lycia.

By 1800 the Saifawa dynasty had been in place for 1,000 years, but Bornu's power and territory had diminished. In 1808 dan Fodio's army of Fulanis destroyed the kingdom's capital, Ngazargamu. Bornu's beleaguered king, called the *mai*, asked an obscure mallam-turned-soldier living in Ngala, south of Lake Chad, to take command of the army. His name was Muhammed al-Kanemi.

As a boy, al-Kanemi had gone to religious school in Murzuk, then moved to Tripoli to study under its scholars. After making the haj he stayed in the Middle East for about a decade to study. He returned to Africa and settled in Ngala, where he earned a reputation as a holy man. When the jihad began, this reputation helped him rally the local forces to repel the Fulani invaders. Word of this had reached the mai.

Under al-Kanemi the Bornu army recaptured the capital and drove back the Fulanis. Al-Kanemi became Bornu's de facto ruler, though he neither deposed the mai nor called himself king. Instead he took the title of sheikh, or shehu. The mai, angry at being turned into a puppet, invited the kingdom of Bagirmi to invade and oust al-Kanemi. In the war that followed, Bagirmi forces overran Bornu, but Bagirmi soldiers accidentally killed the mai. Al-Kanemi soon pushed out the invaders. He later attacked Bagirmi and sacked its capital, where he captured the princess who would become Umar's mother.

In 1814 al-Kanemi built a new capital about 15 miles west of Lake Chad. He called it Kukawa because of the neighborhood's many kuka trees (baobabs). When the first British expedition arrived a decade later, the city was thriving. After al-Kanemi died in 1835, he was succeeded by Umar, one of his forty-three sons. Umar, like his father, alternately fought and appeased his neighbors, which kept the region volatile.

Umar hosted not only Barth but also the explorers Vogel (1854), Rohlfs (1864), and Nachtigal (1870). Their impressions of the sheikh and his nobles are consistent with Barth's. They described a kingdom in decay, rotted by sloth, waste, avarice, and devotion to pleasure. Much of this stemmed from Umar's lax rule. Generous and affable but also reclusive and weak-willed, he preferred religious scholarship to politics. This left a power vacuum that others rushed to fill. At the time of Barth's visit, the man filling most of it was the vizier, Haj Beshir. Naturally this created enmity among some courtiers—worsened, noted Barth, by the vizier's greedy demands of them. Just before Barth arrived, someone had tried to kill Haj Beshir with an arrow as he sat in his courtyard. He kept pistols and carbines near him, and slept with guns. His foremost enemy, 'Abd er-Rahman, was Umar's brother, a tough soldier and schemer who immediately asked Barth if he had any poison.

This was the nest of intrigue that Barth found in Bornu's court.

Nachtigal left a colorful account of the daily meeting of Bornu's Council of State, which Barth also witnessed:

> All appear in the morning at the royal palace, setting aside at the entrance their shoes, head-dress and burnus. They then squat about everywhere in the anterooms and courtyards, alongside the walls and on the ground, chattering and joking, gossiping and hatching plots, until a musical pandemonium of drums, pipes, trumpets and horns galvanizes them and summons them into the reception room and council chamber. On this signal the ruler leaves his private apartments, and enters the extension of the reception . . . ; he is accompanied by some of his brothers and sons and by corpulent eunuchs, who all utter brief, abrupt cries in his praise, for example, "Sagacious! the lion! the victorious!" While he is settling himself on the divan, each of those present hastens to crouch down . . . and to throw dust of the floor on his head, or at least to go through the pantomime of this token of subservience, for on the carefully polished floor it would be difficult to scrape together the necessary quantity of earth.

Unlike the mai, Umar did not hold state while sitting inside a wooden cage. The seating reflected a radiating hierarchy, with the most important and favored courtiers sitting nearest to the ruler. This applied even to people approaching the palace—the lower your status, the farther from the palace you dismounted from your horse.

The sheikh and nobles were supported by a vast, sophisticated bureaucracy of petty officials, all with titles. Among the most important was the hierarchy of *chimas*, or tax-collectors. Every region, territory, and fief had a chima who reported to the bigger chima above him. Chimas collected a general tax and an alms tax (the Qur'an mandates almsgiving). Each village paid a set amount, collected by the village head, who also determined each inhabitant's portion. There were often additional taxes on huts, hoes, and other property. People who lived in more fertile areas paid a special tax. If a murder occurred in a community, it paid a murder tax. Payments were made in cattle, cloth, goods, crops, money, and slaves. The entire structure was also constantly greased by gifts.

Smart chimas tried to protect their constituents from slave raiders and from exorbitant demands by the nobles, since the more people who moved into a chima's district, the more he collected. Greedy chimas soon drove off their sources of income. Peasants, often slaves, were permitted to farm all the land they could till, and to pass it on. But they couldn't sell it—it belonged to the sheikh. Communities often were forced to feed the sheikh's armies as they passed through on a razzia.

A FEW YEARS before Barth arrived, the kingdom of Wadai, northeast of Bornu, had invaded and destroyed Kukawa. When the Bornuese recaptured it, Umar rebuilt it as two towns, both walled, separated by a long broad avenue that was always lively with traffic. "Rides along this main thoroughfare were always of novel and enthralling interest for me," wrote Nachtigal, "revealing a life of such variety and even splendor as a European can scarcely associate with the idea of a Negro town." The sheikh, nobles, and their slaves lived in eastern Kukawa, the regular citizens in the western town. The western town was about one-and-a-half miles square, the eastern one longer and narrower. The clay walls were 30 to 40 feet high and 20 feet thick. Two or three horsemen could ride side by side through the main gates, made of wooden beams reinforced by iron.

Ten days after arriving, Barth and his two servants moved to the western town, into a comfortable clay house with many rooms connected by small courtyards, plus a large adjoining enclosure for their animals. It became known as "the English house." The best way to discourage Kukawa's countless fleas, Barth learned, was "a frequent besmearing of the walls and the floor with cow-dung," though that did nothing to thwart the voracious white ants.

In the next few days Barth got relief in a couple of ways. On April 13 he heard that Overweg was alive, in Zinder, and probably would reach Kukawa in a month. He also found temporary financial relief by borrowing 100 dollars from the vizier, which he used to pay off some of the mission's debts at discounted rates.

He began exploring the twin towns. Kukawa bustled with about 30,000 people. "In this labyrinth of dwellings," wrote Barth, "a man, interested in the many forms which human life presents, may rove about at any time of the day with the certainty of never-failing amusement."

The town's wealthy men advertised their importance by wearing many layers of fine clothing, gaudy with silk and gold stitching. Thus swollen, they waddled with a stately, labored gait. To mount a horse required a boost from several heaving slaves, who then trotted behind their master, holding his sword, gun, and other sundries. The horses, too, were overdressed, burdened with colorful silk and woolen tassels, embroidered cloth and leather, decorative saddles, collars, and pads, jangling brass ornaments, and hanging leather amulets containing Qur'anic verses.

After the lovely Hausa and Fulani women of Kano and Katsina, Barth complained that the Kanuri women were "much more ugly, with square, short figures, large heads, and broad noses with immense nostrils, disfigured still more by the enormity of a red bead or coral worn in the nostril." But they were second to none in coquetry, sashaying through the streets with trailing skirts and flirtatious glances, one breast casually covered by a printed cloth from England, the other left bare. They wore necklaces of amber and agate, silver bracelets on their arms and ankles, silver ornaments in their baroque hairdos. They smiled with teeth stained fashionably brown with a powder made from kola nuts and tobacco.

Kukawa still attracted religious pilgrims from throughout the Islamic world—Morocco, Egypt, Senegal, Timbuktu, and the Middle East as well as Central Africa. The route from the Sudan to Mecca passed through Kukawa, which accounted for some of the pilgrims. So did the sheikh's reputation as a soft touch for religious travelers. Many of them stayed for years, collecting religious welfare by claiming their right to alms. Bornu was also a trade hub, drawing merchants from all four directions.

The city was so crowded with travelers, from such far-flung places, that Barth postponed his study of the Kanuri language to glean geographical information from them. He called them his instructors, and plied them with coffee to keep them talking. They included a remarkable traveler who had roamed from western Mali to Khorasan (northeastern Iran), and from Morocco to Fertit (in today's Central African Republic). This man usually traveled as a dervish.

Another useful informant came from Sennar in Ethiopia. He had deserted the Turkish army after embezzling funds. He fled to Wadai, where he gave military training to the sultan's slaves. He was about to return there, this time as a spy for Sheikh Umar. Another learned man named Ibrahim had crossed the entire continent from west to east, then continued to Mecca. He had spent two years as a hostage in St. Louis on the Senegal coast, and remarked that the English were enthusiastic about distributing Bibles, the French about enjoying the native women. Tales of pilgrims from Mali awakened a desire in Barth to visit Timbuktu.

Barth estimated that Kukawa's main weekly market drew between 12,000 and 15,000 people. The principal currency had changed to cotton strips called *gabaga*, but any cloth could be used as money. Barth noted that no man who owned a cotton shirt would ever starve. The quality of the cotton strips varied considerably, and they were even less convenient than cowries. This led the vizier, after his haj to Mecca, to begin converting Bornu to the cowrie standard. In the process he made quick kills in the local currency exchanges by alternately hoarding shells or flooding the market.

Goods were far cheaper in Kukawa than in Kano or Katsina, and were sold with less clamor—the Kanuris, less vivacious than the Hausas, were less apt to shout out their wares. Barth was no longer surprised to find, amid the snake-charmers, storytellers, and barbers, merchandise from all over Europe as well as Africa. The most valuable items were ivory, ostrich feathers, livestock, and, at the top, slaves, sometimes thousands for sale at a time.

Slaves were classified according to Muslim law, commercial value, and social status. Those born in captivity, for instance, couldn't be sold, but could be given as gifts. Their masters often educated them, arranged their marriages, and gave them wide responsibilities. Many male slaves rose to important positions as military leaders, court officials, or managers of farm villages. Slaves also managed the royal correspondence, the royal stables and stores (grain, meat, rice, butter, wood, etc.), the royal purse, and the royal household. Slaves that served wealthy men often owned land and had their own slaves, and enjoyed more status than poor free men. Such slaves sometimes married free women, even noble women, and their children were born free.

Since these slaves couldn't be sold, kingdoms such as Bornu looked elsewhere for fresh supplies of profitable pagan bodies—hence the razzia. Slaves captured in slave raids or in war could be sold, given away, or retained for use on farms or in households.

These slaves were sorted into commercial categories. Value decreased with age. Old males were the cheapest, followed by old females. Richardson recorded the system of age classifications used in Bornu. For males: children, grown children, those without a beard, those with a beard beginning, those with a beard. For females: children, those with little breasts, those with plump breasts, those with breasts hanging down, old women.

Males were purchased for farm labor, and less frequently for domestic work, which was handled mostly by females. A smaller group of more costly females were sold as singers, dancers, and musicians. The smallest and most expensive category of females was pretty young women, suitable as concubines.

Concubines were not looked down upon. They had privilege, influence, and responsibility. The Qur'an encouraged men to marry their concubines and free them. To Nachtigal concubines seemed "the happiest among the slaves." Those who bore children could not be sold or given away, which made their position even more secure than that of wives, who could be divorced. The children of concubines were born free and inherited equally with the children of wives. Many African rulers, including Umar, were children of concubines. (Richard Burton reported that the Wanyamwezi people of Africa's lake regions left all their property to their concubines' children, on the theory that they needed more help.)

The Qur'an limited men to four wives, but the number of concubines was constrained only by a man's wealth and appetites. Some men took full advantage. The vizier's harem, for instance, contained between 300 and 400 women, a rough estimate both dumbfounding and hilarious. "In assembling this immense number of female companions for the entertainment of his leisure hours," wrote Barth, "he adopted a scientific principle," collecting "a sort of ethnological museum" of women. He wanted concubines from all the tribes of the Sudan and beyond. Among his collection was a Circassian.

"I have often observed that, in speaking with him of the different tribes of Negroland," continued Barth, "he was at times struck by the novelty of a name, lamenting that he had not yet had a specimen of that tribe in his harim, and giving orders at once to his servants to endeavor to procure a perfect sample of the missing kind." Barth remarked that the vizier took "a hearty interest in each of them," and grieved when one died in 1851.

(When the vizier expressed shock that Europeans drank alcohol, Barth dryly responded that Europeans also liked women, but "did not indulge in this luxury on so large a scale as he did, and that therefore he ought to allow them some other little pleasure.")

Unhappy concubines posed some dangers. Clapperton described a jittery merchant from Tripoli who slept with a dagger and a loaded gun, fearful of being strangled by his harem. The sheer number of heirs produced by large seraglios—the vizier had seventy-three sons—led to internecine intrigues and even murders. Barth attributed the decline of the Songhai empire to the abundant scheming offspring of royal concubines.

But the main worry of a man with a harem was the difficulty of controlling the sexual impulses of a throng of attractive young women. Lyon mentioned a sultan with fifty concubines who, if he suspected their babies' paternity, routinely ordered the newborns strangled.

Such paranoia created a market for the most rare and expensive of all slaves: eunuchs. Only castrated males could be entrusted to spend their days surrounded by another man's precious harem. Eunuchs were despots, watchdogs, and tattletales. They oversaw the harem's meals, baths, walks, and visits. The concubines often hated them.

Eunuchs, like harems, were signs of conspicuous consumption. Sheikh al-Kanemi kept 200 castratos. Every year, his son Umar received a tribute of dozens of eunuchs from the pagan kingdoms of Bagirmi and Mandara, southeast of Lake Chad.

The Qur'an forbade castration, so wealthy Muslims either got their eunuchs from pagans or sent intact young male slaves off to be castrated by non-Muslims, including Christians—the Coptic monks of Egypt, for instance, ran castration centers for the Muslim market.

The procedure was brutal. The genitalia were entirely cut away. To stop the bleeding, the wound was packed with ashes or doused with boiling oil or butter. Sometimes the healed wound resembled female genitals; such eunuchs were especially valuable. Barth wrote that only one in ten survived the operation. The practice so appalled him that he urged Christian governments to give its abolishment precedence even over slavery.

As recompense for their mutilation and the acrid fate of living among temptations they could never enjoy, eunuchs received power, status, and occasionally wealth. They were also showered with compensatory luxuries. When Denham could not hide his distress at the pitiful sight of some freshly disfigured young males, Sheikh al-Kanemi's chief eunuch scoffed, "Why, Christian, what signifies all this? they are only [Bagirmis]! dogs! kaffirs! enemies!—they ought to have been cut in four quarters alive, and now they will drink coffee, eat sugar, and live in a palace all their lives."

AFTER THREE WEEKS in Kukawa, Barth took a field trip to Lake Chad. He rode east with two companions, a Bornu military commander and a member of the sheikh's horse guard. As they approached the lake, the grass grew more lush. Barth expected to see open water but instead was confronted by a wall of tall papyrus and reeds, with marshy openings choked by water lilies and other vegetation. The water often came to the riders' knees. It was sweet and fresh. Islands rose above the shallow bottom.

The mission was supposed to map the lake's borders, but Barth soon realized the task was impossible, since the lake's indistinct outline constantly changed. The surface teemed with waterfowl, crocodiles, and hippopotamuses. In the evenings, clouds of mosquitoes tormented Barth's party and their horses.

Several times they glimpsed the mysterious people who lived on the lake's islands. The Kanuris called them Budduma, "people of the grass," but they called themselves Yedina. They spoke their own language and followed their own customs. The young males collected as many beads and ornaments as possible, and wore all of them around their necks as a marriage gift for their future wives. They poled themselves around the lake in small reed boats and wooden boats up to 50 feet long, with low gunwales and high pointed prows. The Yedinas fished, raised cattle on their islands, and traded with certain mainland villages. They were also notorious pirates who raided the shoreline and vanished back into the lake's wilderness of reeds and channels.

"No sultan has any power over these islanders," wrote Denham. "They will pay no tribute to any one, nor submit to any prescribed government. . . . The Bornou people say, 'the waters are theirs; what can we do?' "

This remained true when Barth visited. On his second day at the lake he met some Yedinas at a shoreline village. They wore only a leather apron and a necklace of white beads. He questioned them closely about the Chad and collected a short vocabulary of their ancient language. He described them as "handsome, slender, and intelligent." Barth's companions were amused by his habit of writing everything down.

When he got back to Kukawa, a caravan was about to leave for Murzuk. This was his first chance to send word about Richardson's death and the expedition's precarious state. His packet included letters, dispatches, vocabularies, itineraries, pleas for instructions and funding, and Richardson's eight precious journals. "We had no means whatever, but considerable debts," mused Barth, "and, without immediate aid by fresh supplies, the surviving members could do no better than to return home as soon as possible."

The trip to Lake Chad had whetted his enthusiasm for another journey. He wanted to see the remote kingdom of Adamawa, 450 miles to the south, never visited by a European. He believed that Adamawa held the answer to several essential geographical questions: Were the Niger River and Lake Chad connected by a web of tributaries, as some geographers believed? Was the large tributary that earlier explorers of the Niger had called the Tchadda the same river called the Benue in Adamawa?

He needed to leave soon, before the rainy season turned the roads into quagmires. Two things held him back. He wanted to talk to Overweg about the expedition's future, and he was broke. On May 5, thunderclaps announced rain, jolting him into action. He borrowed more money to buy provisions and a horse, and prepared to depart.

But the next day he heard that a European was approaching Kukawa, and on May 7 learned that Overweg was camped a few miles outside of town. The news so excited him that he immediately saddled up and galloped off to meet his colleague, forgetting to cover his head and almost suffering sunstroke.

Overweg looked tired and sickly. He had nearly died in Zinder. His luggage hadn't caught up with him and he was penniless, so he had no clothes except the rags he wore. Despite his fragile health and Richardson's death, Overweg had no desire to go home. He remained enthusiastic about exploring Lake Chad and the surrounding regions.

That was what Barth had hoped to hear. Invigorated once again, he left two weeks later for the kingdom of Adamawa. The rains had begun.

15

A Mystery Solved

ADAMAWA WAS A YOUNG KINGDOM. AN EMIRATE IN THE LARGER empire of Sokoto, it had been founded by a Fulani scholar and warrior named Modibbo Adama. He had joined dan Fodio's jihad and conquered the pagan region called Fombina, in present-day Cameroon and Nigeria, for Islam. Adama named the new emirate after himself, and in 1841 built a new capital, Yola. After his death in 1847, his son Muhammed Lawal became emir.

Muhammed Lawal and his vassal lords devoted themselves to conflicts with each other and to razzias. These raids sometimes crossed into the territory of Bornu, a provocation reciprocated into Adamawa by slave-hunters from Bornu. Because these borderlands were remote and lawless, bandits preyed on villagers and travelers. The region oscillated between tension and terror. Yet the two kingdoms maintained a thorny détente that echoed the one between Bornu and Sokoto. In fact, as Barth prepared to leave for Adamawa, messengers from there arrived in Kukawa to protest a recent razzia into their territory by a Bornu commander.

Barth made it a point to meet these messengers and question them about their country. He also enlisted one of them as his tutor in the Fulani language, Fulfulde. He even arranged to travel with them back to Adamawa. On the eve of their departure Sheikh Umar insisted on sending along a Bornu officer named Billama. Given the strained relations between the two kingdoms, Barth had misgivings that Billama could taint him in the eyes of Adamawa's emir. But he had no choice, and besides, he was elated to be heading into the mysterious realms watered by the Niger's tributaries.

South of Kukawa they passed ancient villages of the Shuwas, native Arabs. The Shuwas maintained the distinct culture of their ancestors, who had migrated from the Middle East centuries earlier. South of Maiduguri, a large town of about 10,000, fields of young corn stretched for miles, "an uninterrupted scene of agriculture and dense population." Sometimes the group was joined by pilgrims coming from Mecca. One man was returning to Hamdallahi, southwest of Timbuktu, with a highly profitable cargo from the East—books in Arabic.

A week out of Kukawa, the blue-green mountains of Mandara broke the monotonous plain. They reminded Barth of the Tyrolean Alps. He had been trying to learn whether these southern peaks held snow, as had been reported of Mount Kilimanjaro. The question puzzled his instructors from Adamawa. Fulfulde had no word for snow. But Barth's informants excited him by declaring that the peaks were sometimes white. This was true, Barth soon learned—white with clouds.

They entered the lawless country of the Marghis. Farmland appeared less frequently and was replaced by dense forests and bogs where tall grass hid treacherous craters, including the deep tracks of elephants. Nearly every afternoon brought torrential rains.

The natives were pagan farmers who tried to live amid their fields, but marauders and slave-raiders often destroyed everything. Barth's group passed many abandoned villages and neglected farms. "It is really lamentable," wrote Barth, "to see the national well-being and humble happiness of these pagan communities trodden down so mercilessly by their Mohammedan neighbors."

One village fortified itself against cavalry attacks by digging deep pits into the path. Sometimes as Barth's group rode by, desperate people came to the road in hopes of hearing news about their stolen relatives. "These unfortunate and distracted lands," wrote Barth, "where the traveler has every day to observe domestic happiness trodden under foot, children torn from the breasts of their mothers, and wives from the embraces of their husbands."

The pagan Marghi people (also called Mandara and Wandala) wore nothing but a thin leather thong. "I was struck by the beauty and symmetry of their forms," wrote Barth. He particularly admired one woman: "a really beautiful female in the prime of womanhood, who, with her son, a boy of about eight or nine years of age, formed a most charming group, well worthy of the hand of an accomplished artist. The boy's form did not yield in any respect to the beautiful symmetry of the most celebrated Grecian statues." What other explorer thought to compare black Africans to icons of Western art? Africa was expanding Barth's concept of beauty. The lower lip of this lovely young mother was pierced by a thin metal plate about an inch long, shaped like an arrowhead. Barth now considered this adornment a minor blemish that left her only "a little disfigured." (Denham also commented on the Mandara women's "celebrity of form: they are certainly singularly gifted with the Hottentot protuberance.")

Barth questioned the villagers in his usual thorough way. "Seeing that I was a good-natured sort of man who took great interest in them," they sent him a pot of corn beer. But it was "bad muddy beer," so instead of getting tipsy he wrote down 200 words of their language, a distinct dialect that he later connected to the language of pagan Musgu, southeast of Lake Chad.

They came to the border of Adamawa. The next segment was one of the journey's most dangerous. The group had grown to five horsemen, twenty-five armed footmen, several slaves, three camels, six pack-oxen, and three asses. But their real strength lay in Barth's four muskets and four pairs of pistols. At some villages armed men forced them to go around fields of corn. Other men tried to seize two of the slaves traveling with them.

A passing traveler told Barth that two women in Yola were as white as he was. "This was not saying much," wrote Barth, "for my arms and face at that time were certainly some shades darker than the darkest Spaniard or Italian." But the news intrigued him. Explorers often heard rumors about white tribes living in deepest Africa, wayward descendants from Phoenicia or Atlantis. Barth began asking every traveler he met about these white beauties. His fellow travelers teased him, interpreting his interest as romantic longing.

In the village of Mubi, Barth thrilled the chief, "a learned man in a retired spot," with a gift of ten sheets of paper, more than he had ever seen at once. The explorer dazzled and entertained people along the route with his watch, compass, telescope, and chronometer. (His compass and chronometer, he wrote, "were now the most precious things which I had on earth.") Also popular were his music box and map of Africa, since the villagers were surprised to see that their continent stretched so far south.

These marvels led to the assumption that he had magical powers, so he was in demand for medical services. One woman said she had been pregnant for two years and asked for something to help her finally eject a child. Others wanted Barth to write charms—to catch a new husband, drive out devils, cure impotence. He refused. This irritated his fellow travelers, since with the payments "we might all have lived in the greatest luxury and abundance."

Barth himself was viewed as a marvel. Most people in this remote area had never seen a white man, much less a European. The observer became the observed. They followed him or crowded into his tent, laughing and staring. One Fulani girl, about fifteen, proposed marriage. Barth chivalrously replied that if he were staying, he would gladly accept. When he dragged himself up a hill to get a bearing with his sextant— his strength was sapped by the constant wetness and the beginnings of fever—people trailed him, the Muslims dressed in simple shirts, the pagans in leather thongs with large leaves attached behind. Afterward he sat on the rocks and "wrote from their dictation a short vocabulary of their language," Zani. He delighted them by repeating their words.

Barth had been devoting much time to his lessons in Fulfulde, since "nothing but the knowledge of this very language could enable me, to make full use of the opportunity to me." By this point he could understand "a great deal of the household talk of the people, and could keep up a short conversation."

"These tribes," wrote Barth in the preface to the German edition of *Travels and Discoveries,* "cannot but look upon the white stranger, who suddenly appears before them as if he were fallen from the sky, and regard him with the most profound suspicion, before they become convinced that this wonderful being has the same human feeling as themselves and similar, if not the same, principles of action, notwithstanding the total difference of his color, his appearance, his manner of living, and his unintelligible and apparently absurd and foolish activity."

Unlike other contemporary explorers, Barth imagined himself into the natives' perspective. Most explorers were satisfied to present Africans from the outside, as exotic, strange, baffling, savage. By contrast, Barth learned their languages in order to question, probe, investigate. He was interested in Africans as people, not simply as curios. This intimacy allowed him to put himself empathetically into their place. In the passage above, written as the shadow of imperialism was about to touch Africa, he portrayed himself as the strange, baffling creature, and gave Africans the powerful insight that the freak with white skin was simply a human like themselves.

In some villages the novelty that drew crowds wasn't Barth but his camels—almost as rare in these tropical regions as white people, and even funnier-looking. At one hamlet where the group rode by without stopping, the women "managed to pass under the bellies of these tall creatures, in the hope of obtaining their blessing, as they thought them sacred animals."

Barth couldn't resist making multiple sketches of the striking Mandara Mountains, which resembled broken cuspids. The group passed slave villages, where laborers lived and worked fields for their absent masters in Yola.

Barth's party had been living on various porridges and batter cakes made from guinea corn, supplemented by wild fruit. But deep in Adamawa the corn crop had failed because the men had all gone off to war. The group's diet, and the horses', changed almost exclusively to the only food the natives could offer—peanuts. Barth liked them roasted, but they typically came boiled into a disagreeable pap. The occasional alterative was a cold paste of red sorghum that nauseated him. The group got so weary of peanuts that at a fork in the road they chose the longer route, in hopes of finding better fare that evening in a Muslim village. But the villagers refused to provide any food at all, and the men went to bed hungry.

THE NEXT MORNING, June 18, 1851, his companions were surly, but Barth felt "cheerful in the extreme . . . for to-day I was to see the river." He meant the Benue. This river, an unsolved mystery, was his main reason for venturing into Adamawa.

Twenty years earlier, the Lander brothers, Richard and John, had descended the Niger River to the Gulf of Guinea in a small boat. That finally settled questions about the river's direction and delta. During the trip the Landers also probed the mouth of what seemed to be the Niger's largest tributary, a river they called the Shary or the Tchadda. It spilled into the Niger from the east, about 250 miles upstream from the sea.

A British shipbuilder named MacGregor Laird surmised that a trading post at this confluence could harvest the riches of Africa's interior. He founded a venture called the African Inland Commercial Company and hired Richard Lander as a guide. In 1832 and 1833, Laird's two iron steamers chugged up the Niger to the confluence, proving that larger ships could do it. But forty of the forty-nine Europeans died, including Lander. Laird was ruined and the dream of a trading post was scrapped.

In 1841–42 another British expedition took this dream back upriver. It was organized by an evangelical abolitionist and member of Parliament named T. Fowell Buxton. The African people, he wrote, needed "to be awakened to a proper sense of their own degradation." He proposed to rouse them through a string of trading posts, treaties that banned slavery, and clear Christian principles. He also wanted to build a model farm at the confluence of the Niger and the Tchadda, to be managed by Africans trained in European agriculture. Pagan Africa would be redeemed, he said, by "Bible and plough."

Buxton persuaded the English public to donate £4,000 toward this project. The government provided the ships. Of the 159 Europeans who went, 55 perished. The sailors nicknamed the river "the Gate of the Cemetery." The scheme collapsed.

Appalled by the human cost of these missions, the public and the government lost interest in West Africa. Charles Dickens spoke for many in his scathing essay about the Buxton expedition: "Such means are useless, futile, and we will venture to add . . . wicked. No amount of philanthropy has a right to waste such valuable life as was squandered here, in the teeth of all experience and feasible pretence of hope. Between the civilized European and the barbarous African there is a great gulf set. The air that brings life to the latter brings death to the former."

Meanwhile the Tchadda's source remained unknown. Was it Lake Chad, as its name, reported by the Landers, suggested? Did the Tchadda connect to the great river far to the east, the Benue? Could the two rivers be one and the same?

Barth thought so, based on his informants. Today he expected to discover the truth. As he neared the river, he passed parallel rows of tall anthills. Next came marsh with deep pits and tall grasses. And then he stood on the bank of the Benue.

"It happens but rarely," he wrote, "that a traveler does not feel disappointment when he first actually beholds the principal features of a new country, of which his imagination has composed a picture." But the Benue, he added, "far exceeded my most lively expectations."

By luck he had struck the Benue at its junction with another big river, the Faro, falling into the Benue from the south. The rivers ran through a desolate plain against the backdrop of the Alantika Mountains. Their riverbanks were 25 to 30 feet high. Based on signs in the landscape, Barth estimated the Benue could rise 60 feet during the seasonal inundation, an awesome volume of water.

Tremendously excited, he was moved to write the most heartfelt passage in *Travels and Discoveries*:

> I looked long and silently upon the stream; it was one of the happiest moments of my life. Born on the bank of a large navigable river, in a commercial place of great energy and life, I had from my childhood a great predilection for river scenery; and although plunged for many years in the too exclusive study of antiquity, I never lost this native instinct. As soon as I left home, and became the independent master of my actions, I began to combine travel with study, and to study while traveling, it being my greatest delight to trace running waters from their sources, and to see them grow into brooks, to follow the brooks and see them become rivers, till they at last disappeared in the all-devouring ocean. I had wandered all around the Mediterranean, with its many gulfs, its beautiful peninsulas, its fertile islands—not hurried along by steam, but slowly wandering from place to place, following the traces of the settlements of the Greeks and Romans around this beautiful basin, once their *terra incognita*. And thus, when entering upon the adventurous career in which I subsequently engaged, it had been the object of my most lively desire to throw light upon the natural arteries and hydrographical network of the unknown regions of Central Africa. The great eastern branch of the Niger was the foremost to occupy my attention. . . .

Bursting with exuberance, he jumped into the river, despite the many crocodiles. Illness had weakened him and he couldn't fight the current, so he went with it, playfully dipping under the water. Each time he surfaced, the people shouted that he was looking for gold, and when he emerged, they were certain he had become a rich man.

His practicality recovered, Barth faced the tricky task of getting all the goods and animals across the river, 800 yards wide. He nervously examined the ferries—two crude dugout canoes, 25 to 30 feet long, but just 18 inches deep and 16 inches wide. Many damp trips later, everything and everyone was across. The horses swam. So did the camels, eventually, after much roaring and beating. The group also crossed the Faro, 600 yards wide but only 2 feet deep.

As a cap on this triumphant day, the first village they came to helped them to break their peanut diet, providing not only guinea corn but meat.

Barth went to bed elated. The mystery of the Benue was solved. Though the Niger was nearly 700 miles to the west, he had no doubt that the Benue was same river called Tchadda. He noted that only Europeans used that name for the Benue, an error that stemmed from wishful thinking about the river's connection to Lake Chad. He predicted that the Benue would become a highway into the heart of Africa for European commerce and antislavery principles. He was half-right. Thirty years later the Royal Niger Company penetrated to Yola and began its long exploitation of Adamawa.

BARTH ENTERED YOLA at noon on June 20, twenty-two days after leaving Kukawa. The town had no walls, and consisted of conical huts with spacious courtyards, except for the clay houses of the emir and his brothers.

It was a hot, humid Friday, the Muslim holy day, and the town looked deserted. The emir, Muhammed Lawal, was praying and refused to see them. The townspeople, however, were eager to see Yola's first European visitor. Hundreds collected to salute Barth and shake his hand, fatiguing him. No white beauties appeared.

The next day Barth assembled a generous gift and went to the emir's palace. After sitting for more than an hour on the damp ground in the sun, which aggravated his fever, he was dismissed. He consoled himself by conversing with another of the astonishing travelers that he found all over Africa—this one an Arab who had wandered throughout eastern

Africa, and even to Bombay and Madras. He gave Barth an eyewitness account of Lake Nyassa, later made famous by Livingstone.

On Barth's third day in Yola the emir finally received him and the Bornu officer, Billama. Barth presented his letter of introduction from Sheikh Umar, which described the explorer as a learned Christian from a great nation who was curious about Adamawa.

Then Billama startled Barth by presenting more letters. The emir read them with growing anger. They claimed the rights to a piece of Adamawa's territory on Bornu's border, the very territory recently violated by a razzia from Bornu and the reason that messengers had been sent to Sheikh Umar. After raging at Billama, the emir turned his fury on Barth, accusing him of visiting under false pretenses, with an enemy of Adamawa, to spy for a European power. He kicked them out. Barth realized that Sheikh Umar and Haj Beshir had used him in a plot to scare the emir. He suspected that the ploy had ruined his chances to explore Adamawa.

The people of Yola continued to besiege Barth with requests for charms, medicines, and handshakes. It was hot, with smothering humidity. His fever worsened. When two young Fulanis asked him to recite the Qur'an's introductory prayer with them, he irritably refused. "I have always regretted my refusal," he wrote, "as it estranged from me a great many people; and although many Christians will object to repeat the prayer of another creed, yet the use of a prayer of so general import . . . ought to be permitted to every solitary traveler in these regions, in order to form a sort of conciliatory link between him and the natives."

On June 24 the emir's foreign secretary visited Barth to deliver his ruler's message: Barth represented a great nation, and the emir was but the slave of the sultan of Sokoto; so if Barth wanted to explore Adamawa, he would have to come back with a letter from the sultan. To soften this diplomatic brush-off he sent Barth a horse and two slaves, with a note that he was now ready to accept Barth's gift.

Barth, offended in several ways, curtly replied that under the circumstances he could neither accept the gift nor send anything to the emir. He had not come to Adamawa as a bartering merchant, he added, but as the representative of a sovereign power who expected friendly treatment. The volatile emir reacted immediately: Get out of my town this instant.

Barth and his party hastily packed. He was so weak with fever that he had to grip the pommel to stay mounted. On the way through Yola he fainted twice. Over the next several days, as the fever surged and ebbed, he dosed himself with quinine.

He wasn't the only one sick. The rains always brought on the fever season. Illness joined the region's usual threats and dangers. Armed men lurked in the trees, waiting a chance to attack. Barth also had personnel problems. At a village en route, a servant bought three slaves and some ivory to sell in Kukawa, and tried to slip the heavy tusks onto Barth's already weak and overloaded camels. Even when Barth was feverish, not much escaped his notice. He fired the servant. This same man had told the Bornu officer Billama, as they left Yola in haste, that if the angry emir pursued them to kill Barth, the Muslims should leave the infidel to his fate. Billima angrily rejected the idea.

Barth's other servants fell severely ill. He treated them with emetics and laudanum. Midway through the journey, fever hit him so hard that he took the unprecedented step of resting for three days. He swallowed more quinine and slathered his chest with blistering paste.

Sickness and fatigue didn't keep him from observing, questioning, and note-taking. He listened to boys recite verses of the Qur'an phonetically, "with utter disregard of the sense," and noted that these children were often treated like slaves by their teachers. He recorded that when two Marghis were in litigation, they settled it with fighting cocks on "the holy granite rock of Kobshi." The loser not only conceded the case but returned to find his hut in flames. These same pagan Marghis also practiced inoculation against smallpox.

They rode through the monotonous plains south of Kukawa, and entered the town on July 22, twenty-eight days after getting ejected from Yola. The vizier had missed Barth, and sent him a bounteous supper. When they met the next day, Haj Beshir, all innocence, asked how Barth had been received in Yola, then quickly changed the subject to "a long conversation with me respecting the form of the earth and the whole system of the world."

Fever was raging in Kukawa. Nachtigal noted that in Bornu it began when the watermelons were ripe. Stagnant pools of water were fetid with dead animals and offal. People died in droves, and women could be heard wailing day and night. Charm-writers did brisk business as people draped themselves with even more amulets than usual.

Barth's poor health worsened. Haj Beshir urged him to leave for healthier regions, perhaps an exploration of Kanem, northeast of Lake Chad. The suggestion intrigued Barth, but first he had business to sort out.

A small resupply of goods valued at £100 had finally arrived, but the merchandise was worth far less in Kukawa. Barth sold it "to keep the mission in some way or other afloat." He paid the most pressing debts and distributed obligatory gifts to important friends, their wives, and even their chief servants. The scant remainder he saved for further explorations. "All this disagreeable business," he wrote, "which is so killing to the best hours and destroys half the energy of the traveler."

Three days after his return he began a long account of his trip to Adamawa for the Foreign Office—the route, people, customs, politics, vegetation. He also trumpeted his discovery of the upper Benue, and urged the Foreign Office to mount a naval expedition to explore it. This letter put into motion what became the Baikie expedition, which went up the Benue three years later, changing European views of travel in West Africa and eventually leading to the Royal Niger Company. Barth also outlined the expedition's prospective plans: to explore the Bahr el Ghazal east of Lake Chad and the pagan kingdom of Bagirmi to the south. The mission, he added, was in dire straits.

A few days later, on August 6, Barth recorded his "inexpressible delight" at getting a packet from Europe, including many letters and several issues of the British journal *Athenaeum*. The letters reassured him of Europe's interest in the mission, "although as yet only very little of our first proceedings had become known."

Encouraged by this and eager to make the case for more funding, Barth reported to Palmerston about the mission's other recent achievements. The Arab carpenters hired by Richardson had reassembled the boat. In mid-June, while Barth was in Adamawa, Overweg launched it at Maduwari as Sheikh Umar watched from shore. Christened the *Lord Palmerston*, the boat flew the Union Jack. Its fluttering white sails had frightened some swimming Yedinas and agitated a herd of hippos. Overweg had just returned from an extensive navigation of Lake Chad.

Further, Sheikh Umar and Haj Beshir had suddenly changed their minds about signing the commercial treaty with Britain. Three months earlier they had rejected the proposal, alarmed by Arab traders who told them the treaty would bring hordes of greedy Englishmen to Bornu (and incidentally cut into the Arabs' business and end the lucrative slave trade). Umar and Haj Beshir also objected that English traders might pollute Bornu with that popular Christian duo, Bibles and liquor.

But on August 6 a courier told the sheikh that the ambitious governor of Fezzan was back from Istanbul and may have gotten permission to invade Bornu. "The effect of this news upon the disposition of the sheikh and the vizier to enter into friendly relations with the British government was remarkable," wrote Barth. That evening they agreed to sign the treaty and begged Barth to urge Her Majesty's Government to thwart the Turks' plans. Barth, eager to flood Palmerston with good news from the mission, wrote on August 8 that he had concluded the treaty. He hadn't. There would be another year of delays and evasions before the sheikh signed.

In early August, Barth also witnessed the Eid al-Fitr, the Muslim holiday that ends Ramadan, the month of fasting. A cannon shot set the festival in motion. The sheikh and his court rode through Kukawa in a magnificent cavalcade. The sheikh wore a snow-white burnoose. His nobles wore gorgeous tobes in many vivid colors and patterns of cotton and silk. The cavalrymen—Barth estimated there were at least 3,000—also wore metal helmets like those of medieval knights, "ornamented with most gaudy feathers."

The famous prancing horses of Bornu were dazzling as well. A protective metal plate of iron, brass, or silver adorned their heads. Only their hooves showed beneath thick quilted pads or mantles of light chain mail. Marching behind came 6,000 to 7,000 foot soldiers, some with matchlocks, others with bows and arrows. Then followed musicians beating drums, kettledrums, and cymbals, and blowing trumpets, horns, and pipes. The parade proceeded through thousands of onlookers, all dressed in their holiday best, to a special tent outside of town. There the sheikh briefly prayed before leading the cavalcade back into town, where the banqueting began.

On August 21, Barth wrote Palmerston that he and Overweg were about to leave for a long journey to Kanem and perhaps the Bahr el Ghazal. If they succeeded, they would consider *"the direct object of the Expedition as completely attained"*—the exploration of Lake Chad—"and shall forthwith turn our eyes and our thoughts Southward . . . *if but the means will be sufficient* and if H. Br. M's Government and Your Lordship personally will think it worth while." They intended to search for the headwaters of the Nile and continue to the Indian Ocean.

At almost this same time, Consul Crowe was writing to Palmerston from Tripoli with news of Richardson's death, contained in letters Barth sent from Kukawa three months earlier. The question was what to do next: recall the Germans or support them?

While their future was being decided thousands of miles away, Barth and Overweg prepared to leave for Kanem, north of Lake Chad. Barth wrote that the journey was "in the interests of science and as a medicinal course for restoring my health." Historically the region belonged to Bornu, but was also claimed by Bornu's enemy, Wadai, a kingdom northeast of the lake.

Consequently, Kanem was an anarchic no-man's-land. The Germans intended to hook up with "the horde of the Welad Sliman," a nomadic tribe of mercenary Arabs in the pay of the vizier, who supplied them arms for a share of their booty. All the tribes in Kanem considered them enemies and called them Menemene—the Eaters—because of their predatory habits. They were also, wrote Barth, "certainly the most law-less robbers in the world."

16

"The Horde of the Welad Sliman"

O N SEPTEMBER 11, 1851, AFTER FORTY DAYS IN KUKAWA, BARTH left for Kanem. Overweg would join him a week later. Barth was still feverish and weak but, as always, departure for the unknown lifted his spirits. "Nothing in the world makes me feel happier," he wrote that day, "than a wide, open country, a commodious tent, and a fine horse."

His mood didn't sour even after he forgot to close his tent that night and clouds of mosquitoes tormented him. Nor did he let the next morning's biting flies sink him. "Inconveniences," he shrugged, and then spent the day idling in the serenity of the rolling treeless landscape, feeling "quite happy and invigorated."

He was traveling with two Welad Sliman horsemen. They began living up to their reputations the following evening. When a villager balked at an unreasonable demand, one of the Arabs beat him. Two days later Barth's small group came across a flock of sheep. The Welad Sliman simply grabbed the finest one, "notwithstanding the cries of the shepherd," wrote Barth, "whom I in vain endeavored to console by offering him the price of the animal." When Overweg arrived with forty-five more Welad Sliman, such events multiplied.

Despite fatigue from fever, Barth continued to write down everything, from descriptions of nomadic herders and fishermen to details about the lacustrine vegetation. He reported an "electric fish, about ten inches long, and very fat"—a catfish—whose charge could numb a man's arm for minutes. Barth's rocky health wasn't improved by these long exploratory days in the saddle. On September 19, in the midst of a rigorous excursion to find the mouth of a small river, he fainted as he tried to mount his horse. It was the prelude to a severe attack of fever that evening. His companions thought he was dying.

The next day the group rested at a camp on the edge of a river. "We had a good specimen to-day," wrote Barth, "of the set of robbers and freebooters we had associated with in order to carry out the objects of the mission." When a small caravan of Tebu people crossed the river near Barth's group, the Welad Sliman seized their entire cargo of dates.

Barth's troupe crossed the river the following day. The ferry consisted of six calabashes yoked together, on which the passenger sat, pushed by two swimmers. From this shaky perch Barth managed to take several measurements of the river's depth and contours. On the other side, the Welad Sliman filched three sheep for supper. They also kindly cleared a spot for Barth's tent. Then during the night they stole one of his valuable seasoned waterskins.

("A new skin recently greased with goat or sheep fat is abominable," wrote explorer Francis Rennel Rodd, "as the water becomes strongly impregnated with the reek of goat. But water from a good old skin can be almost tasteless, though such skins are hard to come by. Some of the water one has drunk from goatskins beggars description; it is nearly always grey or black, and smelly beyond belief.")

The rulers of Bornu did nothing to protect the region's beleaguered villagers from freebooters, yet squeezed the people for tribute. The villagers also paid off marauding Tuaregs. The Welad Sliman simply took what they wanted. Four days after stealing the dates, they plundered some cattle-herders, taking not only their milk but the containers. The herders appealed to Barth and Overweg, who recovered the vessels, empty, and apologized with some small presents. During the next day's travel, while Barth bought milk from some cattle-herders, the Arabs stole one of the herders' horses. Later that day the robbers snatched another cargo of dates, plus the ox carrying them. "And yet the people who were thus treated were subjects of the King of Bornu," wrote Barth bitterly, "and the Welad Sliman were his professed friends and hirelings."

Despite the violence and lawlessness, Barth tried to focus on his scientific mission and his faith in knowledge. "There was a feeble spark of hope in me," he wrote, "that it would not always be so, and I flattered myself that my labors in these new regions might contribute to sow here the first germs of a new life, a new activity."

There were compensations for his observant eye, starting with the peculiar landscape. To the north, sand hills rolled into the Sahara. To the south, marshy flats and lagoons led to the blue waters of the lake. On the grassy plain in between lived farmers and herders. The Arabs shot a beautifully patterned snake that Barth measured at 18 feet, 7 inches, with a 5-inch diameter. The natives cut it open for the fat. After noting lots of elephant tracks and dung near the shoreline, Barth finally saw "one of the most interesting scenes which these regions can possibly afford"—a herd of ninety-six elephants, "arranged in a natural array like an army of rational beings, slowly proceeding to the water." He sketched them.

Two days later, while the group was trying to find its way out of a "labyrinth of lagoons," Barth's horse panicked while trying to cross a deep bog and fell on its side, with Barth underneath. As both creatures thrashed to extricate themselves, the horse kicked Barth several times in the head and shoulders, without severe damage. "I had on this occasion a good specimen of the assistance we were likely to receive from our companions in cases of difficulty," wrote Barth, "for they were looking silently on without offering me any aid." Like vultures watching an animal stuck in a mudhole.

On October 1 they reached the outskirts of the Welad Sliman's main camp. About 250 horsemen formed a welcoming line and greeted them with musket fire and wild war cries. At the Arabs' urging, Barth and Overweg responded with the traditional gesture, galloping straight up to the line of horsemen and saluting them with pistol shots. ("This is a perilous sort of salutation," wrote Denham, who knew firsthand. As he and his Arab companions galloped to greet the sultan of Mandara, they trampled and killed a mounted onlooker and broke his horse's leg.) Barth and Overweg were shown a spot to pitch their tents. "We had now joined our fate," wrote Barth, "with that of this band of robbers."

For Barth the trip's main purpose was to solve another geographical puzzle. The Bahr el Ghazal was a sandy valley lined with vegetation that sometimes contained water. Barth's question: was it a source for Lake Chad, or an outlet? He asked the Welad Sliman's young leader to arrange an excursion there, about 200 miles east. No, said the man, impossibly dangerous. Then maybe they could explore the eastern side of Lake Chad? Perhaps, said the man, since they were about to go raiding in that direction. In several ways this was not what Barth had signed up for, though he shouldn't have been surprised.

The raiders didn't move for several days. Barth, still weak from fever, welcomed the time to recuperate. He began learning Tebu. He also developed a taste for camel's milk, which he began to prefer. "Milk, during the whole of my journey, formed my greatest luxury," he wrote. But the milk in Kukawa disgusted him because the Kanuris added cow's urine to it, to keep it from going sour.

One night there was some excitement when a prize female slave, captured as booty and destined for the vizier's harem, ran off. The next morning they found her necklace, bloody clothes, and gnawed bones.

Like any group of outlaws, the Welad Sliman attracted desperadoes and runaways. Barth was constantly pestered in camp by 'Abd-Allah, "a renegade Jew" with a compulsive need to relate his adventures. He had fled Tripoli after committing murder. He eventually sought asylum among the Welad Sliman, who granted it upon his instantaneous conversion to Islam. He became a silversmith. After he had amassed a small fortune, the Welad Sliman stripped him of everything. He and two other "renegade Jews" left to travel through the Sudan, but 'Abd-Allah eventually returned to the Welad Sliman and became a freebooter.

The Arabs broke camp on October 11 and rounded the northern edge of Lake Chad, heading southeast. Their camels carried empty sacks to hold plunder. They traveled in an atmosphere of threat and aggression, constantly on alert for attacks, their own or an enemy's, since everyone in the region hated them. Scouts raced off to check every rumor about possible victims or assailants. Despite the oppressive heat, the horde camped in shadeless places to foil ambush by foes and wild beasts. It was physically and psychologically exhausting.

Barth and Overweg didn't know the Welad Sliman's objective or destination. On the route toward pillage Barth dutifully recorded vegetation, geography, animal sightings, names of villages, and currency (white Bornu shirts). His information often came from the native peoples they passed, since they knew the region "so much better than that band of lawless robbers who took no real interest in it except as regarded the booty which it afforded them."

On October 17, after an early start, they reached the edge of their goal—the territory of the Woghdas, a Tebu tribe. The Welad Sliman prepared themselves for violence in time-honored ways, with fiery speeches and fierce cries. Galloping warriors waved white banners. To hide their approach, they camped without fires. "But as soon as it became dark," wrote Barth, "very large fires were seen to the southeast, forming one magnificent line of flame"—beacons summoning the resistance. The Woghdas would be ready for them.

The order was given to remount and proceed. They rode toward the fires all night through high grass. Barth was feverish and exhausted. At dawn they entered a landscape of small valleys dotted with fields, sheep, groves of date palms, and freshly deserted villages. The corn and millet were just ripe, waving in the wind. The warriors of the Welad Sliman had ridden ahead, leaving Barth and Overweg with the young boys tending sixty camels. These youths honored their heritage by chasing down the sheep, ransacking the huts, and torching them as a few remaining villagers fled.

The juvenile horde whooped down the valley and descended on the next village. The natives were waiting and ambushed them. Barth and Overweg spurred their horses through the trap. The group began to look for the main body of horsemen. It was noon and hot. Everyone was worn out from riding all night, but they couldn't dismount to rest for fear of the natives.

They found the main troupe amid its plunder. The Wodghas had hidden much of their livestock as well as their wives and children, so the booty was disappointing—15 camels, 300 cattle, and 1,500 sheep and goats. The empty sacks now bulged with corn.

The raiders camped near a well, but before they drew water, the Wodghas attacked. After a furious counterattack, the Welad Sliman decided to keep moving. "I was now so totally exhausted that I was obliged to dismount at short intervals and lie down for a moment," wrote Barth. They camped at sunset. After being in the saddle for thirty-four hours, wrote Barth, "I fell senseless to the ground, and was considered by Mr. Overweg and our people as about to breathe my last."

A good night's sleep partially revived him, but that afternoon he was staggered by a severe attack of fever. As he lay in his tent, he heard galloping horses and war cries, but was too torpid to move. The Wodghas were approaching. "I received this news," wrote Barth, "with that indifference with which a sick and exhausted man regards even the most important events."

The native army attacked at dawn. Even then Barth couldn't summon the energy to get up until Overweg shouted that the Arabs were beaten and they needed to run for their lives. Barth dragged himself up, grabbing his firearms and a double-sack holding his most important possessions—no doubt his journals and scientific instruments. He mounted and told his servant to hold onto the horse's tail, then fled to the west just as the native army entered the camp from the east. The

Welad Sliman rallied and drove off the Wodgha, who dispersed with their spoils.

Back in camp, the main loss aside from four horses was the Germans' luggage and Barth's tent. The Arabs pursued the natives and recovered most of it, but not the Germans' cooking utensils or provisions.

The dead included four Arabs and thirty-four Wodghas. Overweg tended to the wounded. The Welad Sliman were incensed by the natives' insolent attempt to recover their property, but they were too fearful of ambush to decamp in the dark. They left the horses saddled all night. 'Abd-Allah, the renegade Jew-turned-Muslim, thought he was about to die and frantically sought a razor to shave his head in repentance for sin, in keeping with Jewish tradition. Early the next morning the raiders began a hurried retreat toward their home camp. At night the women wailed for the dead.

Barth and Overweg continued to Kukawa, arriving on November 14. The excursion had been an expensive, appalling failure. Neither of Barth's reasons for going had been fulfilled: he had not reached the Bahr el Ghazal, and his poor health had deteriorated further. Because of his sickness, the Kanem section of his journal "always remained in a very rough state," an added disappointment. More pressing at the moment, he and Overweg had lost their remaining provisions, which represented all their worldly wealth. After two months with the horde of the Welad Sliman they had little to show except the taint of bad company.

In Kukawa the sheikh and the vizier were about to leave for war with Mandara, south of Bornu in what is now Cameroon. "And, being desirous of employing every means of becoming acquainted with new regions of this continent," wrote Barth, "we could not but avail ourselves of this opportunity, however difficult it was for us, owing to our entire want of means, to make the necessary preparations for another campaign, and although the destination of the expedition was not quite certain."

On November 25, 1851, ten days after returning to Kukawa, Barth and Overweg passed through the city gates with the army of Bornu.

17

Razzia

THE OFFICIAL REASON FOR THE MILITARY EXPEDITION WAS TO PUN-
ish the vassal state of Mandara for disobedience. The real reason
was that the "coffers and slave-rooms of the great men" of Bornu were
empty. The lawless Welad Sliman and the legitimate government of
Bornu were both motivated by greed, but the mercenary Arabs didn't
bother to disguise or rationalize their conduct.

A Bornu military campaign moved with ponderous, gaudy pomp.
The boom of a great drum signaled the break of camp. Twenty thousand
men set off to the drum's deep cadence, along with 10,000 horses and
10,000 beasts of burden. Barth described the scene:

> . . . the heavy cavalry, clad in thick wadded clothing, others in
> their coats of mail, with their tin helmets glittering in the sun, and
> mounted on heavy chargers . . . the light Shuwa horsemen, clad only
> in a loose shirt and mounted upon their weak, unseemly nags; the
> self-conceited slaves, decked out gaudily in red bernuses or silken
> dresses of various colors; the Kanembu spearmen, almost naked,
> with their large wooden shields, their half-torn aprons round their
> loins, their barbarous head-dresses, and their bundles of spears;
> then, in the distance behind, the continuous train of camels and
> pack-oxen. . . .

The pack animals were burdened with "tents, furniture, and provisions and mounted by the wives and concubines of the different chiefs, well dressed and veiled." The vizier and the sheikh each brought "a moderate number" of concubines—eight for Haj Beshir, twelve for Umar, all dressed in white burnooses. Four fan-bearers in multicolored attire followed the sheikh, as did shrill musicians. Everyone, wrote Barth, was "full of spirits, and in the expectation of rich booty, pressing onward to the unknown regions toward the southeast."

The army moved over the countryside like locusts. The courtiers brought their own provisions, but the soldiers were expected to supply themselves and their horses from the fields and livestock they passed. "To the ruin of the country," noted Barth. Cornfields were stripped, livestock seized.

He and Overweg had neither provisions nor money to buy any, but the sheikh and the vizier kept them well fed, at first: rice boiled with milk, bread and honey, sheep and sorghum. The Germans spent most evenings in intellectual tête-à-tête with the vizier, whose curiosity matched theirs. Haj Beshir's travels to Egypt and Mecca had enlarged his perspective and excited his interest in foreign matters. "Our conversation at some of these African *soirées* with the vizier," wrote Barth, "became sometimes so learned that even Ptolemy with his '*Mandros oros*' was quoted." On another evening, "a disputation arose of so scientific a character that it might have silenced all those who scoff at the uncivilized state of the population of these regions."

They often discussed slavery. Barth urged Haj Beshir to abolish it in favor of agriculture, industry, and trade. The vizier agreed that slave-hunting was a sordid business, but no other commodity paid as well, and Bornu needed the money for European firearms to protect itself against enemies—firearms that were also used, noted Barth, to hunt down and enslave or massacre yet more people. The high profits from slavery also led to a taste for luxuries that could only be sustained by capturing and selling more slaves. "Such is the history of civilization!" wrote Barth acerbically. He concluded that European nations were hypocritical for condemning the slave trade while profiting from the gun trade that fueled it. The vizier offered to end slave-trading in Bornu—though not domestic slavery—if the British government would send Bornu 1,000 muskets and four cannons.

Haj Beshir was one of the two great friends Barth made on his journey (the other was Sidi Ahmed al-Bakkay, the sheikh of Timbuktu). "I repeat that, altogether, he was a most excellent, kind, liberal, and just man," wrote Barth of Haj Beshir, "and might have done much good to the country if he had been less selfish and more active."

These African soirées were often lighthearted. One evening the conversation turned to Major Dixon Denham, who had accompanied a razzia into Mandara down this same road twenty-five years earlier. Led by Arabs, supported by troops from Bornu and Mandara, the razzia had ended in disaster. When the raiders attacked a Fulani village protected by a palisade fence, the villagers rained down arrows and spears, some of them poisoned. An arrow grazed Denham's face. Two found his horse.

Then the Fulani horsemen attacked. In retreat, Denham's wounded horse stumbled and threw him. Fulani spearmen surrounded him. He expected to die. He later realized that they didn't slice him up because that would damage his valuable clothing. They stripped him naked, cutting his hands and puncturing his side. As they argued over the spoils, Denham darted into some woods. Several Fulanis pursed him. He escaped by tumbling down a ravine into a river. A mounted slave from the razzia scooped him up. He rode naked and bareback behind the slave for hours to the camp of the defeated. Someone took pity on the peeled Christian and gave him a tobe; it was crawling with vermin. Oudney, whose intense dislike for Denham was reciprocated, informed Her Majesty's Government about this episode in one laconic sentence: "The Major . . . lost everything & got stript to the Skin & has several arrow wounds but none of any consequence."

Barth related Denham's story at the soirée. An old mallam who had participated in the battle mordantly remarked that the naked Denham had revealed "all the insignia which mark the difference between the faithful and unfaithful"—that is, the circumcised and the uncircumcised. Other explorers were better prepared. Before his trip in disguise to Mecca, Burton underwent circumcision and often insisted on its absolute necessity for European travelers in Muslim lands. Rohlfs was saved more than once because he had the foresight to leave his foreskin in Europe before traveling through North Africa in the guise of a Moorish doctor.

Barth used the time on the road to deepen his study of the Kanuri language. Since he had no money, he offered his tutors "a needle pension, the needles being very useful in the encampment for buying provisions." Three needles bought enough food to feed a horse for one day; six bought meat. He also began compiling a vocabulary of Mandara by spending time with two slaves from there, questioning them in Kanuri.

It was December, but the heat remained oppressive. In midafternoon the thermometer in Barth's tent registered in the mid-nineties. Since he had no means, he had packed light. He left his heavy tent in Kukawa and brought the flimsy one issued by Richardson, now so threadbare that everything inside it cast a shadow. At night temperatures dropped into the fifties, frigid for Central Africans. Barth and Overweg loaned their long johns, in an unspecified state of ripeness, to the grateful sheikh and vizier. In one of his few attempts to think like a businessman, Barth surmised that a European merchant could make a handsome profit by shipping warm clothes to the Sudan in winter.

By mid-December they were in Mandara. Its sultan had retreated into the country's steep rocky mountains, nullifying Bornu's military strengths—cavalry and spearmen. The vizier didn't really want to fight anyway, and had been hoping for instant surrender. When the sultan sent a present of ten comely female slaves, suddenly the crisis was over. Sheikh Umar turned back toward Kukawa. Haj Beshir, with most of the army, decided to continue south for a razzia into the pagan kingdom of Musgu. Barth and Overweg, he added, would keep him company.

The Germans hesitated, as morality and politics required. After all, they represented the abolitionist British government. Barth no doubt remembered the government's rebuke of Denham for accompanying a razzia. But the two explorers quickly persuaded themselves to join the expedition. Though they couldn't stop the slavers, they "might prevent a deal of mischief," wrote Barth, "and might likewise have a fair opportunity of convincing ourselves whether what was related of the cruelty of the Mohammedans in these expeditions was true or exaggerated."

Missing from these naïve, high-minded sentiments was Barth's constant core motivation: his irrepressible scientific curiosity about a new place. The eager first sentence of his next entry exposed his true rationale: "At length we proceeded onward, entering new regions never trodden by European foot." Denham had been more honest. He dismissed the moral judgment of politicians far away: "Such events . . . must sometimes be the consequence of exploring countries like these. The places I had visited were full of interest, and could never have been seen, except by means of a military expedition, without still greater risk."

THE FIRST THINGS Barth noticed about the changing country were the animals, starting with a scorpion that stung his shoulder and paralyzed his right arm for two days. The vizier gave a lion cub to Overweg, who was also traveling with a small ferocious cat with upright pointed ears, perhaps a caracal. These young predators ate boiled milk and rode atop camels. The swinging motion and intense heat soon killed them. Barth marveled at nests, probably weaver birds', that hung from branches like purses. Elephants were numerous. Their deep tracks turned some areas into dangerous moonscapes that lamed several horses and led to broken human bones. Barth likened elephant meat to pork, though it played havoc with his bowels. He preferred giraffe, "the greatest of our African luxuries."

Barth condemned the expedition's purpose but also criticized its execution. The vizier's army made short marches, camped sloppily in indefensible places, and often rested for days—all, in Barth's opinion, "unmistakable proof of an effeminate court."

He knew something about the people of Musgu from Denham's account. Denham described a delegation of thirty Musgu chiefs who rode unruly horses into Mandara to beg the sultan not to desolate their country with a razzia. As a bribe, they offered 50 horses and 200 of their own people as slaves. Their appearance, wrote Denham, was extraordinary. They

> were covered only by the skin of a goat or leopard, so contrived as to hang over the left shoulder, with the head of the animal on the breast; and being confined round the middle, was made to reach nearly half way down the thigh, the skin of the tail and legs being also preserved. On their heads, . . . coming quite over their eyes, they wore a cap of the skin of the goat, or some fox-like animal; round their arms, and in their ears, were rings of what to me appeared to be bone; and round the necks of each were from one to six strings of what I was assured were the teeth of the enemies they had slain in battle: teeth and pieces of bone were also pendant from the clotted locks of their hair, and with the red patches with which their body was marked in different places, and of which colour also their own teeth were stained, they really had a most strikingly wild, and truly savage appearance.

Denham's Arab companions insisted to him that the Musgu were Christians. He didn't get the joke.

The Musgu women were equally striking. They removed several lower front teeth to make room for a silver lip disk that dragged the lower lip down onto the chin. Large silver studs pierced their noses. Natchtigal mentioned that when Musgu women talked, their silver clattered. There was no demand for Musgu concubines.

Barth heard rumors about the current Musgu ruler, Prince Adishen. He had 200 wives and sometimes performed sex in public with them. He also offered his wives to guests. Barth, always fair-minded, cautioned that it would be unjust to draw conclusions about an entire tribe from the behavior of one lunatic. He added, with comical condescension, "although, of course, they regard the relation of the sexes in a simpler point of view than we do."

These were the impressions of Musgu barbarity that Barth carried with him into their territory. The Bornuese also considered the Musgus contemptible uncivilized pagans. So Barth was surprised by the first village they reached, abandoned by its fleeing inhabitants. The fields of grain were orderly. The comfortable houses were made of clay rather than grass, with meticulously thatched roofs. Each tidy courtyard contained a clay granary 12 to 15 feet high, with an arched clay roof. Bundled hay was wedged 15 feet up in the trees to protect it from grazing animals. Pleasing order and architecture. Pastoral, not barbaric.

A stand of locust trees, the most magnificent Barth had yet seen, and obviously prized by the villagers, rose 80 feet, with a similar horizontal spread. To Barth's dismay the vizier chose that spot for his camp and lopped off large branches to make temporary fences. The soldiers busily pillaged the fields and houses. The line between civilized and barbaric began to blur.

A product of his era, Barth assumed that certain attributes and practices, including clothing and dwellings, divided the civilized from the barbaric. When the elements got mixed—nakedness with skilled architecture—it upset his categories of thinking. This was frequently the dilemma of a European in Africa: how to reconcile African refinement with African barbarity? Most explorers didn't try, choosing certainty over nuance and ambiguity. Barth was open-minded enough to widen his thinking.

A day later Prince Adishen and his retinue came to greet the vizier. At first sight they lived up to their wild reputation. They were nearly naked and rode bareback. To glue themselves on, they cut a wide wound on their horses' backs. When galloping, riders slashed their own legs and pressed them to the horses' flanks.

The Bornu courtiers and even their slaves saluted the pagan chief "with scoffs and importunities." Adishen ignored them, sprinkling sand onto his head in subservience, yet somehow retaining his dignity. He made a deal with the vizier: free rein to harvest slaves in Musgu in exchange for retaining his position and exempting his immediate lands from pillage. He complained to the vizier that the Fulanis were stealing cattle and people from his western territory. The vizier assured him, without discernible irony, that he was now under the protection of Bornu. Haj Beshir sealed the deal with a gift of nice clothing. The entire time, wrote Barth, "the self-conceited courtiers, in their proud consciousness of a higher state of civilization, treated [Adishen] with contempt and scorn."

The courtiers disgusted Barth, but so did Adishen, another African leader who sold out his people for his own benefit. The vizier, devotee of realpolitik, shrugged that Adishen was useful as a buffer between Bornu and the aggressive Fulani tribes to the west.

CHRISTMAS DAY 1851 was cheerless for Barth and Overweg. They had hoped for a special holiday dinner of giraffe, but provisions were scarce because of the vizier's promise not to pillage Adishen's neighborhood. They settled for a meal of coffee with milk.

Three days later they reached a big village called Kakala. "The country was pleasant in the extreme," wrote Barth. Extensive fields, luxuriant trees. Kakala's artificial ponds reminded him of home. Unlike every other African place he had visited, the Musgus here didn't leave their dead out for the hyenas, but buried them in rounded vaults, sometimes adorned with urns. "I nowhere more regretted having no one at hand," wrote Barth, "to explain to me the customs of these people than I did on this occasion."

"This occasion"—a disquieting euphemism. For as he studied the cemetery, "absorbed in contemplating this interesting scene," hell began to engulf the villagers of Kakala. Everything became chaos and screams. Bands of horseman galloped in all directions, chasing villagers fleeing "in wild despair." Barth, flustered and probably panicked, joined a passing group of horsemen. He was desperate to find the vizier. He eventually followed the deep boom of the drum to the main force.

Some villagers had resisted. Three Bornu horsemen were dead. Between 500 and 1,000 Musgus had been captured for slavery. "To our utmost horror," wrote Barth, "not less than one hundred and seventy full-grown men were mercilessly slaughtered in cold blood, the greater part of them being allowed to bleed to death, a leg having been severed from the body."

In the next sentence he began a detailed physiognomy of Musgu males, evidently based on the dead and dying before him—protuberant foreheads, thick lips and eyelashes, wide nostrils and high cheekbones, knock-knees and short beards, copper earrings and necklaces made of twisted rope.

It's an eerie moment. Perhaps it was just his scientific habit to observe and record. Perhaps it was a psychological reflex to preserve his humanity while witnessing such a profound desecration of humanity all around him.

TWO DAYS LATER the army reached the village of Demmo, on the edge of wide, shallow water. Small rivers and sheets of water saturated Musgu. Studying the panorama, Barth mulled over European misimpressions about the equatorial landscape. Expecting a dry barren plateau, Barth and Overweg had found fertile plains, broad watercourses, variegated forests, and rippling hills. This would be startling geographic news in London and Berlin.

The landscape around Demmo interested Barth's companions for a different reason—the water prevented them from pursuing the village's men, many of whom were escaping across it in canoes. But they had left behind women, children, horses, and cattle. The army fell upon them.

"The whole village," wrote Barth, "which only a few moments before had been the abode of comfort and happiness, was destroyed by fire and made desolate. Slaughtered men, with their limbs severed from their bodies, were lying in all directions, and made the passer-by shudder with horror."

How should a man dedicated to science and knowledge treat such scenes? How should he react to them? Barth didn't allow himself to be paralyzed. He chose not to avoid or omit them—though he never mentioned rape, which almost certainly occurred—nor did he sensationalize them. That would have distorted and falsified reality. For the same reason, perhaps, he didn't wallow in moral outrage. He observed intently, described what he saw in detail, condemned it, and then determinedly looked away for something else to examine.

The day after Demmo he wrote, "I deeply regretted that the circumstances under which we visited this region did not allow me to collect all the information I wished; but, roving about the encampment, I endeavored to pick up what I could." He proceeded to give a thorough description of Musgu architecture, noting that the thickness of the houses' clay walls had resisted the fires, but the charred roof timbers and reeds, now rubble inside the walls, had not. It sometimes seems as if Barth's main objection to the razzia was its interference with the scientific endeavor:

> . . . nothing can be more disheartening to the feelings of a traveler who is desirous of knowledge than to visit these beautiful countries under such circumstances, when the original inhabitants are either exterminated, or obliged to seek their safety in flight; when all traces of their cheerful life are destroyed, and the abodes of human happiness converted into desolation; when no one is left to acquaint him with all the significant names which the various characteristic features of the country must necessarily bear, especially those numberless creeks, swamps, and rivers which intersect this country in all directions.

Barth's intellectual willpower could be peculiar and chilly. Despite nightmare scenes, he kept his focus firmly on his scientific mission. He continued to count, measure, and describe. What sort of psychological contortions were required?

In DEMMO, amid carnage and frustration, the new year of 1852 arrived. Barth's thoughts drifted to the future. He hoped to be home by the end of the year. Instead, he later wrote, "I was to remain three years more in these barbarous countries, amid constantly varying impressions of discovery, of disappointment, of friendly and hostile treatment, and under all sorts of affliction, distress, and sickness."

The next day the chief of Demmo, who had escaped, was persuaded to return and swear subservience to Bornu, the destroyer of his village. Were the chief's wives and children now among the razzia's spoils? Were his brothers and sons lying dead on the village paths? For once Barth didn't get the details. The nearly naked chief put on a black tobe as a reward for his new allegiance, as the courtiers mocked him. In a horrifying entertainment to amuse the jeering nobles, the chief pulled up the tobe to expose his privates. His audience laughed. And then, for a finale, he blew a tuneless ditty on a little bugle. He completed his degradation by offering to lead the vizier's army to a large neighboring town full of booty.

The next day the army moved on, led by the chief in his new black tobe. They rode through a landscape "exceedingly beautiful, richly irrigated and finely wooded." The fields around the villages were fertilized with manure, an advanced practice Barth had seen nowhere else in Central Africa. All the villages they passed were newly deserted. The inhabitants were fleeing toward the safety of the Logone River. The army set fire to the villages and hurried onward.

At the Logone, several Shuwa horsemen plunged in, intending to cross and reach the villagers on the other side. But predators became prey when the deep river swept the horsemen into the grasp of a dozen Musgus in canoes. The army turned around, sullen at being deprived of human spoil. Barth and Overweg, by contrast, were "greatly satisfied with our day's work," having reached this major river, which Barth estimated at 400 yards wide.

On the way back to Demmo, at another channel, four Musgus swam in the deepest water, evidently scouts. Musketeers began shooting at them, without effect. The vizier, angry at the day's lack of plunder, ordered some Kanembu spearmen into the water. "A very singular form of combat arose," wrote Barth, ". . . which required an immense deal of energy." The combatants kept themselves above water with churning legs while thrusting and parrying with spears. The outnumbered Musgus killed two Kanembus, but soon three Musgu corpses floated downstream. The fourth man escaped.

Over the next two days the army divided the booty collected so far. This was "accompanied by the most heart-rending scenes," wrote Barth, "caused by the number of young children, and even infants, who were to be distributed, many of these poor creatures being mercilessly torn away from their mothers, never to see them again. There were scarcely any full-grown men." The men, too troublesome to take along, had been slaughtered.

The civilized Bornuese turned the pagan Musgus into subhuman barbarians, a psychological rationalization necessary to justify horrible acts committed for economic and geographic gain. The imperial powers of Europe would soon apply the same rationale to the entire continent.

ON JANUARY 5 part of the army left for an excursion into a new area. Overweg had seen enough and stayed in camp, but Barth saddled up, "determined not to let any opportunity pass by of extending my geographical knowledge."

They crossed several bogs and water-fields, often getting stuck. The delays pleased Barth because they gave the Musgus time to escape. All the villages were empty. All were burned. Barth noted that the misery of the razzia didn't end when the raiders left. Since granaries as well as houses were torched, the survivors faced famine. This scorched-earth policy was deliberate, the vizier told Barth. Famine was the only way to crush the pagans' love of independence. The tactic would have been familiar to generals in Europe and the United States.

The army now came to a stream, narrow but deep, with an island in it. A dozen Musgus stood on the island, mocking the invaders. Enraged, the soldiers fired several volleys from their muskets. None of the Musgus were scratched. Barth explained this grim farce by noting that the muskets were inaccurate, the powder low-grade, and the balls made of such lightweight pewter that they couldn't penetrate the mockers' wicker shields—which, he characteristically added, he later found to be 40 inches long, 16 inches wide at the top, 22 at the bottom.

The angry musketeers commanded Barth to turn his superior weapons on the mockers. When he refused, they called him Useless One. This was one of his Bornu nicknames, given because he seemed to have few skills except asking questions and taking notes, and even declined to make himself useful by writing talismans. Barth acknowledged that he was less popular than Overweg, whose nickname was Tabib, or Doctor, because he spent much time providing medical help and also repairing the natives' watches or other mechanical devices. Barth sniffed that Overweg would do better to spend such time on his notes and journals.

On January 7 the vizier commanded the army to turn toward home. The lush countryside of Musgu continued to fascinate Barth. One morning, lolling in the shade of a tall locust tree on the grassy bank of a clear stream, he gave himself to "the recollections caused by the ever-varying impressions of such a wandering life, which repays the traveler fully for all the hardships and privations which he has to endure, and endows him with renewed energy to encounter fresh dangers."

This seems willed, considering that at present his wandering life was attached to a murderous army still pillaging its way through Musgu. The raids and atrocities had not stopped, but Barth had gotten his fill of viciousness. He began avoiding some opportunities for information. "The distance of the field of battle," he wrote, "spared us the sight of the slaughter of the full-grown men." He noted that the feuds between neighboring Musgu villages kept them from communicating danger to each other. The clay houses, on the other hand, conical and beautifully ornamented, "bore testimony to a degree of order, and even of art, which I had not expected to find among these tribes."

On the morning of January 11, as the vizier's arsonists torched another village, they nearly toasted the resting army, which had to flee the flames. That afternoon, camped beneath some towering locust trees, the army was routed by swarms of bees that emerged from Musgu hives. Barth took bleak satisfaction in such misadventures. He constantly mocked the army as inept, referring sardonically to "this vain and cowardly host," "these great deeds," "this inglorious victory."

On the border with Bornu the army stopped to divide the newest loot. A Musgu leader there—"this despicable chief," in Barth's words—added to the plunder by helping a raiding party capture 800 of his own people. In two months of terror the razzia had captured 10,000 cows and more than 3,000 slaves, a haul the vizier considered mediocre. Most of the captives were women and children.

Barth called Musgu "the African Netherlands" because of its natural defenses of swamps, dense forests, and countless waterways. He believed its people were doomed. Hostile factions split it internally, and it was besieged on all sides—by Bornu from the north, Fulani raiders from the west and southwest, Logone peoples from the northeast, Bagirmis from the east. "All these people hunting them down from every quarter," wrote Barth, "and carrying away yearly hundreds, nay, even thousands of slaves, must, in the course of time, exterminate this unfortunate tribe."

They reentered Kukawa on February 1, 1852. Barth tried to put the best face on the excursion. "We had certainly not entered those regions under such circumstances as were most desirable to us," he admitted, "but, on the contrary, we had been obliged to associate ourselves with an army whose only purpose was to spread devastation and misery over them. Nevertheless, situated as we were, while we could not prevent this mischief, we were glad that we had been enabled to see so much."

Barth had disproved some assumptions about equatorial Africa: that it was barely habitable or was cut off from the Sudan by high mountains. He had disproved the idea that the tribes there were nearly "wild beasts." He had seen fertile lands and thriving crops, and he was convinced that European commerce could tap this region from the west by water.

————

NEITHER SUPPLIES NOR instructions had arrived in Kukawa from the British government. The expedition remained broke, its future in limbo. There was a strong possibility that it had been canceled because of Richardson's death. To raise money Barth sold his heavy Tripolitan tent and bought cloth to line his small tent, which no longer kept out rain or sun. He decided that if new supplies didn't arrive soon, he would take the direct route back to Tripoli. But first, he wrote, he wanted "to try my fortune once more in another direction . . . I resolved to make a last desperate attempt to accomplish something before I finally left the country."

He turned his thoughts southeast, toward the pagan kingdom of Bagirmi.

18

Captive in Bagirmi

O N MARCH 4, 1852, HIS SPIRITS BOOSTED BY GIFTS OF COFFEE FROM the vizier and sugar from a mallam, Barth rode off toward Bagirmi. He was accompanied by two young servants and one pack-camel, sparsely loaded. Overweg stayed behind to continue exploring Lake Chad.

Barth kept his plans flexible, since there was a strong chance that none of them would work out. Most ambitiously he dreamed of pen-etrating east beyond Darfur to the upper course of the Nile. Failing that, he would try to go north to the bellicose kingdom of Wadai, east of Lake Chad. At the least, he intended to spend time in Bagirmi's capital of Massenya, in present-day Chad. But even this was doubtful. The sultan of Bagirmi's unofficial consul in Kukawa was a haughty eunuch who also oversaw Sheikh Umar's harem. He had not been encouraging.

Bornu and Bagirmi had a volatile history. Bagirmi had invaded Bornu in 1819. Later that year al-Kanemi, Umar's father, retaliated by invading Bagirmi. "Then we entered their land and destroyed their towns and burnt their food and their houses," he wrote in a letter to his sisters and daughters. The next year Bagirmi attacked again. Again al-Kanemi retaliated, with even greater devastation. The haughty eunuch was stolen from Bagirmi during these wars, as was a Bagirmi princess who became al-Kanemi's concubine and Sheikh Umar's mother.

In 1824, Bagirmi once more invaded Bornu. This time Bornu met the attackers with two cannons, recently delivered by Oudney, Denham, and Clapperton as gifts from the British government. The cannons cut the Bagirmis to pieces. Hostilities flared for the next eleven years, until Sheikh Umar forged a peace in 1835, perhaps influenced by his mother. Bagirmi began paying Bornu a yearly tribute of slaves and eunuchs, its famous specialty. At the time of Barth's visit, Bagirmi was subservient but hardly friendly, and its leaders no doubt remembered the British cannons of 1824. Barth, Britain's new representative, couldn't count on a warm welcome.

HE FOLLOWED THE marshy southern contour of Lake Chad until he hit "the great road" heading south. Passing armies had ravaged the region for decades. To thwart intruders, the gates of the villages were often so narrow that Barth's camel had to be unloaded to pass through.

Nine days after leaving Kukawa, he reached the small vassal province of Logone and its capital, Logone-Birni. As etiquette demanded, Barth waited on his horse while the sultan's people prepared quarters for him. Logone-Birni was a tumble-down place, reflecting its embattled position between bigger powers. Logone paid an annual tribute of 100 slaves and 100 tobes to both Bornu and Bagirmi. It was also pressured from the southwest by the ever-expansive Fulanis.

Its forty-year-old sultan, Yusuf, greeted Barth from behind a curtain of matting. After satisfying himself that Barth "was something like a human being," he summoned the stranger behind the curtain and shook his hand. Barth attributed the sultan's melancholy countenance to being the ruler of a country incessantly harassed by bigger neighbors. The explorer presented his gifts. "Poor as I was at the time," he wrote, ". . . I had determined to give away my Turkish trowsers, of very fine brown cloth, which I had scarcely ever worn."

That evening the sultan sent Barth four enormous bowls of sorghum pudding with meat and broth, followed the next morning by bowls of gruel sweetened with honey, and then more bowls of hasty pudding. Barth estimated it was enough to feed 200 people. He gave most of it to some travelers going home to Bagirmi, in hopes they would become his advance publicists there.

He took a short cruise down the Logone River. The water was so inviting that he surrendered to the temptation for a bath and jumped overboard. As in Adamawa, the agitated spectators assumed he was diving for gold. By the time he emerged, a large shouting crowd had gathered. They were disappointed to see him merely wet, not aglitter. Unbeknown to Barth, the travelers from Bagirmi witnessed this alarming uproar, and instead of becoming Barth's publicists, they later spread warnings about his disruptive presence.

Denham had visited Logone-Birni, the farthest any European had advanced into this region. "I was firm in my purpose," wrote Barth, "of extending my discoveries beyond my predecessors." He began by chiding Denham for careless errors. Denham had miscalculated Logone-Birni's position, misidentified the Logone River as the Chari, and mistook the town's language (they used Bagirmi only with outsiders and spoke their own language, related to Musgu).

On March 16, despite the sultan's pleas to stay, Barth moved on. He was eager, in one of his favorite phrases, "to penetrate into unknown regions, never before trodden by European foot." He was moving east now, in the marshy land between the Logone and Chari rivers. He passed fields of corn, onions, and cotton. Warthogs became plentiful, as well as crocodiles and hippos, and for the first time he saw tracks of the rhinoceros, greatly feared by the natives.

At the Chari, much bigger than the Logone, Barth relaxed in the shade while the ferrymen sought permission to take him to the other side, into Bagirmi. But the answer was no. The Bagirmi travelers whom Barth had fed in Logone-Birni had recently crossed, and they warned the village chief of Asu not to admit the dangerous white stranger. They added that the vizier of Bornu himself had warned them that this stranger might overthrow the sultan's kingdom.

Stymied, Barth tried to untangle who was behind this refusal. Haj Beshir, the vizier of Bornu, was certainly a schemer. Perhaps he didn't want Barth to visit Wadai, Bornu's sworn enemy. Or maybe the sultan of Logone wanted to force Barth back to Logone-Birni, where he could extract more gifts. The Bagirmi travelers who bad-mouthed him had bought goods in Kukawa to sell in Massenya; maybe they thought Barth was a competing merchant. Any or all of these intrigues were possible. Meanwhile, Barth was stuck on the western side of the Chari.

He retraced his steps for two miles, feinting a retreat, then walked north to another village. The next day before dawn his small group walked to the ferryboat landing across the river from the Bagirmi village of Mele. A boat appeared and took them across. Barth immediately appreciated "the fine figures of the females, their comely appearance and very becoming head-dress." About a mile down the road, while congratulating himself on outflanking his subverters, he saw a horseman approaching—a servant of the chief of Asu, en route to warn Mele not to admit the white stranger. Barth and his party turned off into the stubble fields, toward the river. The intense heat and the futility of escape persuaded Barth to rest in the shade and await his fate. Cattle grazed on the luxuriant marsh grass. Beautiful birds—ducks, ibises, pelicans, snakebirds, marabou storks—fished the wide water.

The chief of Mele appeared with a troupe of armed men. Barth could not proceed, said the chief, without permission from the capital. Fine, Barth agreed, as long as he was given decent quarters and provisions while waiting. Everyone returned to Mele while a man galloped off to Massenya to seek permission.

Thus began a farce of African bureaucracy.

Mele bored Barth. The food was mediocre, the mosquitoes vicious. He passed the time sitting riverside in the shade, watching the birds, crocodiles, and manatees. After six days of this, the messenger returned from Massenya. The sultan was away at war. The lieutenant governor commanded Barth to move to a larger village upriver, which would furnish him with milk and fish until the sultan sent a decision.

After a four-day march Barth and his escort reached the appointed village, but the chief refused to obey the lieutenant-governor's order and turned them away. In temperatures that reached 110 degrees, they retraced their steps to another village. Barth asked if he could await the sultan's verdict in Logone-Birni, but the Bagirmis said no, once he entered the country, he couldn't leave without the sultan's permission. They decided to move slowly toward Massenya and await instructions.

Two days later they stalled in a dreary village called Bakada. A messenger left for Massenya, ten miles away, promising to return the next day with an answer for Barth. In an otherwise cheerless place, wrote Barth, "it was my good luck to obtain quarters in the house of a man who forms one of the most pleasing recollections of my journey." His name was Haj Bu-Bakr Sadik, "a spare old man, of very amiable temperament, to whom I became indebted for a great deal of kindness and valuable information."

Bu-Bakr had visited Mecca three times and fought many battles throughout Central Africa. He lamented his country's destruction by war and slavery. Barth was tremendously relieved to find such intelligent company to help him pass the time. With Bu-Bakr's help he gathered the region's history as well as vocabularies of the Bagirmi and Maba languages. In conversation Bu-Bakr was never idle, always sewing, or scraping roots for medicine, or selecting indigo to dye his tobe. To avoid the sin of waste, he would pluck single grains of corn from the ground.

Barth and Bu-Bakr had ample time to converse. The rider to Massenya didn't return from Massenya for a week, and then brought the frustrating command to keep waiting.

Barth also passed the hours by questioning pilgrims who came through the village. He investigated the large black worms that swarmed by the millions in Bagirmi, devouring crops. He did battle with white ants, which ate his couch poles and sleeping mats, and "finished a large piece of my Stambuli carpet." He noticed that the women in particular suffered from a larval worm that ate away the little toe.

He often visited Bakada's dismal market, hoping in vain for something decent to eat. "The only luxury offered for sale . . . was a miserable lean sheep; and, as a representative of foreign civilization, there was half a sheet of common paper." He didn't have much purchasing power anyway. His wealth consisted of 3,000 cowries, worth about 1 Spanish dollar, plus some beads, cheap mirrors, and lots of needles. He paid for most things with needles, and was grateful to the geographer and explorer Charles Beke for suggesting that he bring them. The people nicknamed him the Needle Prince. They also called him Father of the Three, because he wore stockings inside thin leather slippers inside heavy shoes.

To keep from going mad with boredom he explored Bakada's crops, soils, livestock, water, landscape, and miscellaneous other areas. But after two weeks he had squeezed every drop of information from Bakada, and the place was closing in on him. The breaking point came when Bu-Bakr, his main diversion and consolation, left on April 13 to see his wife in Massenya. The old man promised to visit the lieutenant governor on Barth's behalf and to send an answer within two days.

Those two days were slow torture. Because he owned only one weak camel, he wrote, "I had taken scarcely any books with me, . . . and the little information which I had been able to gather was not sufficient to give my restless spirit its proper nourishment, and I felt, therefore, mentally depressed."

When he hadn't heard from Bu-Bakr by the end of the second day, his patience snapped. At dawn, his eighteenth in Bakada, he and his servants loaded his camel and started back north. He asked no one's permission.

AT THE FIRST VILLAGE they reached, Barth eagerly bartered some beads and needles for butter, milk, and a fowl, his first decent food in weeks. The familiar villages along the route looked different now, because of new thatching done to prepare for the imminent rains. Reports about his movements preceded him, and people began seeking him out for medicine. As usual he refused payment, but one group of villagers offered it in a way "so delicate and becoming" that he accepted—without a word, they tied a fat sheep to the branches of the tree shading him. That night two hyenas rushed into camp to snatch the sheep. Barth shot one. Firebrands kept the other at bay until sunrise.

After four days he was near Mele, his entry point into Bagirmi thirty-two days earlier. He had a premonition that his exodus was about to end, so he decided "to put a bold face upon matters." He ordered the sheep slaughtered, unrolled his ant-eaten Stambuli carpet, and relaxed upon it like a lord, awaiting his dinner and his fate. But for once his information was incomplete, and his pose was undermined by its offensiveness: "At that time I was not aware that in this country none but the sultan and a few high dignitaries were allowed to sit on a carpet."

The next day at Mele he gave the chief a present and asked to be ferried across the river. The chief, still a good bureaucrat, said the trip had to be cleared with the "officer of the river," currently unavailable but expected soon, so please take a seat. Barth settled in his tent to wait.

Eventually the chief entered with several people. Messengers from the lieutenant governor had arrived with the order to stop Barth from leaving. As the explorer began "quietly expostulating," more people crowded into the tent, a common occurrence. But this time they jumped Barth and clamped irons on his ankles.

Luckily, he wrote later, the ambush was so quick and unexpected that it prevented him from drawing his guns and perhaps shooting someone, which would have been a fatal mistake. They took his luggage, firearms, "and, what grieved me most, they seized my chronometer, compass, and journal." A slave grabbed one of Barth's pistols, mounted Barth's horse, and rode off to get instructions in Massenya.

Barth spent the next four days in his tent, "fettered like a slave, resigned to my fate." He calmed himself by reading Mungo Park's first journey, one of exploration's most entertaining but appalling narratives. "I could never have enjoyed the account of his sufferings better than I did in such a situation," wrote Barth, "and did not fail to derive from his example a great share of patience."

On the fourth day Bu-Bakr arrived on Barth's horse and angrily ordered Barth's fetters removed. He was taking the explorer to Massenya. Barth had already compartmentalized the episode as "a useful lesson for future occasions." His property was returned except for the missing pistol. Despite his poor treatment in Bagirmi so far, he added, "I was prepared to endure every thing rather than to forego seeing the capital." But he understood why his weary servants felt differently, "for, having no mental interest, they felt the material privations more heavily."

Not that he wasn't frustrated and fed up. The bad food, the interminable delays, the exhausting bureaucratic hithering and thithering, all of it worsened by searing heat and maddening insects—Bagirmi had drained his patience, and it provoked an outburst atypical in both its self-pity and condescension: "People in Europe have no idea of the situation of a solitary traveler in these regions. . . . a traveler in these countries is no better than a slave, dependent on the caprice of people without intelligence and full of suspicion."

He thought he deserved better treatment. But why? Because he was a visitor? But he was uninvited and allied with Bornu. Because he was pursuing knowledge, not riches? But why should the Bagirmis take his word for that? Because he represented a powerful government? But that distant government had nothing to do with Bagirmi, and its motives were unknown. Because he was white and educated? That probably comes closest to his sense of entitlement.

Barth was usually astute enough to realize that no explorer in Africa had a right to a friendly reception. He knew this even in Bagirmi. Later in his detention there he noted, "a traveler in a new country can not expect to be well treated." He was also far more patient and empathetic than most explorers of Africa. But Bagirmi drove him around the bend. His pique there is understandable. It is also, in several ways, a low point in *Travels and Discoveries*.

THEY REACHED MASSENYA on April 27. Barth was kept waiting outside the gate in the intense afternoon sun for an hour and a half. He couldn't resist sarcasm: "I was not allowed to enter the holy precinct of this ruined capital," he wrote, "without further annoyance." He didn't consider the possibility that he was being put in his place for running off.

The lieutenant governor received him cordially. Barth told him that he represented a government that wanted only to be friends with all the world's princes, but poor treatment and poor food had convinced him he wasn't welcome in Bagirmi, so he had tried to leave. The lieutenant governor handed over Barth's missing pistol and told him he had to wait for the sultan's return. He was quartered in an airy house visible from everywhere in town, so he couldn't step outside without being observed.

In this new place he began his usual investigations. The town was seven miles in circumference but was only half-inhabited, and was half-ruined by wars and deprivations. Bagirmi squeezed Logone and several other small provinces for tribute, but was itself squeezed by the larger kingdoms of Bornu and, to the north, Wadai. Bagirmi's great geographical disadvantage, noted Barth, was its isolation. No caravan route to the north passed through its territory. Consequently, Islam had reached Bagirmi late, and the country remained durably pagan and poorly educated.

In such a place Barth seemed especially suspicious. Many Bagirmis assumed he was a Turkish spy. A pilgrim convinced some townsfolk that the explorer was a dangerous creature called an "Arnaut," "the only people in the world that wore stockings."

He was accused of witchcraft because of his habit of popping outside to check the weather's direction whenever storm clouds gathered. The clouds usually broke up; it wasn't quite rainy season. The people of Massenya became convinced that he was depriving them of rain by making the clouds disappear with his gaze. This accusation by the lieutenant governor made Barth the Rain King laugh out loud. But he shrewdly added that he would be glad to soothe the lieutenant governor's worries by leaving the country. And if such permission were given, he added, he would pray for rain—but at the moment he was praying for the opposite, since swollen rivers would cut him off from Bornu. This answer did not dispel the Bagirmis' suspicions.

Even this remote place offered stimulating company and friendship. A man named Haj Ahmed had worked in the famous goldfields of Bambuk in western Mali and had traveled the caravan routes between Timbuktu, Kano, Agadez, and Tuat. He had made the haj to Mecca, fought battles and traveled all over the Middle East, and finally settled in Medina, Islam's second holy city, where he became a servant in the Great Mosque. He had been sent to Massenya to ask the sultan to contribute some of Bagirmi's famous eunuchs to the mosque. A year-and-a-half later he was still waiting for an answer. He was essentially under house arrest, perhaps suspected as another Turkish spy.

Barth's favorite companion in Massenya was a thin old Fulani named Faki Sambo, "who alone contributed to make my stay in the place endurable. . . . I shall never forget the hours I passed in cheerful and instructive conversation with this man." Faki Sambo had studied in Egypt and traveled observantly throughout eastern Africa and the Middle East. He knew "all the branches of Arabic literature" and had read Aristotle and Plato in Arabic. He was now blind but his mind remained vigorous, and he loved to discuss the splendors of Islamic history, especially in Moorish Spain, and the distinctions between the religion's many sects. Barth never forgot the day he found him "sitting in his court-yard, in the midst of a heap of manuscripts which he could then only enjoy by touching them with his hands."

Barth admired Faki Sambo more than anyone else he met on his journey except Sheikh al-Bakkay of Timbuktu, perhaps because the old scholar reminded him of his own best self—erudite, curious, passionate about learning, broad-minded, a seeker and traveler governed by rigorous principle. Their admiration was mutual. Barth called him an enlightened person, "in his inmost soul a Wahabi"—a devotee of one of

Islam's strictest sects—"and he gave me the same name, on account of my principles."

WEEKS PASSED. Barth welcomed almost any diversion. One day Bagirmi's large black ants forced themselves on his attention, "attacking my residence with a stubborn pertinacity which would have been extremely amusing if it had not too intimately affected my whole existence." The raiders struck after dawn, marching into his house in an endless line 1 inch wide. Their target: the corn in Barth's storeroom. He was lying on a couch in their path, and their fierce attack "soon obliged me to decamp." He mustered reinforcements and counterattacked with clubs and fire. "But fresh legions came up, and it took us at least two hours before we could fairly break the lines and put the remainder of the hostile army to flight." Such mock heroics passed the time. These ants stole so much corn, noted Barth, that hungry natives sometimes followed them home and stole it back.

He got sick and cured himself by living for five days on "an infusion of the fruit of the tamarind-tree and onions, seasoned with some honey and a strong dose of black pepper—a sort of drink which must appear abominable to a European, but which is a delightful treat to the feverish traveler in those hot regions."

People pestered him constantly for medicine. The patients who interested him most were the young females, "among the finest women in Negroland." Some of Bagirmi's princesses enjoyed visiting the white oddity, ostensibly for medicine. One of these, "a buxom young maiden, of very graceful but rather coquettish demeanor," complained about a sore eye and asked Barth to examine it. He approached her "very gravely" and inspected her eyes intently and protractedly before declaring them "sound and beautiful." The young woman pealed with laughter and flirtatiously repeated, "beautiful eyes, beautiful eyes." Barth's conduct with attractive young African women was always partly proper and prudish, partly charmed and amused.

Another pretty young woman fetched him to see her sick mother. The patient evidently required follow-up visits, because Barth remarked that the daughter was always delighted to see him and asked "some very pertinent questions" about why he was living without a woman. "She was a very handsome person," he wrote, "and would even have been regarded so in Europe, with the exception of her skin, the glossy black of which I thought very becoming at the time, and almost essential to female beauty." A remarkable, complicated statement whose depths and implications Barth seemed unwilling to explore, physically or psychologically.

Unlike his contemporary explorers, Barth mentioned hundreds of Africans by name and often provided a few sentences of biography. But nearly all of the many young women he described, and whose company clearly delighted him, remain nameless. With Barth, the reason can never be imprecision or lack of interest. Victorian stuffiness? Chivalry? Sexual awkwardness? Perhaps a bit of each. Evidence is sparse, and all is speculation.

WEEKS TURNED into months. He had set foot in Bagirmi on March 18 and reached Massenya on April 27. May and June dragged by. On July 3, after an absence of six months, Sultan 'Abd el Kader finally returned to Massenya, "displaying a great deal of gorgeous pomp and barbaric magnificence." The sultan, mounted on a gray charger, rode with his nobles and officers amid 700 or so horsemen in full array. He wore a yellow burnoose. On either side, a slave shaded him with an umbrella, one red, one green. Six more slaves, their right arms sheathed in iron, fanned him with ostrich feathers on long poles. A rider on the war camel beat the kettledrums hanging on each side of the hump. Musicians blew horns and pounded smaller drums.

Next came the cavalcade of royal concubines, 45 of them (a fraction of the sultan's harem of 300 to 400). Black cloth covered them head to toe. Alongside each walked a slave. The baggage camels were followed by seven captured pagan chiefs. The fate of these men was execution or emasculation, after "allowing the wives and female slaves of the sultan to indulge their capricious and wanton dispositions in all sorts of fun with them." For six months of war, the sultan's share of the booty came to only 400 slaves.

'Abd el Kader's return sharpened Barth's desire to leave, but the sultan put off seeing him. Three days passed. On July 6, 1852, a thick packet of correspondence arrived for Barth from Kukawa. It was, he wrote, "one of the most lucky days of my life."

19

Letters from Home

IN MAY 1851 AS BARTH TRAVELED TO ADAMAWA, THE GREAT EXHIBI-
tion of the Works of Industry of All Nations—better known as the
Crystal Palace Exhibition—opened in Hyde Park, London. Europe had
never seen anything like this extravagant display, which epitomized
the pride and self-confidence—critics said the arrogance—of Victorian Britain.

As the first crowds were gaping at the Crystal Palace, the Foreign
Office was wondering what had become of the African expedition. Lord
Palmerston didn't know that Richardson had died months before, that
the money had run out, that Barth and Overweg were desperate for
instructions about the expedition's future. He didn't even know where
the explorers were.

Barth's letters about all these matters, along with Richardson's trunk
and journals, left Kukawa with a caravan at about the same time the
opening crowds were marveling at the Koh-i-Noor, the world's largest
diamond, recently seized in India for the British Empire. Barth's letters
took three-and-a-half months to reach the British consulate in Tripoli.
By the time they reached Palmerston, it was mid-September and the
two Germans were riding with the Welad Sliman.

On September 22, Palmerston wrote in a memo, "I think that Mr.
Richardson's death ought not to make any difference as to the providing

funds for the expedition." The Germans, he continued, had been persuaded to go to Africa by the British government and should not be left unsupported. Two days later he told his undersecretary, Henry Unwin Addington, to instruct the explorers to prolong the expedition, with Barth in charge. Palmerston authorized them to use their best judgment about the expedition's direction from Lake Chad—whether east toward the Nile, southeast toward Mombassa, or "a westerly course in the direction of Timbuktoo." Addington dispatched this letter to Tripoli on October 7.

At almost the same moment, Richardson's widow was departing Tripoli with her husband's effects. She had received the £60 pension requested by Richardson before he left for the interior. (In March 1852, Mrs. Richardson would ask the Foreign Office's permission to publish her husband's journals, because she needed the money. Crowe, the British consul in Tripoli, who intensely disliked Richardson and thought he had bungled the expedition, opined that since Richardson had been traveling at the expense of the FO, all his papers belonged outright to the government. But he supposed he wouldn't object to publication as long as the FO vetted the proofs and deleted anything "which might be inconvenient." Richardson's account appeared in two volumes in 1853.)

IN LATE DECEMBER 1851, politics rearranged the Foreign Office. Palmerston had repeatedly exasperated Queen Victoria by his habit of sending communiqués to British ambassadors and foreign governments without seeking her opinion, much less her approval. Despite her rebukes, he didn't change his practice. When Louis Napoléon staged a coup d'état in France on December 2, Palmerston supported it, though he knew the queen did not, and he compounded the offense by officially endorsing France's new government. It was too much. On December 26 the queen demanded his resignation. He was replaced temporarily by Earl Granville. Lord Malmesbury took the position at the end of February 1852.

Five days after Palmerston's ouster, Chevalier Bunsen, the vigilant

Prussian ambassador who had placed Barth with the expedition, wrote to Granville to protect the interests of the mission now in Prussian hands. Bunsen evidently was operating on old information from Barth. He told Granville that the two Germans expected to leave Bornu in May, and intended to travel east to the Nile or Zanzibar, as Ritter and von Humboldt had envisioned.

All of this was incorrect. Bunsen also pressed the government on several financial matters. He asked the Foreign Office to reimburse Barth for paying off Richardson's debts, to increase the payment due each man in Bornu from £200 to £500, and to increase the sum due at the end of the journey from £200 to £300. Next to each of these requests in Bunsen's letter was written, in red ink, "*Done.*" The problem was how to get the funds to Bornu.

(Bunsen also solicited financial aid for Barth from his countrymen. King Friedrich Wilhelm IV of Prussia gave £150. Several private individuals joined Prince Albert, Queen Victoria's German husband, to contribute £60. The Königsberg Society for Natural Sciences donated £300, but since Bunsen was certain that Barth would follow his German mentors' wishes and go east, the chevalier sent the money to Mombassa. Barth never got it.)

Bunsen also noted that the explorers were constantly asked for "real English goods," especially cutlery, but Richardson had furnished the mission with nothing but cheap merchandise from Tripoli. Granville authorized Bunsen to spend £65 on English manufactures and submit the receipts for reimbursement. The chevalier bought 6 dozen scissors, 23 pounds of steel cutlery, 5 dozen small looking-glasses with brass covers, 2 gross of silver rings, some copper finger rings, 2 silver watches, 2 pocket compasses, 4 thermometers, 8 dozen army razors and 3 dozen "fine razors," several music boxes, 4 pairs of pocket pistols, a pair of double-barreled pistols, 5,000 needles, and some colored handkerchiefs. The receipts were duly filed by FO clerks.

The goods were shipped from London on January 19, 1852, and reached Tripoli on March 6. Two weeks later they left with a caravan heading to Murzuk, where Gagliuffi would forward them to Kukawa. But the consul regretted to inform the FO that the region between Murzuk and Kukawa was "in a state of so much excitement and agitation, that it is feared no caravan will venture to leave Mourzouk for many months to come, either for Soudan or Bornou." He added the disturbing news that all the money and merchandise sent long ago for the mission also remained stalled in Murzuk. Around this time, Barth left for Bagirmi, unaware of any of this.

In early June 1852 the new consul in Tripoli, Major G. F. Herman, informed Lord Malmesbury on the consulate's distinctive pale blue paper that £400 was en route to Gagliuffi for Barth and Overweg. He had instructed Gagliuffi to use another £300 to settle Richardson's debt with the merchant Sfaksi, Gagliuffi's partner. Herman hoped the money would reach Murzuk in time to leave with a small caravan then forming for Bornu. If not, he wrote, "the transmission of the money across the desert will I fear be attended with infinite difficulty—great risk and considerable delay." He assumed the expedition was in severe straits, and so had ordered Gagliuffi to "embrace every means of execution in his power, not actually bordering on culpable rashness."

In late June 1852, Gagliuffi wrote that he would do his best to send the money, but warned that a fresh war had broken out between the Tuaregs and the Tebus in the territory between Murzuk and Bornu. Caravans were not risking the trip. He added that for people who didn't know Central Africa "it is impossible for them to comprehend the difficulty one has in sending money into the Interior, as whoever has the charge of it runs a great risk of being murdered, unless accompanied by a strong caravan." He warned that the money probably wouldn't get to Kukawa before the explorers left there after the rains in August.

It would be wise, he continued, to reward Sheikh Umar and Haj Beshir for their treatment of the explorers. For the sheikh he suggested a saber, a cuirass, an iron carriage, some revolvers, and a steel helmet with a plume. For the vizier, a saber, some revolvers, a watch, and a large telescope. (This request crept through the Foreign Office's bureaucracy.

Ten months later, boxes containing Gagliuffi's suggestions, minus the carriage, left England for Bornu.)

A month-and-a-half into his stint as consul, Herman was distraught about the expedition's precarious state and appalled by its former director. In late July 1852 he wrote a letter to Malmesbury in which someone, probably Undersecretary Addington, who handled correspondence, felt compelled to draw a thick black censor mark through several intemperate adjectives. Herman put the blame squarely on Richardson for the financial severities being suffered by Barth and Overweg and the usurious loans they had been forced to take. "All this might have been avoided," wrote Herman, "had but a modicum of the foresight which ought always to preside over the organization and conduct of such expeditions been observed." In his view Richardson's "culpable negligence" verged on the "incomprehensible."

This drew a rebuke from Malmesbury via Addington: blaming Richardson was beside the point; focus instead on helping Barth and Overweg accomplish their mission.

In late June, Gagliuffi informed Herman that the earlier batch of money, goods, and correspondence—which included about £300 in currency and £450 of merchandise, plus Palmerston's letter of October 7, 1851, directing Barth to continue the expedition—had left Murzuk on April 6 with a caravan bound for Kukawa. After a journey of about 1,000 miles the caravan reached Kukawa on June 24, 1852. Overweg took delivery. It was the expedition's first communication from Tripoli since July 1851. The next day Overweg forwarded the correspondence to Barth in Bagirmi.

Barth opened Palmerston's directive on July 6, "one of the most lucky days of my life; for, having been more than a year without any means whatever, and struggling with my fate in the endeavor to do as much as possible before I returned home, I suddenly found myself authorized to carry out the objects of this expedition on a more extensive scale, and found sufficient means placed at my disposal for attaining that object." The letter had been inching its way to him for nine months.

BARTH OFTEN COMPLAINED bitterly about the expedition's lack of means and his consequent sufferings. He sometimes felt that the British government had turned its back on him, and he sometimes ascribed this neglect to anti-German attitudes. Considering the immense lag between Barth's requests and his receipt of a response, he understandably misinterpreted lack of communication as lack of interest.

But the Foreign Office correspondence tells a different story. The FO did everything in its power to support the mission. It invariably approved requests for more funding, and worked strenuously, though often unsuccessfully, to ease the mission's travails. After receiving Barth's desperate letters about Richardson's death and the mission's straits, the FO sent £1,400 in currency and goods, and Malmesbury authorized Consul Herman to draw an additional £500 if necessary. ("But Lord Malmesbury trusts [in the draft letter, Malmesbury crossed out Addington's softer "hopes"] that there will be no occasion for this further outlay.") All this was on top of Richardson's blown budget. But wars, thieves, and distance isolated Barth and repeatedly separated him from the funding he urgently needed.

The Foreign Office correspondence also makes clear that British officials admired Barth's energy, tenacity, and scientific productivity. They often refer to his courage and enterprise. Yet the appreciative nouns are frequently modified by the adjective "Prussian" or "German," clearly a qualifier as well as a descriptor. Barth, with his tetchy pride, sensed this. Friction was inevitable.

Portrait of Barth done after his journey.
(*Courtesy of Boston Public Library*)

Barth in 1864.
(*Courtesy of the
Heinrich-Barth-Institut*)

Adolf Overweg.
(*Courtesy of Boston
Public Library*)

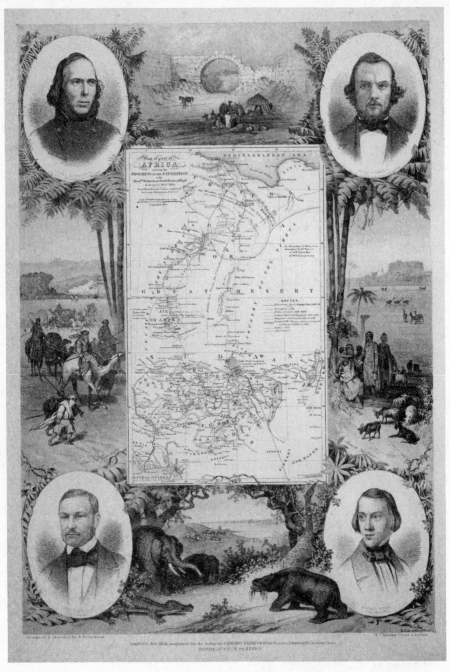

Frontispiece from *An Account of the Progress of the Expedition to Central Africa* by cartographer August Petermann (1854). The lithograph, by Ferdinand Moras, depicts scenes from the journey. The portraits, clockwise starting from top left, are of Richardson, Overweg, Vogel, and Barth. (*Beinecke Rare Book and Manuscript Library, Yale University*)

Letter of transit carried by Barth. On the back of it he wrote, "Safe-conduct given to Dr. Barth by the Sultan of Bagirmi in the case he might choose to visit his country once more; he having been ill-treated before in the absence of the Prince." (*British National Archives*)

My Lord,

The death of a wealthy Ghadamsee residing in this place having obliged the other merchants, natives of that important Commercial town, to send an Express to Ghadames, I shall of course make use of this excellent opportunity, to forward to Government a short account of my last Proceedings together with a Copy of the Letter of Alkuttabu the great chief of all the Tawarick tribes bordering on the so called Niger, wherein full security of life & property is guaranteed to the English visiting his territories; with a Map representing that part of the celebrated River, which is enclosed between Gao, or Gogo towards the N.W. & Say towards the S.E. This map, on a large scale as it is laid down, will I am sure be of very great interest to Government as well as to the Public.

But before making a few remarks it seems first necessary, to state & to assure Government, that I am not only alive, but also in tolerable health

Letter sent to the Foreign Office by Barth from Kano to rebut reports that he was dead.
(*British National Archives*)

Hausa	Emghedesi	English
	katara	
kátăra	tshissōkĕn	haunch
hankárkări	irárdishân	ribs
tshignia	tarĕmâ	thigh
káffa pl. kafăḫu	kê pl. kĕĕo	leg
guĭa	tâmar	knee
dombûbu	kê dê uenni	lower part of the le
tàfi n káffa	kê-nta táffa	sole of the foot
digge	tarámín dĕrô	heel
ḟasŏtshi	kê eunne dedûa	toes
fâta	kûru	skin
mătătshe	abún	dead body
kasámta	shinsher	excrement
ai	áfûna	life
haifuâta	sarĕji	birth, birthda
mutŭa	buĕo	death
gaya	edŏk	burial
cosheŭa	tasáskŏot	grave
beki	asakkŏnoŏkŏ	cradle
imrê	áddŭba	wedding meal
	tigi	marriage
biñi	haiánhar	business
binna	an haia	

Page from one of Barth's vocabularies, comparing Hausa, Emgedesi, and English.
(*British National Archives*)

THE DENDAL IN KÚKAWA.

From Heinrich Barth, *Travels and Discoveries in North and Central Africa.*

KÚLU-KEMÉ, THE OPEN WATER OF THE TSAD.

From Heinrich Barth, *Travels and Discoveries in North and Central Africa.*

MUSGU CHIEF.

From Heinrich Barth, *Travels and Discoveries in North and Central Africa.*

MÁS-EÑA—RETURN OF THE SULTAN FROM THE EXPEDITION.

From Heinrich Barth, *Travels and Discoveries in North and Central Africa.*

SONGHAY VILLAGE.

From Heinrich Barth, *Travels and Discoveries in North and Central Africa.*

TIMBUKTU, FROM THE TERRACE OF THE TRAVELER'S HOUSE.

From Heinrich Barth, *Travels and Discoveries in North and Central Africa.*

20

Resurrection and Death

BARTH SPENT THE MORNING OF JULY 6 EXULTING OVER HIS TROVE OF correspondence, especially the letter from Palmerston that made him the expedition's leader and assured him of funding. He also received many letters from colleagues in Europe praising his splendid scientific contributions thus far. The letters revitalized him and opened new prospects of future discoveries. One small detail marred his happiness: "For the present, however, I was still in Bagirmi."

The bundle of dispatches fueled the Bagirmis' suspicions about Barth. Spy? Scout? Assassin? His position wasn't helped by a high-handed letter from Barth's patron, Sheikh Umar, to the sultan. The same day the bundle arrived, a delegation of agitated officials visited Barth. He thought they were about to put him back in irons. Instead they asked for his journal. Certainly, he said. But first he read aloud from it, translating English and German passages about the geography and ethnography of their country. The delegation, delighted, contributed additional information, but took the journal anyway. The sultan gathered all of Massenya's learned men to inspect this runic volume. None of them could read it. Barth's blind friend, Faki Sambo, assured them it was purely scientific. Stumped but still suspicious, they gave it back.

Since returning, the sultan had avoided Barth, worried that the stranger might poison or hex him. On July 8 he risked an audience, summoning the infidel to the palace. Barth entered a courtyard where courtiers lolled. A doorway covered by a reed mat led to an interior chamber. No one presented himself as the sultan, so Barth loudly asked whether 'Abd el Kader was present. A voice from behind the mat answered yes.

Palmerston had empowered Barth to make commercial treaties with foreign governments on Britain's behalf, a role he took seriously. Speaking in Arabic translated into Bagirmi by Faki Sambo, Barth began the diplomatic spiel he would use throughout Central Africa. It expressed a prelapsarian moment in European-African relations, or at least in Barth's conception of them, since he believed everything he said. He told Bagirmi's invisible sultan that Britain wanted to be friends with all the earth's princes and to trade with them, though never in slaves. He added:

> . . . all who were acquainted with us knew very well that we were
> excellent people, trustworthy, and full of religious feelings, who had
> no other aim but the welfare of mankind, universal intercourse,
> and peaceable interchange of goods. I protested that we did not
> take notes of the countries which we visited with any bad purpose,
> but merely in order to be well acquainted with their government,
> manners, and customs, and to be fully aware what articles we might
> buy from, and what articles we might sell to them.

Barth then presented his modest gifts, including one showstopper, a repeater watch from Nuremberg. Then he asked permission to leave the country immediately, since he had been a prisoner for four months and had business in Kukawa.

The sultan remained silent and hidden, as he would in later visits. As soon as Barth returned to his quarters, two officials showed up to ask, on the sultan's behalf, if Barth happened to have a cannon with him. Well, no. In that case they wondered whether he would make one. Disappointed again, they left. The next day the sultan offered Barth a pretty female slave. "Although sensible of my solitary situation," he replied, "I could not accept such a thing." He again asked permission to leave. The sultan answered that his guest couldn't possibly depart without gifts, which would require some thought.

Days again turned into weeks. Barth, burning to get back to Kukawa and begin his future, remained mired in Bagirmi. His friend Bu-Bakr urged patience—"the most momentous words for any traveler in these regions," fumed Barth.

Not that he was idle. He worked on his historical and ethnological accounts of Bagirmi and Wadai, which would cover forty-two densely written pages. He compiled vocabularies of twenty-four regional dialects, which ran to forty-six pages. He worked on a detailed map of Central Africa. It's astonishing that he found the energy to do all this despite sickness and the psychological stress of indefinite detention.

He also began replies to his recent correspondents. One of them was William Desborough Cooley, the British historian and geographer. His book of 1841, *The Negroland of the Arabs Examined and Explained; or, An Inquiry into the Early History and Geography of Central Africa,* attempted to re-create the history and geography of the western Sudan through rigorous engagement with old travelers' accounts and Arabic sources such as Al-Idrisi and Al-Bakri. Cooley sifted these sources for verifiable facts and cross-checked them against modern European travel accounts. Comparing all these sources, he believed, would yield a strong facsimile of truth about Central Africa's past as well as the location of historical places and landmarks.

He was able to demonstrate that the half-legendary empires of Mali, Ghana, and Songhai had been real, and he roughly positioned them geographically for the first time. From old and new sources he extracted a detailed, complex history of black Africa that contradicted hazy European assumptions about the continent's savagery. Cooley also avoided most of the era's racial and cultural biases. He reminded readers that bloody executions by African leaders weren't so different from English laws that burned women at the stake for counterfeiting money or that hanged hundreds of people for minor crimes such as pilfering.

Cooley's book was immediately influential among Europe's African-ists, but met its greatest resistance in Britain. Barth admired it so much that he carried it to Africa and often consulted it. On April 1851, a few days after he first arrived in Kukawa, he wrote Cooley an introductory letter that began, "Sir, It is from a warm love of science that I quite a stranger to you take the liberty of addressing you the following lines." He expressed his esteem for *The Negroland of the Arabs*, "sincere as it is without the least prejudice and going on with a firm step from point to point"—a perspective and method like Barth's own. Rereading the book in Africa, he told Cooley, increased his appreciation. He thought Cooley would like to know that on-the-ground observations were confirming the accuracy of the old Arab historians and many of Cooley's specula-tions. "I am able to put truth in the place of conjectures," wrote Barth, "and to give life to vague accounts of former times."

Cooley's response, written in January 1852, reached Bagirmi with the packet of letters in July. His tiny handwriting in pale ink contrasted strongly with Barth's bold dark penmanship. The letter was a peculiar mixture of praise, advice, querulousness, bruised egotism, and conde-scension. Cooley regretted not meeting Barth in London and welcomed Barth's compliments about his book, "as it has been received here with discouraging coldness," despite "the revolution effected by me in the comparative Geography of Africa."

He swatted away several of Barth's suggested corrections to his specu-lations. Barth was right, but Cooley's reaction was typical of him. He ridi-culed any new information by explorers that contradicted his armchair conjectures. For instance, he mocked all the eyewitness reports of snow on Mounts Kenya and Kilimanjaro because they clashed with his theory about possible temperatures at the equator. This habit eventually under-mined his influence and earned him the nickname "the stormy petrel."

Cooley praised Barth for sending back "a larger amount of valuable information, then [sic] has been as yet appended to the narrative of any African traveller, Burckhardt alone perhaps excepted; and doubtless you now possess much the loss of which would be deplorable."

Which brought him to his key point: advice about where Barth should go next. He understood that Barth intended to try for Africa's east coast. "Now my dear sir," wrote Cooley, "only reflect on the checks given to the progress of geographical discovery by the obstinate hankering after intractable problems, such as those connected with the Poles, the Mountains of the Moon, Timbuctoo, and etc. etc., which had led to nothing but waste of energy and disappointment." Traveling east from Bornu, he continued, would be another waste. Barth would be leaving Islamic Africa and entering regions with fierce tribes unacquainted with white men and uninterested in establishing commercial relations with them. The languages would be drastically different, so he would be unable to command and control his servants. He would certainly be plundered and probably killed.

"I confess," wrote Cooley, "that your present design of rushing on blindfold in the hope of groping your way for 2000 miles through barbarous nations appears to me quite desperate and likely only to end in your destruction." He begged Barth to consider "the fearful and notorious sacrifice of life that has hitherto attended African Expeditions," and "to retract your rash promises and to embrace safe counsels. The world applauds success much more than self sacrifice. It will avail you nothing to make discoveries if you do not live to tell them. Where the interests of science are concerned, it is evident that discretion is the better part of valour."

Barth replied to this well-meaning but patronizing letter on July 24 from Bagirmi. He began respectfully, one scholar to another, describing his historical accounts of Wadai and Bagirmi, his collection of vocabularies, and the subdivisions of Fulani tribes. Then this: "As for *my further proceedings*, Sir, I pray you, at least not to take me for a child. It has never been my intention nor will it ever be to rush on blindfold into any situation whatever." He added, not quite truthfully, that he had never planned to go east and had always left open other possibilities, depending on circumstances. And circumstances now compelled him "to turn my face Westwards, in order to finish my researches in that quarter."

_____

COOLEY WAS NOT the only deskbound scholar who presumed to dictate Barth's path, though he was in the minority about which path to take. Nearly all the recent letters from Europe, wrote Barth, assumed that he and Overweg "should be able, without any great exertion, and in a short space of time, to cross the whole of the unknown region of equatorial Africa, and reach the southeastern coast." He admitted that he had once hoped to make that journey, but after more than two years in Central Africa he now believed that it would take years more of expensive hardship. Neither his health nor his means were up to it.

So he was relieved when Palmerston held out the possibility of Timbuktu—certainly distant and difficult to reach, but not unthinkable, despite Cooley's opinion. "To this plan, therefore, I turned my full attention," he wrote, "and in my imagination dwelt with delight upon the thought of succeeding in the field of the glorious career of Mungo Park." Park's account had been his sole literary companion in Bagirmi, and perhaps helped tilt him toward Timbuktu.

DESPITE THE RAIN KING'S powers, the violent downpours began. As he moldered in Massenya, Barth knew that the many rivers separating him from Kukawa were swelling and would soon be impassable. His sense of urgency intensified. The sultan, however, remained silent.

Barth grasped at any scrap of hope. On August 1 slaves began to hoe the soil in his courtyard to plant okra. Barth took this as a sign that he would soon be free, since otherwise his camel, which stayed in the courtyard, would destroy the okra seed.

He got another sign on August 6 when the sultan sent him fifty shirts. And, the messengers added, permission to leave soon. Barth kept one of the finer shirts, of light silk and cotton. He gave thirty as gifts to his servants, his host, and friends such as Faki Sambo, Bu-Bakr, and Haj Ahmed, who was still waiting for eunuchs and freedom. Barth saved seven of the best shirts to send to England as examples of Bagirmi manufactures.

But still he couldn't quite leave. His escort to Kukawa was a servant of Sheikh Umar's head eunuch, and this man needed a few more days to close a deal for five slaves that he and his master would sell in Kukawa.

On the morning of August 10, Barth was awakened by his host's servant and told he could pack his camel and go. Barth didn't believe him and rolled back over. His host entered and confirmed the news. After three-and-a-half months of confinement in Massenya, the moment had really arrived. "My heart bounded with delight," wrote Barth, "when, gaining the western gate, I entered the open country, and once more found myself at liberty."

THE RETURN JOURNEY to Kukawa was sodden. The rain rarely let up. They swam flooding rivers and streams separated by bogs and marshes. "I led rather an amphibious life," wrote Barth.

Released from immobility, he didn't want to stop moving. His exhausted servants did everything possible to delay him, desperate to rest and dry out, but he was relentless: early starts, long days, rain be damned. He stayed wet and developed rheumatism, which troubled him for the rest of his life.

Barth made it to Kukawa in just ten days, his servants dragging behind. Overweg learned he was approaching and galloped out to meet him. They hadn't seen each other for five-and-a-half months, and their reunion was joyful. Barth thought Overweg looked weak and exhausted, but that small cloud quickly passed as they talked excitedly about the projects ahead. Barth settled into his old rooms and reacquainted himself with such luxuries as coffee with sugar.

He spent the next day writing letters. From Dr. Dickson in Tripoli he requested more purgatives and emetics, since he and Overweg would be in the interior for the foreseeable future. He sent a long letter to Lord Malmesbury at the Foreign Office to report that he was back in Kukawa, "in perfect health and in the very best spirits." He assured him that the mission was going well scientifically. He had established that the river system of Adamawa was unconnected to Lake Chad. He had brought back a full account of Bagirmi and Wadai. Overweg had been exploring the lake.

Financially, he continued, things remained dicey, a theme he expanded in a letter that day to Consul Herman in Tripoli. A caravan had arrived with 1,000 dollars and 750 dollars' worth of merchandise—helpful, but not nearly enough. The expedition's debts came to more than 3,000 dollars, mostly because of the horrible terms accepted by Richardson from the merchant Sfaksi.

On this same day, Gagliuffi also sent a letter to Consul Herman, informing him that he had consigned 450 dollars and a box of fine English tableware to a Tebu merchant who was going to Kukawa. No one had wanted to transport money because of the danger, but Gagliuffi persuaded the merchant by buying "half a camel" from him to carry the box and then sweetening the offer with another £10. But Gagliuffi added that neither he nor the merchant could be held responsible "for what may occur on the road between this and Bornou."

(Instead of going straight to Kukawa, the merchant went to his hometown of Bilma and settled in for a weeks-long wedding celebration. He sent the caravan ahead to Kukawa, without the money or the tableware. By the time he got to Kukawa, Barth was gone. The vizier sent the money and tableware on to Barth in Zinder, but missed him by a few days. From there, the cash and cutlery disappeared.)

Barth also attended to pressing matters in Kukawa. Three days after returning, he met with Sheikh Umar. The sheikh wanted Barth to ask the British government to establish a consulate in Kukawa. He also wanted Barth to fill the post, a sign of his trust in the explorer. Barth agreed to push for a consulate, but he himself had other plans—to extend his scientific explorations west and perhaps reach Timbuktu.

The sheikh was pleased—not because Barth would be furthering science but because he wouldn't be going east to Wadai and signing a commercial treaty with Bornu's enemy. This response strengthened Barth's suspicion that the vizier probably had schemed to trip him up in Bagirmi.

BARTH AND OVERWEG talked often about the future. Overweg still looked drained and seemed unable to recover his strength. They decided a change of air might help. On August 29, Overweg left to explore a seasonal river that fed Lake Chad. He returned on September 13 but had pushed himself so hard during the excursion that he was exhausted and didn't eat that evening.

Fevers arrived with the rains. September was the unhealthiest month in Kukawa. To escape town the Germans took long rides every day. On September 20 they went north. Overweg, an avid hunter, "was so imprudent as to enter deep water in pursuit of some water-fowl," wrote Barth, "and to remain in his wet clothes all the day." (Barth had been guilty of the same thing on his return trip from Bagirmi.) That night Overweg was too spent to eat. The next morning he couldn't get up. Barth earnestly advised him to take a sudorific, but "he was so obstinate as not to take any medicine at all." His illness worsened throughout the day.

The next day, September 22, "his speech became quite inarticulate and almost unintelligible." This symptom alarmed even Overweg. To recover, he urged Barth to take him to the house of their friend Fugo Ali in Maduwari, eight miles southeast of Kukawa on the lake. Fugo Ali had been Overweg's navigator on Lake Chad. The explorers started for the village the next day, but Overweg was so weak that the short trip took two days. Barth left him with Fugo Ali and returned to Kukawa to finish some dispatches.

That evening one of Overweg's servants rushed back with the news that Overweg was worsening.

> I mounted immediately, and found my friend in a most distressing condition, lying outside in the court-yard, as he had obstinately refused to sleep in the hut. He was bedewed with a cold perspiration.
> . . . He did not recognize me, and would not allow me or any one else to cover him. Being seized with a terrible fit of delirium, and

muttering unintelligible words, in which all the events of his life seemed to be confused, he jumped up repeatedly in a raging fit of madness, and rushed against the trees and into the fire, while four men were scarcely able to hold him.

Toward morning he finally collapsed onto his bed and grew quiet. Barth asked if wanted anything. Overweg urgently indicated that he had something to tell him. He struggled to speak but couldn't make himself intelligible. "Hoping that he might have passed the crisis," wrote Barth, "I thought I might return to the town." And he did. His conduct was astounding. Was Barth clueless? Heartless? Frightened? Resentful of Overweg's neglect of his health? No explanation can excuse his conduct at this crisis, when Overweg clearly needed care and solace.

Early the next morning, September 26, Overweg's servant woke Barth in Kukawa. Overweg had not spoken since Barth's departure and his condition was alarming. Barth again rode toward Maduwari. He was met by Fugo Ali's brother, in tears.

"Is the foreigner dead?" asked Barth.

"Yes."

Barth spurred his horse into a gallop.

At Maduwari, according to an account left by Overweg's servant, Barth wept over his companion's body, a detail omitted from the explorer's own account. When he emerged from the hut, he told Overweg's distraught teenaged servants, Dorugu and Abbega—slaves whom Overweg had freed—not to worry, he would take care of them. The villagers, who knew Overweg well from his long stays there, began lamenting him.

Barth and Fugo Ali washed Overweg's body and wrapped it in a white cloth. They dug a grave in the shade of a hajilij tree. No one spoke. Barth put some of Overweg's personal effects into the hole. They covered the body with boughs, then dry grass, then dirt. To protect the grave from hyenas and scavengers, they finished with branches of thorn.

"Thus died my sole friend and companion," wrote Barth, "in the thirtieth year of his age, and in the prime of his youth. It was not reserved for him to finish his travels, and to return home in safety; but he met a most honorable death as a martyr to science."

OVERWEG IS THE least knowable of the expedition's three Europeans. The glimpses of him in the accounts of Richardson and Barth are brief, and he left no publishable journals. He was clearly energetic and amiable— easier to like, Barth admitted, than his European companions. Barth enjoyed his company and his skills, but was sometimes exasperated by his boyish carelessness and naïveté. In the days leading up to his death, Barth's concern for him is clear, but so is his irritation. The behavior that contributed to Overweg's death—repeatedly exhausting himself despite his weakness, plunging into the lake after waterfowl and staying in wet clothing, refusing medicine—suggests a young man who considered himself indestructible. Barth called him imprudent and obstinate.

These flaws were magnified for Barth by what he saw as Overweg's irresponsibility toward their mission and toward science. Earlier in the journey, Barth recorded that Overweg "laughed at me when, during moments of leisure, I finished the notes which I had briefly written down during the march." In contrast, Barth approvingly noted that Richardson took pains with his journal. As a scientist, Overweg was as tireless and enthusiastic as Barth, but far less meticulous and conscientious. Barth's candid epitaph for Overweg appears in *Travels and Discoveries* hundreds of pages before the actual death scene:

. . . it is greatly to be regretted that my unfortunate companion, who seemed never fully aware that his life was at stake, did not take into consideration the circumstance that he himself might not be destined to return home, in order to elaborate his researches. If all the information which he occasionally collected were joined to mine, those countries would be far better known than they are now; but, instead of employing his leisure hours in transcribing his memoranda in a form intelligible to others, he left them all on small scraps of paper, negligently written with lead-pencil, which, after the lapse of some time, would become unintelligible even to himself. It is a pity that so much talent as my companion possessed was not allied with practical habits, and concentrated upon those subjects which he professed to study.

It took tremendous discipline for an explorer to keep a detailed journal despite hunger, thirst, sickness, danger, fatigue, and the myriad problems and mundane tasks that besieged a traveler in remote places. To neglect one's notes must have been a constant temptation. Overweg habitually succumbed to it.

After Overweg's death Barth tried to salvage his companion's memoranda but could decipher nothing but a few names, like a maddening story made of scribbles and occasional characters. Except for some measurements of latitude and a few astronomical observations, Overweg's two-and-a-half years of research perished with him in Maduwari. He remains the figure who urgently wanted to tell us something, but waited too long.

THAT EVENING BARTH returned to their house in Kukawa. During his absence in Bagirmi, Overweg had found a layer of gypsum in the courtyard and used it to cheer up their quarters with whitewash—typical of both his boyish good spirits and his squandering of time. To Barth the place now seemed "desolate and melancholy in the extreme."

They had intended to make another surveying excursion on Lake Chad, and Barth had hoped to make another attempt at exploring Kanem. But "any longer stay in this place had now become so intolerable to me," wrote Barth, "that I determined to set out as soon as possible on my journey toward the Niger—to new countries and new people."

21

Westward

Two days after Overweg's death, Barth resumed a letter he had started earlier to Cooley:

> Circumstances have changed. . . . Yesterday at noon I laid my sole companion and fellow traveler in the grave and am now lonely and companionless in these regions where nobody does understand my doing, the Director of my own expedition—but nevertheless I am in good health and best spirits—as far as circumstances allow and shall not give up the least point—I am not a man who is afraid of death in such a cause, but I shall be the more prudent and circumspective, and it will please God I trust to give me success, and after that safe return home redeemed by the sacrifice of two lives out of three.

He also worked on official correspondence. He informed Consul Herman about Overweg's death, the new plan to go west, and the need to be resupplied down the road. He asked again for a letter in Arabic that introduced him as a representative of the British government, not merely an expeditionary. He advised Herman to "look sharp" to keep Gagliuffi's private interests and partnership with the merchant Sfaksi from harming the mission.

He also urged Herman to lobby for a British consulate in Kukawa. The sheikh had promised to give the consul a spacious house, "with three milk cows ready for him, if they do not die in the meanwhile." Sheikh Umar, added Barth, was sending several cases of gifts to the queen, accompanied by an envoy instructed to visit the marvels of England and report back to the sheikh. Barth asked Herman to arrange free passage for this envoy and "to instruct that fellow a little how he has to behave in England." Barth also enclosed Overweg's papers in a separate envelop to be delivered to Chevalier Bunsen, adding "you will be so kind not to open the packet." This instruction would be held against him.

Next Barth wrote a long letter to the Lord Secretary in the Foreign Office about all these matters. He emphasized the wisdom of sending a consul to Kukawa to cement relations with Bornu. The sheikh was sending an envoy and the vizier hoped to send his son to England soon. Barth hoped that the government would take advantage of this open door. (Britain would not send a representative to Bornu until after 1900.)

This letter, dated October 10, 1852, reached the Foreign Office in London on February 19, 1853. The news about the envoy's approach excited a lot of correspondence between Tripoli and London about how to deal with this person, house him, translate for him, transport him to England. For decades the British government had been trying to establish relations in the Sudan. Now that Barth was thrusting the opportunity upon them, they were unsure how to react.

Barth informed the Foreign Office that he hoped to reach the Niger River at the village of Say. Beyond that everything was "extremely uncertain." He doubted he could make it to Timbuktu, but hoped he would be able to map the unknown course of the Niger between that city and Say. He asked the government to send a cache of money, merchandise, and new instruments, especially thermometers, to Zinder, 400 miles west. Beyond there he would be hard to reach.

His departure was delayed when a Tuareg horde invaded the lands between Kukawa and Zinder. Two months after Overweg's death, things had simmered down enough to go. Sheikh Umar and Haj Beshir wished him well and added a parting gift of two fine camels.

ON THE MORNING of November 25, 1852, Barth passed through Kuka-wa's western gate. The day felt momentous. Bornu had been his base for nearly twenty months. Ahead lay unknown regions and dangers. The lands between Bornu and Timbuktu were boiling with wars and brig-ands. He was uncertain whether supplies would reach him before he lost touch with Tripoli. He was alone, the sole representative of the British government in Central Africa. If he managed to reach Timbuktu, 1,200 miles away, he didn't know whether the sheikh there would welcome him or kill him. The last undisguised European to enter the legendary city, Major Gordon Laing, had been murdered. (René Caillié, a French-man, had later visited briefly, but in disguise.)

If Barth survived the journey and Timbuktu, he still had to get home. He could go north to Morocco like Caillié, or continue west to the Atlantic, or descend the Niger to the Gulf of Guinea. Any of these routes would be far shorter than retracing his steps. Everything about the future and the territory ahead was murky and fraught. But Barth, as always when undertaking a new journey, was upbeat.

"I felt unbounded delight," he wrote, "in finding myself once more in the open country, after a residence of a couple of months in the town, where I had but little bodily exercise."

His troop numbered ten. In addition to several tag-along travelers, there were Dorugu and Abbega, the boys whom Overweg had bought and set free and who were now under Barth's care, plus a payroll of four. After many bad experiences with workers who quit, Barth had devised a new strategy: no one got paid until they returned with him to Hausa-land. Mejebri Ali el Ageren, an Arab from an oasis in eastern Libya, had a salary of 9 Spanish dollars per month—a princely amount—plus two horses and permission to trade on his own. Barth hired him as a trouble-

shooter to overcome problems with the natives of the many lands they
would pass through.

Next down the pay chain was Barth's main servant, Muhammed el
Gatroni. He received a horse and 4 Spanish dollars per month, with a
bonus of 50 dollars if the mission succeeded (that is, if Barth lived). This
remarkable man deserves an aside for his unsung career in the exploration of Africa. He served not only Barth but several subsequent travelers whom Barth inspired. A Tebu from the desert village of Gatron (or
Gatrun) in southern Fezzan, el Gatroni was about eighteen when the
Richardson expedition began. Barth called him "the most useful atten-
dant I ever had; and, though young, he had roamed about a great deal
over the whole eastern half of the desert and shared in many adventures
of the most serious kind. He possessed, too, a strong sense of honor, and
was perfectly to be relied upon." He was the only person who stayed
with Barth throughout the expedition's five-and-a-half years, except for
a short break when Barth entrusted him to take Richardson's journals
and effects to Murzuk.

Years later, when Barth was writing *Travels and Discoveries* in London, he met a French teenager named Henri Duveyrier who dreamed of
exploring the Sahara. Barth advised him to learn Arabic and, if he ever
went to Central Africa, to hire el Gatroni. Duveyrier took this advice,
and el Gatroni accompanied the Frenchman on some of the travels that
made him famous. In Germany, Barth's example inspired Karl Moritz
von Beurmann to undertake an expedition into Bornu in the early 1860s.
Barth recommended el Gatroni, who guided von Beurmann to Kukawa
but not onward to Wadai, where von Beurmann was murdered. Barth
also inspired his countryman Friedrich Gerhard Rohlfs, who followed
Barth's suggestion and hired el Gatroni for his journey to Bornu in the
mid-1860s. A few years later Rohlfs arranged for el Gatroni to lead Gustav Nachtigal on part of that explorer's five-year odyssey through Central Africa.

Nachtigal described his "respectful awe" upon first meeting the
famous guide in 1869. He wrote that el Gatroni "was not a man of many

words. A quiet friendly old man, he was by no means indifferent to the joys of life; he seldom, however, allowed the equanimity which was the result of his temperament and his rich experiences to be disturbed." Nachtigal often called el Gatroni old, but he was only a year or so older than the thirty-five-year-old Nachtigal. His life of rough travels was carved on his face.

When el Gatroni strongly advised Nachtigal against a dangerous trip to Tibesti, the explorer asked him to recommend someone else as a guide. "The worthy man, however, rejected this proposal with some indignation," wrote Nachtigal. " 'I have promised your friends in Tripoli,' he added, 'to bring you safe and sound to Bornu, just as I also guided thither your brothers, 'Abd el-Kerim (Barth) and Mustafa Bey (Rohlfs). With God's help we shall achieve this purpose together. Until then I shall not leave you, and should misfortune befall you among the treacherous [Tebu], I want to share it with you.' "

WHEN THEY RESTED in the afternoon heat, Barth's lion's skin kept him "delightfully cool," and warmed him during the cold nights, when temperatures dropped into the low 40s. His legs now hurt constantly from rheumatism, which periodically lamed him. He treated it with shea butter. He also had a foot disease, probably a fungus from being constantly wet on the trip back from Bagirmi. But in general his mood was cheerful because of the prospects ahead.

They passed the old Bornu capital of Ngazargamu, built near the end of the fifteenth century and sacked by dan Fodio's jihadists in the first decade of the nineteenth century. It had been a grand place, with high walls six miles in circumference. Judging by the outlines still visible on the ground, the royal palace had been extensive and made of baked brick, a craft forgotten in Kukawa. By contrast, the dimensions of the ruined mosque were small, which led Barth to conclude that only the courtiers practiced Islam, as in Kukawa.

He found no signs of a madrasah, or college, attached to the mosque, as was the custom in centers of Islamic learning. This led him to a broader speculation that scholarship in Bornu "has always been a private affair among a few individuals, encouraged by some distinguished men who had visited Egypt and Arabia. . . . it cannot be doubted that this capital contained a great deal of barbaric magnificence, and even a certain degree of civilization, much more so than is at present found in this country; and it is certainly a speculation not devoid of interest to imagine, in this town of Negroland, a splendid court, with a considerable number of learned and intelligent men gathering round their sovereign, and a priest writing down the glorious achievements of his master, and thus securing them from oblivion." But that vision was hard to conjure among these ruins, where the forest now grew right up to the crumbling walls and the only inhabitants were two ostriches.

As they moved west, flat plains filled with corn and millet gave way to rolling forested hills and then to undulating red sands and fields of peanuts and beans. Baobab trees yielded to tamarinds and doum palms. Farther west they came to mountains, lakes, and ravines, and the fields changed to cotton, wheat, and onions. Guinea fowl proliferated and joined the menu. Elephants, warthogs, monkeys, and splendidly horned oryxes and addaxes all appeared by sign or sight. The architecture, the crops, and the natives' physiognomies and personalities all changed along with the landscape, reflecting Carl Ritter's theories about the environment's influence on humans.

Barth wrote it all down with his customary specificity. At a tiny Fulani village named Yamiya, he recorded that 120 fine cattle were getting watered from the well, which "measured two fathoms in depth; and the temperature of the water was 80° at 1.20 P.M., while that of the air was 84°." Accuracy, he noted, was easily sabotaged. Even vigilant travelers could pass along misinformation. At one place, for instance, he asked a man for the village's name but didn't quite hear it, so he asked another man, who replied, "Mannawaji." Barth wrote it down but soon realized that the word meant "he doesn't want to answer." A traveler who didn't understand Kanuri would have invented a phantom village, whose real name was Gremari.

He also criticized the assumption of some geographers that recording a village's name and geographical position was enough. "But to me the general character of a country, the way in which the population is settled, and the nature and character of those settlements themselves, seem to form some of the chief and most useful objects of a journey through a new and unknown country."

The roads were rivers of trade, busy with merchants carrying cotton, natron, earthenware. The people of Gashua lived up to their reputation for thievery by carrying off the Arab troubleshooter's blanket one night, while the sleeping troubleshooter was wrapped in it. When he woke up and resisted, they threatened him with spears until he let go. To discourage further depredations Barth fired some shots "and with a large accordion, upon which I played the rest of the night, I frightened the people to such a degree that they thought every moment we were about to ransack the town."

They reached Zinder on Christmas, but Barth didn't even mention the holiday. He was more concerned about how long he would have to wait for the supplies needed to continue his journey. Zinder was on Bornu's western edge. "No place in the whole of Sudan being so ill famed," wrote Barth, "on account of the numerous conflagrations to which it is subjected." Tuaregs harassed it from the north, Fulanis from the south, pagan Hausas from the west. The people of Zinder spoke Hausa, which would be Barth's primary language for the next six months and 600 miles.

He settled in to wait for provisions. He spent most of his time working on his journals and reports. Before venturing into the dangerous territories to the west he wanted "to send home as much of my journal as possible, in order not to expose it to any risk." Additional risk, that is, since his papers still had to cross about 1,400 turbulent miles to reach Tripoli.

The year's salt caravan had arrived from Bilma. The Tuareg traders danced and played music all day and night. Annur, the old chief of

Tintellust, was in town, but treated Barth coolly because of Richardson's insulting behavior.

Some years earlier, Dorugu, the young servant whom Barth had inherited from Overweg, had been stolen and sold into slavery from a village about fifty miles southwest of Zinder. Barth had told the boy, who was twelve or thirteen, that if the opportunity arose, he could rejoin his father. On their first day in Zinder, Dorugu heard that his father, a drummer, had passed through town the day before. Some Hausa men offered to take Dorugu to him, but he was afraid they would sell him instead. Barth didn't mention any of this and evidently didn't make much effort to reunite the boy with his father. On the other hand, Dorugu didn't make much effort, either, judging from his own account, and didn't ask Barth for help. Perhaps he wasn't keen about leaving his adventurous life with the explorer for life in a small farm village.

On January 20, 1853, four weeks after Barth reached Zinder, his parcel arrived. Two packages disguised as loaves of sugar held 1,000 dollars in cash, mostly Spanish dollars. But there were no new scientific instruments and, dishearteningly, no letters. He bought two sturdy baggage camels and spent 300 dollars on trade goods for the journey, including "red common burnooses, white turbans, looking-glasses, cloves, razors, chaplets."

Ten days after the money arrived, he left Zinder feeling flush and healthy. His foot disease was gone and he had 2,000 dollars' worth of money and merchandise. But his wealth increased the dangers of the road in the borderlands between the pagan kingdoms and the Fulani kingdom of Sokoto, "the scene of uninterrupted warfare and violence." As he left Zinder, the pagan Goberawa were massing for war against the Fulani town of Katsina, his next destination.

Instead of roving ahead of his baggage camels as he preferred, Barth stuck with the group for safety. For the same reason, they sometimes joined bands of salt traders. The principal crop had changed to rice. At wells, following the custom of the country, the horses of travelers drank before any waiting natives.

AROUND THE SAME TIME that Barth was unwrapping those sweet loaves of cash, the envoy from Bornu reached Tripoli. He delivered Barth's letters informing the Foreign Office of Overweg's death and the new plans about Timbuktu. Herman forwarded the news to England, where it wouldn't arrive until late February. Herman, who always looked for the dark cloud, wrote to the foreign secretary, "From the information I have obtained from several Arabs here who have long resided at Timbuctoo—so great are the obstacles both moral and physical which our enterprising traveler will have to encounter that I entertain the most serious apprehensions for his safety."

His opinion of the envoy from Bornu, Ali ibn Abdullah, was equally bleak. He asked Lord Russell, the foreign secretary, to reconsider transporting him to England. "He is simply a black slave of the Sultan's," wrote Herman, "—so illiterate that he is utterly incapable of furnishing the slightest information of interest even on the primitive state of his own country, much less of comprehending for any useful purposes the more complicated civilization of Europe."

This opinion would have surprised Barth, who elicited intriguing information from all manner of people and did not consider Kukawa primitive. Herman wrote that the envoy would be housed and fed at the consulate while awaiting Lord Russell's further orders. Then Herman left for a brief sabbatical. His letter evidently got lost in the transition from Lord Russell to the new foreign secretary, Lord Clarendon.

In Herman's absence, his vice-consul, R. Reade, wrote to the FO that the envoy spoke only the language of Bornu and would need an interpreter in England. Reade recommended himself. Clarendon approved the trip for both of them, but they didn't get out of Tripoli fast enough. When Herman returned, he angrily delayed Reade's plans. He re-sent his letter about the envoy to Clarendon, using exactly the same description. He added that Reade would be useless as an interpreter since he didn't speak the envoy's language. Reade must have been crestfallen when his expense-paid trip to London was snatched from him. Herman added that sending the envoy to England was presently unwise because of his poor health. Ali ibn Abdullah had blood in his urine, an enlarged prostate, and pain in his groin, abdomen, and back—chronic gonorrhea.

After reading this dispatch, Clarendon wrote to Chevalier Bunsen for his opinion about the envoy question, and included Herman's description. Bunsen smoothly demolished the consul's condescension. He began by referring to the envoy as "the Black Diplomatist," then continued, "He cannot help being *black*, because black is the normal colour of all the Bornuese: as to the distinction between Slave and Servant, I do not suppose it to be very strict in the Interior of Africa. However I must observe that if Mr. H. calls the country a *primitive one*, this is rather a severe or hasty expression: because not only are they *Mohammedans*, but are, comparatively speaking, of a *superior* African civilization. . . . I daresay the 'useless Black' speaks his Bornoo language in perfection. . . . In short, perhaps, he turns out to be the best man they could send—and what more could they do?" Bunsen also pointed out that if Britain offended the envoy and thus Bornu, the new treaty could be put into doubt.

Meanwhile other possible complications arose. The undersecretary of the Foreign Office, Addington, sent a memo to Clarendon about the sticky consequences of bringing the envoy to England if the man was indeed a slave. The abolitionists would raise a ruckus and insist that he be freed, as British law demanded. That could cause a diplomatic breech with Bornu. Better to treat the envoy well in Tripoli and send him home, advised Addington. Clarendon ordered it done. He also ordered the FO's actual interpreter in Tripoli, Frederick Warrington, son of former consul Hanmer Warrington, "to extract all the information he can from the Sheikh's Envoy."

Herman showed some finesse by telling the envoy that the British government was unwilling to risk his precarious health by requiring him to make an arduous trip into the severe northern climate of England. The envoy, already homesick and shivering in the relatively cool temperatures of Tripoli, jumped at this reprieve and bolted for Bornu.

Herman itemized the consulate's expenditures for hosting the envoy: travel expenses, medicines, gifts ("two complete dresses"), fees for baths, and so on. The cost for the envoy's six-month stay came to about £20.

In his description of the sheikh's gifts for the queen, Herman reverted to form. Ethnologically, he wrote, the items might shine "a faint gleam of light" on the people of Bornu and "may possibly prove of interest, but in other respects, with the exception of an elephant's tusk, they are intrinsically of no value." Another opinion that would have shocked Barth.

In London the Foreign Office catalogued the gifts and forwarded them to Buckingham Palace, with a chart that listed their names in Kanuri and Arabic. In a column labeled "Remarks," the chart described or explained each item. The gifts included samples of men's and women's clothing (such as "kajee anagoodoo," a man's pantaloons); a wide array of agricultural products (corn, millet, indigo, gum Arabic, dried fruit, dates, beeswax, and a vegetable called "wabooloobull"); medicines (for instance, a concoction for colds made from a thorn tree and a medicine for weak eyes called "feedery chumlumleny"); utensils (water basket, wooden soup tureens, baskets with silk and cotton, dishes with grass covers); rhino horn and animal skins (lion, leopard, gazelle). There were spears, shields, war bells, and daggers with fish-skin covers. There was a horse whip made from a giraffe's tail and a slave whip made from a hippopotamus tail.

Queen Victoria's reaction to this fascinating collection is unrecorded, but she did send a thank-you note.

AT THE END of January 1853, at about the same time that Barth was unwrapping the loaves of cash in Zinder and the envoy from Bornu was entering Tripoli, Chevalier Bunsen sent a memo to Lord Russell, then foreign secretary. He noted that the African mission's thermometers, barometers, and astrological instruments all seemed to be damaged or broken. Barth and Overweg were unable to measure many things accurately—a lost opportunity. Bunsen suggested that the mission be resupplied with instruments. He also recommended sending a third scientist skilled in astronomy and botany, which weren't Barth and Overweg's strengths. Naturally, he knew just the German for the job, a young man named Eduard Vogel. He would not expect a salary, just expenses for travel and instruments.

Russell immediately agreed. Britain, he wrote, might never again have such an opportunity to scientifically explore Central Africa. "And I consider the enterprise so hazardous," he continued, "that in my opinion we would do well to add a third to the adventurous pair already employed by us."

Bunsen and Russell didn't know that Overweg had been dead for four months. Russell wanted two British sappers to accompany Vogel as assistants, which led to a stream of letters between the Foreign Office and the Board of Ordnance about pay rates and employment conditions. Less than a week after Bunsen recommended Vogel, the deal was done. Russell wrote Herman in Tripoli that the German and two sappers would be starting for Tripoli by the end of February.

Two weeks later, on February 19, the Foreign Office in London received Barth's letters about the death of Overweg and other matters. Sending Vogel took on a new urgency. Russell wrote Barth to tell him that he would be getting an assistant. (Barth would not get this news until May 1854, when it was fifteen months old.) Two days later Russell was replaced by Lord Clarendon, who also wrote Barth a letter, approving his plan to try for Timbuktu. A bit redundant—Barth had been en route for three months.

At almost the same time, Herman got a letter from Gagliuffi. No caravans had dared to leave Murzuk for two months because of massive unrest throughout Central Africa. Sending anything to Barth was impossible. No one would risk their lives to do it. "If our intrepid traveler proceeds as far as Sokoto," wrote Herman to Clarendon, ". . . it will be wonderful if he is not murdered by the natives, and if he should go on to Timbuctoo the risk will be a hundredfold greater."

22

The Prospect of the Niger

Barth's party covered the 140 miles between Zinder and Katsina in five days, without problems. Katsina's market surpassed Zinder's, and Barth made "considerable purchases," mostly cottons and silks from Kano and Nupe that were coveted farther west. He listed them with his usual precision: 75 "woman-cloths"; 35 black tobes from Kano and 20 from Nupe; 20 varieties of silks; 232 black face shawls for Tuaregs; 4 fine burnooses; half a dozen "sword-hangings" of red silk; and a large supply of tobacco, which was esteemed in Timbuktu. All together he spent 1,308,000 shells, or about 525 Spanish dollars (£105). He complained that the exchange rate in Katsina was 2,300 shells per dollar instead of the standard 2,500.

On his first visit to Katsina he had been held hostage for ten days by the greedy emir, Muhammed Bello Yerima, who hoped to squeeze some riches from the penniless white stranger. This time Barth got stuck here by politics. Because of the war brewing between the Goberawa and the Fulani, Barth's party couldn't leave until they knew where the warfront would be. Barth's guide told him to be ready to move with an hour's notice, which kept him on stressful alert.

So did the ants in his quarters. One day after sitting on a clay bench there, he got up and found a big hole in the back of his tobe. The ants, whom Barth couldn't help admiring as "these clever and industrious miners," had eaten through the clay wall of his house and chewed into his clothing, all in the space of an hour.

Other creatures in Katsina also besieged him. He gave the avaricious emir a generous gift—a superior blue burnoose, a red caftan, two turbans, a red cap, two loaves of sugar, and, the emir's favorite, a pocket pistol. But the man wanted more, and schemed to keep Barth and his rich baggage in Katsina. He was thwarted by Barth's new friendship with the vizier of Sokoto, visiting to collect Katsina's annual tribute to the sultan. (That year it came to 800,000 cowries plus a superb horse worth almost as much. Barth estimated the sultan's income from tributes at more than 100 million cowries, or about £10,000, plus the equivalent amount in slaves and cloth.) This vizier protected Barth from the emir's intrigues but not from his greed. Eventually the emir cadged another pocket pistol from the explorer. "He had a cover made for the pair," wrote Barth, "and used to carry them constantly about his person, frightening every body by firing off caps into their faces."

Barth also felt under siege from people seeking medical treatment. Every morning when he woke up, his courtyard was crowded with 100 to 200 patients, once including a blind horse whose owner asked Barth for a cure.

A caravan of 500 camels arrived from the north, "but without bringing me even a single line, either from my friends in Europe or even from those in Africa." This was doubly disappointing since the chances of getting correspondence after leaving Katsina were almost nil.

February turned into March. Barth felt more and more restless. War was approaching but so was the rainy season. He had decided it would be wise to travel to Sokoto with the vizier and his troop of fifty horsemen. On March 21 they finally left Katsina for Sokoto, 170 miles due west.

Barth enjoyed the beautiful landscape of deleb palms, shea-butter trees, and massive kapok trees, interspersed with fields of tobacco and yams. Wherever they stopped in the evenings, the vizier urged Barth to come inside the village's walls for safety, but he preferred his tent and the open air. He relied on the protection of his guns. The thatch huts in villages were often stiflingly hot and sometimes infested with vermin. They were also highly flammable, and Barth worried that if his stock went up in flames, so would the mission.

The signs of war were everywhere—abandoned villages, destroyed villages, villages barricaded with heavy timbers or intricate moats and earthworks. To escape detection the group sometimes traveled after dark. The vast wilderness of Gundumi, about 50 miles from Sokoto, was ideal for ambushes, and had to be crossed in a thirty-hour forced march. Even the energetic Clapperton, noted Barth, called this trek "the most wearisome journey he had ever performed in his life." Partway through, Barth noticed that the boy Dorugu was exhausted and told him to climb onto a camel. The grueling slog killed several camels and one woman.

The group collapsed into sleep on the far side of Gundumi. The sultan of Sokoto, Aliyu, was at a war camp nearby. Barth felt that his mission couldn't succeed without Aliyu's blessing. The sultan sent for him that evening. Barth passed through the campfires of the sultan's army and found the ruler seated beneath a tree on a platform of clay. He motioned for the Christian to sit on the ground before him.

Aliyu, the son of Muhammed Bello and a Hausa slave, was about forty-five, stout, and moon-faced. He received Barth "with the utmost kindness and good-humor." The sultan had followed Barth's movements with the greatest interest, including his trip to Adamawa. Barth made his diplomatic pitch for a commercial treaty with Britain, and also asked for a carnet to help ease his way toward Timbuktu. Aliyu immediately agreed to both requests, saying "it would be his greatest pleasure to assist me in my enterprise to the utmost of his power, as it had only humane objects in view, and could not but tend to draw nations together that were widely separated from each other."

The sultan's cheerful goodwill lifted Barth. Perhaps it would be possible to reach Timbuktu. The next morning he put together a package of fine gifts, including a pair of silver-ornamented pistols in velvet holsters, a burnoose of red satin with a yellow satin lining, and many other items of clothing and luxury. The presents delighted Aliyu, especially the pistols. He again agreed to Barth's two requests but insisted that the explorer delay his journey until the military campaign ended. Barth nodded, having no other choice. But he had little faith in Aliyu's success. The sultan struck him as weak and indolent.

That evening Aliyu sent Barth 100,000 shells to defray his household expenses during the delay. That same night, hyenas entered camp and tried to carry off a boy, mauling him badly. The camp's desolate location and atmosphere disturbed Barth. The next day, as soon as Aliyu took his army to war, Barth gathered his group and departed for Wurno, where Aliyu kept a residence, to await the sultan's return. It was April 3, 1853.

WHENEVER BARTH SPENT more than a few days in a large African town, he always distributed alms to the poor. In Wurno he bought an ox to feed them. But Wurno dispirited him. It was expensive and even filthier, he wrote, than the worst places in Italy. Its leading citizens mirrored their ruler, Sultan Aliyu, in their lack of energy and courage. They shrank from engagement with the belligerent pagans threatening them from several directions. Wurno's merchants warned Barth that travel to the west was impossible because of roving war parties. He began to doubt whether he would be able to proceed. Still, he spent his days collecting information about the western country, and he took long daily rides to stay in shape.

After two-and-a-half weeks in Wurno, he needed a respite. On April 20 he left for the capital, Sokoto, twenty-five miles to the southwest. En route he passed the tiny village of Degel, where Usman dan Fodio had hatched the jihad that transformed Central Africa. In keeping with Barth's frequent theme that the present leaders of Africa's empires paled next to their great forebears, he commented, "But such is the degraded state of these conquerors at the present time, that even this village, which, if they had the slightest ambition or feeling of national honor, ought to be a memorable and venerable place to them for all ages, has been ransacked by the Goberawa, and lies almost deserted."

After pausing for a good lunch of boiled onions seasoned with butter and tamarinds, he reached Sokoto. He remembered Clapperton's first impressions of it as brimming with energy and prosperity, but Barth saw mostly poverty and misery, the result of depredations from all sides. The roads were so dangerous that not a single Arab merchant now visited. Bello's former palace was badly decayed.

In the market Barth spent another 70,000 shells on supplies. The town was famous for leather goods, and he filled a leather bag with dates for the journey ahead, in hopes that he would be able to take it.

He also visited the house just outside of town where Clapperton, during his second trip into Central Africa, had died of dysentery twenty-six years earlier. Clapperton had returned from his first expedition with high praise for Muhammed Bello's generosity and intelligence. He also brought back a commercial treaty signed by Bello, in which the sultan agreed to give access to British merchants and to give up slavery in exchange for a couple of cannons and some firearms.

But Clapperton's return trip didn't go well. Sokoto and Bornu were at war, and Bello wouldn't let Clapperton proceed to visit al-Kanemi in Kukawa. Stalled in Sokoto, Clapperton sickened and died. When his servant, Richard Lander, returned to Europe with this news, Bello's reputation plummeted. Barth defended Bello, pointing out that he had been harassed by native revolts as well as war, and had been pressured by Arab traders who felt threatened by Clapperton's commercial proposals. Barth also suggested that Clapperton might have insisted too adamantly on visiting Bornu. These views probably didn't endear the German to Clapperton's many British admirers.

In a passage that sounds self-descriptive, Barth dismissed the common European suspicion that Bello had poisoned Clapperton: "The amount of fatigue, privations, and sickness to which this most eminent of African explorers was exposed on his circuitous journey, by way of Nupe and Kano, from the coast as far as this place, explains fully how he was unable to withstand the effects of the shock which mental disappointment exercised upon him; nay, it is wonderful how he bore up so long, if his own hints with regard to the state of his health are taken into account."

Barth greatly admired Clapperton's energy and accuracy, which he contrasted several times with Denham's sloppiness. He probably also admired Clapperton's openness to Africa and Africans. Clapperton described the vizier of Sokoto as "my good old friend . . . for whom I felt the same regard as if he had been one of my oldest friends in England, and I am sure it was equally sincere on his side." During Clapperton's first visit, when the vizier's favorite son died of smallpox, the explorer went to console him. They sat together silently for an hour. "Unable to alleviate his grief," wrote Clapperton, "I took him by the hand; he pressed mine in return; and I left this disconsolate father with heaviness of heart."

AFTER FOUR DAYS in Sokoto, Barth rode back to Wurno and continued to await the sultan's return. He found relief from Wurno's shortcomings in the company of a scholar named 'Abd el Kader dan Taffa, a rich repository of knowledge about the kingdom of Songhai, once the region's greatest power. He also spent much time reading a manuscript entitled *Tazyīn al-Waraqāt* by Usman dan Fodio's younger brother, Abdullahi, about the history of the western part of the Fulani kingdom. Abdullahi was a warrior who conquered many places during the jihad. Even more learned than dan Fodio, he wrote at least seventy-five works on Islamic law, religion, and science. After the jihad, dan Fodio awarded him a large kingdom in the western lands, called Gwandu, unknown in Europe before Barth visited. Dan Fodio's son, Bello, was given the larger eastern portion, the Caliphate of Sokoto.

Tazyīn al-Waraqāt was a strange document that mixed history, poetry, theology, eulogy, and literary theory. Two samples of its poetry and themes:

They cut off at a blow the heads of the unbelievers
With swords the blades of which are bright.
Whetted arrows, transfixing, assist them,
While under them are fine horses.

Turn aside towards the winding streams of the loved ones of Maji
And drink from the streams the water of the white cloud.
Let tears flow on their dwellings there
And cure the heart of the sorrows which have entered it.

Such pleasures aside, Barth urgently wanted to leave. The rainy season was pending, and reports said the roads were getting more dangerous. He also felt "sorely pestered by begging parties, the inhabitants of Wurno and Sokoto being the most troublesome beggars in the world"—quite a superlative, given Barth's experience.

When Aliyu returned, Barth immediately sought his blessing and a letter of transit. On May 8 he left Wurno and set his course southwest. Once past Sokoto, he would enter regions, in his beloved phrase, "never trodden by European foot." The gateway to these regions was the Fulani kingdom of Gwandu.

To cross the 150 miles between the capital town of Gwandu and the Niger River, Barth needed the good will of the kingdom's ruler, Khalilu. This son of Abdullahi lived like a monk. His own subjects rarely glimpsed him except on Fridays when he went to the mosque. To a European and a Christian he was "most inaccessible."

Barth, quartered in the house of Gwandu's chief eunuch, tried to get an audience with the sultan by insisting on presenting his gifts in person. He was told to forget it. During his three weeks in Gwandu, Barth never saw Khalilu or even heard his voice from behind a screen. The sultan surrounded himself with a small mafia of handlers who controlled him and ran the kingdom. Paranoia, seclusion, and avarice made Gwandu a nasty kleptocracy.

Barth tried to outflank the mafia by hiring one of its members as his intermediary. Instead the man used his position to worsen Barth's standing with the sultan, then demanded extravagant gifts to fix what he had broken. He also insisted on gifts for the rest of the cabal.

Barth sent Khalilu the same generous packet of goods given to the sultan of Sokoto, minus the fancy pistols. But the mafia had heard about the pistols and told Barth he couldn't leave Gwandu until their sultan got equal treatment. After many futile attempts at negotiation, Barth handed over the guns.

In the midst of these shakedowns Barth met a learned man who showed him an ancient manuscript. As he began reading, he became tremendously excited. The quarto volume in his hands was a history of one of Africa's great kingdoms, Songhai, "from the very dawn of historical records down to the year 1640 of our era." It was more proof—scarcely believed when Barth reported it in Europe—that Central Africa had an old written tradition. The manuscript, entitled *Tarikh al-Sudan*, was written by Abderrahman es-Sa'di (Barth incorrectly ascribed the work to Ahmed Baba, a famous scholar of Timbuktu and the teacher of es-Sa'di). It provided an eyewitness account of the horrible consequences of the invasion of Timbuktu by a mercenary Moroccan army in the 1590s.

"I saw the ruin of learning and its utter collapse," wrote es-Sa'di, a man after Barth's own heart, "and because learning is rich in beauty and fertile in its teaching, since it tells men of their fatherland, their ancestors, their annals, the names of their heroes and what lives these led, I asked divine help and decided to record all that I myself could gather on the subject of the Songhay princes of the Sudan, their adventures, their achievements, their history and their wars. Then I added the history of Timbuktu from the foundation of that city, of the princes who ruled there and the scholars and saints who lived there, and of other things besides. . . ." Barth spent several days reading it and copying passages.

The rainy season roared into the area as well, bringing heat, bugs, fevers, rheumatism. Militarily the district was "plunged into an abyss of anarchy." Barth didn't dare venture many yards from the town's walls, much less make his usual excursions into the countryside. His doubts about reaching the Niger grew again.

But even the dangers of the road seemed better than the draining corruption of Gwandu. After more gifts to his extortionate intermediary, Barth managed to extract a letter of transit from Khalilu. He was allowed to leave on June 4. He proceeded west toward "that great African river which has been the object of so much discussion and individual ambition for so long a period"—the Niger.

IN THE SWAMPY valleys of the province called Kebbi, Barth worried most about war parties, but the worst bloodthirsty attackers were mosquitoes. As a refuge from these maddening pests, every villager built an elevated hut, 8 to 10 feet off the ground, entered by a ladder—"the most essential part of even the poorest dwelling in the province of Kebbi."

He passed familiar scenes: fields of corn and rice, beautiful landscapes, devastation. In one fertile valley he rode by "an uninterrupted line of large walled towns. But most of them are now deserted and destroyed." Thousands of people had been uprooted or turned into slaves. "Life and death in these regions are closely allied," he wrote.

In these volatile conditions, any traveler caused alarm. When Barth's small group came across a wayfarer sitting beneath a palm tree and enjoying its fruit, "we could not help greatly suspecting this man to be a spy, posted here by the enemy in order to give them information of the passers-by." Barth had to restrain his Arab troubleshooter from killing the man. The next day they came across a solitary pilgrim, a Jolof from the Atlantic coast heading to Mecca. He was walking with a small bundle on his head, a double-barreled gun on his shoulder, and a sword hanging at his side. Barth, perhaps feeling abashed by yesterday's overreaction, was buoyed by "this enterprising native traveler" and gave him a small present to help him along.

In the town of Birnin-Kebbi the people told Barth that reaching the Niger was unlikely because of turmoil in the countryside. In Zogirma he fired two bodyguards and replaced them with two old warriors, paying each man a salary of one new black head-shawl, one flask of rose oil for his wife, and 1,000 cowries for household expenses while away. But they only stayed with him from June 9 to 14, so he soon had to start looking for other guardians.

They saw signs of war parties—hoofprints of horses, destroyed villages, withering cornfields, starving cattle. It became impossible to buy corn for their animals. Despite the urgent warnings of villagers, Barth continued to camp outside the walls each evening. "I again enjoyed an open encampment," he wrote, "which is the greatest charm of a traveling life."

In the Valley of Yelou, just across the border between present-day Nigeria and Niger, the vernacular language changed from Hausa to Songhai. Barth had mastered Hausa and was still studying Fulfulde, the Fulani language. He began looking for a guide fluent in Songhai to tutor him but failed to find one. He tried to pick it up on his own, "and, in consequence, felt not so much at home in my intercourse with the inhabitants of the country through which I had next to pass as I had done formerly."

They were angling northwest to hit the Niger. Barth was humming at the prospect. "This celebrated stream," he wrote, "the exploration of which had cost the sacrifice of so many noble lives." Other than the Nile, no other African river had so excited the curiosity of Europe. (This would soon shift to the Zambezi and the Congo because of the journeys of Livingstone and Stanley.)

On the morning of June 20 he reached the famous river. While waiting for ferries to cross from the town of Say, he gazed at the "noble spectacle" of the Niger and duly recorded its width and current-speed. But his response seemed more de rigueur than wholehearted.

Several things were dampening his enthusiasm. The intense heat and humidity left him "almost suffocated, and unable to breathe." It was the prelude to fever. He also needed to decide how to proceed from here. The first rains had started and would soon become torrential. He had been advised in Gwandu not to try following the river's long upstream arc to Timbuktu, which resembled a flattened upside-down U, but rather to cut across country and hit the river again west of Timbuktu. Others had given similar advice. Barth knew that Mungo Park had already traveled the upper part of the river (though his record of it was lost when he was killed). The Landers had traveled the lower river. But no European foot had trod the territory south of the Niger's arc. That's what Barth decided to do.

His reactions in Say illustrated the emotional peaks and letdowns of exploration. He had reached a major goal, the Niger, but couldn't afford much exultation because he had to move on before the rains worsened and the war caught up with him and his supplies ran out. Barth rarely mentioned the psychological toll of constant stress, and handled it well. He always mustered the energy and will to continue, to pursue the promise of the region ahead, the next landscape, the new peoples and languages.

At first the cheerful governor of Say was delighted to welcome the town's first Christian visitor. (Park had floated right by.) Because of the recent conflicts, even traders had stopped passing through, and Say was suffering. The governor hoped that Barth could arrange for a European steamer to visit and fill the town's market with luxuries. When the governor learned that Barth wasn't there as a trader, his welcome turned to alarm—because, wrote Barth, "in exposing myself to such great dangers, I could not but have a very mysterious object in view . . . and he asked repeatedly why I did not proceed on my journey."

After four days in Say he eased the governor's mind by striking inland, toward the northwest and Timbuktu.

23

"Obstructed by Nature and
Infested by Man"

NO EUROPEAN HAD EVER DESCRIBED THE LANDS WHERE BARTH
now ventured. His route would take him across what is now
southwest Niger, northern Burkina Faso, and central Mali. He had a
rough idea of the distance between Say and Timbuktu, based on geographers' estimates of that fabled city's location. But its position had
never been fixed and the estimates were grossly incorrect. This would
cost Barth dearly in time, effort, and expense, illustrating why accurate
maps were crucial.

He left Say on June 24, 1853. As always, the prospect of unfamiliar
people and places galvanized him. Within hours this mood was swept
away by a fierce sandstorm followed by three hours of violent rain.

At first the landscape rippled with hills and cornfields. In exchange
for Barth's modest passage-gifts, the village chiefs sent him fowls, sheep,
even heifers. Butterflies sipped from wildflowers in green pastures. The
tracks of cattle mixed with those of elephants and, for the first time
since Bagirmi, rhinos.

Four days out of Say he met a merchant heading north, and entrusted
letters to him. They never arrived. Barth later heard that disease had
killed the merchant before he reached Kano. Given the distances and
difficulties, it seems miraculous that any letters ever reached the coast.
Oudney, Clapperton, and Denham kept in touch with the outside world

through Tebu couriers who traveled back and forth between Lake Chad and Murzuk, 800 miles, carrying little more than a waterskin and pounded corn. For fuel they burned dung caught in bags beneath their camels' tails. They traveled in pairs because odds were that only one would survive.

The landscape, pounded by rains, softened into marsh, then bog. They crossed flooding rivers and streams. At the Sirba River, 70 yards wide and 12 feet deep, they haggled with natives who put the smaller packages into calabashes and swam them across. The humans and the larger bundles made the trip on loose bales of reeds, as an audience of villagers watched the entertainment from the river's high banks. Barth noted that the men smoked small pipes nonstop and wore their hair in long plaits hanging over their faces, things he hadn't seen before. Copper rings began showing up on women's arms and legs. The method of carrying water changed as well. A jug on the head was replaced by a yoke across the shoulders, with a pitcher on each side held by netting. The sight reminded him of Germany.

The rains were capricious. Most stretches of terrain were sodden, but others suffered drought and the tease of oppressive humidity. Huts shimmered in the heat. Corn seedlings wilted. Emaciated cattle licked the soil for salt.

The extremes of rain and drought made travel more arduous. Good provisions grew more scarce. So did native hospitality. Barth found the Songhais to be the least welcoming people of his journey. Sometimes they refused his request for accommodations and told him to keep moving. Sometimes he obliged, but other times he used threats to claim a space for his soggy, exhausted group. His usual supper changed from fowls or lamb to millet with a vegetable paste made from tree-pod beans. His breakfast was cold vegetable paste with sour milk (thin yogurt). He supplemented this diet with wild fruit.

Two weeks into the journey, guinea worm attacked one of Barth's servants. Of all the horrible afflictions in Africa, Barth dreaded guinea worm most. At the time, its source was unknown, but Barth correctly guessed that the main cause was stagnant water. The parasite enters the body when people drink from ponds or standing pools that contain water-fleas carrying the worms' larvae. The larvae dig their way out of the intestine, meet other burrowing larvae, and mate. The males die and the females excavate their way to the surface, which takes about a year. When about to emerge, the worm secretes acid to form a blister, usually on the leg or foot, that causes burning pain. When the blister pops, the worm's white head squirms out. The parasite, which may be 2 to 3 feet long, must be tugged slowly and gently. The extraction takes months, all of it excruciating. Sometimes a person is infested with dozens of worms. No wonder Barth dreaded the disease. It often made his servant "the most disagreeable person in the world."

Barth, too, had become infested, but his parasite was human: Weled Ammer Walati. El Walati, as Barth called him, was an Arab scoundrel from the Mauritanian desert west of Timbuktu. Barth ran into him at a village about 350 miles from Timbuktu. El Walati was handsome and slender, with "very fine expressive features." He wore a black tobe and a black shawl around his head. "His whole appearance, as he was moving along at a solemn thoughtful pace," wrote Barth, "frequently reminded me of the servants of the Inquisition."

At first he beguiled Barth. He had "roved about a great deal" among the Tuaregs and the Fulanis, and knew the territory ahead. He lived in Timbuktu and claimed to be a close friend of the sheikh. He spoke six languages and told fascinating tales about the region's history. All this was catnip to Barth. He hired the man as a fixer to ease his passage through several hundred miles of unknown territories en route to Timbuktu. El Walati was "altogether one of the cleverest men whom I met on my journey," wrote Barth, "in spite of the trouble he caused me and the tricks he played me."

The tricks began a few days later at the town of Dori. Barth didn't want to pause anywhere very long. He hoped to stay ahead of rumors about his presence. Dori, for instance, was full of salt traders who would broadcast news about this stranger wherever they went. But in Dori,

Barth learned that he was now traveling at El Walati's leisurely pace. The Arab always had a deal brewing, and he made excuses, or made himself scarce, until the deal was done. He quickly sold the horse that Barth gave him as part of his salary and bought seven oxen, with an eye toward selling them at a great profit in Timbuktu. The intricacies of this deal kept them in Dori for nine days.

Barth used the delay to write a long letter to Consul Herman about his plans and his route. He put it inside a package addressed to a Fulani friend in Sokoto, with instructions written in Arabic to forward it to Tripoli. But the traveler carrying the package crossed so many high rivers that by the time he reached Sokoto, the outer envelope and instructions had dissolved. The English inside looked like gibberish to Barth's friend, so he gave the letter back to the messenger, who put it in his cap as a charm. Barth found it there a year later while passing back through Gwandu. Meanwhile the Foreign Office had grown alarmed by the explorer's silence and had begun to suspect the worst.

BARTH DESCRIBED THE territory beyond Dori as "unsettled provinces obstructed by nature and infested by man." He considered this the most dangerous stage of his journey to Timbuku and expected it to take about twenty days. It took almost twice that long, partly because of the city's incorrect position on maps, partly because of heavy rains and flooding, and partly because of El Walati.

When Barth's group left Dori, so did a large band of armed men who insisted on offering their protection. A similar band had recently made a similar offer to a wealthy sherif, who was later found murdered. Barth refused to proceed until the men wheeled back toward Dori.

His group passed villages terrified by rumors of approaching warlords. Four days beyond Dori, 150 to 200 belligerent herders surrounded them, shouting and shaking their spears "with warlike gesticulations." "The affair seemed rather serious," wrote Barth rather casually. He pulled his gun. El Walati saved them by shouting that Barth was a

friend of the sheikh of Timbuktu, and was bringing him books from the
east. The men dropped their spears and crowded around Barth to ask his
blessing. He complied, "although it was by no means a pleasant matter
to lay my hands on all these dirty heads."

The main hazards during this stretch were heavy rains, flooding
rivers, and swamps. Everything and everyone stayed wet. These discomforts were worsened during the day by biting flies that penetrated
their clothing. At night, "of mosquitoes there was no end," wrote Barth.
If he closed his tent to keep them out, the sweltering humidity made
the interior stiflingly hot. If he sought a breath of air outside, shoals
of mosquitoes attacked. Either way, sleep was nearly impossible. The
insects also maddened the animals. Barth typically downplayed insects
as inconveniences, but during this portion of the journey he mentioned
them often, along with his constant exhaustion.

Every African explorer complained about these pests. Denham was
especially vivid about the "millions of flies and mosquitoes beyond all
conception." At one point his eyes swelled shut and his hands were so
puffy from bites that he couldn't hold a pen. He tried to escape the bugs
by sleeping in the middle of herds of cattle, or by lighting damp vegetation to make smoky fires. On bad nights even the horses overcame their
terror of fire and sought relief by hanging their heads in the smoke.
Denham could be almost operatic on the subject: ". . . another night
was passed in a state of suffering and distress that defies description:
the buzz from the insects was like the singing from birds; the men and
horses groaned with anguish; we absolutely could not eat our paste and
fat, from the agony we experienced in uncovering our heads."

IN EARLY AUGUST, four days after the dirty-haired spearmen, Barth
entered the territory of Dalla, part of the Caliphate of Hamdallahi
("Praise to God"). Dalla's ruler, like Hamdallahi's emir, was a fanatical Muslim "who would never allow a Christian to visit his territory."
Hamdallahi had been founded by fundamentalists inspired by the jihad

of dan Fodio. Its capital city was about 150 miles due east of Barth's position. He expected trouble from that direction. Just to the north of him
began territory controlled by Tuaregs. Barth knew how Tuaregs treated
Christians. His route to Timbuktu was a tightrope between these dangers. To escape detection for as long as possible, he assumed the identity
of a Syrian sherif. He was still trying to travel fast and stay ahead of
rumor, but the rains and El Walati kept slowing him down.

Despite these anxieties, he continued to collect information. Many
of the villages were built for war, with strong fortifications and gates
too narrow for loaded camels. Some towns had towers and crenella-
tions that reminded him of Bavarian castles. He noticed that travelers
began using a different greeting as they passed on the road. The value
of certain trade goods changed. His darning needles, once ignored,
were now highly desired, but his small needles, treasured in Bagirmi,
were regarded with contempt. Near Kobou, now just across the border
between Burkina Faso and Mali, Barth's group encountered masses of
black and red worms covering the paths, "marching in unbroken lines
toward the village."

The closer he got to Timbuktu, the more people drank tea. In Songhai villages, he noticed, "there is no end of smoking," and people danced
every night—behavior reported in the eleventh century by the Anda-
lusian geographer Al-Bakri. Such amusements were forbidden by the
fundamentalist regime in Hamdallahi, and were a constant source of
conflict with the tobacco-loving dancers of Timbuktu.

But in general Barth wasn't happy with the quality of his findings.
He hadn't had time to master Songhai or to do his customary deep inter-
viewing. "I must apologize to the reader," he wrote, "for not being able
in this part of my journey, which was more beset by dangers, to enter
fully into the private life of the people."

Their route now angled more to the northwest, into the domain of
Tuaregs. El Walati began working a profitable con. He advised Barth to
deflect the Tuaregs' suspicions by sending gifts to the chiefs whose lands
they were crossing. El Walati insisted on serving as Barth's intermediary.

Then he entered the village or camp, sold Barth's gifts, and announced the imminent arrival of an important and wealthy Syrian sherif. When Barth appeared, the chief demanded presents. El Walati would commiserate with the exasperated explorer about such outrageous greed. This hustler epitomized the Hausa proverb, "You do not give a hyena meat to look after."

Barth soon sniffed out the scam but bit his tongue. He was afraid that without El Walati he would never reach Timbuktu. He also believed that if he crossed the Arab or fired him, El Walati would betray him to the Fulanis or the Tuaregs for a reward. Barth felt trapped between the fanaticism of the Fulanis, the violent avarice of the Tuaregs, and his fixer's cunning.

The journey was repeatedly delayed by El Walati's entrepreneurial shenanigans. "As long as my friend El Walati had something to sell," wrote Barth, "there was no chance of traveling." The Arab used the proceeds from selling Barth's goods to wheel and deal all along the route. In one place he "helped" Barth bargain for oxen, but the price included a 50 percent commission for himself. Farther down the road he sold one of the new oxen and mournfully told Barth it had been stolen. In another village Barth was puzzled by the hostility toward his group until he learned that El Walati had gotten married there four years earlier and absconded with all his wife's property. Barth had to bail him out to avoid violence.

By that point the explorer's tongue was almost bitten through. "It was only by degrees that I became acquainted with all these circumstances," wrote Barth, "while I had to bear silently all the intrigues of this man, my only object being to reach safely in his company the town of Timbuktu."

Sometimes Barth couldn't help admiring El Walati's cleverness. When some Tuaregs stole the fixer's tobacco pouch, he pulled out one of Barth's books—it happened to be Lander's *Journey*—and threatened the thieves with it as if it was the Koran. The pouch reappeared.

Several times Barth narrowly escaped detection as a Christian. One Tuareg chief, after talking to Barth, refused to believe he was a Syrian sherif, pegging him as a Berber from the north. Barth almost blew his own cover twice. At Bambara, about 75 miles from his goal, he met an Arab from West Africa who had been everywhere between Mecca and the Atlantic port of St. Louis in Senegal. Barth couldn't resist peppering the man with questions, including many about the Arabs west of Timbuktu. The man soon grew suspicious, because he had never met an Arab from the Middle East, as Barth purported to be, who knew so much about West Africa. Barth talked his way out of it.

At another place, a Tuareg chief entered Barth's tent unexpectedly and caught him reading a book—Cooley's—written in characters that were not Arabic. Barth's sun-darkened skin and mastery of Arabic allayed the man's suspicions. Yet Barth's looks were different enough, and his supposed pedigree as a Syrian sherif was exotic enough, that he attracted unwanted attention wherever he went. People wanted to see him, talk to him, ask for his blessing—and incidentally request a small gift. The women pestered him for tobacco.

In several places he was again taken for a rain king and implored to use his powers. He always refused, but since the rainy season had started, he often got credit for downpours. (After one of these coincidences, the town's governor praised Barth as a rain god. This man was later shocked to learn that the rainmaker was a Christian. This greatly amused the sheikh of Timbuktu, who jibed the governor about appealing for rain to an infidel.)

The landscape now consisted of flat marshes and sheets of water laced by, in Barth's words, "a labyrinth of creeks, backwaters, and channels." At Sareyamou, Barth gave up land travel and hired a boat for 10,000 cowries. Using 18-foot poles, the boatmen pushed the vessel through a maze of narrow watercourses flanked by a "sea of reeds." The boatmen worked to the rhythm of songs about the deeds of Askia, the great king of the Songhai empire in the late fifteenth century.

Barth had been fighting illness since Say, so he enjoyed this respite from hard travel. He did have to get out and walk through shallow water several times each day, and in the boat his feet stayed immersed in sloshing water, aggravating his rheumatism. But he relished the novelty of fresh fish dinners and the watery scenery, which included the massive heads of hippos breaking the surface.

On the evening of their fourth day afloat, the channel opened into the Niger. The river was a mile wide here and looked immense, unspooling beneath a rising new moon and a sky fractured by lightning. Barth's servants stared "with real awe and almost fright." And then all eyes shifted to follow the water rolling northeast toward Timbuktu, twenty-five miles downstream.

In Kabara, Timbuktu's port town, Barth heard that the sheikh was away, trying to settle a dispute between some Tuaregs and Berabishes. "This piece of information produced a serious effect on me," he wrote, since "this whole region is plunged into an abyss of anarchy and misrule." Barth had premised the entire journey on hopes that the sheikh would protect him if he made it to Timbuktu. His situation was delicate, "for as yet I was an outlaw in the country, and any ruffian who suspected my character might have slain me, without scarcely any body caring any thing about it." Having no alternative, he sent El Walati to Timbuktu to feel out the sheikh's brother about the possibility of entering the city under his protection.

Meanwhile, Barth took up quarters in Kabara, about eight miles away. His presence immediately attracted bloodsuckers. As he sat eating a plate of rice, a Tuareg ruffian entered with a spear and sword. He sat down and glared at Barth from within his head-shawl. Barth told him in Arabic and Fulfulde that he was dining and couldn't speak to him. The Tuareg replied by calling himself a great chief and demanding a gift. Barth demurred. The Tuareg warned that he was a great evil-doer about to do great harm. "After a very spirited altercation," wrote Barth, "I got rid of him."

During the next hour, 200 armed men crowded into his house. They squatted on his floor and stared at him, talking among themselves about this stranger who stared back while lying across his smaller luggage and guarding the larger boxes behind him. Barth took advantage of this frightening situation to write a detailed description of the men's clothing and weapons.

After they cleared out, Barth went to bed. El Walati returned around midnight with the sheikh of Timbuktu's brother, Sidi Alawate, and several companions. To reduce the torment from mosquitoes, the guests were taken to the second-floor terrace, and given supper. Then Barth joined them to meet Sidi Alawate. "For the present I was entirely in his hands," wrote Barth, "and all depended on the manner in which he received me."

El Walati had told Sidi Alawate that Barth was a Christian under the protection of the sultan of Istanbul. Alawate asked Barth for proof. This was precisely why Barth had asked the British government several times to get him a letter of protection from Istanbul. Such a letter would often have eased his way during the journey. But he never got one. Barth talked his way around Sidi Alawate's request, and the man agreed to protect him until his brother, the sheikh, returned.

After they left, Barth tried to sleep but tossed restlessly until dawn. Nine-and-a-half months after leaving Kukawa, he was about to enter Timbuktu. It was September 7, 1853.

24

Golden City

For centuries before Barth's arrival, the word "Timbuktu" conjured magic in Europe. Timbuktu was gold, mystery, exotic isolation. Its geographic position was unfixed, like a dream's. Accounts of it were few but enticing. In 1324 when Timbuktu belonged to the kingdom of Mali, Mali's emperor Mansa Musa made a haj across Africa to Mecca. En route he passed through Cairo and into legend. His caravan of 60,000 included 12,000 slaves dressed in silk, 500 of whom walked with golden staffs. Eighty camels carried 300 pounds of gold each, which Musa spent lavishly. The fame of this spectacle circulated throughout Europe and the Middle East, and generated fabulous tales about golden cities somewhere in the heart of Africa.

The Moroccan traveler Ibn Battuta visited Timbuktu in 1353. He was struck by the inhabitants' learning, religious devotion, and beautiful clothing, and also by the number of concubines and naked women. About 150 years later the Spanish Moor Leo Africanus stayed in Timbuktu. Though unimpressed in most ways, he admired the king's many golden plates and scepters. He too commented on Timbuktu's abundance of scholars, who came from all over northern Africa to study and teach under the patronage of the king. Leo wrote that the most profitable commodity in Timbuktu's market was books—probably an exaggeration, since the city's wealth was based on gold, salt, and slaves, but the observation reinforced Timbuktu's reputation for learning. Like Ibn Battuta, Leo was also impressed by Timbuktu's lighter side. He described its people as peaceful and highly social, singing and dancing in the streets until one o'clock every night.

In Europe these tales and fragmentary reports got inflated to the proportions of myth. Timbuktu began appearing on maps that were fanciful not only for where they placed the city, but for portraying it as a city of gold. Africa's El Dorado inspired dreams. Governments coveted its wealth. The Portuguese evidently sent several missions to Africa's interior in the mid-1500s, though it's doubtful they reached Timbuktu.

For the next couple of centuries Europe's interest in Timbuktu subsided as countries turned their focus to India, the Far East, and the Americas. But in 1788 a group of prominent British citizens, led by Sir Joseph Banks, who had circumnavigated the globe with Captain James Cook, formed the Association for Promoting the Discovery of the Interior Parts of Africa. Better known as the African Association, the group's purpose was to erase the "stigma" of geographical ignorance about Africa. "The map of its interior is still but a wide extended blank," noted the association's manifesto. The association began sending explorers into Africa with three main goals: to trace the Niger River, investigate commercial possibilities, and geographically pinpoint Timbuktu.

Their first recruit, the American John Ledyard, died without getting far. So did Irishman Daniel Houghton. The Scot Mungo Park reached the Niger alone on his first expedition and survived, but on his second trip he was afraid to stop at Timbuktu and was killed farther downstream; none of his forty-six companions survived. Subsequent missions, whether from the north coast, the west coast, or by river, also ended fatally. Friedrich Hornemann (German), Jean-Louis Burckhardt (Swiss), Henry Nicholls, Major John Peddie, Captain Thomas Campbell, Dr. Joseph Ritchie—all died in Africa, though Ritchie's subordinate, Captain G. F. Lyon, survived to write about their journey to Murzuk.

Since reaching Timbuktu meant glory, the city also inspired hoaxes. In 1816 an American sailor who sometimes called himself Robert

Adams, other times Benjamin Rose, caused a sensation in London by claiming that he had been shipwrecked on the African coast and taken to Timbuktu as a slave, where he lived for five months. A publisher smelled a bestseller and paid Adams to describe his adventures. Adams was soon discredited by his absurd errors, including the howler that Timbuktu, renowned as a center of Islamic learning, had no mosques. Other shipwrecked sailors with similar stories came forward in 1821 and 1824, and were likewise sunk by their silliness.

In 1824 the French Société de Géographie offered 10,000 francs to anyone who reached Timbuktu and—the small print—returned alive. The British were determined to get there before the French. The following year the African Association launched another explorer toward Timbuktu from Tripoli—Major Alexander Gordon Laing.

Captain Hugh Clapperton, recently back from his three-and-a-half-year journey to Bornu and Sokoto, felt that the prize of Timbuktu was being handed to an upstart. Whoever reached the fabled city first was assured of fame, and Clapperton believed, with some justice, that he had earned the right to it. When he was ordered to send Laing advice about traveling in Africa, he at first refused. Even after complying, he remained determined to beat Laing to Timbuktu by taking the shortcut through "the white man's graveyard" of tropical West Africa. Just three months after returning to London from Bornu, he took ship back to Africa.

His small party, which included his servant Richard Lander, struck inland from Badagri on the Guinea Coast. Malaria soon wracked them. Lander lost his mind several times with fever. Dr. Robert Morison died. He was followed to the grave by Captain Robert Pearce and a servant, George Dawson. Clapperton and Lander made it to Sokoto, where they got stranded and Clapperton died of dysentery.

Meanwhile the dashing and supremely confident thirty-two-year-old Laing had been in Tripoli preparing his expedition and falling in love with Emma, daughter of the eccentric British consul, Hanmer Warrington. Two days after marrying Emma in July 1825, Laing left

for Timbuktu. (Consul Warrington refused to let the newlyweds con-
summate their marriage, on the grounds that Laing was unlikely to
return.) Seven arduous months later, in the section of the Sahara called
the Tanezrouft, about two dozen Tuaregs began shadowing Laing's caravan of forty-six men. One night as he slept, his escort of Arabs betrayed
him to the marauders. The Tuaregs fired muskets into Laing's tent, then
attacked with swords and spears, hacking until they were sure he was
dead. He should have been.

"I have five sabre cuts on the crown of the head," he wrote to Consul
Warrington, "and three on the left temple; all fractures, from which
much bone has come away. One on my left cheek, which fractured the
jawbone, and has divided the ear, forming a very unsightly wound. One
over the right temple, and a dreadful gash on the back of the neck, which
slightly scratched the windpipe &c. I am nevertheless, as already I have
said, doing well, and hope yet to return to England with much important geographical information." He wrote the letter with his left hand,
since his right arm was maimed.

Several of Laing's servants had escaped the attack by running into
the dunes. The next day, after the caravan departed, they tied Laing to
his camel and proceeded. He rode 400 miles in this wretched condition before reaching an oasis where he was taken in by an Arab chief
named Sheikh Sidi Muhammed—the father of the man who would
become Barth's protector in Timbuktu. Laing convalesced there for
three months. Then a plague, probably dysentery, struck the village,
killing the sheikh and sickening Laing. But the apparently invincible
explorer survived again. He left for Timbuktu.

In mid-August of 1826, after traveling for more than a year and
2,000 miles, he became the first European in centuries to see the legendary city. It disappointed him. Instead of glitter, he found sand and
mud. In his only surviving letter from Timbuktu he downplayed that
reaction, focusing instead on his achievement. He also mentioned that
he had been searching the city's written records, "which are abundant,"
a discovery whose significance he didn't fully comprehend.

His timing was bad. Just a few months earlier, the Fulani fundamentalists of Hamdallahi had conquered Timbuktu. The Christian
stranger was unwelcome. Five weeks after Laing arrived, Hamdallahi's
ruler ordered him expelled. On September 22 he started north toward
Morocco with an escort of Berabish nomads. A few days into the desert,
they murdered him. His journals disappeared.

A YEAR AND A HALF later a poor Muslim traveler walked into Timbuktu.
Its inhabitants barely noticed him, just as he had planned. His name
was René Caillié, a French dreamer inspired by Defoe's Robinson Cru-
soe. No summary can do justice to Caillié. To achieve his life's goal of
seeing Timbuktu, he worked for years, saving money for the journey.
To improve his chances of survival, he lived for months among Moors
in North Africa, learning their ways and languages. He also perfected
a cover story, told many times during his long trek through Islamic
lands: my parents were Egyptians who took me to France as a boy, and
now I am returning to my Muslim faith and roots by traveling overland to Cairo.

Caillié started for Timbuktu from Africa's west coast in 1827. After
a year of appalling ordeals, including guinea worm, he reached the city
in April 1828. Reality shattered his dream. "I looked around," he wrote,
"and found that the sight before me did not answer my expectations. I
had formed a totally different idea of the grandeur and wealth of Timbuktu. The city presented, at first view, nothing but a mass of ill-look-
ing houses, built of earth. Nothing was to be seen in all directions but
immense plains of quicksand of a yellowish white color. . . . all nature
wore a dreary aspect, and the most profound silence prevailed; not even
the warbling of a bird was to be heard."

He estimated the population at 10,000 to 12,000, and described the
people as cheerful and gentle. Tuaregs prowled the town's outskirts and
sometimes entered to take whatever they wanted. Caillié heard about
the recent murder of Laing and decided not to linger. After staying only

two weeks, still in disguise, he went north with a caravan through the Sahara to Morocco, another hellish journey.

When he reached Europe, his trials didn't end. Though he collected the 10,000-franc prize, the Legion of Honor, and a small government pension, some people doubted his account, which couldn't be verified. The British, who wanted the laurel of Timbuktu for themselves, and who knew that their man Laing had gotten there first, were especially ungracious. Consul Warrington was driven nearly insane by Caillié's claim. For him the loss of British prestige was compounded by his son-in-law's death and his daughter's grief. He accused Caillié of somehow acquiring Laing's missing papers and then colluding with the French consul and the pasha of Tripoli to defraud the public.

Caillié's book, published in French and English in 1830, was a best-seller but disappointed serious readers looking for thorough information about Africa's interior. Though incredibly intrepid and tenacious, Caillié was no scholar, and his need to stay disguised impaired his ability to collect material. This too played into the hands of his British detractors. "We shall offer no opinion on whether M. Caillié did or did not reach Timbuctoo," wrote John Barrow, second secretary of the Admiralty and a founder of the Royal Geographical Society, ". . . but we do not hesitate to say, that, for any information he has brought back, as to the geography of Central Africa, or the course of the Joliba [Niger], he might just as well have staid [sic] at home."

The accusations and insinuations of fraud devastated Caillié. "I must confess," he wrote at the end of his account, "that these unjust attacks have affected me more sensibly than all the hardships, fatigues, and privations, which I have encountered in the interior of Africa."

No European would reach Timbuktu again until Barth, so for twenty-five years no one could prove or disprove Caillié's account. Doubts about it festered. In 1833 the French government cut off Caillié's pension. His travels had shattered his health. He died in 1838, aged thirty-nine, impoverished. Such were the laurels of being the first to return from Timbuktu.

Barth no doubt nettled some people in England by corroborating most of Caillié's account and by praising him as "that very meritorious French traveler." Barth might have been describing himself when he added, "Following close upon the track of the enterprising and intelligent, but unfortunate Major Laing, who had been assassinated two years previously on his desperate journey from Timbuktu, Caillié naturally excited against himself the jealousy of the English, to whom it could not but seem extraordinary that a poor unprotected adventurer like himself should succeed in an enterprise where one of the most courageous and noble-minded officers of their army had succumbed."

WHILE EUROPE SPUN fantasies about golden desert kingdoms and explorers lost their lives pursuing a chimera, Timbuktu's actual history unfolded in ways that were fantastic enough. Always a pawn in desert politics, it was swept by savagery, scholarship, tolerance, and fundamentalism.

The place began around 1100 A.D. as a Tuareg seasonal encampment, where the edge of the Sahara touched the big northern bend of the Niger. Perhaps there was a well nearby, perhaps associated with a slave woman—the common translation of Timbuktu was "the well of Buktu." Barth dismissed this, attributing the name to a Songhai word for "hole" or "womb," because the town was built in a hollow among the sand hills. Others said the place was named after an old woman, Tin Abutut, who watched the Tuaregs' goods near the well, and whose name in Tamasheq meant "woman with the big naval."

Whatever the etymology, by the twelfth century Timbuktu was a flourishing trade hub where "the camel met the canoe." Africa's ancient cultures, Islamic and pagan, rubbed together there: Arabs, Moors, and Tuaregs from the north, black tribes from the south, Hausas and Fulanis from the east. Gold from mines in the south was traded for salt from desert mines in the north, and for goods from the Barbary Coast.

As it grew, Timbuktu began attracting Muslim scholars. This reputation increased after Mansa Musa conquered it in the fourteenth century and encouraged scholars to settle there. Musa also returned from his haj with an Egyptian architect who built the town's Djingereber mosque and its attached school, which attracted hundreds of scholars. (Religion and learning are intimately connected in Islam. The Arabic word for mosque is the masculine *jami*; the feminine form, *jami'a*, means university.)

The Malian empire waned, and in 1433 the Tuaregs took back the city, which they considered theirs. Several decades later the rising empire of Songhai, led by Sonni Ali, conquered Timbuktu and massacred many people, including scholars. The town withered as Gao, the Songhai capital 250 miles downstream, prospered.

When Sonni Ali died in 1492, he was succeeded by the visionary Askia Muhammed. Askia expanded Songhai into a great kingdom that covered much of central Sudan—Barth likened him to the renowned expansionist kings of Spain and Portugal. Askia also revered learning. Under the patronage of him and his successors, Timbuktu entered its true golden age. For the next hundred years the city blossomed as a center of Islamic learning. "Salt comes from the north, gold from the south, and silver from the country of the white men," said a proverb, "but the word of God and the treasures of wisdom are only to be found in Timbuktu."

Hundreds of scholars and mystics congregated there and taught hundreds—some estimates claim thousands—of students. Most of the scholarship was religious, but also included mathematics, astronomy, Islamic law, rhetoric, geography, botany, medicine, and music. The schools used Arabic translations of works by Plato, Aristotle, Ptolemy, and Hippocrates. There were also books in Hausa, Fulfulde, Tamasheq, and Songhai. Ahmed Baba, perhaps Timbuktu's most celebrated scholar, wrote at least seventy works in Arabic. He had a library of 1,600 books, which he said was among the city's smaller collections.

Timbuktu's golden age ended brutally in 1591. Sultan al-Mansur of Morocco sent an army of mercenary Spaniards, Berbers, and Arabs, known as the Arma, or Ruma, across the desert to Songhai. Their 4,000 muskets decimated the Songhais, who carried bows, spears, and swords. Timbuktu and Gao were overrun. The Arma, garrisoned in these towns, soon married into the population and became part of the ruling caste.

Timbuktu's libraries were plundered during the war. Its scholars, suspected as agitators and traitors, were jailed for five months, then forced to walk across the Sahara to Marrakesh. Sixty-four days. For many it was a death march. The survivors were imprisoned. Timbuktu's tradition of learning was temporarily erased.

The sultan released the scholars from prison after two years, but refused to let them go home, where they might cause trouble. The celebrated Ahmed Baba wrote a poem of longing for Timbuktu:

> *O traveler to Gao, turn off to my city.*
> *Murmur my name there and greet all my dear ones,*
> *With scented salams from an exile who longs*
> *For his homeland and neighbors, companions and friends.*

This forced exile lasted about a decade, until the sultan died. By then all of Timbuktu's surviving scholars had died in a plague, except one. Ahmed Baba alone returned to Timbuktu, where he spent twenty years before his death in 1627.

For two centuries, while Europe's imagination turned Timbuktu into an isolated mystery and a metaphor for the most distant and desirable place imaginable, the real Timbuktu baked in its sand and dust, and rebuilt itself into a commercial hub for trade in gold, salt, and slaves. Learned men gathered there again.

Waves of violence continued to disturb it. The Fulani jihadists of Hamdallahi conquered it in 1826. Hamdallahi's founding ruler, Ahmadu Lobbo, banned tobacco and decreed that men and women must be segregated. Residents of Timbuktu, a relatively cosmopolitan center of trade, learning, and pleasurable diversions, considered such ideas preposterous and acted accordingly. This resistance boiled over in 1844 when the

Tuaregs retook the city. Lobbo starved the rebels by stopping corn from moving downriver.

In 1846, Sheikh Ahmad al-Bakkay, who was trusted by all parties and adept at skating the thin edges between them, brokered a compromise. Timbuktu would pay tribute to Hamdallahi but would be left alone, with no occupying army. The town would be run by a Songhai administrator and a Fulani judge and tax collector. Serious matters would be referred to the ruler of Hamdallahi. Sheikh al-Bakkay had no official position but exercised considerable influence as a holy man, scholar, power-broker, and liaison to the Tuaregs. The Tuaregs, unpredictable and unfit for politics, remained a wild card. The compromise chafed all the parties. The precarious balance between them could be upset by almost anything.

That was how things stood as Barth prepared to enter the city.

25

In Timbuktu

WITHIN A MILE OF LEAVING THE GREEN MARGINS OF THE NIGER at Kabara, Barth was in the desert. The sand was powdery, like fine sugar. Its color was buttery or, in the right frame of mind, golden. Thorn bushes and dusty stunted trees lined the sandy road to Timbuktu. Rags fluttered from branches—fetishes offered in hopes of a new shirt. Donkeys were nearly invisible under their immense loads of river grass, sold as fodder in the city. About halfway into the eight-mile trip came a notorious stretch called "He Does Not Hear," where Tuaregs regularly robbed and killed travelers, beyond earshot of port and town.

The sky was overcast, the daylight blurred by blowing sand. At first Timbuktu's beige silhouette was indistinguishable from this murk. When it emerged, Barth also saw a group of riders coming to welcome and inspect him. He tensed. If they suspected him in any way, he would be turned back or worse. In the traditional greeting, he raised his gun and spurred his horse into a gallop, pulling up sharply as he reached them.

They exchanged many salaams. One of the men complimented Barth in Turkish, a language familiar to any Syrian sherif. But Barth hadn't spoken Turkish since his excursion around the Mediterranean and had almost forgotten it. The moment "might have proved fatal," he wrote, "not only to my enterprise, but even to my own personal safety." But he recovered and muttered a Turkish phrase, then urged his horse forward, anxious to avoid questions and enter the city.

His protector, Sidi Alawate, quartered him in a house catercorner from the sheikh's. Until the sheikh returned, Alawate instructed Barth, the explorer must submit to voluntary house arrest—no excursions, no visitors. This was immediately violated by droves of curious people who entered the house with Barth's luggage, eager to examine and question the stranger. He ignored them. He was surprised that word of the traveling Christian hadn't beaten him here, but knew that his cover story would soon crumble.

At this moment of triumph, just as he reached his goal and felt momentarily safe, exhaustion and illness finally overcame his willpower. He collapsed with severe fever. "Yet never were presence of mind and bodily energy more required," he wrote, "for the first night which I passed in Timbuktu was disturbed by feelings of alarm and serious anxiety."

The next morning brought the first death threat. The sheikh's nephew and rival, Hammadi, had learned Barth's true identity and had informed the Fulani judge that the infidel among them must be killed. Barth wasn't alarmed, at first, since he had the protection of Sidi Alawate.

This illusion evaporated within hours. Barth had already promised Alawate a generous gift, but once the Christian became public news, Alawate seized the chance to bleed him. He demanded another formidable gift, including burnooses, waistcoats, tobes, English razors, two pistols and gunpowder, 10 Spanish dollars, "and many other articles." The next day he demanded the same again.

Barth was exasperated, but his health and mood had improved, and he felt energized by making it to Timbuktu. "I began to enter with spirit upon my new situation," he wrote, "and to endeavor by forbearance to accommodate myself to the circumstances under which I was placed."

Since he couldn't go out, he went up. His house had a terrace on the second floor, where he could exercise and view the northern part of the city. He saw a small market, round huts made of matting, and many clay houses, some low and ugly, some with two stories and architectural ornamentation. Nearby rose the earthen mosque of Sankore, with its striking four-sided pyramidal minaret studded with projecting wooden beams. Built in the fourteenth century, Sankore had been the heart of Timbuktu's golden age of scholarship. Like the city, it had deteriorated. Sheikh Ahmad al-Bakkay had recently restored it. Barth couldn't see either of the city's other ancient mosques: the Djingereber, built in 1335 on the orders of Mansa Musa, or the Sidi Yahia, built in the fifteenth century. Surrounding everything, the Sahara.

Though Barth could see a slice of the city from his terrace, people also could see him. When exercising or sketching, he often had to step back out of sight. He was grateful for the terrace, but it also confined him in a prison of perspective. He wanted the ground's-eye view, down with the people. For the moment, that was too dangerous.

He wrote a letter to the British vice-consul at Ghadames, W. Charles Dickson, informing him that he had reached Timbuktu, "which so many daring spirits have in vain attempted to reach! May I be more fortunate than the late Major Laing and return in safety." He ended, "May God Almighty lead me safe back to the sea!"

Morning in Timbuktu began before dawn, when the muezzins' high plaintive song called the faithful to the day's first prayer. This was answered by a chorus of crowing roosters, which inspired bawling goats and braying donkeys. Soon after came the aromas of cooking fires, and then the thudding rhythms of women pounding millet with tall wooden pestles.

On his third day of confinement Barth was down with fever again when an unfamiliar servant rushed in to say that a mob was coming to storm his house, and he must run for his life. Barth smelled a ploy by Sidi Alawate and his pal El Walati to steal all his goods. Instead of fleeing, he loaded his guns and armed his servants. When Alawate and El Walati sauntered into the house, they were shocked to find Barth's militia protecting the storeroom. They left grumbling about Barth's crazy pluck. He began posting armed servants on the terrace at all times.

In a scholarly footnote to this episode he observed that when the servant warned him to leave, she also advised him to secure all his animals. He responded that he had only one animal there, his horse. He later learned that in Timbuktu's idiosyncratic jargon, the word for animals had come to mean any moveable property—a link, surmised the linguist, to the days when Timbuktu's people lived mostly in the desert and owned mostly livestock.

That afternoon Sidi Alawate stormed Barth's house with several learned and aggressive men, who pressured Barth to renounce Christianity and become a true believer. The infidel professor never declined a chance for intellectual exercise. He challenged them: if they could prove Islam's superiority to Christianity, he would convert. The scholars eagerly agreed and the theological jousting began. After breaking many lances against the adamantine German, the learned Muslims retired from the field.

Sidi Alawate showed up every day with a new list of gifts required to maintain his indiscernible protection. He said he used some of the gifts to grease the town's important people, but Barth doubted whether any of the goods got beyond this blackmailer and his coconspirator, El Walati. The explorer's stock of merchandise dwindled at an alarming rate.

His fever surged and faded. He was exhausted but felt too threatened to sleep much, and kept his loaded weapons at hand. He spent most of his time either on the terrace or in an open area downstairs where he could see anyone who entered.

On September 26 at three o'clock in the morning, clamorous music woke him from a feverish sleep. The music heralded the return of the sheikh, whose house was about twenty-five paces from Barth's across a tiny square. Barth desperately needed the sheikh's goodwill, but was too ill to rise from bed the next day and pay his respects. He sent his regrets. The sheikh, with the humanity that characterized him throughout Barth's stay, urged the visitor to rest. He also sent a generous gift—two oxen, two sheep, two large vessels of butter, and camel-loads of rice and corn. He assured Barth of safe passage toward his homeland, though he added that, to thwart poisoners, Barth probably shouldn't eat anything that didn't come from the sheikh's household.

The next afternoon, still ill with fever, Barth crossed the narrow street to meet his prospective benefactor and to present his first gift, a new Colt six-shooter. No other person in Africa would be as crucial to Barth as this man.

Ahmad al-Bakkay al-Kunti belonged to the Kunta family, an Arab-Berber clan influential throughout western Africa since at least the fourteenth century. The Kuntas were famous as merchants, scholars, and Sufi holy men. Barth wrote that they were "distinguished by their purer blood and by their learning above almost all the tribes of the desert." They also functioned as intermediaries who brokered arguments, especially between the merchants of Timbuktu and the Tuaregs, and between the Tuaregs and other desert factions. "It is really surprising," wrote Barth, "that a family of peaceable men should exercise such an influence over these wild hordes, who are continually waging war against each other, merely from their supposed sanctity and their purity of manners." When Barth arrived, al-Bakkay had been away mediating a dispute. The sheikh was also renowned as a poet and scholar, who attracted many religious students to Timbuktu. Barth later described him as the city's "eminent religious chief—the Pope of Timbuktu, as I might call him." The explorer had come more than 1,200 miles in hopes that a man with these qualities would welcome him.

Al-Bakkay rose and greeted the explorer affably. "At the very first glance which I obtained of him," wrote Barth, "I was agreeably surprised at finding a man whose countenance itself bore testimony to a straightforward and manly character." The contrast with Sidi Alawate, the sheikh's younger brother, was a wonderful relief. Al-Bakkay was fifty, "rather above the middle height, full proportioned, with a cheerful, intelligent, and almost European countenance, of a rather blackish complexion, with whiskers of tolerable length, intermingled with some gray hair, and with dark eyelashes." He wore a simple tobe, trousers, and fringed head-shawl, all black.

The two men felt an immediate rapport and fell into easy conversation, "an unrestrained exchange of thoughts," wrote Barth, "between two persons who, with great national diversity of manners and ideas, meet for the first time." The sheikh praised Laing, the only other Christian he had ever seen, and lamented his murder and missing papers. He again pledged that he would arrange Barth's safe passage from the city, with an escort to take him beyond the reach of the emir of Hamdallahi.

Barth left in good spirits, his hopes vindicated. He had started the day feeling gloomy—it was the anniversary of Overweg's death. He had confided to his journal that he felt so frail he half-expected to follow his companion to the grave. But he also hoped that when another year had passed he would be almost home. Al-Bakkay had strengthened that prospect by assuring him that he could leave Timbuktu soon. After three and a half rigorous years in Africa, he was feeling the pull of home.

Four days later these hopes blew up. "If at that time I had known," wrote Barth, "that I was still to linger in this quarter for eight months longer, in my then feeble condition, I should scarcely have been able to support such an idea; but fortunately Providence does not reveal to man what awaits him, and he toils on without rest in the dark."

ON THE FIRST DAY of October twenty men armed with muskets rode into Timbuktu from Hamdallahi. They carried orders from Emir Ahmadu Ahmadu: Drive out the Christian and seize his goods. The sheikh's scheming nephew issued a statement that the emir must be obeyed immediately, and if Barth resisted, to kill him.

Timbuktu's delicate balance of power wobbled. The Songhai and Fulani appointees felt compelled to obey Ahmadu Ahmadu but were reluctant to clash with Barth's influential protector, Sheikh al-Bakkay. The sheikh wanted to keep his promise to Barth, but by temperament he was a mediator, not a fighter. The explorer judged him too timid to defy the emir.

But the sheikh surprised Barth—surprised all Timbuktu. He had long resented the despotism and fundamentalism of the ruler of Hamdallahi. The new demand offended him. He also saw this as an opportunity to ingratiate himself with Britain, a wealthy nation that might show its gratitude with weapons, books, and other valuable gifts, or might even make possible Timbuktu's independence from the puritanical overlords of Hamdallahi.

Al-Bakkay ignored the emir's order. But he told Barth that it was now unsafe for him to leave. Everyone knew what had happened to the last Christian expelled from the city—Laing, murdered in the desert. The sheikh's concern seemed sincere, but Barth's continuing presence also provided an excuse to defy the emir.

The sheikh was not all strength and insight. Like Barth, he fell for El Walati's charm. This scoundrel and his partner, the sheikh's brother Alawate, persuaded al-Bakkay to hold Barth hostage until the British government sent a large ransom of goods. Barth was instructed to write a letter explaining the conditions. The avaricious duo also convinced the sheikh to demand that Barth turn over his horse and guns.

Barth was an infidel and an illegal alien in Timbuktu, with a death threat on his head. Without al-Bakkay's protection, he was finished. In such circumstances most people would choose discretion. Barth replied to the sheikh that Britain would not send "so much as a needle" until he had safely returned home. As for his horse and gun, he added, neither would leave his house "until my head had left my shoulders."

This grim standoff among all parties was broken a few nights later. A party of armed Tuaregs, known to be unfriendly toward the sheikh, cantered into town from the Sahara. This was Timbuktu's historical nightmare—squeezed between the ferocious desert tribes of the north and the severe Fulani peoples to the south.

Al-Bakkay, alarmed at the momentum of events, woke Barth at two o'clock in the morning and told him that they must keep armed watch from his terrace throughout the night. Tomorrow, he said, they would leave the city for a tent camp seven miles away. They would return when Timbuktu was less dangerous for them both.

Barth was more pleased than alarmed. The sheikh was still protecting him. And after being cooped up for a month, he would finally be outside and on horseback, on the move. The future looked threatening, but at least he would meet it in the open air.

THE SHEIKH'S CAVALCADE left the next morning. People lined the narrow streets to get a look at Barth, an invisible scandal for the past month. They rode seven miles into the desert. Barth was lodged in a tent made of camel's hair. Other tents were bright white cotton. Despite the threats hanging over him, Barth felt elated as he took in fresh air and fresh scenes. Camels, cattle, and goats grazed the sandy hills. White pigeons massed in the trees. Donkeys led by slaves carried water from a well. The sheikh's young sons, aged four and five, scampered around camp. In the evenings there was melodious chanting of verses by al-Bakkay's students and animated conversations by the cook fires.

Al-Bakkay's resistance to Hamdallahi pleased Barth, but his strategy troubled him. The sheikh wanted to send for reinforcements from his allies among the Tuaregs, especially a great chief named Alkutabbu who could protect Barth on his getaway. But Alkutabbu was several hundred miles away, which meant that Barth wouldn't be leaving anytime soon.

After two days the sheikh and the explorer returned to town to test the political temperature. The Fulani governor, who struck Barth as a man of good sense, was in a bad position. He was holding off the city's judge, who was insisting that the governor obey Ahmadu's order. But the governor also tried to discourage the sheikh from summoning Alkuttabu, because he didn't want trouble between the Fulanis and the Tuaregs.

The sheikh sent the summons anyway. To demonstrate resolve to their enemies, al-Bakkay asked Barth to fully arm himself whenever he crossed the street for a visit. Barth objected that he wanted peace, with no violence, but the sheikh insisted. He also asked Barth to rapidly fire his six-shooter in front of his house to exhibit that weapon's frightening potency.

El Walati continued his weasel ways. He gave a pistol to al-Bakkay's nephew and enemy, Hammadi, and told the sheikh that the gift had come from Barth, insinuating that the explorer was arming the sheikh's foes. But al-Bakkay was waking up to the scoundrel's true nature, and to Barth's integrity; he dismissed the story. Then Barth let El Walati ensnare himself with his own cleverness. The explorer had left some camels and other goods in a village outside the city, intending to collect them on his return trip. El Walati, figuring that Barth would never survive Timbuktu, had sold the camels before the explorer ever left the village. Barth had learned of it, so he offered the missing camels to the sheikh as a gift and told El Walati to deliver them. The snake couldn't squirm out of that trap, and the sheikh cut him off. Immune to shame, El Walati was later offended when Barth refused to hire him for the return journey from Timbuktu.

Throughout October, al-Bakkay moved Barth in and out of town like a chess master, responding to moves by the opposition that Barth sometimes grasped, sometimes didn't. Barth certainly felt like a pawn. In mid-October he wrote to Vice-Consul Dickson in Ghadames that al-Bakkay intended to use him as an instrument "to overturn the whole empire of Hamdallahi and found a new empire in its stead, under his own auspices." Barth added that he hoped to stay out of trouble and to leave in early November.

Barth called the trips into the desert "going to the tents." The schedule was irregular—a couple of days at the tents, then several days in Timbuktu, then overnight at the tents. The bucolic charm of tent life began to fade. He missed his books and writing table. Sleeping in the cold damp air aggravated his rheumatism.

Near the end of October, in a show of defiance, the sheikh took Barth on an excursion. They went first to the port of Kabara, a Fulani stronghold. Despite the danger, Barth was eager to go. He wanted to collect information about the river in flood and the changes it caused in the countryside. They drew a crowd, and Timbuktu's governor rode out to keep an eye on them. After a leisurely lunch the sheikh took Barth to see the Djingereber, or "Great Mosque," built by Mansa Musa. Barth wasn't allowed inside, but "its stately appearance made a deep impression upon my mind." The mosque was in the Fulani section of town. As Barth was measuring it, a throng gathered and followed them. But the people were more curious than hostile, and several offered Barth their hands. The emir's dictum hadn't yet poisoned everyone against the infidel.

He gathered information about every aspect of Timbuktu, from any available source. He estimated the town's settled population at 13,000, swelled by 5,000 to 10,000 during the heavy trading season from November to January. Few goods were made in Timbuktu. The city's economy relied solely on foreign commercial traffic. He confirmed Caillié's accuracy on most counts and commiserated with "the very unfavorable circumstances in which he was placed."

He apologized that his own circumstances made a thorough investigation of the market impossible. Then he wrote thirteen pages about it, detailing everything from the products offered to their prices and origins. The main trade goods were gold, salt, and kola nuts. Most of the salt came from the isolated mines of Taoudenni, a hellhole worked by slaves since 1596, about 450 miles due north into the Sahara. European goods reached the market from Morocco—tea and cutlery from England, cotton cloth from Manchester. The city's business, as in Agadez, was conducted in an idiosyncratic idiom that patched together Songhai, Hausa, Tamasheq, Fulfulde, Arabic, and tribal dialects, reflecting the city's history of scholarship, violent occupation, and cosmopolitan trade.

Timbuktu was both less and more than Barth had expected. Europe had overrated its political and commercial importance, he wrote. Its real treasure lay in being "the seat of Mohammedan learning and Mohammedan worship," epitomized by its three great mosques. He heard rumors about large libraries of ancient books, some destroyed by the Fulanis, but others hidden away.

THE SHEIKH MOVED Barth in and out of town throughout early November. The tedium of life at the tents grated. "I was deeply afflicted by the immense delay and loss of time," he wrote, "and did not allow an opportunity to pass by of urging my protector to hasten our departure." He tried to fill the days by studying Songhai, which he disliked "on account of its deficiency in forms and words." He also studied the local dialect of Tamasheq, the Tuareg language, whose wit and subtleties delighted him.

Sometimes the stints at the tents were lightened by diverting visitors whom he questioned closely. He welcomed even hostile guests since they relieved his boredom. One day a relative of the sheikh's accused Barth of visiting Timbuktu to scout it for conquest. Such suspicions would be justified in the near future, but Barth's motives had so little connection to imperial ambitions that he treated the charge as an absurd joke. He had made the difficult trip to Timbuktu, he told his accuser, because the British government had heard that the natives "fed on sand and clay," so his government sent him to learn how it was done "in order to provide in a similar way for the poor in our own country." As the accuser looked bewildered, the sheikh roared with laughter.

Barth's favorite times at the tents were spent talking to al-Bakkay about the Qur'an, Christianity, the Paraclete, the coming of the Messiah, and other bottomless theological subjects. Their talks deepened their respect for each and for their different religions. (Barth noted, however, that al-Bakkay's open-mindedness did not extend to Jews—a result, he wrote, of the still-influential jihad against Jews preached in this region at the end of the fifteenth century by al-Maghili. Barth himself makes several anti-Semitic remarks in *Travels and Discoveries*.)

Al-Bakkay even began defending Barth's faith against irate Muslims—not that the explorer shrank from self-defense. Barth, who could quote portions of the Qur'an in Arabic, regretted that he didn't have more time to study and discuss the fine details of Islam. He loved to see the young students writing verses of the Qur'an on their wooden tablets, and to hear them reciting. "There was nothing more charming to me," he wrote, "than to hear these beautiful verses chanted by sonorous voices in this open desert country, round the evening fire, with nothing to disturb the sound, which softly reverberated from the slope of the sandy downs opposite. A Christian must have been a witness to such scenes in order to treat with justice the Mohammedans and their creed."

Though Barth enjoyed the sheikh's invigorating intellectual company, al-Bakkay was often unavailable, either plotting strategies or enmeshed in family life. He had only one wife and no concubines. "I can scarcely imagine that there is in Europe a person more sincerely attached to his wife and children than my host was," wrote Barth, undermining the European stereotype of the lascivious African Arab.

In mid-November events accelerated. Another messenger arrived from Hamdallahi with a direct order for the sheikh: Hand over the Christian. Al-Bakkay ignored it. On November 17 more messengers from Hamdallahi entered the city carrying the same message. The Berabish tribe that had murdered Laing also took an oath to kill Barth. On the last day of November, while Barth was at the tents, news arrived that a troop from Hamdallahi had come to Timbuktu with orders to take Barth dead or alive. He slept that night with his pistols tucked into his sash.

The next afternoon at two o'clock thirteen armed men rode toward the tents. Barth gathered his weapons—a double-barreled rifle, three pistols, and a sword—and went outside. There he met the sheikh, holding his new Colt six-shooter. Barth kneeled and aimed his rifle. The horsemen pulled up. Their leader shouted that he had a letter from the emir for the sheikh. Al-Bakkay shouted that he would receive it in town and warned them not to come any closer. After conferring, they wheeled back toward Timbuktu.

Later that day the sheikh and Barth returned to town. The next morning a messenger delivered the emir's latest unvarying order: Give up the Christian and all his property. Al-Bakkay was as irritated by the messenger's low birth as by the letter's high-handed tone. A similar letter went to the Fulani governor. Another, addressed to the people of Timbuktu, was read aloud at the Great Mosque of Djingereber. It threatened to punish them if they didn't seize Barth or allowed him to escape.

The townspeople now expected violence. Barth could hear gunfire all over the city as people tested their weapons. The Moroccan merchants sensed an opportunity to look altruistic while protecting their self-interest. They had been scheming against Barth since his arrival. They didn't want British merchants cutting into their business. They now advised the sheikh to abandon the Christian for the sake of the city.

The crisis distressed Barth—not for himself but because of the turmoil he was causing. He had hoped to visit and investigate Hamdallahi, and to befriend the emir for Britain. He regretted that Timbuktu and his friend al-Bakkay were now threatened because of his presence.

The sheikh reacted differently. Timbuktu was his city and Barth was his guest—a sacred responsibility. He had been sidestepping the emir for two months, but the despotic letter stung him into boldness, perhaps boosted by his expectation that the great Tuareg chief would soon arrive with reinforcements. Al-Bakkay replied to the emir with a long defiant poem that alternately defended Barth and chided Ahmadu Ahmadu, sometimes cuttingly.

"Tell the host of the Fulan," it began, "—I say, shameful! I am attacked in a great and weighty matter. Ye have sought my guest . . . the free guest of a free man. . . . My guest is my honor." He rebuked the emir for being ignorant of the laws of Islam, unlike the very man he wanted to fetter and plunder. He mocked the emir, in meter, for acting as if this solitary stranger far from home posed a threat: "Really, my astonishment is unlimited." He continued, with the cultural disdain of "white" Arab-Africans for black Africans, "No daughter nor son of Ham was my parent, nor will I obey the sons of the lazy Ham." Barth had come from a country at peace with Muslim nations, noted the sheikh, and he had already traveled unharmed through many Islamic lands. So how dare Ahmadu Ahmadu declare war on this man and his nation when the emir was nothing but "a simple chief, a ruler of huts at the extremity of West Africa."

This letter bomb left for Hamdallahi on December 2.

THE FOREIGN OFFICE had completely lost touch with its solitary explorer. The plans hatched for Barth in London and Tripoli seemed rational but were utterly unconnected to his reality. For instance, Britain's plans to explore the Benue River. Barth's letters about reaching the Benue in mid-1851 got to London in early 1853. In them Barth strongly recommended that Britain mount an expedition up the Niger River and the Benue, to open the heart of Africa to British trade.

This started a flurry of letters between the Foreign Office and the Admiralty. Lord Clarendon, the foreign secretary, wanted an expedition to leave as soon as possible. The Admiralty, still stinging from criticism of the deadly Niger excursion of 1841, agreed to an expedition but insisted on thorough preparation. In June 1853, Clarendon dispatched the news to Barth that a steamer would be leaving for the Benue in a year's time. Clarendon asked Barth to find a native who knew the river, and to have this guide meet the boat at the confluence of the Niger and the Benue. And, he added, please try to induce the regional chiefs to leave stacks of wood for fuel at intervals along the riverbank.

These absurd requests demonstrate how ignorant the Foreign Office was not only about Barth's location, but about African realities and geography, and about what was feasible for a solitary European traveling in unknown Islamic Africa. When Clarendon wrote these instructions, Barth had almost reached the Niger at Say. By the time the explorer received them in December 1854, the boat had already steamed from Britain to the Niger and up the Benue, and was almost back to England.

Similarly, in late August 1853, Consul Herman in Tripoli got a letter from Barth written in Katsina nearly six months earlier. Herman informed Clarendon of this message and wrote that he hoped Barth would get the dispatch about the approach of his new assistant, Vogel, and would turn back to Kukawa to meet him. In fact, Barth was about to enter Timbuktu. "He has not given me the slightest insight into his movements or plans," complained Herman to Clarendon.

In November 1853, Herman was still in the dark. "I regret that I am unable to convey to your Lordship any positive intelligence of Dr. Barth," he wrote to Clarendon. Herman was reduced to reporting guesses and rumors. He noted that a caravan that might have carried dispatches from Barth had been plundered by Tuaregs. The native grapevine put Barth in Sokoto in July. (He had been there in April, and by July was beyond the Niger.) Herman hoped that his letters would reach Barth before he got too far west. But he was already there.

AT ABOUT THE same time that Herman was writing to Clarendon, Barth started a letter to Chevalier Bunsen about his situation in Timbuktu. After mentioning the various death threats ("I hope they will not succeed"), he added that he had nevertheless been working hard. He enclosed a long dissertation about towns and villages along his route, with the etymologies of their names. He included a list of tribes and their subdivisions. He wrote about the principal places of an ancient people called the Tombo. He added extracts, copied from the old manuscript in Gwandu, about the history of the Songhai kingdom. He sent precise routes and a detailed map.

After pages and pages of this he turned to new developments in his own situation, including the standoff with the thirteen riders at the tents and the recent ultimatum from Ahmadu. He noted that this ultimatum included an escape clause: if Barth could prove that he was protected by the sultan of Istanbul, Ahmadu would let him go, but if he was "merely the envoy of a Christian prince," he must die. Barth complained bitterly, again, that a simple letter of transit from Istanbul, which he had often requested from the Foreign Office, could save his life but had never arrived.

Before leaving Kukawa, Barth had written the Foreign Office and the British vice-consul at Ghadames, Dickson, asking for letters of credit and support to be sent ahead along his planned route to Timbuktu. Now he informed Bunsen that he had recently gotten a few lines from Dickson (written in mid-June, delivered in early December). But "it is very much to be regretted," wrote Barth, "that W. Dickson has sent me here but a very *insufficient credit*, upon which I have hardly got the value of ten dollars. Like men in a leaking ship, I rather throw over board [i. e., sell] every thing not absolutely indispensable, scientific and unscientific, to get away from these raging waves. . . ."

He added that because violence and mayhem were seething in every quarter outside Timbuktu, his possible routes home had been whittled down to one: "I must go back by the long road which brought me"— roughly 2,700 miles. He hoped that when the new year of 1854 dawned in less than a month, he would be gone from Timbuktu. "And may the end of next year bring me once more to Europe," he wrote in closing. "Here nothing is to be depended on. Merciful God protect me."

26
Stuck

W HEN BARTH WAS PREPARING TO LEAVE KUKAWA, HE DIDN'T know which route he might take home from the Niger. His main options: 1,400 miles north through the Sahara to Morocco, 1,200 miles west to the Atlantic, 1,000 miles south to the Gulf of Guinea. He tried to prepare for each possibility by writing letters to Britain's African consulates for any help they could provide. To cover the Moroccan route, for instance, he wrote to the consul in Tangier, Drummond Hay. He asked Hay to solicit letters of recommendation and safe passage from the sultan of Morocco, and perhaps from important merchants, and to forward them to Timbuktu. Barth's letter from Kukawa, dated October 16, 1852, reached Tangier on April 21, 1853.

Hay immediately wrote to Lord Clarendon in London and to Consul Herman in Tripoli that he would not write to the sultan on Barth's behalf. "For by doing so," he explained, "I should probably seal the hard fate of the poor wanderer." Hay reminded them that the last European who attempted the route between Morocco and Timbuktu, the British doctor John Davidson in 1836, had carried a protective letter from the sultan. Yet Davidson had been murdered in southern Morocco, almost certainly on the sultan's orders, and probably at the insistence of Tangier's merchants. The Moorish powers, wrote Hay, would take any measure to protect their lucrative trade with Timbuktu in gold and ivory.

"No Moor can understand that a European gentleman would expose his life for scientific purposes or to solve a problem in Geography," wrote Hay. "They take it for granted the object of the Christian or his Government is to get information on Trade and thus in their ignorance conclude it would be made use of to their prejudice." Thus a request from the British government to protect Barth would be his death warrant. Hay was probably right. Barth later felt this suspicious hostility from the scheming Moorish merchants in Timbuktu, which contributed to his decision not to return home by the Moroccan route.

Hay did what he could. He asked the British vice-consul at Mogador (Essaouira), 400 miles down the Atlantic coast, to find someone trustworthy who was going to Timbuktu and could take Barth in hand. He also placed £200 at the vice-consul's disposal to assist Barth or to pay his ransom if he was kidnapped or enslaved instead of killed.

Barth remained unaware of these strategies and subsidies. In Timbuktu he complained in his journal that the Foreign Office hadn't sent him the requested letter of transit from the sultan of Morocco. What he called negligence was actually concern, and perhaps helped save his life.

AFTER THE EMIR'S ULTIMATUM and the sheikh's stinging response, Timbuktu tensed, its opposing forces expecting an explosion. In early December two groups of Tuaregs arrived, 100 fighting men. They considered Timbuktu a Tuareg town and would support the sheikh against the Fulanis. In a fiery speech that same day at the Djingereber mosque, the city's Fulani judge exhorted the crowd to attack the Christian and his allies—al-Bakkay, the Tuaregs, and the city's governor. A friend of the governor, who knew the judge for a cowardly blowhard, stood up and urged him to lead them into battle right then. When the judge hemmed and hawed, the crowd dispersed.

Meanwhile the Tuaregs were having second thoughts. Fighting for Timbuktu against their old enemies was one thing, fighting for an infidel quite another. In several encounters their chiefs accused Barth of false beliefs, such as not acknowledging Muhammed as the only prophet.

They had stepped into Barth's intellectual wheelhouse. He replied that even Muslims did not consider Muhammed the only prophet—they honored Moses, Jesus, and many other holy men also revered by Christians. And in one crucial way, he reminded his accusers, Islam gave pride of place to Jesus, teaching that Jesus, not Muhammed, would return at the end of the world. We worship the same God and follow the same religious principles, argued Barth, despite "a few divergencies in point of diet and morals." So it seemed to him, he concluded, "that we were nearer to each other than [they] thought, and might well be friends, offering to each other those advantages which each of us commanded."

This was not only rhetorically masterful but characteristic of Barth's open-mindedness. His reasoning usually won over the Tuaregs. In stubborn cases he fascinated them with scholarship: the etymology of their tribal name, historic accounts of their ancient dwelling places, maps of Africa and Arabia. And of course his theology and scholarship were always sweetened with gifts. His disarming acumen didn't make the Tuaregs any more trustworthy in the long run, but did secure their momentary respect and loyalty, desperately needed.

On December 9, Barth and the sheikh went back to the tents with their Tuareg allies. The following day a party of twenty-five riders approached from Timbuktu. The delegation was peaceful and made two requests: Give us a copy of the Christian's letter of protection from the sultan of Istanbul, and don't bring the infidel back into town. Al-Bakkay agreed to show them copies of letters written on Barth's behalf by several Muslim rulers, but rejected the second demand. To emphasize his autonomy, he took Barth back to Timbuktu later that day.

Another week of stalemate passed. Ahmadu threatened to cut off Timbuktu's supply of corn unless Barth was forced from the city. The governor left for Hamdallahi to discuss the impasse. At the same time, the son of the Berabish chief who had murdered Laing suddenly died. The superstitious people of Timbuktu took this as an omen, since Barth was rumored to be Laing's son. The Berabish clan that had sworn to kill Barth recanted its oath. These developments lowered the city's political temperature. The emissaries from Hamdallahi seemed satisfied to await Ahmadu's response to al-Bakkay's defiant letter.

Christmas came and went. On December 26, al-Bakkay jauntily assured Barth of his pending departure and showed him the healthy camels they would take. But the explorer had lost faith in these declarations.

The new year turned. "I had long cherished the hope," wrote Barth, "that the beginning of 1854 would have found mè far advanced on my homeward journey; but greatly disappointed in this expectation, I began the year with a fervent prayer for a safe return home in the course of it."

BACK IN TOWN, Barth was cheered by the arrival in the market of good dates, tea and sugar, and "the luxury of a couple of pomegranates." During his first months he had eaten pigeons almost every day. Sometimes at the tents there would be roasted goat or ostrich eggs. Then as now, Timbuktu was known for its delicious flatbread, baked every morning in tall egg-shaped ovens made of clay. Barth typically ate this bread with milk for breakfast, had some couscous at about two in the afternoon, and after sunset ate a dish of millet sauced with squash and bits of meat. All of it came from the sheikh, who also sent another dish late, often after midnight, which Barth considered excessive and gave to his servants.

When the flooding Niger reached its apex in early January, Barth lobbied the sheikh for another excursion to see it and measure it. The river almost licked the city's walls. Boatmen unloaded their goods within 500 yards of the Djingereber mosque. Creeks streamed over the Sahara, "a marvelous and delightful spectacle." The journey invigorated Barth but also stirred up the Moorish merchants, who spread the rumor that he had been looking for British gunboats coming upriver from Gao.

Three days later Barth was back at the tents. His health, though still precarious, had improved. But on January 14 he suddenly crumpled with the worst fever of the journey, accompanied by violent shivering. Al-Bakkay suspected poison. Barth had just drunk some sour milk given to him by a Berabish man, an intimate friend of the sheikh's but also a member of the clan that had murdered Laing. It speaks volumes that al-Bakkay immediately assumed this man had put clan and religious fervor above old friendship.

Barth didn't think the milk caused his illness, but the man had been acting surly, unsatisfied with Barth's gift to him. Bad-tempered from acute illness, Barth lashed out at him—"I ordered him away in a very unceremonious manner." So unceremonious that even his own servants and friends among the sheikh's entourage, "without paying any regard to my feeble state, gave vent to their feelings against me as a Christian"— another reaction that speaks volumes. Only al-Bakkay didn't waver, sending Barth tea and visiting often to check his condition. The explorer felt better the next morning. His friends came to his tent one by one to apologize. If Barth did the same to the Berabish man, he didn't record it.

The pendulum continued its slow swing between the town and the tents. Barth's patience was thinning. He kept preparing to depart and pressing the sheikh for a date. The answer never changed—soon.

January turned to February, "with utter disappointment at the failure of my expected departure, and with nothing but empty promises." When he accused the sheikh of not keeping his word, al-Bakkay replied with a smile, well, if a person has only one fault . . .

The sheikh said he couldn't leave until his brothers arrived, until the Tuareg chief arrived—always some excuse. Under Barth's relentless pressure, in early February al-Bakkay finally leveled with the explorer and confessed that the delay wasn't caused by politics but by his wife's pregnancy—he didn't want to leave until she gave birth, in perhaps a month. He begged for Barth's understanding. Barth sighed and agreed, having no other choice.

Another troop of armed men arrived from Hamdallahi. More were

expected soon. They carried an edict from Ahmadu: a tax of 2,000 shells
on each slave in Timbuktu. One way or another, the emir was determined to bring the sheikh and the city to heel.

Near midnight on February 16 the sheikh's big drum announced
the approach of his older brother Sidi Muhammed. Al-Bakkay wanted
Muhammed to watch over the family's interests in Timbuktu while he
accompanied Barth on the first part of his journey. Sidi Muhammed,
like his brother, was cheerful and sociable, but also martial and com-
manding. He clearly doubted the wisdom of al-Bakkay's stance and
questioned Barth sharply. Barth didn't take offense. He acknowledged
that he was a stranger, a foreigner, a Christian, and a big problem.

BARTH USED THE following ten-day lull to put together another thick
packet for Europe, addressed to Vice-Consul Dickson in Ghadames. On
February 26 he entrusted it to some merchants going north. He didn't
know that Dickson had left Ghadames for the war in Crimea. The packet
languished in Ghadames, with lamentable consequences that Barth
didn't learn about for months.

The day was unlucky for him in another way, too, but this one was
instantly clear. A large troop of armed men, including 10 musketeers,
entered town under the command of Ahmadu's fierce uncle. They delib-
erately marched past Barth's house to intimidate him. In response, the
explorer opened his door to display his firearms and the men ready to
use them. The incident unnerved one of Barth's men, who quit.

The next day things darkened. Another troop of 100 men arrived
from Hamdallahi bearing two letters for the sheikh, one friendly, the
other threatening reprisals if Barth wasn't thrown out. The three Kunta
brothers discussed their options. After spending time with Barth, Sidi
Muhammed had agreed to help protect him, though grudgingly. This
was reflected in the lukewarm defense of Barth that he wrote that night
to the delegation from Hamdallahi. His main argument: Barth wasn't

any worse an infidel than Laing. Barth noted that this would allow his opponents to reply that the current infidel wouldn't be treated any worse than the previous one, who had been murdered.

A messenger from Ahmadu came to the sheikh's house with the same unchanging demand. Again, al-Bakkay replied that Barth was his guest and therefore under his protection. Consequently the only choices were honorable peace or war. The messenger retorted that the second option was more likely. Events again seemed to be coming to a head.

Barth went home "to refresh myself with a cup of tea, and then made preparations for the eventual defense of my house, and for hiding the more valuable of my effects." He returned to al-Bakkay's around midnight and found the sheikh holding a double-barreled gun, surrounded by 40 men armed with spears and muskets. For the rest of the night the sheikh entertained the group with stories about Moses and the life of the Prophet. At five o'clock Barth went home "and endeavored to raise my exhausted spirits by means of some coffee."

The emissary from Hamdallahi rode into town that morning with 60 men but didn't approach the sheikh's quarter. By that time more than 200 defenders had gathered at al-Bakkay's house. Despite the posturing, neither side seemed keen on fighting. After another conference that evening between the Kunta brothers, Sidi Alawate was dispatched to probe the emissary's intentions.

The sheikh came to Barth's house after midnight with surprising news. Only one of the recent letters—the friendly one—had been written by Ahmadu. The threatening letter had been written in Kabara at the insistence of the Moorish merchants. Al-Bakkay had assured the emissary that if Ahmadu stepped back, Barth would leave Timbuktu soon—even sooner, he added cheekily, if Ahmadu would pay for the departure with public funds.

But al-Bakkay was sugarcoating the facts. The next day the emissary came to the sheikh's house and accused Barth of being a war chief and a freebooter who must leave immediately. Luckily for Barth and al-Bakkay, 60 warriors from the Kel Ulli, a ferocious tribe of Tuaregs allied with the sheikh, arrived that afternoon "with great military demonstrations and beating of shields." The Kel Ullis were infamous for "totally annihilating" two other powerful Tuareg tribes. They were distinguished, wrote Barth, "by three qualities which, to the European, would scarcely seem possible to be united in the same person, but which are not infrequently found combined" in Tuaregs: valor, thievishness, and hospitality. In his vocabulary of Tamasheq words and phrases, Barth used this illustrative sentence: "The Kel-ulli are expert in stealing." They were welcome allies, but volatile. Barth saw them as the perfect escort to whisk him from Timbuktu.

He had started a letter to Bunsen about these incidents, adding to it as events developed. Written in the stress of the moment, his letters reveal far more impatience than the cooler version in his book. "Though entirely innocent," he wrote to Bunsen, "I shall be the pretended and alleged cause of great revolutions in this stupid little city of the desert. If I were not a quiet man, with my whole mind turned to scientific acquisitions, and to a happy return home, I should very likely be able to set up for the petty dictatorship of Timbuktu. On the other hand, these annoyances, and (as yet, at least) bloodless quarrels afford me some amusement, for these continual disappointments about my departure wholly unfit me for study."

Several days later, after the arrival of the Kel Ullis, he added to the letter that he expected to leave soon with them. "But I do not yet give way to joy, for the cup may be snatched from my lips a thousand times before I taste it. I study quietly, and wait, and keep on my guard; for I always have to expect deception. . . . In short, I hope for the best, and prepare for the worst."

THE CUP WAS snatched away. Al-Bakkay, still a father-to-be, dillydallied. Three days later, on March 4, this excuse disappeared when the sheikh's wife gave birth. Al-Bakkay assured Barth that they would leave in three days. The explorer wanted to believe him but couldn't. Sure enough, the very next day al-Bakkay decided to wait for the arrival of the Tuaregs' main chief and his warriors, who were said to be approaching. People in the vicinity began moving their flocks far way to save them from these marauders.

On March 7 another Kunta brother, 'Abidin, entered Timbuktu and racheted up the tension. 'Abidin opposed al-Bakkay's protection of Barth. He chose to lodge with Hammadi, their nephew and al-Bakkay's enemy. This instigated a quarrel between al-Bakkay and his older brother Sidi Muhammed. Barth listened quietly. Like the explorer, Sidi Muhammed had lost patience with al-Bakkay's stalling. Why didn't he defuse the situation by leaving town with the Christian? And why, asked Sidi Muhammed, should they fight the entire Fulani kingdom for the sake of a single person, especially an infidel? Al-Bakkay, master of procrastination, dodged the question by promising to send for Barth's horses the following day, in preparation for departure.

Things seemed to be coming to yet another head. Barth went home and finished packing so he could leave on quick notice. In a continuation of his letter to Bunsen, he noted that 'Abidin's arrival might force al-Bakkay into action. He also inserted a map of the countries south of the middle course of the Niger, then unknown to Europeans, and asked Bunsen to correct a small portion of a map sent previously. He spent a paragraph summarizing his scholarly disagreement with Cooley's placement of the ancient capital of Ghana. Lastly he attached the subdivisions of the powerful tribe El Aarib. All this while unsure of his fate.

The next day Sidi Muhammed and Sidi Alawate went to confer about Barth with their brother 'Abidin and nephew Hammadi. The explorer was kept in the dark about their discussion. That afternoon al-Bakkay made his own visit to 'Abidin and half-promised (his specialty) to depart with the Christian in two days, on March 10. The sheikh was trying to buy time until the great Tuareg chief arrived. He evidently still hoped to use this force to fight for Timbuktu's independence from Hamdallahi.

March 10 arrived. The Kunta clan repaired to the tents, not in preparation for a journey but to celebrate the birth of al-Bakkay's son. Five oxen were slaughtered for a supper that began after midnight. "Nothing during my stay in Timbuktu was more annoying to me, and more injurious to my health," wrote Barth, "than this unnatural mode of living, which surpasses in absurdity the late hours of London and Paris." Considering what his stay had been like, the statement is flabbergasting. Two more cows were slaughtered the next day. Crowds of people came to feast on enormous dishes of rice and meat, some of them five feet in diameter, and so heavy that six men hoisted them. The celebration featured the usual displays of horsemanship and gunfire. Some of the Berabish guests carried new double-barreled guns bought in the north from the French, whose designs on the territory south of their toehold in Algeria had started to alarm al-Bakkay.

Barth described the festivities and chatted up the interesting guests. He tried to enjoy himself, but he was twitching with exasperation at the interminable delays. He grumped about being separated from his books and his morning coffee, and about the choking clouds of wind-blown dust.

On March 15 he started a letter to Lord Clarendon by noting that he had sent two packets of considerable scientific importance, including maps. He hadn't written the foreign secretary earlier, he said, "as I did not like to entertain Your Lordship with a detail of my hopes and fears. . . . I have preserved my life and liberty during my stay in this place merely with a loaded gun in my hand and a pair of loaded pistols in my girdle; else I would have fallen a sacrifice to the intrigues of hostile men long ago."

THEY HAD BEEN back in town for three days when yet another crisis arose. At a raucous meeting the Moorish merchants and the Fulanis from Hamdallahi swore an oath to drive Barth from Timbuktu before sunset. If the infidel defied them, vowed Ahmadu's martial uncle, he would kill him with his own hands. At that point Sidi Alawate, who had crashed the meeting, stood to declare that Barth would see both sunset and sunrise in Timbuktu, but would leave tomorrow morning. And if he didn't, he was theirs to dispose of. Barth knew none of this. It was March 16.

Sidi Muhammed woke Barth before sunrise and instructed him to mount up and follow him. Barth wanted to wait for al-Bakkay, but Muhammed brusquely refused. Barth was leery but said nothing. "As a stranger," he wrote, "I could neither expect nor desire these people to fight on my account." He mounted his horse, fully armed.

Muhammed said they were going to the tomb of Mukhtar, the oldest of the Kunta brothers, on the town's outskirts. People peered at them from doorways as they passed through the brightening streets. Fulani horsemen began shadowing them but dropped off once they left town. Instead of going to the tomb, Muhammed led Barth to the tents.

Muhammed's attempt to avoid trouble incensed his brother. In midafternoon the sheikh sent an angry note to the tents asking Muhammed to return immediately, since the Fulanis were about to storm Barth's house and seize his goods. Muhammed, abashed, ordered the beating of the great drum to call together the camp's warriors. This troop, including Barth, galloped toward Timbuktu. They stopped to say the evening prayer, then approached the city in the dark. The Tuaregs beat their shields and yelled war cries. Barth fired a shot to give the sheikh their location. Al-Bakkay arrived with a large force that included Tuaregs, Arabs, Songhais, and some Fulanis. They were welcomed with a joyous song.

"The spectacle formed by this multifarious host," wrote Barth, "thronging among the sand-hills in the pale moonlight, was highly interesting, and would have been more so to me if I could have been a tranquil observer of the scene." Unfortunately, he added, he was "the chief cause of this disturbance."

Fearing treachery within the group, his friends warned him to stay in the midst of the Kel Ullis so he couldn't be stabbed in the dark. They edged toward the city, but war drums had also summoned the Fulani forces. The armies confronted each other across the night. Barth foresaw carnage if they tried to enter the city. "I protested repeatedly to the sheikh," he wrote, "that nothing was more repugnant to my feelings than that blood should be shed on my account, and perhaps his own life endangered."

Messengers galloped back and forth. A deal was struck: if the Fulanis didn't pillage Barth's house, al-Bakkay would keep the Christian outside the city. Under this fragile détente, the sheikh's forces turned back toward the tents. They got lost in a maze of creeks and didn't arrive until three o'clock in the morning, tired, cold, and hungry. "Such was the sole result of this night's campaign," wrote Barth.

THE FLOODWATERS OF the Niger had receded, leaving a patina of green vegetation near Timbuktu—and also millions of newly hatched insects. Worst were the big biting flies. They "almost drove me to despair," wrote Barth. His horse, Blast of the Desert, suffered so badly that Barth built fires so the animal could stand in the smoke. While Barth was stuck in camp, the sheikh continued to make excuses about leaving, so Barth took grim pleasure when his host visited one day and got bitten so viciously that he bled.

Four days after the armed standoff outside Timbuktu, the Kunta men gathered in hopes of resolving their differences. They met for lunch at the tomb of the oldest brother, Sidi Mukhtar. Sidi Muhammed, Sidi Alawate, al-Bakkay, and 'Abidin all came, along with their nephew, Hammadi, Mukhtar's son. Though Hammadi and 'Abidin were his sworn enemies, Barth was struck by their graciousness toward him. After lunch the family conferred for more than an hour, but disbanded hastily, which Barth took as a bad sign.

The next day, adding to his letter to Bunsen, Barth related all this and ended, "My thoughts are all towards home, where I must at all events stay some time to recover myself, before I can undertake any thing new. My return is long delayed."

Ahmadu hadn't forgotten about Barth or the insolence of al-Bakkay and Timbuktu. Instead of punishing the city with force, he turned again to a different weapon—taxes. This time he imposed a fine of 2,000 shells on every adult in Timbuktu for not saying their Friday prayers in the mosque. His agents also raided houses and confiscated many pounds of tobacco, an illegal pleasure. (Islamic scholars had been debating tobacco since the sixteenth century. Timbuktu had always been firmly protobacco, and the city's inhabitants enjoyed it with gusto. Tobacco became one of the town's important trade commodities. Timbuktu's most famous scholar, Ahmed Baba, wrote a treatise defending its use. When Hamdallahi outlawed it, al-Bakkay composed eloquent protests that irked the puritanical jihadists.)

At the tents Barth desperately turned his restless mind to anything that would keep him from going mad with tedium and bug bites. He complained so much about boredom that al-Bakkay sent a nephew to the tents so the explorer would have someone educated to talk to. The antics of the sheikh's young sons also entertained him. So did the Berabish tribesmen hanging about, who casually dropped the tantalizing information that there were letters for him in Azawad, about 150 miles north of Timbuktu. Aside from a brief note from the vice-consul of Ghadames in early December, he hadn't received a single line in English or German for nearly a year. The letters in Azawad gave another spur to his desire to escape Timbuktu.

The sheikh kept promising and delaying, partly out of concern about Ahmadu's maneuvers. The emir sent yet another delegation from Hamdallahi with orders to impose yet another levy. The merchants of Timbuktu pleaded with al-Bakkay not to go, fearful of what Ahmadu might do in his absence. Ahmadu fed these fears by sending a bigger peacemaking gift to Hammadi, the sheikh's enemy, than to the sheikh himself.

Barth was sick of these petty intrigues and postponements. He was also running out of goods and had to sell a broken musket to get cowrie shells to pay for his needs. Then on March 31 the sheikh had Barth's luggage brought to the tents. On April 3 the sheikh's provision bags arrived, followed over the next week by his books, horses, and several people who would be going on the trip. On April 11, al-Bakkay himself appeared. Barth allowed himself to hope.

Too soon. Another week passed before the sheikh finally gave the word. Even then, on the day of departure, al-Bakkay overslept as Barth paced. Once up, the sheikh indulged in a protracted goodbye to his beloved wife and sons. The caravan finally got underway at eleven o'clock.

It was April 19, 1854, more than seven months since Barth had entered Timbuktu. He was exhilarated to be traveling at last in the direction of home. He expected to reach Sokoto in forty or fifty days. "But I had no idea," he later wrote, "of the unfavorable circumstances which were gathering to frustrate my hopes."

27

Released, More or Less

Eduard Vogel, Overweg's replacement, reached Tripoli in March 1853. With Consul Herman's mother-hen help he began organizing a caravan for Kukawa. Herman had been appalled by Richardson's poor management and preparation. He was determined to prevent a similar debacle on his watch, as far as he was able. Under Herman's supervision, Vogel's list of provisions and gifts grew to cover many pages.

A promising astronomer and botanist, Vogel had trained at the University of Berlin and had been working at Bishop's Observatory in London. He was twenty-four years old. He didn't speak Arabic or any African languages and had never traveled outside Europe. Two soldiers from the Corps of Royal Sappers and Miners, James Church and Edward Sweeney, were assigned to him as assistants. Addington from the Foreign Office wrote to Lord Raglan, "How will English Sappers and Miners work under Germans without any Military Man to keep them straight?" The question was prescient.

Herman wrote Lord Clarendon that this trio were "absolute tyros." But the consul, never one to rest in optimism, quickly moved on to the gloomy downsides. He worried that Vogel was unsuited for an African expedition. "The slightest exposure to the sun so sensibly affects him," he wrote, "that I at times question if he will ever be able to accomplish the objects of his mission."

A few days later, his pessimism darkening, Herman began a letter to Clarendon, "Exploratory expeditions to Central Africa appear to be pursued by an unerring fatality." The tyro Sweeney had collapsed with fever and congestion of the lungs, liver, and spleen. Herman asked for a replacement, since he suspected that if anything happened to Corporal Church, which in his view was likely, Vogel couldn't reach Kukawa on his own. The German was amiable, zealous, and no doubt a superb astronomer, wrote Herman, but was also frail and "as helpless and inexperienced as a child." Sweeney's replacement, John Macguire, got to Tripoli in late July.

The caravan reached Kukawa in January 1854, around the time that Barth was wondering whether he'd been poisoned in Timbuktu. The next month Vogel began a letter to the Foreign Office with his customary exuberant greeting: "Sir!" in huge script, centered on the page. He reported that Sheikh Umar had warmly welcomed them, lodging them in Barth and Overweg's old quarters. The rest of his news was unsettling. No one in Kukawa had heard anything from Barth. Nor had the dispatches sent to Barth through Kukawa ever left the city—the vizier had not forwarded any of them to Kano or Sokoto for reasons of political intrigue. Worse, the supplies forwarded to Zinder for Barth's return trip from Timbuktu had been lost to pillagers, who also murdered the caravaneer. If Barth survived his journey west and turned back toward home, no resources awaited him.

Later that month Consul Herman wrote to Lord Clarendon with thrilling news: after a year of silence and mystery, dispatches had arrived from Barth. He was not only alive, he had made it to Timbuktu. But his situation was perilous. He hoped to leave soon and reach Kukawa by March—that is, next month. Herman planned to instruct Gagliuffi to send 800 Spanish dollars to Barth at the first opportunity. Once in Kukawa, continued Herman, Barth could hook up with Vogel and go south to meet the steamer on the Benue in July. (This would have surprised Barth. He knew nothing about a Benue expedition, and he had no intention of prolonging his stay in Africa.)

Barth had included a request from al-Bakkay for "a series of Arabic books," most on Islam, but also on history, medicine, poetry, and any other works of interest. The Foreign Office eventually approved the request and a box of books began making its way across Africa to the scholarly man who had saved Barth's life. Al-Bakkay owned an Arabic copy of Hippocrates given to him by the sultan of Sokoto, who had gotten it from Clapperton. Such books, wrote Barth, "have had a greater effect in reconciling the men of authority in Africa to the character of Europeans than the most costly present ever made to them."

BARTH'S EXHILARATION at escaping from Timbuktu soon turned to frustration. The sheikh moved at a turtle's pace, which then slowed, stalled, and stopped. Al-Bakkay was trying to mediate a dispute between two Tuareg tribes before a war erupted. The offending tribe was moving west toward Timbuktu. To preserve peace in the region, the sheikh needed to stick with the tribe. His diplomatic obligations conflicted with his pledge to Barth. Ten days after leaving Timbuktu, al-Bakkay turned the caravan back toward the city.

The retreat depressed Barth. It piled another delay on top of all the others. "My feelings may be more easily imagined than described," he wrote. "An immense amount of Job-like patience was required." The delay also complicated his journey—the rainy season was beginning, and the many rivers he needed to cross were rising. But he exercised his remarkable ability to observe a situation impersonally, calling the sheikh's decision "altogether right."

Al-Bakkay was also distracted by news that the French army had made a sortie to Ouargla (Wargla), about 400 miles south of Algiers. This inflamed fears that France intended to invade Tuat or even Timbuktu. Al-Bakkay was already worried about French ambitions in the western Sahara. That was partly why he wanted an alliance with Britain. Now he wondered whether he should rally the Tuaregs to attack. Barth advised against it since that would let France justify farther incursions, though he doubted that the French were interested in military ventures across the desert—another example of his naïvely unimperialistic thinking. But he did sign a letter, written by the sheikh and sent to the French consulate in Algiers, forbidding the French from penetrating any farther into the interior. When Barth left Europe, Britain and France had been rivals, almost enemies. But while he had been out of touch, the two countries had tiptoed into a delicate alliance, cemented by the Crimean War. This letter to Algiers eventually caused a small diplomatic commotion.

For almost a week the sheikh's small caravan crept back toward Timbuktu. Al-Bakkay mediated as they moved, but got nowhere with the Tuaregs. He didn't want to take Barth too close to the city, where animosity toward foreigners had been freshly stoked by the French rumors. He stopped the caravan several days outside Timbuktu and told Barth to wait there for his return. Barth worried that al-Bakkay's many distractions would keep him from coming back, but was reassured when he left behind his beloved cook.

Barth passed the time conversing with visitors from the Songhai villages and Tuareg tribes in the vicinity. They talked beneath the trees along the river or in Barth's tent, now four years old and so "mended and patched" that the original material had nearly disappeared. The topic was often religion. A troublesome Tuareg chief tried to incite the camp against Barth for being uncircumcised. Barth shut him down by pointing out that if circumcision was a mark of Islam, then all Jews and many pagans must be as holy as Muslims.

He was struck anew by the regal Tuareg men and their independent women. They were monogamous but free of jealousy, "and the degree of liberty which the women enjoy is astonishing." Barth grew fond of a young Tuareg named Kungu who expected to die young like his brothers. He mounted his horse by using his iron spear as a pole vault. One group of Tuaregs urged Barth to marry one of their daughters and join them.

Some of the older Tuaregs had seen Mungo Park descending the Niger. One of Barth's visitors described Park's odd boat and his straw hat and gloves. Another old chief had been wounded in the leg by a British bullet. Park's policy on his second expedition—when in doubt, shoot—had left corpses and bad feelings along the Niger. Laing feared for his life because of it, and may have been murdered partly in revenge for it. Barth admired Park but deplored his gun-happy policy. Because of it, some Tuaregs still considered all Europeans *tawakast*—wild beasts— a mirror image of European stereotypes about Africans.

Camping next to the river, Barth's group had to be alert for lions and especially crocodiles. Some of these monsters were 18 feet long. They ate two cattle and bit off a man's foot while the caravan waited for the sheikh.

Barth's group was camped near a Tuareg tribe which, by the rules of hospitality, had to provide food for the sheikh's students and servants— more than two dozen people. For nomads living close to the bone, these extra mouths were a hardship. After several days the hosts tried to escape early one morning, but the sheikh's party quickly packed and followed their meal ticket. The tribe no doubt joined Barth in yearning for the sheikh's return.

ON MAY 17 the camp learned that al-Bakkay was back from Timbuktu and waiting nearby. Barth's party found him sleeping under a caper bush. Their galloping horses didn't awaken him. "Such was the mild and inoffensive character of this man," wrote Barth, "in the midst of these warlike and lawless hordes."

When the sheikh woke up, he smiled at Barth and promised no more interruptions. He also handed him a packet of letters that had been sitting in Azawad for two months. "I can scarcely describe the intense delight I felt at hearing again from Europe," wrote Barth. He tore open two letters from Foreign Secretary Lord Russell and one from his successor Lord Clarendon, all written in February 1853. He got a letter from

Chevalier Bunsen and another from Consul Herman, but was extremely disappointed not to find anything from his family or friends. Yet the packet did include an *Athenaeum* from early 1853 and ten *Gaglignani's Messengers*, an English-language newspaper printed in Paris. Sitting in his ragged tent, he devoured this old news from home, so wonderful to read in the heart of Africa.

WITHIN A FEW DAYS they passed the place they had reached on the first aborted attempt. Barth started to believe they were truly launched. He felt released, psychologically as well as physically, and expressed his joy in the manner of a happy scientist—in a torrent of observation, description, detail, and data. Every tree, bush, and berry got its due—figs, kapoks, broom, caper bushes, doum palms. The caravan was slogging through a network of creeks and swamps that laced the northern bank of the Niger. Some of them were choked with water lilies. The landscape gave Barth ample opportunity to use one of his favorite words: labyrinth.

The damp triggered his rheumatism, but the trade-offs were worth it. After climbing spines of land, they could often glimpse the Niger, dotted with boats, hippos, cattle. Whenever possible Barth set up his tent to overlook the river, "which had now almost become a second home to me, and with its many backwaters, islands, and cliffs, afforded me a never-failing source of interest."

They passed many villages and Tuareg encampments. Barth catalogued their names, subdivisions, numbers, and livestock. He described the Songhai villages' crops of wheat and tobacco, their dikes for irrigating rice fields, their butter and milk, the names of their wells. He marveled at Tosaye, where the broad Niger takes a sharp turn south and gets squeezed into a gorge only 150 yards wide.

He took side trips into history and etymology. At Bourmen he ruminated on the old legend that an Egyptian Pharaoh once reached this obscure place 2,200 miles from the Nile Delta. He decided the story might hold some truth. Another spot on the river was famous as the place where Tuareg women had held out their bare breasts to beg mercy from attackers from a clan of relatives, the gesture meant to remind the raiders that these breasts had suckled their blood kin; the gesture was in vain.

As always, the chief attractions were the people. At Bamba he met descendants of the Arma (or Ruma), the ruthless musketeers sent by the sultan of Morocco at the end of the sixteenth century to conquer and occupy the region of Timbuktu. The occupiers had intermarried with the natives and fallen from power, but their scraggly descendants still distinguished themselves by wearing a band of red cloth in their head-shawls.

Barth was beguiled by the daughter of a Tuareg chief, "one of the finest women that I saw in that country." She noticed his admiration and half-joked that they should marry. Barth said he would gladly take her away, if only he had a camel strong enough to carry her: "her person rather inclined to corpulency, which is highly esteemed by the Tawarek." He gave her a mirror, "which I was always accustomed to give to the most handsome woman in an encampment, the rest receiving nothing but needles." Later in the journey this policy caused trouble in one camp when the women began vying for the award and Barth gave it to one of the competitors' daughters.

(His brief dalliance with the plump Tuareg beauty had a coda. In 1896 a Frenchman named Lieutenant Hourst started down the Niger from Timbuktu. Because the region's people esteemed Barth's memory, Hourst told everyone he was the explorer's nephew, which often helped him out of sticky situations. At one point on the Niger Bend he was stalled by an old Tuareg chief. While waiting, Hourst learned that the pretty woman who had charmed Barth was still alive and living nearby. Hourst immediately asked to meet his "uncle's" old crush, but she happened to be away. He sent warm greetings and a folding mirror "to the lady who might have been my aunt if she had not been so fat, or if Barth's camels had been better able to carry heavy loads." She turned out to be the sister of the recalcitrant chief, who was so pleased with Hourst's flattery that he not only let him go but provided him with guides. "My dear 'uncle'! my brave 'uncle'! my providential 'uncle'!" wrote Hourst, "—yet once again had you drawn a sharp thorn from the foot of your nephew when the happy thought occurred to you of relating your love affair with a daughter of the Kel es Suk.")

THE CARAVAN PROGRESSED slowly around the Niger's lazy curve. The sheikh was using the trip to barnstorm, glad-handing every Tuareg chief and village chief along the route. He was also fond of sleeping late. Barth called it "sham traveling" and bit his tongue with frustration. "As if I was destined to spend my whole life in this region," ran one typical entry, "we this day only moved on three miles." But the slow pace did allow Barth to observe everything closely and to lay down the river's course precisely. (According to Hourst, al-Bakkay traveled so slowly partly because he was defusing death threats against Barth along the way, though Barth never knew this.) To cover the 100 miles between Bamba and Gao, the ancient capital of the Songhai empire, took four weeks.

Old texts called Gao "the most splendid city of Negroland," with a circumference of six miles. Now it was a miserable dump, 300 huts surrounded by rubbish and swamp. The heat and humidity were staggering and unhealthy. Barth was eager to push on. This was the place where he and al-Bakkay had agreed to part.

The explorer put his papers in order and wrote letters. He wanted to send off copies of his notes and the route from Timbuktu to Gao "in case of any mischance befalling myself." The legs of his writing table had broken off, so he wrote with a board across his knees. "It is impossible for me," he wrote in a letter to Lord Clarendon, "to praise in too strong terms the kindness hospitality and steadfast protection which the Sheikh El Bakay has bestowed upon me during my long stay in these quarters." He urged Clarendon to take advantage of al-Bakkay's preference for the British over the French by sending merchants soon. He praised the decision to send Vogel but added that it would be some time before they could meet, and he quashed the idea of joining Vogel in another expedition:

> . . . by my protracted stay in these countries, by constant exertion & want of proper food, but perhaps more than all by anxiety the greatest enemy of the African traveller I have been debilitated in such a degree, that I find it absolutely necessary to visit Europe before I shall be able to undertake something so eminently difficult. Indeed I must thank God if I reach home in safety, for my way is still a long one.

The packet he gave al-Bakkay to send from Timbuktu included letters for the Foreign Office, the Royal Geographical Society, and many friends. It didn't reach Europe until 1857, having spent more than two years in Ghadames.

The lull before parting was bittersweet. Barth and his friends from Timbuktu had grown fond of each other. In the mornings, as he took the air outside his tent, they gathered around him for conversation. One morning they asked him to read aloud from his European books, for the sound of the languages. He read the Bible in Greek and some passages in English, and recited a poem in German—the latter a big hit because "the full heavy words of that language" reminded them of their own. Another day they asked him to put on his European clothing, so he dug out his black suit. They admired the fine cloth and the trousers but found the frock coat comical. In Central Africa, wrote Barth, they were right.

As their time left together grew short, he and the sheikh continued their genial wide-ranging talks. They had been almost constant companions for nine-and-a-half months. Finally the day arrived when Barth was to cross the river and continue his journey home. His entry for July 9:

This was the day when I had to separate from the person whom, among all the people with whom I had come in contact in the course of my long journey, I esteemed the most highly, and whom, in all but his dilatory habits and phlegmatic indifference, I had found a most excellent and trustworthy man. I had lived with him for so long a time in daily intercourse, and in the most turbulent circumstances, sharing all his perplexities and anxieties, that I could not but feel the parting very severely.

Barth esteemed al-Bakkay, but couldn't resist pointing out his flaws. The explorer sometimes judged the sheikh a timid procrastinator, but that seems unfair, considering the violent forces he had to balance. He risked his life by defying Ahmadu Ahmadu. He outmaneuvered not only the emir, but enemies in Timbuktu, including scheming members of his own family, while also dealing with constant threats from bellicose Tuaregs. He was also kind, generous, loyal, open-minded, and invigorating company. Because of him, Barth survived Timbuktu.

When he reached the opposite bank of the Niger, Barth fired two shots in farewell, as al-Bakkay had requested. Then he turned and began jotting notes about the sandy downs of this new shore, and the paths that led away from the river toward the east.

28

Rumors and Consequences

After separating from al-Bakkay, Barth quickened the pace. No more leisurely mornings or layovers, no more short days. Barth roused his people early and pushed them to do at least 15 miles a day. One morning, to slow him down, they hid a camel behind some bushes and told him it was missing, but he found it and got everybody moving. Their first goal was Say, the port town where Barth had crossed the Niger more than year earlier.

They stayed wet. If they weren't crossing creeks and bogs, they were getting drenched by rainstorms. Barth's fever and rheumatism kicked up, and he dosed himself with medicine. Their guide left them and his replacement didn't show up. Barth, impatient, pushed on anyway. Because of the river's loops and back channels, they sometimes got lost or hit deep impassable streams and had to backtrack. One day, disoriented in a maze of channels, they ran into a group of farmers who set them straight and also offered to share their meager meal—each of them carried a ball of pounded millet and some curdled milk. Barth gave them needles. They parted after reciting together the opening prayer of the Qur'an.

Barth wrote down mile-by-mile descriptions of the river, noting places where navigation would be obstructed by rapids, narrows, or large rocks. As landmarks, he listed the names of villages, whether thriving or abandoned, and mapped his route. He was writing for the British merchants that he expected to follow him.

Hippos and crocodiles were common, and sometimes frightened their animals. One day a blizzard of locusts flew into their faces, a sign of fertile regions ahead. Fields of corn and rice appeared. Villages became more frequent. More people meant more risk of thievery, so Barth began firing his gun at night in warning. But his group was also able to eat better, trading for grains, milk, and meat. "Nothing renders people in these countries so communicative," he wrote, "and, at the same time, allays their suspicions so much, as a little trading."

Everywhere they stopped, people visited, seeking presents or medicine or conversation with the foreigner. Barth was surprised that so many people knew all about his stay in Timbuktu and the events there. Occasionally one of al-Bakkay's people entertained visitors by reading the satiric poem sent by the sheikh to Ahmadu Ahmadu.

About 100 miles upriver from Say, Barth heard the Hausa salute and was offered one of his favorite foods, fura, a drink made of water mixed with millet flour and powdered sour cheese. These things, he wrote, signified Hausaland and "transported me once more into a region for which I had contracted a great predilection."

A few nights later they heard war drums close by, so they broke camp before dawn and continued toward Say. They reached the town on July 29, thirteen months since Barth first stood on the banks of the Niger. The governor was lame with rheumatism, so Barth gave him some medicine. In gratitude, the governor gave Barth a small piece of sugar, "a great treat to me, as I had long been deprived of this luxury."

He briefly considered continuing down the Niger to the sea. "But such an undertaking was entirely out of the question," he wrote, "on account of the exhausted state of my means, the weak condition of my health, and the advanced stage of the rainy season, which made it absolutely necessary for me to reach Sokoto as soon as possible." After three days in Say, he left the Niger and started overland.

Though the route was familiar, the landscape had been transformed

by rain. Landmarks had vanished behind lush vegetation. Barren plains
had become fields of swaying millet. Insects were flourishing as well—
fleas, hairy ants, and especially mosquitoes. A typical complaint from
this part of the journey: "Owing to the number of [mosquitoes], repose
was quite out of the question."

One aspect of the region remained unchanged—devastation caused
by war. Barth passed villages thriving a year ago but now abandoned.
The desolate scenes revived his anger about the region's rulers, Sultan
Khalilu of Gwandu and Sultan Aliyu of Sokoto, "both of whom were
accelerating the ruin of their nation."

On August 9 at a village midway between Say and Gwandu, Barth
confirmed a rumor heard from the governor of Say: Sheikh Umar of
Bornu had been deposed by his brother, and the vizier Haj Beshir was
dead. The news dismayed Barth but didn't surprise him. The vizier's
greed and strong influence over Umar had made him many enemies in
Bornu. 'Abd er-Rahman, Umar's martial brother, was first among them.
He had once asked Barth for poison, with an obvious target.

The coup had occurred the previous November. Barth later learned
the details: Anger about the vizier's high-handed ways was threatening to become violent, so Umar ordered a curfew and put the vizier in
charge of enforcing it. The vizier's men immediately rumbled with the
supporters of 'Abd er-Rahman. The next day Umar called together the
entire court and appeared in his red robe, worn when issuing punishments. He blamed 'Abd er-Rahman for inciting the previous night's violence. 'Abd er-Rahman insulted the vizier and accused his brother of
having "the spirit of a sheep." He stormed from the room and rode out
of town with his followers.

Umar and Haj Beshir pursued him. There was a skirmish. When it
became clear that Umar's forces were losing, Haj Beshir fled to Kukawa.
As Umar was surrendering to 'Abd er-Rahman, who agreed to let his
brother live, Haj Beshir was gathering as many of his possessions as possible, no doubt including his favorite concubines. He bolted toward the

Chari River, intending to cross and escape. But a Shuwa chief detained him at the river's edge. In Kukawa a mob plundered his house. 'Abd er-Rahman sent emissaries to Haj Beshir, promising on the Qur'an that if he returned he would be pardoned. At first the vizier refused, distrustful. But eventually hope, and perhaps the promise of comfort, won out. As soon as Haj Beshir set foot in Kukawa, 'Abd er-Rahman had him seized and strangled with a bowstring.

Aside from sadness about the death of his old friend, Barth worried what these developments meant for Vogel, the mission, and his own plans. If he couldn't get home through Kukawa and the Tebu country, he would have to take the dangerous route through Aïr. The possibility made him shudder.

OUTSIDE OF GWANDU a horseman recognized him with an exuberant "Marhaba!"—"Welcome!" The friendly greeting made Barth exceptionally happy. It was, he explained, "one of those incidents which, though simple and unimportant in their character, yet often serve to cheer the solitary traveler in foreign countries more than the most brilliant reception." It was a foretaste of the homecoming he longed for.

In Gwandu he ran into a man whom he had entrusted the previous year with a letter to be delivered in Sokoto. Asked if he had done so, the man pulled a small leather case from his hat and extracted a tattered paper. "Here is your letter!" he said. The envelop, with its Arabic instructions to forward the parcel to Tripoli, had been ruined by rain and river crossings. The recipient in Sokoto couldn't read the English inside, so he returned the ragged document to the messenger. He had been wearing it in his hat as a charm ever since. In worse news, a fire had destroyed the precious store of books Barth had left here.

Gwandu's monkish Sultan Khalilu again refused to meet Barth. Though the explorer had given him many handsome presents on his first visit, and though he now desperately needed aid, the miserly sultan

offered next to none. As before, the leader of Gwandu's mafia tried to
squeeze Barth, but this time he sharply refused, offering only a trivial
present to be given on his way out of town.

After four days he left for Sokoto, arriving on August 26. His old
haunts were almost unrecognizable because the entire town was now
"enveloped in one dense mass of vegetation." His friends greeted him
joyfully and made him comfortable. "While my Mohammedan and
black friends thus behaved toward me in the kindest and most hospitable manner," he wrote, "the way in which I felt myself treated by my
friends in Europe was not at all encouraging, and little adapted to raise
my failing spirits."

He had expected a sort of long-distance homecoming here—some
supplies, certainly a thick packet of letters. He was astonished, and
dejected, to find nothing at all for him, no words of concern or encouragement, nothing that acknowledged his efforts or even his existence.
The only information about Europe came from a liberated female slave
from Istanbul who told him that five Christians had come to Kukawa.
This further perplexed him. Wasn't he still the director of the expedition? Shouldn't these Europeans have tried to get word and assistance to
him? "I could only conclude from all this that something was wrong."

Spurred by an even greater sense of urgency, he stayed in Sokoto
only three days before making the one-day journey to Wurno. Sultan
Aliyu was there and welcomed him warmly. He knew all about Barth's
stay in Timbuktu, even the initial shabby treatment by Sidi Alawate. A
generous man, Aliyu offered Barth bountiful dishes, so tempting after
the poor rations of the previous weeks. But Barth had to turn down
these rich foods because of dysentery, which wracked him for a week.
As he was recuperating, the disease again "broke out with considerable
violence," completely draining his strength. He slowly recovered on a
regimen of Dover's powder (a mixture of ipecacuanha, opium, saltpeter,
tartar, and licorice) and a diet of pounded rice mixed with curdled milk
and mimosa seeds. He wasn't able to get on a horse until September 22.
Even then he remained weak.

The disease had laid him up for nearly a month. He was eager to move on, but his companions also were ill and unfit for travel. He decided to wait until early October when the rainy season would be almost over. Meanwhile he and Sultan Aliyu often conversed. Barth found him cheerful, intelligent, and broadly curious, but also lazy, weak, and uninterested in protecting his subjects from war and depredation—his constant complaint about African rulers.

On October 5 he began the 260-mile trip from Wurno to Kano. He was still feeble, "dragging myself along in the most desperate state of exhaustion." In the evenings he sometimes collapsed with fatigue before his tent was up. His camels also were in bad shape. Throughout the trip from Timbuktu they often died and had to be replaced, unsuited for hard travel in the hot and humid rainy season. "The quantity of water that we had to sustain from above and below was not only destructive to animals," wrote Barth, "but likewise to men, and I myself felt most cheerless, weak, and without appetite." They traveled one section of the route at night to avoid thieves who expected them to leave in the morning. As they approached Kano, there were fields of corn, rice, cotton, and indigo, and many herds of cattle. He began to eat better and recovered some of his strength.

After twelve days they reached the gates of Kano. Barth was frail and exhausted but keyed up. After the dashed expectations of Sokoto he was eager to collect the supplies, money, and, perhaps most important, the letters from home that he was certain must be waiting for him in this major center. It was October 17, 1854.

NOTHING. Not a single line, nor any relief. "I was greatly disappointed," he wrote, "in finding neither letters nor supplies, being entirely destitute of means, and having several debts to pay in this place—among others, the money due to my servants, to whom I had paid nothing during the whole journey from Kukawa to Timbuktu and back. I was scarcely able to explain how all this could have happened," he continued, "having

fully relied upon finding here every thing I wanted, together with satisfactory information with regard to the proceedings of Mr. Vogel and
his companions, whose arrival in Kukawa I had as yet only accidently
learned from a liberated slave in Sokoto."

'Another staggering blow. No sign that people from home were thinking of him. No hint that the British government was concerned about
him. No word that Vogel was looking for him to supply help. No con-
firmation that his scientific peers appreciated the reams of information
he had been collecting and sending despite every imaginable hardship
and obstacle. No encouragement to go on. These psychological stresses,
piled on top of the dangers and deprivations of African travel, as well as
his chronic physical ailments, would have crushed most people. Barth
staggered but took action.

The next day he sent his most trusted man, el Gatroni, to Zinder,
160 miles away, to fetch the 400 dollars and the British ironware stored
there when he left for Timbuktu. Barth hoped the cache had survived
the revolution in Bornu. He also expected el Gatroni to find the expedition's new supplies waiting there. Next, Barth arranged temporary
credit with a Kano merchant by giving him nearly everything of value
he had left, including a six-shooter. Then he went to work, completing a
survey of Kano begun during his first visit.

"Severe fits of fever attacked me repeatedly," he noted. To counter
them he used "uninterrupted exercise." The city's climate was malign
for Europeans. Horses didn't do well either—two of his three swelled
up and died, including his great companion Blast of the Desert, who
had carried him "during three years of almost incessant fatigue on my
expedition to Kanem, to the Musgu country, to Bagirmi, to Timbuktu,
and back to Kano."

As he waited for el Gatroni's return, he mulled over two other
rumors from the Sudan grapevine. On October 29 he heard that a British expedition had steamed up the Benue River. He had urged this mission on the government two years earlier but hadn't heard a word about
it since. He traced the rumor to a man in Kano who had seen the steamer

on the Benue. Barth questioned him closely and was convinced that the rumor was true.

Barth wouldn't know the details for many months. The mission had left Britain in early June 1854. When its commander died soon after the boat reached the island of Fernando Po in the Gulf of Guinea, Dr. William Balfour Baikie assumed command. Baikie, who later became Barth's friend and supporter, took the 100-foot steamer *Pleiad* up the Niger for 700 miles. In early August the *Pleiad* entered the Benue and ascended it for 250 miles. At the end of September Baikie turned around, reaching the Niger on October 20, while Barth was in Kano. By February 1855 the *Pleiad* was home.

Every previous excursion on the Niger had proven deadly to Europeans, mostly because of fever. But the *Pleiad*'s entire crew—twelve Europeans and fifty-four Africans—survived because of an experimental therapy—prophylactic doses of quinine. This success altered the course of African exploration. The voyage also proved Barth's conviction that the heart of Africa could be opened to commerce through navigation of the Niger's watershed.

The second thing on Barth's mind was the situation in Kukawa. Conflicting rumors swirled through Kano, but in early November news arrived that Umar had been restored to power and his brother 'Abd er-Rahman was in prison. (At first Umar spared his brother's life, because of his mother's insistence, but two months later the sheikh had him strangled.) Umar's reinstatement relieved Barth. He knew Umar would welcome him in Kukawa, which meant that he could take the shorter and safer route home through Tebu country rather than risking Aïr.

First, he had to muster the means to leave Kano, so he eagerly awaited el Gatroni. The faithful servant returned after an absence of three weeks. He brought nothing but a few letters from the Foreign Office, written in Arabic on Barth's behalf to Sultan Aliyu of Sokoto and to the chiefs of the Fulanis. Barth noted wryly that they were very nice letters and would have done him a lot of good two years ago.

But el Gatroni found nothing else for him in Zinder. The cache had disappeared during Bornu's civil unrest. The supplies forwarded to Zinder by the British government also were gone—Vogel's servant had come from Kukawa, said el Gatroni to the dumbfounded Barth, and taken all of them away.

"It was now that I heard that the news of my death had been every where believed," wrote Barth.

THE FOREIGN OFFICE had not heard from the explorer for months. The last dispatch received by Consul Herman had been written in March 1854 while Barth was at the tents outside Timbuktu. During Barth's silence, Herman did receive many disturbing reports about violence and new wars in the lands the explorer would have to cross if he ever left Timbuktu. Then in late October Herman opened a disturbing dispatch from Vogel, written in July. Herman immediately wrote in his lugubrious way to Lord Clarendon at the Foreign Office:

> My Lord,
>   It is with the deepest regret that I have the honor of reporting to Y. L. [Your Lordship] that Dr. Vogel, in a private letter to me, dated Kouka the 10th July last, announces the death of Dr. Barth at [Maradi] about 100 miles E. N. E. of Sokoto.

Herman noted that Vogel's source was credible, that the region near Maradi was convulsed by violence, and that no word had arrived from Barth in months. "All tend to induce the sad conclusion," wrote Herman, ever a devotee of the worst, "that the report of his death will prove but too true a tale."

Clarendon got this letter in early December and informed Chevalier Bunsen, who forwarded the news to Barth's parents and siblings in Hamburg. "And thus," wrote Barth later, "my family was thrown into the deepest grief, in consequence of the rumor of my death." They held a funeral, and "all my effects were buried."

A month passed. At the end of November, Herman sent another letter to Clarendon. This time he wondered whether Barth had been buried prematurely. Herman suggested some countertheories that underscored the uncertainties of communication in Central Africa, and the opacity that resulted. He noted that the reports about Barth's death from Vogel and Sheikh Umar had come from only one person, who might not be so credible after all. (The source was a malicious servant of Vogel's who lied about Barth's death in hopes of stealing his provisions. Vogel was too green to recognize the man's machinations until after the damage was done.)

Second, continued Herman, the predatory bands of Tuaregs infesting the Maradi region might have intercepted Barth's dispatches, which would explain his long silence. Third, a large caravan from the area where Barth supposedly died had recently arrived in Kukawa, and no one in it had heard this news, which would have flashed through the rumor mill. And lastly, none of Barth's servants had shown up in Kukawa to claim their wages, as they surely would have if the explorer were dead. For all these reasons, concluded Herman, "there exists a ray (a faint one I grant) of hope that Dr. Barth may yet be restored to his friends and the world of Science."

This dispatch reached London in late December. Clarendon passed the faint hope along to Bunsen, who no doubt informed Barth's family.

ON NOVEMBER 10, 1854, the day after receiving the news of his death, Barth wrote a long letter to Lord Clarendon from Kano. He began with restraint. He said he was enclosing a large detailed map of the Niger between Gao and Say, as well as a letter from the great chief of the Tuaregs that guaranteed safety to all British travelers in his territory.

In the second paragraph his frustration spilled out. "But before making a few remarks," he wrote, "it seems first necessary, to state & to assure Government, that I am not only alive, but also in tolerable health; for I have become aware, that not only the rumour had been spread of my death, but that in a hurry, which certainly does not seem justifiable, *the supplies* which partly I had left here, partly had ordered to be deposited here in the firm and loudly proclaimed intention, to return to Hausa, *have been withdrawn from me as from a dead person.*"

As a consequence, he continued, he was stuck in Kano with a debt of more than 500 dollars and no means whatsoever. "I have been plunged into a state of great perplexity & difficulty, just when I hoped to repose at length from my perilous labours & find a little comfort." He didn't know how this "ill-founded" rumour began, but he couldn't understand why someone had ordered his things seized and removed, especially since he had sent four dispatches from Timbuktu and another from Gao on July 5, which "must by this time also have arrived." And if they hadn't (which was the case), Consul Herman should immediately trace them because they contained much valuable information, including four detailed maps of Central Africa.

After this outburst he recovered himself and reported his news, while simultaneously reminding Clarendon of his recent accomplishments on behalf of a government that had seemingly abandoned him. About his trip to Timbuktu: "I may say without the least exaggeration that *my arduous & perilous undertaking has been crowned with the most splendid success,* much more so than I ever might have anticipated with the most sanguine hope." He noted, with some overstatement, that he had spent seven months there "getting a correct insight into the whole sphere of life of this Queen of the desert, which from time immemorial has excited the most vivid interest of all Europe, & of England in particular."

He had become intimate friends with the city's "eminent religious chief," Sheikh al-Bakkay. He had laid the foundations for political and commercial relations between Britain and Central Africa by signing agreements with Timbuktu, Sokoto, and the large kingdom of Gwandu, which was unknown in Europe until his visit. He had mapped the Niger between Timbuktu and Say, and had gathered much invaluable information about the unknown history of Songhai.

He added—with amusing exaggeration, considering what he had been through—that after living for several months among the western Tuareg tribes, "I have made them accustomed to see Christians among them, have reconciled their hatred against our religion, have concluded cordial friendships with several of their most distinguished men, and have got full franchise and promise of security from their chiefs for any English visiting their territory."

"So my undertaking may truly be said," as he said so himself, "to have been crowned with an unparalleled success." He asked Clarendon to reward al-Bakkay handsomely for protecting him, principally with books in Arabic. And he hoped that with God's help he would soon follow this dispatch to Europe.

MEANWHILE he remained stuck in Kano. His supplies were gone, most of his horses and camels were dead, and he was broke. Still, he hoped that one of the letters from Zinder would prove helpful. Vice-Consul Dickson had written him from Ghadames in late 1853 to say that two Ghadamsi merchants were holding property of his that could be used as collateral for a loan. Barth approached the merchants and was rebuffed. The merchants took the view that Dickson was far away in the Crimea, so finders, keepers.

Barth appealed to Kano's ghaladima, the city's most powerful man after the emir. He agreed to hear the dispute, and did so in public before a large audience curious to see how the Christian would fare. The merchants' defense: the letter is old and Barth is an infidel. Nevertheless, countered the ghaladima, the infidel's property does not belong to you—make the loan. The merchants demanded their standard usury—an interest rate of 100 percent. Barth agreed that the British government in Tripoli would repay double the 200-dollar loan in four months. He couldn't resist pointing out that the loan would have been unnecessary if his supplies had not been snatched from Zinder.

With the money he bought two horses, a couple of camels, and some provisions. After a month in Kano, he left on November 21. "I then pursued my journey with great cheerfulness." In six months he hoped to be breathing "the invigorating air of the north."

KUKAWA WAS 400 volatile miles to the east. The coup d'état there had ignited fighting throughout Bornu. Though Umar was back on the throne, skirmishes still flared in the countryside. Marauders were taking advantage of the chaos with sprees of pillage. Barth's small party passed villages newly burned or desolated, their unharvested crops left in the fields. The town of Gumel, calm and prosperous when Barth first saw it, was now shattered. Barth called on its emir in the charred ruins of the royal residence. Arab merchants were afraid to travel and warned Barth about the dangerous roads ahead. His group sometimes traveled at night to avoid bandits. At one point they didn't see another person for twenty-five miles, rare in this part of Sudan.

One thing hadn't changed—the region's thieves. At Garki, as the camp slept, a nervy robber climbed a baobab tree, crept along its branches, and stole the tobe and trousers belonging to one of Barth's servants.

On December 1 they broke camp near the village of Bundi, about 225 miles from Kukawa. A few miles later, in the middle of a forest, "I saw advancing toward me a person of strange aspect," wrote Barth, "—a young man of very fair complexion." Barth hadn't seen a white man since Overweg's death more than two years earlier. The fair rider was Vogel.

This chance meeting stunned them with pleasure. They dismounted and sat. Barth broke out his precious store of coffee, and they talked. "For more than two years now," he wrote in the German edition of *Travels and Discoveries*, "I had not heard a word of German or any other European language, and it was an infinite joy for me to be allowed once more to converse in my own language. But our conversation soon turned to subjects that were not so pleasant."

Barth was amazed to hear that nearly all the supplies and money brought by Vogel were gone. He also learned that Vogel had never opened his letter because the address was in Arabic, which Vogel didn't understand, so he had put it aside. Consequently, Vogel had only recently learned that Barth was alive. "I could not help reproaching my friend for having too hastily believed the news of my death before he had made all possible inquiries," wrote Barth, "but as he was a new-comer into this country and did not possess a knowledge of the language, I could easily perceive that he had no means of ascertaining the truth or falsehood of those reports."

Barth was especially disappointed that Vogel didn't have a single bottle of wine. "For, having now been for more than three years without a drop of any stimulant except coffee, and having suffered severely from frequent attacks of fever and dysentery, I had an insuperable longing for the juice of the grape, of which former experience taught me the benefit." He had regained his strength in Asia Minor, he added, by drinking good French wine.

After two hours they parted, with plans to reunite in Kukawa when Vogel returned from Zinder. In *Travels and Discoveries* Barth gave this meeting less than two pages.

Ten days later Barth neared Kukawa. He sent a letter ahead to Sheikh Umar, who dispatched his chief eunuch and thirty horsemen to escort the explorer back into the city with éclat. He was taken to his old quarters, which felt like home, where he found the British sappers Church and Macguire.

"It might seem that I had overcome all the difficulties in the way of complete success," wrote Barth, "and that I could now enjoy a short stay in the same place before traversing the last stage of my homeward journey. Such, however," he continued in the familiar refrain, "was not the case. . . ."

29

Getting Out

THE FIRST PROBLEM, EVERLASTINGLY, WAS THE MISSION'S LACK OF means. Every time Barth assumed that his troubles were over and his stresses would lessen—in Sokoto, in Kano, in Zinder, and now in Kukawa—he instead found bitter disappointment. Vogel, despite the precautions of Consul Herman, had nearly exhausted the mission's resources, with help from thievish servants. Further, he had sent one of those thieves to collect Barth's goods in Zinder, most of which were now missing. Barth had to find a way to finance the 1,500 miles between him and the Mediterranean.

He tried political and ethical leverage on Sheikh Umar. After first giving him a present worth £8, Barth pointed out that unless Umar restored the goods stolen from Zinder during the revolution (the ironware and 400 dollars), and the goods stolen by the person who later fetched Barth's property, peaceable relations with Britain would be impossible. He asked Umar to track down the thieves and to compensate the British government—Barth suggested camels—for its stolen property. This speech inflamed an important courtier against Barth—he had profited from one of the thefts, carried out by his servant. To counter the courtier's influence with Umar, Barth made a handsome gift to the sheikh's brother and urged him to advise Umar to protect Bornu's friendship with Britain. Barth had long since become adept at the moves and countermoves of African politics. Despite his poverty, he also slaughtered fourteen oxen for the people of Kukawa, to stay in their good graces.

While the sheikh mulled things over, Barth turned to another unexpected headache. Vogel and Corporal Church, one of the British sappers, had become enemies. Church was refusing to take Vogel's orders. The other sapper, Private Macguire, didn't share Church's hostility, but supported him out of military and national solidarity. The sappers, who had volunteered for the mission, were charged by the British government to assist Vogel, but neither had accompanied the German scientist on his recent journey to Mandara, and they were now sulking in Kukawa while Vogel went to Zinder.

Barth was "greatly disappointed and grieved" by this conduct. During Vogel's absence he tried to unravel and fix it. Church expected to find a sympathetic ear in Barth, since the explorer was still upset by Vogel's failure to investigate the rumor of his death. The sapper told Barth he had tried to warn Vogel about his dishonest servant Mesaud, but had been brushed off. Mesaud was also the source of the rumor about Barth's death, launched in a scheme to steal the goods in Zinder. Church and Macguire had written about these matters to Consul Herman, and this evidently was the letter that gave Herman faint hope Barth wasn't dead. But when Vogel learned that Church had criticized him to superiors behind his back, he took offense, which offended Church. Church also accused Vogel of wasting the mission's resources, and added that the young German spent several hours every day alone with a female slave of Mesaud's, implying an illicit relationship.

When Vogel returned to Kukawa at the end of December, Barth immediately asked to see the mission's accounts. He found them in order. As for the female slave, Barth learned that Vogel had saved her and her child during a razzia, and simply enjoyed her occasional company. Vogel's "purity and almost virginal chastity of manners," as Barth later wrote, further undermined Church's slur. Vogel conceded that Church had been right about Mesaud. (After Barth's appeal to

Umar, Mesaud was imprisoned for stealing the goods, some of which were recovered.)

Church's real complaint, said Vogel, was that he hated the discomforts of life in Africa. He also hated the energetic Vogel's work habits. (Herman had been wrong about the young German, who was much tougher than he looked.) Church had turned sullen and insolent, refusing to perform his duties as an assistant. Barth saw for himself that all this was true. Church was a difficult character. Barth also saw that these veteran British soldiers resented taking orders from a green young scholar—Vogel was twenty-five—who was German to boot.

Barth asked them to put aside personal animosities for the sake of the mission, no doubt remembering the many times he had done so with Richardson. Otherwise the mission, which should be their highest priority, would be damaged. Vogel and Macguire agreed, but Church was unbending. He declared his intention to go home with Barth.

In *Travels and Discoveries*, Barth blurred all this with a couple of vague remarks. He wrote that Vogel had jumped into the mission with enthusiasm, "giving up all pretensions to the comforts of life" for the sake of science and knowledge. "He unfortunately committed the mistake," continued Barth, of expecting the same dedication from the sappers, whose "ideas were less elevated." These partial truths, intended to protect the public's perception of both sides, didn't stop Church from making damaging accusations later on.

NOT EVERY SURPRISE in Kukawa was unpleasant. Part of the box plundered in Zinder was recovered, including a packet of letters for Barth. Some were three years old, but he read them with great pleasure. And after being deprived of fresh books for years, he luxuriated in Vogel's small library. He also grew fond of his energetic young countryman, Vogel, and relished the chance to converse again with a well-trained scientist.

After Vogel and Macguire left on January 20, 1855, for Adamawa and Bauchi, Barth felt "rather desolate and lonely." His spirits were further lowered by an attack of rheumatism that crippled him for more than a week. Yet he never stopped pestering Umar to send him homeward. He told the sheikh he couldn't delay any longer, "my health having suffered considerably from my five years' stay in these countries." To emphasize his point, on February 20 he rode a few miles outside of Kukawa and pitched his tent. "I felt extremely happy in having at length left behind me a town of which I had become excessively tired."

But he couldn't get away that easily. Umar wanted Barth to move back to Kukawa until they resolved all the issues of theft. Barth suspected that if he returned he would get stuck for another month or two. "Knowing from experience that with these people time is of no value," he wrote, "and finding my health rapidly declining, I had come to the resolution of not waiting any longer." Umar yielded to his determination and sent him five camels, inferior ones, but they nevertheless gave Barth "a slight hope of proceeding on my journey." He bought two more camels and hired a guide.

But on February 28, Umar sent musketeers to bring him back to town. The reason wasn't clear, but a large caravan was approaching and Barth suspected that the sheikh hoped it carried supplies for the mission and hence new gifts for himself. "I thought it prudent, heartrending though it was," wrote Barth, "to resign myself in obedience to the tyrannical will of these people."

The caravan brought nothing for Barth or the mission except a letter from Lord Clarendon that was twenty months old. Barth tried to make good use of this intermission by studying Kanuri and the history of Bornu, and he attempted to improve his health with daily rides. But his journal referred constantly to his physical and mental exhaustion. "All that now remained for me under the present circumstances," he wrote, "was to resign myself in patience, although the delay pressed upon me with indescribable heaviness, and I had scarcely energy enough to endeavor to employ my time usefully." "Altogether my usual energy was gone," he noted, "and my health totally undermined, and the sole object which occupied my thoughts was to convey my feeble body in safety home." Even his usual delight in African company waned; he complained that he hadn't had a happy day in Bornu since Vogel left.

Worries about money also drained his vitality. Two of his camels died during this delay. "Everlasting anxiety about the necessities of daily life eats into [a traveler's] energy," wrote Gustav Nachtigal, "which in any case suffers from the climate, from disease and from intellectual isolation, and this naturally impairs his scientific work."

Around this time, Consul Herman got exciting news from Murzuk. He forwarded it to Lord Clarendon in a letter dated March 13. "I have the honor to report to your Lordship," he wrote, "that the rumour of Dr. Barth's death has most happily proved unfounded." Gagliuffi had received a letter in Italian from Barth, written from Kano in mid-November 1854. Barth said he intended to go to Kukawa and then straight home. Clarendon got this dispatch three weeks later. He immediately informed Chevalier Bunsen and the Royal Geographical Society.

The news came too late to prevent another mix-up. A caravan from the north arrived in Kukawa on March 23, 1855. It brought 1,000 dollars for the mission. But at the time, the Foreign Office still thought Barth was dead, so the packet was addressed to Vogel as the head of the mission, and there was some doubt about transferring it to Barth. "All this mismanagement," he wrote, "in consequence of the false news of my death, greatly enhanced the unpleasant nature of my situation; for, instead of leaving the country under honorable circumstances, I was considered as almost disgraced by those who had sent me out, the command having been taken from me and given to another. There is no doubt that such an opinion delayed my departure considerably, for otherwise the sheikh would have exerted himself in quite a different manner to see me off."

Barth eventually did collect the 1,000 dollars, some of which funded his journey home. Umar also repaid the 400 dollars stolen from Zinder, which Barth used to pay debts, including the salary of el Gatroni.

By mid-April the crushing heat, with daytime temperatures above 110 degrees, was further damaging Barth's health. Sheikh Umar grew alarmed. If Barth died in Bornu, relations with Britain might be strained.

Umar gave the explorer a camel and hinted that he could leave soon. Barth's hopes revived. He bought another camel and made preparations.

On May 4 he left Kukawa again to camp nearby. He returned to town on May 9 to say goodbye to Umar, who had arranged for him to accompany a caravan of Tebu and Daza merchants for the first part of the journey. As a final request, Umar asked Barth to send him a small cannon. (The sheikh died in 1880.)

After one false start and another five-day delay, which almost unhinged Barth, the journey began in earnest. On May 19 they crossed the river separating Bornu from Kanem. "I deemed it one of the happiest moments of my life," wrote Barth; ". . . I turned my back with great satisfaction. upon these countries where I had spent full five years in incessant toil and exertion."

One obstacle did remain: he had to cross the Sahara in the heat of summer. More immediately he had to deal with the monkeys. He was bringing three of them back (species unspecified), tethered to the baggage atop the camels. On the first day's march they kept untying the baggage ropes, and their incessant screeching spooked the camels into stampeding, which plunged the hairy little jockeys into worse hysterics, which further panicked the camels. Things got broken, including a musket. Barth got the monkeys off the camels' backs and shooed them away.

The caravan was skirting the northwestern edge of Lake Chad. Lakeside villagers sold them smelly dried fish for the long desert crossing. On May 30 they struck north into the dunes. "I here enjoyed again the wide expanse of the open desert," wrote Barth, "which, notwithstanding its monotony, has something very grand about it, and is well adapted to impress the human mind with the consciousness of its own littleness, although at the present season, it presented itself in its most awful character, owing to the intense heat which prevailed."

The suffering began. The best way to survive the crossing was by forced march, with short breaks during the most scalding hours. Even in the shade, when they could find any, the temperature was 110 degrees. Humans and animals plodded in a stupor of heat and exhaustion. Sand-winds sometimes intensified the wretchedness and desolation. They wrapped veils around their heads and mouths to block the sand, and tightened their girdles to avert hunger. It was worst for the heavily burdened camels, and for the slaves of the Tebu and the Daza, who staggered under their loads. During one of the night marches, four camels collapsed and died. Slaves deranged by misery tried to hide and get left behind, though that meant certain death. The travelers often had to dig sand out of the wells. Sometimes the water was as sweet as grace, sometimes fetid with dead birds or other filth, too foul to drink. But they always drank.

It took them a month to cover 450 miles to the salt-trading oasis of Bilma, a soothing respite of palm trees and grasses. A few days later Barth's small group separated from the rest of the caravan. The next phase of the journey was the most difficult, across a rocky desert plateau. It was also the most dangerous, infested with bandits. Barth bought as much fodder-grass as he could find, using "dollars, cloves, and the remnant of dried fish which I still had left . . . as my only safety with my small band of people consisted in the greatest speed."

Barth surely knew Denham's description of what lay ahead of them:

The fatigue and difficulty of a journey to Bornou are not to be compared with a return to Fezzan: the nine days from Izhya to Tegerhy, without either forage or wood, is distressing beyond description, to both camels and men, at the end of such a journey as this. The camels, already worn out by the heavy sand-hills, have the stony desert to pass; the sharp points bruise their feet, and they totter, and fall under their heavy loads: the people, too, suffer severely from the scanty portion of provisions, mostly dates, that can be brought on by these tired animals,—and altogether it is nine days of great distress and difficulty. There is something about El Wahr surpassing dreariness itself: the rocks are dark sandstone, of the most gloomy and barren appearance; the wind whistles through the narrow fissures, which disdain to afford nourishment even to

a single blade of wild grass; and as the traveller creeps under the
lowering crags, to take shelter for the night, stumbling at each step
over the skeleton of some starved human being, and searching for
level spots on the hard rock, on which to lay his wearied body, he
may fancy himself wandering in the wilds of desolation and despair.

They made another series of forced marches. At wells they drank
quickly and moved on to avoid human predators. Though they were
heading north, temperatures remained 110 degrees or higher. They
reached a well called Mesheru, notorious for being surrounded by the
bones of slaves whose march to the northern markets had ended there.
"The water of this well," wrote Barth, "which is five fathoms in depth,
is generally considered of good quality, notwithstanding the remnant of
human bones which are constantly driven into it by the gale; but at present it was rather dirty." In the next sentence he noted the remarkable
landscape and commented, "It would form a good study for a painter
experienced in water colors, although it would be impossible to express
the features in a pencil sketch."

The juxtaposition is jarring: pastel artwork and water made gritty by
human bones, its depth measured precisely. The horrors elaborated by
Denham barely seemed to touch Barth. He was insulated by thoughts of
home. When this segment ended after seventeen days, at an oasis called
Tejerri, he wrote to Frederick Warrington, who was coming from Tripoli
to meet him, that he had arrived here on July 5 "after a most agreeable
undisturbed journey of 48 days"—another of his dumbfounding state-
ments, especially since he added that he could barely use his arms and
legs because of rheumatism. He asked Warrington to arrange a warm
bath for him in Murzuk. He also asked him to bring "a bottle of tolerable
wine," and ended, "I hope to get plenty of interesting news from you, and
if it please God, *a few letters*." He must have been almost out of his mind
with happiness now that every step was bringing him closer to home.

They came to the village of el Gatroni, who had a joyous reunion
with his family after years of separation. Barth gave him the prom-

ised bonus of 50 dollars and wished he could double it for his invaluable dependability. El Gatroni treated Barth to a meal of fowls, with a special treat of grapes for dessert.

On July 13, just south of Murzuk, Barth reached the tent of Frederick Warrington, who had escorted the three Europeans out of Tripoli when the mission began. "I could not but feel deeply affected when, after so long an absence, I again found myself in friendly hands, and within reach of European comforts."

But those comforts dangled like a carrot at the end of a stick. "All dangers and difficulties might be supposed to have ceased," wrote Barth. "But such was not the case." The tribes between him and Tripoli were in revolt against Ottoman rule. The Turks and Britain were allied, so the region was dangerous for Barth. But at this point nothing could stop him for long, and he moved on after a delay of six days.

He also learned from Warrington about another troubling development. During his absence, the once-close relationship between Britain and Prussia had been wedged apart by the Crimean War. When Russia moved to expand southward into territories controlled by the Ottoman Empire, Britain, France, Prussia, and Austria attempted to mediate. Russia rejected the terms they suggested and invaded the Caucasus and the Danubian Principalities. By late March 1854, when Barth was on the verge of escaping Timbuktu, Britain, France, and Austria had declared war on Russia. Prussia, however, remained neutral, despite the efforts of Prince Albert and Chevalier Bunsen, who always urged close ties between Britain and Prussia. When Prussia refused to support Britain, Bunsen resigned as ambassador to the Court of St. James's, a post he had held for thirteen years. From Britain's perspective, Prussia's snub resembled enmity.

The rift wasn't sudden. The close relationship between Britain and Germany had long coexisted with an undercurrent of suspicion and resentment about Germany's influence on British affairs. The alliance and the resentment both started in 1714, when George I, the first Hanoverian king of England, arrived from Germany. Georges II through V all married German princesses. Queen Victoria's mother was a German princess, her governess a German baroness. Victoria married a German prince, Albert. One of the royal couple's closest counselors, Christian Friedrich, was a German baron. In some British circles Germany was viewed as a parasite. When Victoria married Albert, some street wit wrote, "He comes to take for 'for better or for worse'/ England's fat Queen and England's fatter purse."

Barth felt the repercussions of all this in Africa and would soon feel them in England. He had been sending his scientific dispatches to Bunsen, who forwarded them to Humboldt, Ritter, and other German scholars, as well as to the Foreign Office. He saw nothing amiss in this practice since his contract specified that he was not in British government service, but was an independent scientist-for-hire, at least until he assumed the directorship of the mission. But after the rift over the Crimea, some people in Britain, especially within the Royal Geographical Society, began grumbling that despite Barth's British paycheck, his first loyalty was Prussia.

In his letter to Clarendon from Murzuk, Barth addressed the issue. He wrote that he had just learned of "the most lamentable division and coolness which had succeeded to the harmony once existing between Her British Majesty's government and the King of Prussia. I have only to mention, that the correspondence formerly passing through the hands of the Chevalier Bunsen was far from being a correspondence with Prussia, but with my friends in England, principally Members of the Royal Geographical Society, sufficient care being not taken at the Foreign Office of private correspondence."

AFTER A COUPLE of tense encounters with the rebels, who said they would have cut his throat if Britain had openly opposed their revolt, Barth neared Tripoli. Four days from it, a messenger from the vice-consul, Richard Reade, met him with a bottle of wine.

On August 28, 1855, after five years and five months in the African interior, he rode into Tripoli. He inhaled the perfumes of the city's renowned gardens. "Yet infinitely greater was the effect produced upon me by the wide expanse of the sea," he wrote. "I felt so grateful to Providence for having again reached in safety the border of this Mediterranean basin, the cradle of European civilization, which from an early period had formed the object of my earnest longings and most serious course of studies." He had an urge to gallop to the beach, leap from his horse, and kneel in a prayer of thanks. But such dramatic gestures were beyond him. Instead he rode quietly through the town's dazzling white walls to his quarters.

He was taking the young servants freed by Overweg, Abbega and Dorugu, with him to Europe. Over the next few days he delighted them with new clothes—trousers of blue wool, tailored jackets of red wool with metal buttons and gold stripes, red wool caps with blue silk tassels.

Barth was impatient to leave Africa. They stayed in Tripoli only four days before taking a steamer to Malta and then to Marseilles, where they boarded a train for the English Channel. Dorugu and Abbega were amazed by all of it—the peculiar utensils called forks, the big houses "without even the least amount of sand," the way people pressed coins into their hands simply because they were black, the swift chuffing carriage that Barth called "Victoria's horse," the women with faces white as chalk and wasplike waists above puffy skirts. And then one morning, remembered Dorugu, "I don't know who it was who told me the name of the town—perhaps it was Abdul Karim [Barth] himself, I don't remember—but the name of the town was London."

It was September 6, less than two weeks since they had left Tripoli. After settling into Long's Hotel on Bond Street, Barth reported immediately to Lord Clarendon, who received him as a hero.

He had completed his labors and now looked forward to the harvest: first the peaceful solitude of composition, then publication of his account, followed by some fame and a professorship. Perils and intrigues, he felt sure, were finally behind him.

30

Problems at Home

THE LONDON PAPERS HAD REPORTED THE RUMOR OF BARTH'S death, but none of them noticed his return. It was a foretaste of the public's response to him and his journey.

By contrast, London's high officials and scientists welcomed him with warm praise. Lord Palmerston, head of the Foreign Office when the mission left Britain, was now prime minister. He and his replacement at the FO, Lord Clarendon, were delighted by Barth's achievements. "I am happy to repeat to you what I have already expressed to you verbally," wrote Lord Clarendon, "the high sense which I entertain of the zeal and ability which you have shown in prosecuting the enquiries in Central Africa on which you have been engaged, and of the fortitude, perseverance, and sound judgment which have enabled you to overcome the many dangers and difficulties with which you have had to contend in the course of your valorous enterprise."

Less than two weeks after returning, Barth sent a long letter to Clarendon asking the government to express its appreciation in cash. He needed money to pay his expenses while he wrote his account, and money to pay for the many detailed maps and illustrations he wanted to include. He made his case with stiff pride and faint grievance.

"I take first the liberty to observe," he began, "that an enterprising man, who under takes difficult & dangerous things, does it as well for his honor and reputation as for ameliorating & improving his position in society." He had joined the mission enthusiastically, he noted, "though I had in the beginning to subject myself to the direction of Mr. Richardson." He had also "sacrificed" his own money for the mission, since the funding provided by government, especially for the two scientific members, had been "rather a little scanty & precarious." After assuming the mission's leadership, he had "done what was possible for a mortal man." He therefore hoped that "Her Majesty's Government will be pleased to confer upon me that measure of distinctionary & pecuniary remuneration, which my services may be considered to deserve." The tortured wording suggests how uncomfortable Barth was when asking for money for himself.

He also hoped the FO agreed that his journals belonged to him and could be published without the government's objection. Having felt the shifting diplomatic winds, he assured Clarendon that he would not comment on France's ambitions in the western Sahara. Nevertheless, as promised to his friend, he enclosed a letter from Sheikh al-Bakkay asking the British government to stop the French from advancing farther south.

He also enclosed treaties, written in Arabic, made with Sheikh Umar of Bornu, the sultans of Gwandu and Sokoto, and two Tuareg chiefs. All of them pledged to protect British merchants. Barth sent a letter from Umar asking "the Sovereign Lady of the English realm" to send gifts: "In the first place, two nice guns, for campaiging. Also, some wonderful cannon balls with some drum instruments, and a large striking clock (or with alarum). Also, some fire instruments, such as brass lamps and candlesticks, and such like. Also a tent. That is all. Also a nice sword, which I described to Abdu-el-Kerim." Umar offered to send his son to Tripoli to take delivery.

Clarendon responded a few days later. Yes, the journals were Barth's property. Clarendon hoped that their invaluable scientific contents would reach the public soon. As for remuneration, Clarendon wanted to consult with Chevalier Bunsen and others. He also had splendid news:

because of Barth's extraordinary feats and service, Queen Victoria had decided to award him a Companionship of the Bath, one of the crown's highest honors, rarely given to a foreigner. Burton, Speke, and Baker, among other famous British explorers, never received it.

Bunsen, now retired in Heidelberg, suggested that the British government pay Barth £600 per year for the journey's five-and-a-half-year duration, and reimburse his personal expenses. The Treasury lowered this to £500 for four-and-a-half years, dating from the time of Richardson's death. Treasury also agreed to give Barth £1,000 upon completion of the first three volumes of his book, and up to another £1,000 upon completion of the last two, on condition that he provide the government fifty copies. A British publisher offered Barth £500, a German publisher £750.

All these terms were agreeable to Barth. With his finances settled, he expected to write in peace. But first he wanted a real homecoming. He left on October 1 for Germany.

"WHEN WE ARRIVED at the gate of his father's house," remembered Barth's servant Dorugu, "he opened the carriage and ran into the house. You could hear a lot of noise in the house." Barth hadn't seen his father, mother, and siblings for six years. For part of that time they thought he was dead, and they had buried him in absentia. No wonder his return to Hamburg was noisy. Gustav von Schubert, his brother-in-law and intimate friend, described how nearly six years in Africa had changed him:

> His intellectual interaction had been completely restricted to and reliant upon the Arab world, which had a lasting effect upon him. He had taken on the serious, honorable, withdrawn, proud, almost haughty demeanor of the sons of the desert. His bold yet thoughtful spirit had proven itself in even the most complex and difficult circumstances—no wonder, then, that he returned with even greater self-confidence than before. His inborn mistrust had

also grown to alarming levels, however, since he had had to remain on his guard at all times in those surroundings. Everywhere he went, he sensed deliberate and calculated attempts being made to exploit him. He had to reacclimatize himself to many aspects of European culture, which was not without its share of difficult and painful experiences for him, especially in the beginning.

How different he seemed, however, when among the family he had gone without for so long—so full of tenderness for parents and siblings! The hard man did not mark the moment of their reunion with any great outpouring of emotion, but over time the peaceful and loving company of his family gave him more and more joy. He remained this way until the end of his days: hard and gruff on the outside, but with a warm and loving inner disposition.

Barth hired a tailor to make warm clothes for Dorugu and Abbega, who were stunned by the cold. He took them with him to visit Overweg's father, and told the Africans, "That is the man whose son gave you your freedom." He also entertained them with a trip to the circus.

Von Humboldt, bursting with pride about Barth's achievements, arranged a lunch for the explorer with Frederick Wilhelm IV, king of Prussia, at the summer palace, Sanssouci. Carl Ritter, Barth's other old mentor, came as well. Frederick offered to help subsidize the German edition of Barth's book. The Prussian government also awarded him a pension of about £140 per year (raised after two years to about £200, to run until 1861).

In subsequent weeks various groups feted and honored Barth. Hamburg gave him a gold medal. The courts of Württemberg, Weimar, and Sardinia presented decorations. The University of Jena gave him an honorary doctorate. Academic societies sent honors. On October 13 he addressed the Geographical Society of Berlin and received an ovation. He was offered a professorship of geography for one semester for £225. Von Humboldt and Ritter were working to secure him a permanent position.

Chevalier Bunsen had other ideas. When Barth visited him in Heidelberg, he advised leaving Germany for England. German universities paid paltry salaries and demanded heavy teaching loads, Bunsen warned, which would leave little time for much else. In England, Barth could make more money for less work and still have plenty of time for travel—which Bunsen correctly suspected was more attractive to Barth than teaching. Staying in Prussia, argued the old diplomat, also would alienate the British government and public, which now resented Germany because of the Crimean War. Though hesitant, Barth decided to take Bunsen's advice.

While Barth was visiting his parents, he got a letter from Dr. Norton Shaw, a well-known geographer who was secretary of the Royal Geographical Society (RGS). Shaw invited Barth to dine with some members of the society before his speaking engagement there in mid-November. Barth immediately responded that the letter surprised him because he had not agreed to speak and did not intend to address any scientific society until after he published his journal. He evidently meant no *British* group, since he had addressed Berlin's Geographical Society two weeks earlier.

"My narrative having been published in extenso," Barth continued, "it will be seen, what has been achieved really and what has been *presumed* to have been achieved, though at least what I myself have ever presumed I do not know."

This cryptic remark and its sarcastic *presumed* had a history. Barth hinted at it in his last sentence to Shaw, assuring the secretary that he felt a strong obligation to "the Scientific public" and to the "eminent Statesmen" who had entrusted him, "although a foreign gentleman," with the mission. He pointedly left out the Royal Geographical Society.

The problems began while Barth was still in Africa. During the mission's early years, he sent his dispatches first to Bunsen, who passed them on to the Foreign Office and to Barth's scientific colleagues in Berlin. This irritated the FO and the Royal Geographical Society, which regularly complained that some of Barth's dispatches were appearing in Germany before the RGS received them. By the time Barth learned of the FO's disapproval, some suspicions about his loyalties had already taken root.

These were worsened by the overenthusiasm of a superb German cartographer named Augustus Petermann, who became closely associated with the mission. Petermann worked at the London Observatory and was indirectly responsible for Barth's appointment—Bunsen learned about Richardson's proposed expedition through Petermann. Whenever Barth sent maps back to Europe, the FO hired Petermann to turn them into finished works of cartography. (His maps are one of the glories of *Travels and Discoveries*.) All this was fine, but Petermann also sent his maps to German publications along with information from Barth's journal.

This didn't sit well with the FO or the RGS. "Of course it is Mr. Petermann's object," wrote Undersecretary Addington in December 1853, "to make himself, for his own profit, and also for his own glory, the historiographer of all the discoveries of Barth and Overweg: but that is not our object, or intention. . . . Drs. Barth and Overweg were members of Richardson's expedition, paid by us, and traveling at our expense," he continued, and any public announcements about the expedition should come from the Royal Geographical Society, "which properly speaking is our natural medium of partial geographical communications." Addington pointed a blaming finger: "The Chevalier Bunsen has always looked upon us as the mere paymasters of the expedition, while the fruits belong to Germany. This is a mistake."

The long delays between dispatches from Barth also fed British suspicions, especially within the RGS, that Barth was giving everything to the Germans. The RGS contributed neither funds nor expertise to the expedition, but because of its eminence and influential members, it felt entitled to be the first to review Barth's reports.

The society's secretary, Dr. Norton Shaw, was particularly antagonistic. In January 1854 he published an article about an RGS meeting at which Barth and Overweg were the butt of criticisms and crude jokes. Shaw wrote that "it might be presumed"—the word that nettled Barth—"that their labours would have been placed at the disposal of the English Government, and the results would have been accessible to English geographers and other promoters among our countrymen. But this has not been the case . . . the information respecting this expedition seems to be of a private character, if we may judge from the manner it is dealt with and the closeness with which it is preserved from English geographers."

If anyone doubted that Shaw's barbs were aimed at the scientists' nationality, he turned explicit: "In connection with Lake Chad and other African names, it may be observed that the Germans are adopting various ways of spelling them, because they find it difficult to say 'cheese.' "

Petermann responded with a nine-page open letter that called Shaw's report "scurrilous and offensive." The cheesy comment, he said, was especially shameful from a representative of the RGS.

Shaw was not only unbowed; he attacked. In June 1855 he again complained to the Foreign Office that the Germans, in particular Bunsen and Petermann, were still conspiring to keep Barth's geographical information from the British. The FO investigated and satisfied itself that Shaw was wrong, but Shaw wrote at least two more accusatory letters that summer before Barth reached London.

Shaw's insinuations may have been encouraged by the society's president, Francis Egerton, the earl of Ellesmere (for whom the Arctic island is named). In his Anniversary Address in May 1855, Ellesmere reported that Barth had moved from Timbuktu to Kano, and had met Vogel. Then he started inserting needles. He said that Barth hadn't sent much information back, so judgment must be postponed about "the importance of the geographical data presumed to have been accumulated during his prolonged absence." Ellesmere's "presumed" was probably another thorn that irked the thin-skinned Barth, who detected an insinuation that he might have spent his "prolonged absence" dallying in Africa instead of using his chronometer.

Some of Ellesmere's other remarks must have grated as well. He noted that Barth had recently sent a map of the Niger between Gao and Say, but undercut this compliment by complaining that Barth hadn't provided any data used to construct the map, or data for any of maps he had sent. And Ellesmere couldn't resist adding that this part of the Niger was "first traversed by Mungo Park." Barth probably wondered, with reason, so what? Park had floated down the river and died without contributing anything to science's knowledge of it. Barth had sent back the first detailed map of an unknown section of the great river. Ellesmere's remark carried shades of the churlish British rejection of René Caillié's claim to Timbuktu, since a Brit had gotten there first.

Ellesmere also complained that many of Barth's maps had not been seen by the RGS because they evidently were in Germany—another falsehood. He "hoped" that Barth would return with "the explanations that are necessary to establish the value of his arduous, protracted, and hazardous labours."

This tone and attitude must have put Barth's teeth on edge. On top of all this, soon after Barth's homecoming in Germany, several British newspapers ran stories criticizing him for excessive spending in Africa. After all his deprivations and penury there, the accusation infuriated him. He was convinced that detractors within the RGS had planted the articles, though the culprit may have been Corporal Church, who had his own reasons for resenting Barth.

When Barth felt wronged, especially in matters of honor and integrity, he never held his tongue, and sometimes planted his foot on it. The patience and compromise he exercised in Africa disappeared when he got back to Europe. His indomitable temperament served him superbly in difficult places but sometimes offended polite European society.

"If in England," he said during his address to the Geographical Society in Berlin, "a few mean-minded individuals, seeking to exploit national enmity under the guise of scholarly questions, have given vent to their feelings in contemptible utterances against the leadership of an English expedition by a German, such an attack must urge me all the more to present as quickly as possible my achievements before the English public in order to justify myself as well as the respected English statesmen, above all Lord Palmerston, who honoured Germans with their trust."

Soon after this, and before reports of it appeared in the British press, Shaw's invitation to address the RGS arrived. In his agitated state Barth felt that the society had *presumed* far too much, and he was in no mood to yield to it, despite its considerable influence. It would be two-and-a-half years before he addressed the Geographical Society.

"I absolutely agree with your response to Mr. N. Shaw," wrote Bunsen to Barth. "Your answer is one worthy of a man and of a German. The Geographic Society has no special claim on you, and N. Shaw is not our friend. Yet I hope all the more that you will not delay your arrival in England any longer than the end of the month," advised Bunsen. "Otherwise you will make it difficult for the English ministry to do everything for you that it wants to. You travelled in the name of the English government as their representative, and you can't damage this relationship with England and the English populace under any circumstance. Don't let yourself challenge politics!"

At the end of November 1855, Barth returned to London to begin writing his opus. He settled into a small house with a garden in St. John's Wood near Regent's Park. He hoped to work undisturbed. Almost immediately, the calm shattered on several fronts.

THAT OLD FOX G. B. Gagliuffi, British vice-consul in Murzuk and merchant extraordinaire, had recently been on leave in London. He evidently met with his boss the foreign secretary, Lord Clarendon. According to a letter written December 7, 1855, and marked "Confidential," Gagliuffi told Clarendon that Barth "had availed himself of the means placed at his disposal by H. M. Govt. during that service, to promote German commercial interests in preference to British." Though deeply skeptical of this charge, which violated common sense and contradicted all the commercial treaties Barth had gotten on Britain's behalf, the Foreign Office duly investigated.

Gagliuffi's motive was revenge. He had been sending doleful letters to the FO claiming that he had spent a small fortune outfitting the expedition and hadn't been repaid for his noble sacrifice. The FO had rejected his claims, partly because of letters written by Barth. The explorer had taken Gagliuffi's measure in Murzuk, and though he liked the man and acknowledged his hard work for the mission, he also noted his tendency to do well for himself at every opportunity, which included gouging the expedition. For instance, Barth warned the FO that Gagliuffi seriously inflated the value of the merchandise he provided. When Gagliuffi learned of Barth's caveats, he tried to besmirch him at the FO by appealing to British resentment of Germans. The FO sent Gagliuffi's correspondence about reimbursements to Barth, and asked for a response. The FO evidently omitted Gagliuffi's accusation about promoting German interests, which would have incensed Barth.

His return letter on December 11 was fair, calm, and clear. "There cannot be the least doubt," he wrote, that Gagliuffi had been instrumental in opening Central Africa to British trade and had given crucial assistance to the expedition. His financial grievances, however, lacked merit. Barth explained that when he took over the expedition's finances after Richardson's death, he discovered that Richardson had agreed to crippling terms for a loan from an Arab merchant named Sfaksi—an interest rate of 100 percent, plus other provisos that could swell the original debt from 636 dollars to nearly 3,000. In 1852 in Kukawa, Barth bargained Sfaksi down to 1,700 dollars—still a handsome return, as Barth pointed out. But Sfaksi's partner wanted the entire usurious amount. That partner was Gagliuffi. But the debt had been cleared, wrote Barth, and the FO owed Gagliuffi nothing except gratitude for his fine service as vice-consul—which, Barth graciously suggested, "is well worth a generous consideration from H. M.'s Government." Gagliuffi's claims and his accusation against Barth don't appear again in the official records.

Barth was also under question about Corporal Church, the sapper who had quarreled with Vogel in Kukawa and returned to Europe with the explorer. In addition to his regular soldier's pay, Church had been promised a bonus of £10 to £15 from the Foreign Office if he performed satisfactorily. Barth had written to Clarendon from Murzuk that Church was accompanying him from Bornu because Vogel was "incapable of suffering any longer the arrogance and insolence, which this able but sulky and malicious man was continually manifesting in criticizing and even ridiculing all his doings and proceedings." Despite this insubordination, which also included his refusal to accompany Vogel on several excursions from Kukawa, or finally to do any work at all for the mission, Church asked the FO for his bonus.

Undersecretary Edmund Hammond asked Barth for a report on the matter. Barth was in Hamburg and answered with a brief note that reflected his recent stings from the RGS. Church, he wrote, "would have been an useful man under an English leader, but having had the misfortune of being placed under a German leader, and that moreover a very young one, he thought himself authorized to criticize him, and in doing so followed, as it seems, the insinuation of certain men who make science the battlefield for nationalities."

This peeved Hammond, who disliked Barth and sometimes fanned Shaw's suspicions about documents going first to Germany. Hammond sent Barth's letter to Clarendon, asking for instructions while also slashing at Barth and accusing the Germans of defrauding a deserving British soldier. Hammond found it unsatisfactory, he wrote, that just because Church "did not quite agree with foreign scientific gentlemen he therefore is to be considered solely to blame and mulcted of his reward and denied a character." Clarendon saw things more diplomatically. Since Church's conduct hadn't been altogether satisfactory, "the smaller gratuity (£10) will be sufficient." Barth and Clarendon thought the matter ended, but Church, Hammond, and the British military weren't finished, and it flared up several months later.

Before that happened, however, Barth had another, much uglier confrontation with Norton Shaw of the RGS. An envelope addressed to Barth from Tripoli arrived at the Foreign Office in mid-December 1855. A clerk there couldn't find Barth's address, so he took the envelope to the Royal Geographical Society in hopes of getting it. Norton Shaw took possession. Soon after, Shaw returned the envelope to the FO with a note that its seal was broken. The FO forwarded the opened envelope to Barth along with Shaw's nonexplanation about the seal.

Barth took this as the culminating insult from a man who had repeatedly accused him of shady behavior, and now had opened his private correspondence to seek information he thought the RGS was entitled to. Always thin-skinned in matters of honor, Barth felt flayed by recent slights and accusations. Once again he responded rashly. He returned the envelope's contents—letters from Vogel and Vice-Consul Reade—to Lord Clarendon, with a scathing letter in which he denounced Shaw for opening his private mail.

"How I have merited such an unjust and offensive treatment I am yet to learn," he began. In an aggrieved tone he pointed out that after serving Britain for six years in Africa he had reported to Clarendon even before seeing his family. "Notwithstanding this loyal conduct of mine and notwithstanding my sincere attachment to England," he continued, the FO had forwarded letters addressed to him to the secretary of the RGS, "expressly in order to be broken open by him and then to be returned to me with a sneer. Protesting to Your Lordship," he continued, "that in sacrificing my life it has not been exactly my object to earn shame and insult, I have the honor to sign me Your Lordship's most obedient humble servant, Dr. Barth."

He further embarrassed himself with a petulant postscript: "P. S. In conformity with the views of Your Lordship's office I am preparing an advertisement in the French and German papers, begging my friends to forward all letters of importance, directly to Dr. Shaw, who appeared authorized by Your Lordship, to open my letters."

Clarendon immediately ordered an inquiry into why Barth's packet was sent to the RGS, and he wrote a stern letter to the new president of the society, Admiral F. W. Beechey, asking him to investigate "the outrageous liberty that has been taken with [Barth's] letter by their secretary." Beechey, who admired Barth, immediately agreed.

The FO clerk who took the envelope to the RGS swore that the seal was unbroken when Shaw took possession. Shaw strenuously denied opening it, and suggested that it had somehow been torn during the process of returning it to the FO. Barth doubted this explanation but, lacking any proof to the contrary, had no choice but to accept it. He dropped his charge. Besides, he was embarrassed by his overreaction and mollified by the prompt responses on his behalf by the FO and the RGS. He apologized to Clarendon for his insinuations about the FO.

He also wrote to Beechey at the RGS that he had been hoping for friendly relations with the society's eminent members, but had been distressed by hints of antagonism from "low-minded individuals, who will have easy work to excite jealousy against a stranger." He had not come to England, he continued, "to implicate myself in private quarrels and disputes" but "to be instrumental if possible to further and to promote the knowledge of a Continent, which as yet is so insufficiently known, and to open it for European intercourse." He could do this more readily in England than in Germany, he wrote, because of Britain's power and empire. Beechey soon became one of Barth's strongest supporters.

All this took place in the last two weeks of 1855. Barth hoped that "private quarrels and disputes" were now behind him. But on January 3 of the new year, Shaw, no doubt in retaliation, wrote another letter to Hammond. He accused Barth of funneling astronomical information from Vogel to Petermann, now in Germany, who had published it there several months before the RGS received it. Hammond asked Barth to explain.

Barth replied that in July 1855 he had sent all of Vogel's astronomical observations, plus other information, to Lord Clarendon from Murzuk. He admitted that in his excitement over Vogel's success at finally fixing the position of Yakoba he had sent that one nugget of data to Petermann for the cartographer's delectation. It puzzled him that anyone considered this a big deal, especially since Clarendon had gotten this information and much more. He added that he sent certain information to Petermann because he was doing the maps, not for any underhanded reason.

"I trust that no enlightened man," wrote Barth, "will find a great fault in any communication of a progress in science, if neither the name of the author is kept secret and if due praise is given to the liberality of the Government, which has been the means of making the discovery. And neither of those two conditions, as far as I know, has ever been neglected by Mr. Petermann in any of the communications, which he has made to the Public, though I myself have repeatedly reproached him with publishing them too hastily."

(Petermann sometimes exasperated Barth, who once wrote, "I believe Petermann has really convinced himself that the African expedition was his work, not mine, and that Providence only brought me safely through all those unspeakable dangers thanks to his ideas and his leadership abilities. . . . Despite his great and justifiably rewarded abilities, Petermann is a real loudmouth.")

Clarendon characteristically found the right line through this tangle. He told Hammond he didn't wish to deny information to Petermann, but that Barth "must see the manifest inconvenience" of the cartographer publishing valuable information before it had been given to the RGS. Barth got the point but it baffled him. He was naïve enough, and idealistic enough, to be surprised when anyone put political or national boundaries on scientific information.

DORUGU AND ABBEGA, the freed slaves who had been Barth's servants since he left Kukawa for Timbuktu, had accompanied the explorer to Germany and returned with him to England. Dorugu was about fifteen at the time, Abbega several years older. Barth hoped they would learn English and perhaps some European crafts that would make them useful to future explorers in Central Africa. He also planned to get linguistic help from them for the book on African languages he intended to write after publishing his journal. Meanwhile, as he got to work on *Travels and Discoveries*, he arranged for the teenagers to stay with Reverend J. F. Schön, a missionary and a scholar of the Hausa language who had been on the Niger expedition of 1841.

But by early 1856, Dorugu and Abbega were desperately homesick. They asked Barth to get them back to Africa. He arranged for the Foreign Office to pay their return voyage to Tripoli. He also asked Consul Herman to get them a camel, a trustworthy guide to Kano, and the Arabic passports carried by free blacks in defense against slavers.

As these plans took shape, Barth was attacked by the Anti-Slavery Society, a potent and noisy shaper of public opinion. The society accused Barth of participating in the slave trade while in Africa and of bringing two slaves to England as his servants. The source of these scandalous lies was evidently another man seeking vengeance against Barth: Corporal Church. Barth was stunned, and again felt his honor and integrity under attack.

In the midst of this, the time arrived for Dorugu and Abbega to leave. But they had changed their minds and now wanted to stay, probably with Schön's encouragement, since he too saw them as linguistic resources. Barth, angry that his good intentions for the Africans had blown up in his face and that his efforts to get them home were being shrugged off, refused this change of plans. Then in late February he got word that after boarding their ship in Southampton, the Africans had disembarked with Schön and gone home with him. Barth unreasonably took this as a betrayal by both the Africans and Schön.

(Schön tutored and proselytized Dorugu and Abbega, with the intention of sending them back to Africa as missionaries. They were baptized in May 1857. Abbega returned to Africa later that year. Dorugu followed in 1864. Both quickly abandoned missionary work and applied their new skills to better-paying trades. Dorugu eventually became a schoolteacher. Abbega reverted to Islam and worked as an interpreter for explorers, British officials, and the Royal Niger Company.)

Another irritant for Barth was some more sniping in the press about the mission's cost and his management. Barth felt that the Foreign Office was doing little to defend him. In June 1856 he wrote Undersecretary Hammond "that certain people who from the beginning have done all in their power to vilify the Central African Expedition, spread exaggerated

rumours with regard to the expenditure of that Expedition." He told
Hammond he had asked Admiral Beechey, president of the Royal Geographical Society, to insert a statement in his Anniversary Address that,
according to Francis Galton, an expert on expenditures for exploration,
the mission had cost relatively little. This was true. Barth asked Hammond to clear this statement with Lord Clarendon, "to check at once
those rumours so offensive to every feeling of justice and truth."

The FO, however, did not want to sustain the controversy about
expenses by giving it any more attention. Hammond's terse answer:
"Lord Clarendon considers it will be better not to publish any statement
on this subject. His Lordship knows nothing of the reports to which you
allude, and this may safely be disregarded." Barth took this as a slap in
the face.

Corporal Church continued to agitate and spread venom, writing
letters that cast himself as a wronged martyr. His complaint had been
taken up by the British military, which sent letters to the FO wondering why a brave British soldier was being denied part of his rightful
bonus because of scurrilous remarks by foreigners. Church's plea was
probably boosted by the lionizing of British soldiers in the Crimean
War among the press and public after the heavy casualties caused by
commanders' gross incompetence. In May 1856 the Foreign Office
sent Barth a list of Church's grievances and asked for specific charges
against him.

Barth evidently didn't know about Church's recent machinations and
was surprised to learn of his complaints. Barth's long reply mixed his
usual blunt honesty with cluelessness about its effects. First he expanded
his short comments from the previous October, which he said had been
intended to explain Church's behavior, not criticize it: "For it is easily
understood that the Members of an Expedition are brought into nearer
contact with each other, than is generally the case in the army. Then
Mr. Vogel was a very young man, who of course by his want of experience could not but commit some blunders and thirdly he was a foreigner

and that at a time, when the war and the difference of politics roused national antipathies. . . . All this I said in order to explain and if possible excuse Corporal Church's conduct in criticising and ridiculing Mr. Vogel's conduct. . . . For [Church's] mischievous, malicious and insolent behavior is an undeniable fact."

For Barth, the observing scientist, facts explained phenomena. Undeniable facts were simply data, not criticisms, even when draped with words such as "malicious" and "insolent." It surprised him that Church and the FO didn't understand that.

He added more data. When he reached Kukawa in December 1854, Church had tried to poison him against Vogel, accusing the young scientist of sloppy bookkeeping and immoral relations. After investigating, Barth found both the books and Vogel's character in good order, which in turn cast doubt on Church's honesty. And then, in front of Barth, Church had threatened to smear Vogel if Vogel complained about him to British superiors. Barth noted that Church was also continuing to slur a man named Madi, hired by Richardson in 1850, who had served the mission loyally, "and having been most severely wounded and crippled for life, while defending the boat against the pirates of the lake, has been placed by me upon a small pension."

Church was clearly a nasty piece of work. And yet Barth ends his devastating letter this way: "I frankly confess, that I should feel sorry, if what I have said should deprive him of the higher rewards, which it appears he might have obtained. But I have been called for to vindicate my own conduct."

After the FO forwarded this letter to Church, he had the brass to respond that nothing in it charged him with neglect of duty or want of zeal, so he wanted his money. After all this agitation, the archives go silent about whether Church ever collected that additional £5 bonus. He did, however, receive a watch and chain from the Royal Geographical Society in May 1856 for "his meritorious and intelligent services while employed upon the African expedition under Dr. Vogel."

AT THE SAME CEREMONY where Church was honored by the RGS, Barth received one of the society's most prestigious awards: the Patron's Gold Medal. "For your successful and extensive explorations in Central Africa, your numerous excursions about Lake Chad, your discovery of the great river [Benue], and for your hazardous and adventurous journey to and from Timbuctu." A scientist to his fingertips, Barth highly prized this tribute from his fellow scholars. In his acceptance he thanked the society on behalf of Prussia as well as himself. He also urged the British government to follow up his discoveries by opening a relationship with Central Africa through commerce on the Niger and Benue rivers. This would give the natives "a humane and lawful way" to replace the misery caused by the slave economy. The government ignored this advice for decades.

Barth's accomplishments as an explorer were indisputably prodigious, and British scholars expected that his published journals would carry similar scientific heft. But given his nationality and the previous friction with the RGS, some people questioned the award of the Gold Medal and felt it should have gone to Richard Burton for his journeys in disguise to Mecca (*Personal Narrative of a Pilgrimage to Al-Medinah and Meccah*, 1855), and to Harar in Ethiopia (*First Footsteps in East Africa*, 1856). But even the British candidates for the Gold Medal reportedly felt that no one deserved it more than Barth.

Burton was among the small circle of people whom Barth saw in London while writing *Travels and Discoveries*. The two great African travelers met when Burton returned from the Crimean War in early 1856. Burton wanted to search for the source of the Nile. Barth suggested that he look for the Sea of Ujiji (Lake Tanganyika) described by Arab traders. This became Burton's immediate goal. The British government and the RGS funded the project.

Burton and his assistant John Hanning Speke left for eastern Africa in September 1856. They would be gone nearly three years. After appalling hardships, they became the first Europeans to reach Lake Tanganyika. They heard of an even bigger lake to the northeast, but Burton was too ill to move, so Speke went alone. He found the lake and named it Victoria. On scant evidence, he claimed it the source of the Nile. Despite Burton's violent disagreement, Speke was eventually proven correct. Burton received the RGS's Gold Medal in 1859 "for his various exploratory enterprises," especially the expedition with Speke to the African lakes. Speke got the award in 1861 for the same journey, in particular his discovery of Lake Victoria.

Barth's friends in London also included Rear Admiral William Henry Smyth, an astronomer and one of the founders of the RGS; Dr. William Baikie, director of the Benue expedition; Francis Galton, a polymath who also explored southwest Africa and wrote *The Art of Travel*, an immensely popular handbook about exploratory travel; Desborough Cooley, the geographer and historian; and Sir Roderick Murchison, a geologist and one of the founders of the RGS, which he frequently served as president.

But Barth socialized little, isolating himself in his study to write *Travels and Discoveries*. "My main flaw is this propensity towards loneliness," he wrote to his friend von Schubert, "and that I withdraw from whatever social circle too easily. I have to get myself some more 'cheerful society.'"

"The idea of having to spend time on diversions," wrote von Schubert, "or on social pleasantries or obligations, was completely foreign to him."

He was also yearning for more than male companionship. After he returned from Africa, according to von Schubert, "Barth's deepest longing was to find a life partner." Barth wrote to him, "If I chose well, a life companion would bring my entire life into bloom. I yearn for communion of hearts and snug companionship." But he was unwilling to pause his writing long enough to meet women, much less court one. "I just need my first volumes to come out," he wrote von Schubert, "and then I will find an opportunity to meet a like-minded soul." Von Schubert's wry comment: "This perspective would hardly help him find the woman he longed for to fill the emptiness in his heart."

Barth had hoped to finish the first three volumes by the end of 1856, absurdly optimistic even without all the year's distractions. In November 1856, Barth learned that his father, whom he called his best friend and greatest supporter, had died. He buried his grief by working even harder. The long motionless hours at his desk aggravated his rheumatism and his restless nature.

"How I long for the freedom of a bivouac in the desert," he wrote to von Schubert, "in that unfathomable expanse where, free of ambitions, free from the thousands of little things that torture people here, I would savor my freedom as I rolled out my bed at the end of a long day's march, my possessions, my camels, and my horse around me. I almost regret having put myself in these chains."

In the first half of 1857 more distractions pulled at him. The Foreign Office hadn't heard from Vogel since May 1855. In February 1857 a rumor reached London that the young German had been murdered in Wadai, evidently for naïvely climbing a sacred mountain. Barth thought highly of Vogel's energy, dedication, and astronomical skills. The news upset him. This was soon followed by a report that Corporal Macguire, while en route to Tripoli and home, had been killed six days north of Kukawa. All of Vogel's papers were missing—another blow.

Barth had been urging the FO to send another expedition up the Niger and Benue to fortify Britain's relations in the region, especially with Timbuktu and Sheikh al-Bakkay. The FO finally approved the mission in November 1856, again under the leadership of Dr. Baikie, who had become Barth's good friend. The FO asked Barth to help Baikie plan the trip, and he was pleased to oblige. Yet when the mission's new ship was launched in a public ceremony in March 1857, the FO somehow failed to inform or invite Barth. He took it as another insult.

But most of his attention was elsewhere. He was about to place the first three volumes of *Travels and Discoveries in North and Central Africa* before the public.

31

Last Journeys

THE ENGLISH EDITION OF *TRAVELS AND DISCOVERIES IN NORTH AND Central Africa, Being a Journal of an Expedition Undertaken under the Auspices of H. B. M.'s Government, in the Years 1849–1855* was published in April 1857. Longmans, Green & Company printed 2,250 copies, priced at about £1 per volume. The three volumes covered Barth's journey up to his departure for Timbuktu. The books were beautifully done. There were several dozen pastel lithographs of African scenes by painter J. M. Bernatz, based on sketches by Barth, and many dozen woodcuts and drawings, plus superbly detailed maps by Petermann.

Barth admired the illustrations but wished Bernatz had followed the text's example and included more "enlivening circumstances"—more scenes of Africans busily living their daily lives, instead of so many landscapes, as if humans and human culture were scarce.

Barth had written the book in both English and German, for simultaneous publication. (Eventually there were editions in Dutch, Danish, and French, as well as a U.S. edition.) Considering that English was his second language, the task verged on the heroic. The Germanisms and malapropisms in the English edition were surprisingly few. Water was occasionally "the aqueous element." Adamawa was "the country after which I had been panting so long." He referred to the Bahr el Ghazal, "which it was not our destiny to become acquainted with by ocular inspection," and to messengers who delivered their bad news after "having moistened their organs with a cup of coffee." But in general the writing was plain and clear.

In both languages the reviews were mixed. Reviewers admired Barth's learning, precision, thoroughness, breadth, and endurance. They pronounced him one of the greatest, if not the greatest, of African travelers. Many called the book the most useful and indispensible yet published about the continent. But they also complained that it was clotted with excessive detail, as if Barth had dumped his journal onto the page instead of transforming it into a narrative with general themes. Every reviewer grumbled about the length, grumbles that grew louder with the publication of volumes four and five the following summer, which brought the page count to nearly 3,500, including hundreds of pages of scholarly appendices. "Their great length," commented the *Guardian* about these hefty volumes, "will be an obstacle not easily overcome in the way of their general popularity."

Correct. The first three volumes sold poorly, so the publisher printed only 1,000 copies of the last two. By contrast, David Livingstone's *Missionary Travels and Researches in South Africa*, published a few months after Barth's first volumes, quickly sold more than 30,000 copies, and kept selling. Livingstone was wildly popular, mobbed in public, and in great demand as a speaker.

Barth had met Livingstone in late 1856, just a few days after the missionary returned from his two-year transcontinental journey across Africa, the basis for *Missionary Travels*. The two men remained cordial ever after. Barth admired Livingstone's toughness, integrity, and clear, if unscientific, observations. He may also have recognized a kindred solitary nature. They sent each other their newly published books, appeared together at several talks, and occasionally corresponded.

Barth didn't resent Livingstone's success, but he was baffled by their contrasting receptions. He had spent nearly nine years on this project—traveling, documenting, and writing. He had made discoveries, brought back reams of new information, opened Central Africa for British trade, reached Timbuktu. He had hoped to be rewarded with renown, both scientific and popular. He did earn the admiration of his peers—gold medals from the Royal Geographical Society and the Paris Geographical Society, honorary memberships from Oxford University, the Royal Asiatic Society of London, and several groups in Germany.

But it puzzled him when the public balked at reading thousands of pages of meticulous scholarship and preferred Livingstone's entertaining yet scientifically lightweight chronicle. For Barth, pleasurable reading meant scholarly treatises and histories. High drama meant new scientific findings. He didn't understand that although the public valued scientific discoveries, it craved entertainment. He had smothered his incredible adventures beneath thick layers of information. Livingstone's book was nearly 700 pages long, but compared to Barth's 3,500 it seemed terse. (Barth's tome, in turn, was succinct compared to his mentor von Humboldt's twenty-three volume *Personal Narrative of a Voyage to the Equinoctial Regions of the New Continent.*)

Other factors also were at play. Livingstone had the advantage of being British rather than Prussian, and the British liked their heroes homegrown. After Henry Morton Stanley tracked down the beloved Livingstone in 1871, the British treated Stanley coolly, as an American interloper working for an American newspaper. Sir Henry Rawlinson, president of the RGS, scoffed that it was "not true that Stanley had discovered Livingstone, as it was Livingstone who had discovered Stanley." The irony was that Stanley was Welsh but had changed his name and nationality after moving to the United States.

In *Travels and Discoveries*, Barth often praised his British predecessors in Africa, but he just as often criticized them for sloppiness or inaccuracy. That probably rankled people. So did remarks such as "it seems that the English are more apt to perform a great deed than to follow up its consequences." Nor did he hesitate to scold the government for various shortcomings, from doing too little about slavery to ignoring the rich possibilities of the Sudan.

At several points in the book he also complained bitterly, and unfairly, about the government's lack of financial support for the mission. He sprinkled the book's concluding paragraph with self-congratulation and cranky grievances: "I had embarked on this undertaking as a volunteer, under the most unfavorable circumstances. . . . The scale and the means of the mission seemed to be extremely limited. . . . I had continued in my career amid great embarrassment, carrying on the exploration of extensive regions almost without any means. . . . I resolved upon undertaking, with a very limited supply of means, a journey to the far west. . . ." Such stuff must have been hard for the British to swallow.

His book was also a tougher sell than Livingstone's because he didn't return with a momentous discovery or accomplishment—a transcontinental trek, the source of a great river. He brought home a mass of detail that was far more durably valuable than any one discovery, but the public wanted thrilling headlines, not small print.

Barth was also the victim of bad timing. During his absence Britain had begun shifting its African focus, for strategic and commercial reasons, from the Sahara and the west coast to the continent's east and south. A new wave of explorers ventured into these regions, capturing the popular imagination and deflecting attention from Barth's achievements. Livingstone was lionized after returning from fifteen years in eastern and southern Africa. Burton and Speke excited the popular imagination with their first trip to Somalia in 1854, and brought it to a boil with their great trek of 1856 to 1859 to find the source of the Nile. Francis Galton's popular books about southern Africa contributed to the trend. By the time Barth returned to Britain, his epic journey was geographically out of style.

So was his tone and perspective. The public loved Livingstone's book partly because it was more personal and sensational than Barth's. As noted by the delightfully named periodical *The Ladies' Repository*, these qualities gave Livingstone's book a certain "romantic attraction" that Barth's lacked. The British public did prize books about scientific exploration, such as the journals of Captain Cook or Darwin's *Voyage of the Beagle*, but readers were always more enthusiastic about books such as Mungo Park's that were heavy on alien curiosities, exciting escapes, lurid anecdotes, and extreme trials. Even Burton, a rough scholar, larded his books with personal drama.

The trend toward autobiographical books that emphasized the writer's experiences and Africa's strangeness would accelerate throughout the nineteenth century, epitomized by Stanley's self-dramatizing style ("the roving correspondent meets the command that may send him to his doom") and his egocentric melodramatic titles: *How I Found Livingstone, In Darkest Africa, Through the Dark Continent, My Dark Companions and Their Strange Stories.*

Not coincidentally, as Africa and Africans became the exotic background for a traveler's heroic adventures, imperialism was devouring the continent and its people. Both developments could be justified only by making Africa and Africans less real and less important than European perceptions and ambitions. Barth, by contrast, tended to downplay his personal experiences, and to put Africa and Africans at the forefront. For him Africa wasn't an empty canvas to be filled by his own perceptions, but a vibrant multidimensional place with a long and complex cultural history worth studying.

This suggests another reason that Barth failed to find popularity: his news from Africa was unwelcome. Europe was on the cusp of the imperial age. Curiosity about Africa was hardening into certitude that the continent would benefit from European civilization and religion, by force if necessary. Islam was considered a dangerous and evil opponent of Christian values. Racialist theories were winning adherents, prompted partly by racial unrest in the West Indian colonies. In 1852, for instance, Disraeli argued that, for their own good, the West Indian slaves shouldn't have been freed. British commentators had started proposing that blacks were helpless without white supervision, and that foreign lands populated by dark-skinned people were created by Providence as raw materials to be shaped by white civilization.

"Decidedly, you have to be servants to those that are born *wiser* than you, that are born lords of you," wrote Thomas Carlyle, addressing blacks in his 1849 essay, "Occasional Discourse on the Nigger Question," a polemic against white liberal attitudes about race. "That, you may depend on it, my obscure Black friends, is and was always the Law of the World, for you and for all men."

As Barth was traveling in Africa, Dr. Robert Knox came to prominence as a popular lecturer in Britain, following the publication of his book *The Races of Man* (1850). Knox's theme was "transcendental anatomy"—the superiority of the white race, especially its highest flowering, the Anglo-Saxon. "Race," he said, "is everything: literature, science, art—in a word, civilization depends on it." (Knox took up lecturing after his medical career ended in disgrace when two men were arrested for murdering people to supply corpses for his school of anatomy.) Evidence of culture among Africans was attributed to colonization by Semitic, i.e. light-skinned, people from Egypt, North Africa, and the Middle East.

When Barth's book appeared, the age of imperialism hadn't begun, but the assumptions that later grew like tumors were all in place—that Africa was uncivilized, that it was inhabited by people who were both childlike and savage, people who had no discernible history or culture, no ability to govern themselves, who lived in a state of barbaric chaos. It was a short step from these assumptions to the certainty that Africa could only be saved by imposing European civilization, religion, governance, and commerce. These racial certitudes bred righteousness, which shaped foreign policy. Information that contradicted the going assumptions was ignored or dismissed as naïve.

Barth's open-minded observations challenged these assumptions. He saw—was willing to see—that Africans had their own story. Though he carried some of the age's racial preconceptions, he was willing to go where the evidence took him. He did find ignorance and savagery in Africa, but he also found scholars and sophisticated systems of government and commerce. He called Islam a great religion filled with learned men, though it was often used as excuse for fanaticism and violence. "I have not given up my belief," he wrote, "that there is a vital principle in Islam, which has only to be brought out by a reformer in order to accomplish great things." He pointed out that acts done in the name of Muhammed could be as great, or as evil, as acts done in the name of Jesus Christ.

Barth also brought home proof of Africa's long, rich history and cultural traditions, including a literary tradition. He had the gall to assert that one of his literary discoveries, the *Tarik al-Sudan*, "will be one of the most important additions which the present age has made to the history of mankind, in a branch which was formerly almost unknown."

In his work, Barth tried to cross the barriers between white and black, Christian and Muslim, Europe and Africa. He went to Africa to learn and communicate, not to dictate and control. He wrote about Africans as individuals who belonged to diverse cultures often connected by history and language. In his work Africans are real people with distinct stories, not a dark mass waiting to be molded. He met Africa and Africans on their own terms, and usually in their own languages.

The result was the most extensive trove of knowledge collected about Africa in the nineteenth century. Barth brought back findings that he believed would create a new, richer, more accurate idea of not only African history but world history—volumes of new information on a vast region of distinct cultures, hitherto unknown to Europeans, that had been in constant trade and conflict for ten centuries.

He believed in the enterprise of science: an incremental accumulation of data, an open-minded search for truth, in order to replace ignorance with knowledge. Von Schubert noted "the priest-like seriousness with which he subordinated everything else to this goal."

In addition to scientific knowledge, he brought back psychological understanding. He made clear that Africans could be as intolerant and racist as any Londoner, as certain of their cultural superiority as any Englishman, as politically devious and subtle as any Prussian. They could be loving, cruel, shortsighted, open-minded, scholarly. They would take any measure necessary to protect their business, land, children, or social position. They could be as shrewd, brave, dishonest, trustworthy, and chauvinistic as any European. All these human qualities, in addition to history, also connected Europeans and Africans. As he told a Tuareg chief who accused him of being an infidel, "we were nearer to each other than he thought, and might well be friends, offering to each other those advantages which each of us commanded."

Barth's evidence and attitudes were inconvenient. To see Africans as individuals, to recognize the common humanity beneath the cultural differences, to acknowledge the continent's complex history, cultures, and social organization, would make colonization and rapacious exploitation morally indefensible. Better to substitute expedient assumptions for knowledge. Better to choose an African story that made occupation morally imperative. Better to put Barth's work high on a shelf and forget about it.

THROUGHOUT THE REST of 1857, Barth's relationship with the Foreign Office continued to deteriorate. Before leaving Timbuktu, he had urged al-Bakkay to send emissaries to England to strengthen commercial relations. Soon after his return to London he began pushing the Foreign Office to invite representatives from Timbuktu, Sokoto, and Bornu to England. The Foreign Office hesitated. Such an offer might offend Britain's new ally, France, whose ambitions in Central Africa were clear. Nevertheless in April 1857, Clarendon sent invitations to the African leaders.

By then a delegation from al-Bakkay was already en route to Tripoli. The group included al-Bakkay's son-in-law, nephew, and cousin. They reached Tripoli in June and asked for permission to continue to London. Clarendon sent his approval, and Barth began looking for lodgings. But then Consul Herman realized that the emissaries seemed less interested in trade than in politics. They wanted to lobby the British government to stop France from advancing into the Sahara. Herman also gathered that "something must have passed on this subject between the Sheikh and Dr. Barth."

Clarendon, worried that the delegation could become politically embarrassing, instructed Hammond to see if Barth had told al-Bakkay that Britain would support Timbuktu against France. Hammond asked Barth and reported that the explorer probably had given al-Bakkay that impression, and also had signed a letter forbidding France from penetrating toward Tuat.

Britain couldn't risk the perception that it was plotting against French expansion in Africa. Once again the Foreign Office used the weather gambit. Herman told the Timbuktu delegation that Britain was too cold for them at the moment, but they would be welcome in spring. The emissaries saw through the brush-off and left Tripoli in October. Sheikh al-Bakkay wrote to Queen Victoria to protest this shabby treatment of his ambassadors. He also wrote a gracious letter to Barth, assuring him that he knew the explorer had nothing to do with the government's behavior.

Barth was appalled. He regarded this conduct as an insult to his friends and a repudiation of his diplomacy on Britain's behalf. "Mr. H. [Hammond] had the audacity to tell me to my face," he wrote to Chevalier Bunsen, "that he wished these people were at the bottom of the Red Sea; right after that I was shown a letter sent to the Foreign Office which said that my friend el-Bakay had murdered Laing and that I had his papers."

He was referring to a message sent by the Foreign Office at the end of 1857. It contained two letters from the British vice-consul in Oran, Algeria, stating that Major Laing's murderer had been found, and that a French officer had learned that Barth now possessed Laing's missing papers. The FO asked Barth to comment. The question was routine but arrived without buffering apologies, and the insult wounded Barth anew. "I have had to hack my way through another net of the most disgusting intrigues," he wrote to Bunsen, ". . . how could I possibly consider taking part in any future endeavors in service to this government?"

He was also embittered because he still hadn't received the Companionship of the Bath, promised by the government more than two years earlier. Nor had the Foreign Office bothered to unpack the samples of

African manufactures that he had laboriously collected and shipped to England to help stimulate trade relations. Following Bunsen's advice, he had once hoped to be rewarded with a position at a major British university, but no offers came.

These slights, in addition to all the others, convinced Barth that he and his work were being shunted aside. By May 1858, when he completed the last two volumes, he no longer expected or wanted a future in Britain. He was eager to put the place behind him.

First, as promised, he addressed the Royal Geographical Society, where he now felt like a valued member. His topic was the history, geography, and politics of Central Africa, which he said were connected to each other and to world history by language: "Only the most accurate study of the idioms of all these tribes can furnish us with a thread which may lead us with some degree of security through this ethnographic labyrinth."

The moment his final volumes were printed in August, he left for Germany. "With uncertain future," he wrote ebulliently to von Schubert, "and without any great shining prospects, but free." Within weeks he was refreshing himself in his favorite way—by traveling, this time through Asia Minor.

IN JANUARY 1859 he was back in Berlin and eager to leap into the future. He found an apartment and felt excited about rejoining the city's scientific circles. Von Schubert wasn't optimistic. "I had very little hope that things would turn out well for him, and wrote in my journal: 'Heinrich is always too gruff and unyielding, and yet too modest and too imprudent. His pride doesn't permit him to give in at the right moments. In the river of life he is a bold and persevering swimmer, but not a very agile one.' And I wasn't wrong."

Barth had several influential allies in Berlin. His old mentor von Humboldt wrote to him: "In the last few days I have discussed your wishes very seriously with Ritter and the Regent, and I hope that everything can be arranged according to your desires. I can attest that the ailing King considers it of the utmost importance to get you, the man admired everywhere, a position."

A consulship in Constantinople interested Barth, until he heard the salary. Von Humboldt also tried to secure him the consulship in Damascus, but the Prussian government decided not to refill the position. Barth lobbied for the same post in Siam, unsuccessfully. Then in May, von Humboldt died, ending that vein of possibility.

Barth also explored academic opportunities. Von Schubert noted that the explorer would have had many offers if he had stayed in Germany, but by taking Bunsen's advice and going to England he had lost his moment and also estranged some German scholars. Ritter tried to find him a professorship, but in September he followed von Humboldt to the grave. Ritter had recommended Barth as his replacement, but the government seemed in no hurry to fulfill its promise to give Barth an academic position after his journey. (His other main sponsor, Bunsen, died in 1860.)

Barth himself was part of the problem. His restlessness and adamant autonomy made him leery of any permanent position. "When he was sitting at a desk, he longed to be atop a horse or a camel," wrote von Schubert, "when he was travelling, he missed the appealing stillness of his study. Thus he pursued a fixed, lasting relationship with the university on the one hand, and worked to secure himself a certain amount of independence on the other. It was difficult to bring the two things together."

Nor did his brusque, thorny personality help his job search. "He preferred not to talk about his own deeds at all," noted von Schubert, "and, if they came up in conversation, he spoke of them very modestly. Due to his closed-off nature, he was no great judge of character, which meant he often placed an undeserved degree of importance on the opinions of unimportant people and their press products."

As he cast about for the right position, he stayed busy. He worked on his volumes about the languages of Central Africa. He also helped to establish and raise money for an institute named after Ritter. Its purpose was to fund geographic exploration in unknown regions, especially in Africa. Its first projects, with Barth as director, were expeditions to search for Vogel's papers and to complete Vogel's explorations of the area between Lake Chad and the Nile.

Barth asked the British government to contribute to the institute. He explained why in a letter to the Royal Geographical Society's Murchison: "For the gentlemen of the Foreign Office are well aware, that I have still a just claim upon them." He wanted "a kind of testimonial" from the British about the services rendered by Germans to the Central African Expedition—not only himself, Overweg, and Vogel, but also Ritter, who had recommended Barth; Bunsen, who had secured him the position; and Petermann, who had drawn the invaluable maps. What would this British expedition have been without Germans? But perhaps that was the underlying issue. "May the English learn justly to appreciate the German character," wrote Barth, "and I have no doubt, that the English and Germans will achieve many grand things together, bound in friendly companionship, in time of peace and in scientific pursuits, or in time of war and on the battlefield."

The British government declined to contribute to the institute, another sign of its waning interest in the Sahara and Central Africa, and another affront to Barth. He shouldn't have been too surprised. The Foreign Office had closed the vice-consulate in Ghadames in early 1861 and later that year shuttered the one in Murzuk after Gagliuffi resigned the post.

The Foreign Office further indicated its indifference to Central Africa by its handling of Sheikh al-Bakkay's second attempt to strengthen relations, in late 1860. Al-Bakkay sent a courier to Tripoli with letters to the queen and the FO, again asking them to persuade France to halt its expansion south. And he still wanted to send a delegation to England. To discourage this the new Foreign Secretary, Lord Russell, directed Consul Herman to trot out the well-worn excuse of England's cold weather. But if the sheikh wanted to send a delegation anyway, instructed Russell, tell him that he will have to pay for the delegation's travel costs and expenses in England. This slap in the face not only reneged on the government's earlier invitation, but disregarded the sheikh's gracious hospitality and protection of Barth for so many months in Timbuktu. As intended, the insult destroyed the relationship cultivated so carefully by Barth on Britain's behalf.

· When he learned of it, Barth wrote to von Schubert, "I know that the English are ashamed to the depths of their souls." This was apparent only to Barth. A few months later he was still angry, writing to von Schubert, "The English . . . took what I offered them with open arms and threw it into the mud. The men on the Niger and on the Chad should at least know that I did not lie to them."

In 1861, Barth got the chance to repay part of his debt to al-Bakkay. One of the sheikh's sons was captured by the French in Senegal and accused of being a spy. Barth wrote to the governor there and asked him to spare the man's life in return for the Kunta tribe's many kindnesses to him. Out of respect for Barth, the governor freed the man, who wrote Barth a gallant thank-you in Arabic.

Barth's relations with the British government improved somewhat in 1862 after he finally received the Companionship of the Bath, seven years late—a delay, he told von Schubert, caused "by a clique of jealous officers" in the Ministry of War.

That same year he was nominated for full membership in Berlin's Royal Academy of Sciences, the highest academic honor in Germany. But his own colleagues voted to reject him. According to von Schubert, the rebuff "plagued him bitterly." Again, he smelled personal intrigues.

He was probably right. Few professionals guard their fiefs more viciously than academics, and Barth's news from Africa trespassed on several. Among Germany's intelligentsia, the dominant views about Africa came from Hegel and Schiller, and were epitomized by Hegel's remark that Africa "is no historical part of the world; it has no movement or development to exhibit." Barth's work should have demolished the notion that Africa had no history; instead, self-interested parties tried to demolish Barth. Hence, Leopold von Ranke, Germany's most famous living historian and a follower of Hegel and Schiller, voted against Barth, dismissing him as an adventurer, not a scientist, an opinion that suggested total unfamiliarity with *Travels and Discoveries*. It was convenient for other luminaries from the Royal Academy to agree with von Ranke. In the same year that he was rejected as a mere adventurer, Barth published the first volume of his groundbreaking work on African languages.

Since his return from Africa, Barth had been corresponding energetically with a long list of people throughout Europe. His French correspondents alone numbered at least two dozen and included geographers, diplomats, editors, linguists, Arabists, and archeologists. The volume increased when he assumed the presidency of the Berlin Geographical Society in 1863. He followed any news coming out of Africa and wrote excitedly to foreign correspondents about the expeditions of Speke, Burton, and Baker. He relayed updates about German expeditions, and made sure that any new findings were presented to the Geographical Society.

He was particularly generous toward other explorers, regardless of nationality. The list was long: Livingstone, Burton, du Chaillu, Rebmann, Krapf, Baikie, von Beurmann. He advised the young Frenchman Henri Duveyrier, who became famous for his travels among the Tuaregs, and Gerhard Rohlfs, who would follow Barth to Bornu. He inspired Germany's second-greatest African explorer, Gustav Nachtigal, who also made an epic journey of five years. "Barth, who had to contend with much the same internal and external difficulties," wrote Nachtigal, "I took as my constant example."

Barth was dismayed when politics interfered with the progress of science or put nationality above the free flow of knowledge. He felt his own work had been pushed aside because of politics. The newest friction between politics and science was caused by the "January Uprising" in Poland against Russia in 1863. France and Britain supported the revolutionaries with sympathetic rhetoric. Prussia signed a military agreement to help Russia smash the revolt.

"May the Germans, and the Prussians in particular, succeed in fostering that friendly feeling between the English and the German Nation which the shortsighted policy of their Governments has nearly destroyed," Barth wrote to the RGS's Murchison in May. "Would not my own position in England have been a different one, if I had been backed by those men to whom I had trusted. At all events I promise you for my own part to forward the interests of geography and Geographical Research and Discovery to the best of my ability."

But May also brought good personal news: the government finally gave him an at-large appointment at the University of Berlin, at the modest salary of 1,500 thaler (about £200). "Barth saw the offer as his personal salvation," wrote von Schubert. Elated, the explorer wrote his brother-in-law: "Everyone has to go through some dark times and accepts this calmly, but swimming completely against the current exhausts even the strongest person. Instead of finding accommodation and help, I have fought my way through nothing but resistance whenever I want to do anything at all."

His two courses that fall attracted many students, and this time he was happy in the classroom. "What is more instructive to the youth than geography and sociology, with all their stimulating and inspiring facets?" he wrote to von Schubert. "For me, this area of science is the epitome of all the others, the band connecting all the other disciplines, and as the different branches of science become more aware of the roots that anchor them in life, this science will become more and more important."

Since his return to Berlin he had traveled for several months each year: to Spain in 1861, the Balkans in 1862, the Alps in 1863. He relished his new position partly because it left him free to write and travel. He published two more volumes of his work on African languages, and books about his newest travels. In 1864 he climbed in Italy's Apennines.

"Travelling was Barth's real element," wrote von Schubert. "Following his own instincts, not subject to others' will, able to give his research ideas complete freedom, he always came back from these trips and resumed his day-to-day work refreshed, full of strength and vitality."

In 1865 he spent nearly three months exploring Macedonia, Albania, and Montenegro. He took the highest path through every mountain range, and zigzagged his way through the valleys between them. His health seemed fully recovered. When he returned to Berlin in October he learned that his old friend, Sheikh al-Bakkay, had died in battle, fighting for his beloved Timbuktu.

On November 23, Barth collapsed with tremendous pain in his abdomen. After two days of agony he fell unconscious and died on November 25. He was forty-four.

A few newspapers speculated that his traveler's habit of self-medication had led to accidental poisoning. His relatives requested an autopsy to end the rumor. The doctor found that Barth's stomach had burst from an infection, the result of chronic intestinal disease, probably caused by years of poor diet in Africa. The doctor also found a bullet in Barth's thigh, left there by Egyptian Bedouins in 1846.

His funeral on November 29 drew Berlin's scientific elite. The *Times* of London, which had ignored his return from Africa, reported his death. Murchison wrote an appreciative obit for the *Journal of the Royal Geographical Society*. It ended, "A more intelligent, indefatigable, trustworthy, and resolute traveller than Dr. Barth can rarely be found, and we all deplore his untimely end at the early age of forty-four."

Epilogue

THE TALL MARBLE HEADSTONE THAT MARKED BARTH'S GRAVE WAS destroyed in World War II during the Battle of Berlin. By then his name and his epic journey were nearly forgotten, except by scholars. The length, breadth, and scope of his travels and findings place him among the greatest of African explorers. Some Africanists consider him without peer. Yet his name means nothing to the general public.

Some of the reasons for Barth's obscurity have been mentioned. Another might be that he didn't fit the image of the explorer created by books and art, later amplified by movies. He made his great journey as the age of exploration and discovery was giving way to the age of imperialism. His heroics differed from those of the new model. The imperial heroes weren't self-effacing scientists but self-promoting media personalities like Stanley. Barth emphasized his accuracy and comprehensiveness more so than his courageous adventures, and when he bragged, it was about his scientific discoveries. He didn't fight a lion, or quell rebellious porters with a whip, or shoot his way out of a ring of hostile natives. He didn't act as if Africa and Africans were brutes to be tamed. Though tough and well armed, he never shot or beat a native, unlike nearly every other African explorer. His goal was information, not submission. His method was sociability, not intimidation. "I have never proceeded onward without leaving a sincere friend behind me," he wrote, hardly the creed of a steely-eyed conqueror.

The names of the kingdoms Barth visited are mostly forgotten as well. He was among the last Europeans to witness them before the onslaught of colonialism. Within fifty years the empires he visited and wrote about—Bornu, Sokoto, Gwandu, Adamawa, Bagirmi, Wadai, Hamdallahi—were gone. They survive, as he does, in *Travels and Discoveries*. His work is considered indispensable by modern scholars partly because much of what he recorded was lost or destroyed.

Many of his findings still pertain today: the friction between Islam and other beliefs in northern Africa, and the friction within Islam itself between scholars and anti-intellectual zealots. Few of us know much about Islam or northern Africa's history of Islamic learning and the extensive interactions between cultures there. Barth still has much to tell us.

His news of Islamic Africa's long tradition of literate and learned cultures, and of its ancient manuscripts, has been largely ignored for generations. That is finally changing. Backed by the Ford Foundation and other funders, there is an ongoing effort to find and restore these manuscripts. Timbuktu is the main locus. In the last decade a few scholars there have recovered 700,000 manuscripts, most of which have been kept for hundreds of years by poor desert families as part of their patrimony. Acquired in trade for cows and money, these works are finally going into collections for research and preservation in Timbuktu.

The manuscripts verify Barth's findings. They demonstrate not only a brisk exchange of ideas, but also extensive commercial and personal interactions between cultures in northern Africa. All this has surprised even scholars of Islam, who have typically discounted Islamic learning and its influence in northern Africa. John Hunwick is a historian of precolonial Africa and founder of Northwestern University's Institute for the Study of Islamic Thought in Africa, which is leading the effort to train young African scholars who will translate and interpret the manuscripts in Timbuktu. He has said, sounding like Barth, "We hope, too, to enlighten the general public as to the role that Islam has played in African societies, and to the fact that much of Africa has long enjoyed literacy and an intellectual life—matters that may help to erase some of the unfortunate stereotypes about Africa. . . . [Then] Timbuktu will cease to be seen just as a legendary fantasy, and will be recognized for what it really was—a spiritual and intellectual jewel inspired by the Islamic faith."

ONE OF BARTH'S FAVORITE words was "labyrinth." As a scholar of the classics, he would have known the myth well. The cunning architect Daedalus built an elaborate maze to imprison the Minotaur, the half-man, half-bull that had to be fed human sacrifices. Theseus traveled into the labyrinth to kill the monster, unwinding Ariadne's ball of thread as he went so that he could find his way back out.

"We here trace a historical thread," wrote Barth in the preface to *Travels and Discoveries*, "which guides us through this labyrinth of tribes and overthrown kingdoms." Barth couldn't fail to see himself as Theseus. His Ariadne, the supplier of his thread, was knowledge—history, languages, geography. He used them to find his way into the heart of Africa and to emerge with riches, and he made maps so that others could follow him. Too few know he was there.

Acknowledgments

In Nigeria: Abdalla Uba Adamu, professor at Bayero University in Kano, recommended Nasiru Wada Khalil as a perfect guide to Islamic northern Nigeria; he was right. Nasiru, who works in the Sharia court of Kano, wisely persuaded me to hire Nasiru Datti Ahmed, a secondary school teacher in Kano, as our driver. These two learned, curious men provided guidance of many kinds, as well as amiable company and friendship.

In Timbuktu: Shindouk Mohamed Lamine, chief of the Berabish Oulad Najim, and his wife Miranda Dodd offered valuable help and information while providing hospitality at their home and hotel, Sahara Passion, on the edge of the desert.

The libraries and librarians of the British National Archives, the Royal Geographical Society, Yale University, Trinity College, Wesleyan College, and Central Connecticut State University were indispensable to this book. I am especially grateful to Susan Applegate at the Boston Public Library, who offered to digitize one of the rare copies of Gustav von Schubert's biography of Barth, making possible the fluid translation by Jaime McGill, who was both quick and conscientious.

The Notes make clear my gratitude to many scholars and writers, especially the British authors who tended Barth's low flame for many years: Benton, Bovill, Prothero, Rodd, and, above all, Anthony Kirk-Greene.

I am indebted to Ryszard Kapuścińksi, whose brief comments about Barth in his book *The Shadow of the Sun* first drew my attention to the explorer.

During a conversation about another book subject, my agent, Deborah Grosvenor, jumped on my casual mention of Barth and persuaded me to drop the planned project and pursue the obscure German traveler. She was right, too.

Star Lawrence, my editor at W. W. Norton, saw the subject's potential and gave me the space (and the advance) to explore it. Melody Conroy smoothed countless bumps during the editorial process. Copy editor Fred Wiemer saved me from several embarrassments.

As always, my wife Judith Kaufman has been an endless source of encouragement and balm.

Notes

All quotations from Barth's *Travels and Discoveries in North and Central Africa* are taken from the three-volume edition published by Frank Cass & Co. in 1965, a facsimile reprint of the edition published in the United States by Harper & Brothers from 1857 to 1859. This edition is available digitally.

Chapter 1: Preparations

I took much of the biographical information about Barth's life before the African expedition from Gustav von Schubert's *Heinrich Barth, der Bahnbrecher der deutschen Afrikaforschung; ein Lebens- und Charakterbild auf Grund ungedruckter Quellen entworfen* (Heinrich Barth, Trailblazer in German Research of Africa: A Portrait of His Life and Character Based on Unpublished Sources), published in 1897. Von Schubert was Barth's brother-in-law and one of his few close friends. His book is still considered the best biography, but it is rare and exists only in German. It has now been digitized, thanks to Susan Applegate at the Boston Public Library. The translation used here is by Jaime McGill and was commissioned by me.

Biographical materials about Barth in English are scarce and scanty. The exception is A. H. M. Kirk-Greene's 70-page biographical introduction in *Barth's Travels in Nigeria* (Oxford University Press, 1962), a book of edited extracts from Barth's account. Kirk-Greene, who served as a British district officer in Nigeria (Adamawa and Bornu) before his eminent academic career at Oxford, has been Barth's main champion in English. Between the late 1950s and early 1970s he wrote half a dozen essays about the explorer. His frequent appearance in these endnotes indicates my debt to him.

For a discussion of nineteenth-century science education in the universities of Britain and Germany, see Paul Kennedy's *The Rise of the Anglo-German Antagonism, 1860–1914* (Humanity Books, 1988), pp. 116–118.

Chapter 2: Invitation to Africa

For background on Britain in the Sahara, see especially *Britain, the Sahara, and the Western Sudan, 1788–1861* (Oxford University Press, 1964), by A. Adu Boahen; *Prelude to Imperialism: British Reactions to Central African Society, 1840–1890*, by H. Alan C. Cairns (Routledge & Kegan Paul, 1965); and *The Image of Africa*, by Philip D. Curtin (University of Wisconsin Press, 1964). Boahen also writes about Richardson's antislavery missions in the 1840s. For Palmerston's views on commerce, see Kenneth Bourne's *Palmerston: The Early Years, 1784–1841* (Free Press, 1982).

Richardson's two-volume account of his first trip to the Sahara is *Travels in the Great Desert of Sahara, in the Years of 1845 and 1846,* published in 1848.

Quotations from Foreign Office correspondence throughout the book come from the massive bound volumes about the Central African Expedition in the British National Archives: FO 101/23, FO 101/26, FO 101/30, FO 101/34, FO 101/36, and FO 101/45. Quotations from other correspondence related to the expedition were taken from many different files in the archives of the Royal Geographical Society in London.

Chapter 3: At the Edge of the Desert

For the brutality of the Saharan slave trade, the dispatches from Murzuk, and the friction between Richardson and Crowe, see Boahen, pp. 127–31, 151, 166–75.

For Muslim treatment of slaves, see Ronald Segal, *Islam's Black Slaves* (Farrar, Straus & Giroux, 2001), especially pp. 36–39.

For Lyon on Tripoli, see his *A Narrative of Travels in Northern Africa* (London, 1821), p. 10. For Nachtigal on Tripoli, see his *Sahara and Sudan: Tripoli and Fezzan, Tibesti or Tu,* vol. 1, trans. by Allan G. B. Fisher and Humphrey J. Fisher (Harper & Row, 1974), p. 137. For Richardson on Tripoli, see his *Travels in the Great Desert of Sahara,* vol. 1 (London, 1848), p. 93.

All quotations from Richardson about the Central African Expedition come from his journal, sent home after his death by Barth and published as *Narrative of a Mission to Central Africa,* 2 vols. (London, 1853).

Crowe's comments appear in letters in the FO volumes.

The hadith attributed to Al-Suyuti can be found in, among other sources, *Lit-*

eraturgeschichte der Araber: Von ihrem Beginne bis zu Ende des zwölften Jahr-hunderts der Hidschret (Literary History of the Arabs from Their Beginning to the End of the Twelfth Century), by Joseph Baron von Hammer-Purgstall (1850), vol. 1, p. xli. A similar saying, "The ink of the scholar is more precious than the blood of the martyr," can be found in *Tuhfat al-Fudala* by the renowned Tim-buktu scholar, Ahmed Baba (1556–1627), who was probably quoting Al-Suyuti. Baba is quoted by Souleymane Bachir Diagne in "Toward an Intellectual History of West Africa: the Meaning of Timbuktu," in *The Meanings of Timbuktu*, ed. Shamil Jeppie and Souleymane Bachir Diagne (HSRC Press, 2008), p. 27.

Chapter 4: First Steps

Spellings of African places and names are notoriously various, the result of phonetic guessing. For instance, Richardson's interpreter is referred to variously as Yusuf, Yusef, Yousef, and Youseff, with a last name of Moknee, Mukni, Muck-eni, and Mokumee. Murzuk has also been spelled Murzuq, Mourzuk, Morzouk, and Murzuch. There's Timbuktu, Timbuctoo, Tombouctou, and so on. Barth fur-ther complicates things by his excessive use of diacritics, most of which I have dropped. I also use the typical North African spelling for the name of Islam's founder—Muhammed—rather than Mohammed, as used by Barth.

For the Sahara, see especially *Sahara: The Great Desert*, by E. F. Gautier (first published in 1928), and *The Golden Trade of the Moors*, E. W. Bovill (Oxford University Press, 1968, reprint of 1958 edition).

For Lyon on the south wind, see his *Narrative*, p. 133.

The quotation from Hershel comes from Richard Holmes's *The Age of Won-der* (Pantheon, 2008), p. 443, a study of what Holmes calls the era of "Romantic science."

For a stimulating discussion of caravan travel, see Johannes Fabian, *Out of Our Minds: Reason and Madness in the Exploration of Central Africa* (Univer-sity of California Press, 2000).

Chapter 5: Stalled in Murzuk

Income for the pasha of Murzuk, see Hornemann, *The Journal of Frederick Hornemann's Travels, from Cairo to Mourzouk, the Capital of the Kingdom of Fezzan, in Africa, in the Years 1797–98* (W. Bulmer & Co., 1802), p. 68.

The men and women of Murzuk, see Hornemann, pp. 72–73, and Lyon, p. 336. For red pepper, see Hornemann, p. 73.

Boahen includes much useful information about Gagliuffi.

About the amounts paid to Ghat Tuaregs and others in later chapters: in mid-nineteenth-century Africa, the terminology of currency and the exchange rates can be confusing. For hard currency, Spanish dollars and Maria Theresa dollars from Austria were widespread, equivalent, and standard. Five Spanish dollars equaled one British pound sterling. There was also something called the Fezzan riyal (Barth) or real (Richardson) or rial, based on the Spanish dollar and Spanish reales (eight reales equaled one dollar, hence the famous "pieces of eight"). Based on the figures given in Barth's and Richardson's journals, a Spanish dollar was worth about 1.25 riyals and a British pound was worth 7.25 riyals. As Barth moved through Africa, the types of currency changed, for instance to cowries or strips of cotton cloth, as did the exchange rates.

Chapter 8: Plundered

For the Kel Fadey and the "eyrie of vultures," see "Lords of the Waste: Predation, Pastoral Production, and the Process of Stratification Among the Eastern Tuaregs," by Candelario Sáenz in *Chiefdoms: Power, Economy, and Ideology*, ed. Timothy Earle (Cambridge University Press, 1991, reprinted 1997), pp. 100–18.

When I asked my host in Timbuktu, a Berabish chief named Shindouk Mohamed Lamine ould Najim, about various Tuareg words mentioned by Barth, to see whether they are still in use, "tebulloden" elicited a chuckle and a nod. In some Tuareg tribes, girls once were compelled to overindulge in milk and meat to increase their girth and desirability. Yet the Tuareg had nothing on the Karagwe in eastern Africa. According to James Bruce, the wives of their king, Rumanika, were forced by a man with a whip to drink milk incessantly, and were so obese they couldn't stand up, wriggling to move across the floor. See Alan Moorehead, *The White Nile* (Harper, 1960), p. 47.

The origin and meaning of the word "Tuareg" is unsettled. In addition to the historical meaning cited, Tuareg has been attributed to an old Arabic word meaning "inhabitant of Targa," perhaps once a Tuareg name for the Fezzan in southern Libya.

"Tuareg" comes in many alternate spellings: Tawarek (Barth), Tuarick (Richardson), Touareg (French), and Twareg, among others. The same is true for the Tuaregs' name for themselves: Imoshagh (Barth), Imohag, Imohagh, Imashaghen, Imuhagh, Imajaghan, Imajughen, and Imazaghan are a few of the variations. The Tuaregs' language is usually but not always spelled Tamasheq, Tamashek, or Tamajaq.

The section on the Tuaregs draws especially from *The Pastoral Tuareg: Ecology, Culture, and Society* (2 vols.), by Johannes Nicolaisen and Ida Nicolaisen (Thames & Hudson, 1997); *People of the Veil*, by Francis Rennell Rodd (Lord Rennell of Rodd) (Anthropological Publications, 1970, first printed in 1926);

The Conquest of the Sahara, by Douglas Porch (Knopf, 1984); and *Tribes of the Sahara,* by Lloyd Cabot Briggs (Harvard University Press, 1967). Also helpful were Bovill's *The Golden Trade of the Moors; The Last Caravan,* by Thurston Clarke (Putnam, 1978); and *Azalaï,* by John Skolle (Harper's, 1956). The anthropologist quoted is Henri Schirmer, taken from Porch, p. 65.

A sample of Tuareg poetry and its three main themes, translated by Charles de Foucauld and quoted in *The Pastoral Tuareg,* p. 161:

> *My white camel, O woman with white teeth*
> *I swear by God, it shall not go raiding, shall not leave you*
> *It shall not go away from you to another country*
> *I lead it to the pastures only to visit you with love again*
> *Neither in dreams nor in thought*
> *Shall it go away from you to another country.*

Barth predicted that their camp on the outskirts of Tintellust would henceforth be called the "English Hill" or the "Hill of the Christians." Francis Rennell Rodd, a British explorer who traveled in Aïr in the 1920s, wanted to visit Tintellust to look for traces of Barth, whom he called "perhaps the greatest traveler there has ever been in Africa." Tintellust wasn't on any map, but Rodd's guide knew the village and took him there. As they reached the outskirts, the guide pointed out a place called "the House of the Christians." When Rodd asked why, the guide said that in the olden days three white Christians, not French, had come to Tintellust—not as conquerors, but as friends of Chief Annur—so the thatch huts where they camped had never been inhabited or pulled down. All that remained of the camp, noted Rodd, were "the traces of two straw huts and a shelter, a wooden water trough, and some broken pots." And, of course, the name. *People of the Veil,* pp. 308–13, and also Rodd's reminiscence in the *Geographical Journal,* vol. 124, no. 3, (September 1958), pp. 330–31.

In 2005, Julia Winckler, a British photographer fascinated by Barth, traveled to Tintellust. She, too, was shown Barth's old encampment. A story persists there, says Winckler, that Barth buried treasure nearby, and the villagers still occasionally dig for it. Winckler documented her visit to Agadez and Tintellust with photographs and videos: www.retracingheinrichbarth.co.uk.

Chapter 10: Desert Port

Rodd's *People of the Veil* has a helpful discussion of Agadez and other Sahelian entrepôts.

Kirk-Greene points out that Barth collected so much information not only because of his linguistic skills and omnivorous curiosity, but because he didn't neglect anyone as a source of information. Kirk-Greene adds that the list of people mentioned by Barth as informants is exceptionally long, and that "even trivial acquaintances are described with sensitivity." The reason, he says, is that Barth had little of the "stereotyped Western impatience with the African's 'lack of intelligence' and 'unreliability.' Instead many references and anecdotes imply an understanding of and affection for the people among whom he lived." From "Heinrich Barth: An Exercise in Empathy," in *Africa and Its Explorers*, ed. Robert I. Rotberg (Harvard University Press, 1970). Also helpful on this subject is "Dr. Heinrich Barth as a Diplomatist and Philanthropist," by E. A. Ayandele, in his *African Historical Studies* (Frank Cass, 1979).

For music in Islam, see *The Garland Handbook of African Music*, ed. Ruth M. Stone (Garland, 2000) and "Music and Islam in Sub-Saharan Africa," by Eric Charry, in *The History of Islam in Africa*, eds. Nehemia Levtzion and Randall L. Pouwels (Ohio University Press, 2000).

In *Out of Our Minds*, Johannes Fabian notes that for African explorers, the sense of hearing was the one most likely to be assaulted, because they had no control over the noise around them, especially from drums and other instruments. He also points out that most explorers and early ethnographers rejected African music and dance as immoral, and therefore ignored them as unworthy of consideration.

Rodd comments that Barth's description of Tuareg men leaving the town to defecate is an example of how his "capacity for meticulous observation depended on never missing an opportunity, however strange, of acquiring information."

Emgedesi or Emghedeshie, the distinctive dialect of Agadez, was extinct by the early twentieth century.

In addition to Barth's and Richardson's descriptions of the salt caravan to Bilma, see Bovill and Nicolaisen. Bovill mentions Bilma's singing peak and relates it to the well-known phenomenon of the desert's famous "singing sands."

Tebu is also sometimes spelled Toubou, Tibbu, Tibu, Tubu, Tebou, and Tibboo (Richardson).

A sidelight: *Beau Geste*, P. C. Wren's popular 1924 novel about a troop of French Foreign Legionnaires besieged by Tuaregs in a desert town, is set in Agadez.

Chapter 11: Separate Ways

Clapperton's observations can be found in vol. 2 of *Narrative of Travels and Discoveries in Northern and Central Africa: In the years 1822, 1823, and 1824*, by Dixon Denham, Hugh Clapperton, and Walter Oudney (John Murray, 1826).

Mungo Park, *Travels in the Interior of Africa*, two volumes (Cassell & Co., 1893, reprint edition).

"The absence of news from the outside world seems to have afflicted the explorers almost more than any other hardship," writes Alan Moorehead. "In the hope of finding mail at some outlandish spot they would rouse themselves from their illnesses and march for weeks or even months on end. . . ." *The White Nile*, p. 107.

The burr that Barth called karengia has other names in different parts of Africa, including kram-kram, uzak, and niti. By any name, it's a torment.

Denham noted that people in Bornu sometimes ran down young ostriches and made them pets. He also described how ostriches were hunted. The hunter looked for eggs and then buried himself nearby. When the ostrich returned and settled on the eggs, the hunter jumped up and shot it with an arrow, preferably in the head to keep from damaging the valuable feathers. "Ostriches have a most extraordinary aversion, from nature, to a pregnant woman," continued Denham, "and a sensibility to discovering when such a person is near them, quite astonishing: they will make directly toward her, and, with lifted feet and menaces, oblige her to withdraw. I have even known them single out a woman so situated in the street, and following her to her own door, beat her with their long beaks, and the whole time hissing with the greatest agitation and anger."

Chapter 12: "The Celebrated Emporium of Negroland"

Locusts: Nachtigal, vol. 2, pp. 195–96; Livingstone, *Missionary Travels and Researches in South Africa*, chap. 2; Hornemann, p. 59.

Cowries: some of the prices for goods are taken from *West African Travels and Adventures: Two Autobiographical Narratives from Northern Nigeria*, translated and annotated by Anthony Kirk-Greene and Paul Newman (Yale University Press, 1971), p. 106.

Usman dan Fodio and the nineteenth-century jihads: "The Fulani Jihad: a Reassessment," by Marilyn Robinson Waldman, *Journal of African History*, 3, 1965, pp. 333–55; *A History of Islam in West Africa*, by J. Spencer Trimingham (Oxford University Press, 1962); *Rural and Urban Islam in West Africa*, ed. Nehemia Levtzion and Humphrey J. Fisher (Lynne Rienner, 1987); *West Africa and Islam*, by Peter B. Clarke (Edward Arnold, 1982); Boahen, *Britain, the Sahara, and the Western Sudan; Islam in Africa*, ed. James Kritzeck and William H. Lewis (Van Nostrand–Reinhold, 1969). *Cambridge History of Africa, c.1790–c.1870*, vol. 5, ed. John E. Flint (1976).

The exchange between al-Kanemi and Bello about books is quoted by S. A.

Albasu in "Islamic Learning and Intellectualism in Katsina Outside the Birni: The Yandoto Experience," *Islam and the History of Learning in Katsina,* ed. Ismail Abubakar Tsiga and Abdalla Uba Adamu (Ibadan: Spectrum, 1997).

Barth mentions Kano's dye-pits and tandem cloth-beaters, both of which still operate. Today's residents of Kano take their cotton robes to the beaters the way Westerners take shirts to the cleaners. The beaters pound the cloth with wooden mallets whose heads are as big as a gallon of paint. Central Africans believe that beating the cloth in this way preserves the cotton fibers and gives the cloth a silken glitter, in contrast to ironing, which injures and dulls the fibers.

Kano's market: the only description that rivals Barth's is Clapperton's in his *Narrative.* Another noteworthy description of Kano is Paul Staudinger's in his *In the Heart of the Hausa States,* 2 vols. (Ohio University for International Studies, 1990, reprinted from 1889). The 500-year-old Kurmi market remains as crowded and fascinating as in Barth's day, with many of the same goods on display alongside newer items such as steel pipes, auto and machine parts of every type, old cell phones, wrecked motherboards, and other digital debris. Herbalists now use a bullhorn to sell their folk remedies for stomach troubles and private rashes. Stinking sludge still chokes the Jakara, with the contemporary additions of engine oil and plastic bottles.

Paper: see "Paper in Sudanic Africa," by Jonathan M. Bloom, in *The Meanings of Timbuktu,* ed. Shamil Jeppie and Souleymane Bachir Diagne (HSRC Press, 2008).

The current emir of Kano, Ado Bayero, lives in the palace, where he maintains a large household that includes sixty concubines and many royal slaves.

In northern Nigeria, as in Barth's day, Sokoto is the locus of religious power, Kano of commercial power. The sultan of Sokoto is still the head of Islam in the region.

Chapter 13: An Ending

The letter from al-Kanemi to Bello is quoted by Trimingham in *A History of Islam in West Africa,* p. 209.

Chapter 14: The Kingdom of Bornu

The introductory audience of Denham, Clapperton, and Oudney—the first Europeans to visit Bornu—with Umar's father, Sheikh al-Kanemi, differed from Barth's. The wide street leading to the palace was lined with spearmen on foot, and cavalrymen stood three-deep at the door. The visitors were kept waiting on their horses in the sun for some time. When allowed to enter, they were stopped by men holding crossed spears, who put a hand on their chests. They finally reached the sheikh's inner chamber. He was sitting in a dark room on a carpet. Two men on each side of him were armed with pistols. Another brace of pistols lay in front of the sheikh. About forty-five at the time, al-Kanemi was dressed simply. With "a benevolent smile" he bid the strangers welcome and asked their purpose. All of the British explorers ended up highly impressed by al-Kanemi's intelligence and hospitality, but occasionally appalled by his harsh justice, especially toward women. The explorers were in Bornu from February 1823 to August 1824.

For the history of Bornu, I consulted Trimingham; *The Shehus of Kukawa: A History of the Al-Kanemi Dynasty of Bornu,* by Louis Brenner (Oxford University Press, 1973); *The Kanuri of Borno,* by Ronald Cohen (Waveland, 1967); *The Sultanate of Bornu,* by Dr. A. Schultze, trans. by P. A. Benton (Frank Cass, 1968, reprint of 1913 edition); and vol. 2 of Nachtigal. Natchigal was also helpful on Bornu's court and public life.

Barth spends twenty arcane pages working out the dates and dynasties of ancient Bornu. It's the sort of tedious scholarship that bored reviewers but shows Barth's astonishing breadth of knowledge about African and Arabic sources.

Brenner notes that the constant gift-giving expected in Africa was often called graft by the British. But he adds: "Gift exchange, however, was not bribery as it is understood in the western context; it was not an extra-official or extra-legal activity. Rather, it was an integral part of the system and was considered not only proper but mandatory for all. No one in Bornu would visit, much less make a request of, his superior, without offering him a gift. Conversely, no man of status would long remain respected if he did not constantly reward his subordinates for their loyalty and services."

For slaves, concubines, and eunuchs, I consulted, among others: Segal; Skolle; Bovill; *Three Nigerian Emirates: A Study in Oral History,* by Victor N. Low (Northwestern University Press, 1972); *The African Diaspora in the Mediterranean Lands of Islam,* by John O. Hunwick and Eve Troutt Powell (Markus Wiener, 2002), chap. 8; *Concubines and Power: Five Hundred Years in a Northern Nigerian Palace,* by Heidi J. Nast (University of Minnesota Press, 2005). Bovill notes that eunuchs existed in Europe for centuries, and adds, "The *Soprani* of the Sistine Chapel, 'the musical glory and moral shame' of the papal choir, were not abolished until late in the nineteenth century, but the gelding of boys continued in Italy for some time after that." The tradition of harems continues. For instance, in addition to his allotment of four wives, the current emir of Kano has about sixty concubines. Nast notes that business relationships in Kano are sometimes still cemented by the gift of a concubine.

For the slave market and categories, see Richardson, *Narrative*, vol. 2, pp. 202ff., and Nachtigal, vol. 2, pp. 215ff.

Burton: *Lake Regions of Central Africa* (Horizon, 1961), vol. 2, pp. 23–24.

When Umar's father, al-Kanemi, returned from his victorious invasion of Bagirmi (with Umar's future mother in tow), he wrote a passionate song to the concubine he recovered there, who had been taken in Bagirmi's earlier invasion of Bornu. The song runs for hundreds of words in a high romantic style worthy of the troubadors: ". . . the joy, oh, how exquisite! the recovery of my lost love! a part of myself! . . . Her arched eyebrows reaching to her temples, overhanging eyes than which the moon is less bright, as it shines through darkness! large piercing eyes, whose looks could never be mistaken . . . lips sweeter than honey and colder than the purest water! . . . Who shall now tell of my joy? From her shoulder to her waist, how fair is her proportion! When she moves, she is like branches waved by a gentle breeze! Silks from India are less soft than her skin; and her form, though noble, is timid as the fawn! Let this my joy be proclaimed to all my people!" Translated by Denham and included in his account, vol. 2, app. XIV, pp. 409–10.

The Yedina/Budduma: Denham and Schultze were helpful.

In 1893 the renegade warlord Rabeh sacked and burned Kukawa. Seven years later the French explorer Ferdinand Foureau reached the site and wrote, "The present appearance of [Kukawa] is one of infinite sadness. . . . the crumbling walls, already covered with creepers, the broken huts, and the human skulls which strew the earth amongst broken pottery and gaping, dried-up walls." Quoted in Brenner.

Today, Kukawa is a small dusty place. White visitors are still rare and, based on my experience, not especially welcome. The aged governor declined to answer questions, denied a request to walk around town, and essentially told me to keep moving. Nevertheless, two helpful residents showed me the former location of the sheikh's palace. The once-towering clay walls are now modest cinder block. The walls surround mostly sand, but there's also a cinderblock building, not much bigger than a large garage, with a tin roof. Inside are two crumbling mud-brick mounds with squat wooden doors—the graves of al-Kanemi and Umar. In the sandy wastes west of town is a forlorn memorial: a kuka, supposedly the capital's namesake tree, enclosed by a low broken wall. Barth wrote that al-Kanemi chose the spot for his new capital because of a young baobab tree there. I heard a refinement of this local legend: the tree now inside the broken wall was a sapling when the adolescent al-Kanemi used to lean against it and dream of glory, which is why he later chose this spot for the new capital of Bornu. It's a pleasing story flawed only by impossibility; the sheikh spent his boyhood far from Kukawa.

After the allied European forces defeated Rabeh, the British assumed control of Bornu. The regional capital was moved to Maiduguri, 80 miles south, where the sheikh built a handsome new palace. According to a story that echoes the one about al-Kanemi's founding of Kukawa, the sheikh proclaimed that he would walk around Maiduguri reciting the Qur'an, and would build his new palace wherever he finished. The moment occurred beneath a tamarind tree that still grows in one of the palace's courtyards. The current sheikh of Bornu continues the unbroken line of direct descent from al-Kanemi and Umar.

Chapter 15: A Mystery Solved

Helpful on Adamawa: Hunwick, Boahen, Trimingham, and especially Kirk-Greene's "Barth's Journey to Adamawa," in *Heinrich Barth: Ein Forscher in Afrika, Leben-Werk-Leistung*, ed. Heinrich Schiffers (Franz Steiner Verlag GMBH, 1967). Kirk-Greene ends his essay, "In original discovery, geographical, historical, and linguistic, Barth has no peer in the annals of Fulani history."

Barth's quote about learning Fulfulde comes from the "Introductory Remarks" to his *Collection of Vocabularies of Central-African Languages* (Justus Perthes, 1862). Barth considered his trip to Yola disappointing in some respects, but linguistically it was rich. For instance, he noticed that the Batta language was related to the Marghi and Zani languages, and also sometimes resembled the Musgu language, "which itself is related to the various dialects of Kotoko. All these languages have some general points of affinity to the South African languages."

The passage from Barth's Preface to the German edition is quoted by Kirk-Greene in his article on Barth's empathy.

For earlier river expeditions up the Niger, Curtin and Boahen were helpful. Dickens's essay, "The Niger Expedition," appeared in *The Examiner* on August 19, 1848, and was reprinted in *Miscellaneous Papers*.

The many spellings and names of the Niger and Benue rivers suggest the unsettled state of geographic knowledge about these river systems. The Niger was also called the Isa, Quorra, Kworra, and Kwara. The Benue was called the Shary, Shari, Tchadda, and Chadda. Lake Chad was also spelled Tschad and Tchad.

Kirk-Greene comments that Barth's description of the Benue "stands in the annals of West African exploration alongside Mungo Park's classic account of his first glimpse of the Niger."

Gold in the Benue: after Barth's dispatch about Adamawa reached England, John Hogg, a British naturalist and member of the Royal Society, wrote, "the country of *Adamawa* may hereafter become as celebrated for this precious metal as *California* and parts of Australia are in this *new golden age*." "Notice of Recent Discoveries in Central Africa by Drs. Barth and Overweg . . . ," from *Transactions of the Royal Society of Literature*, vol. IV, new series (November 19, 1851), p. 4.

For a fuller account of the *Lord Palmerston*, see "What Became of the Boat?" by Kirk-Greene, *West Africa*, May 23, 1959, pp. 489–90. Nobody knows the answer to his question.

My description of Eid al-Fitr also draws upon Nachtigal's report, which is much fuller than Barth's: vol. 2, pp. 279–84. See Denham as well for several wonderful descriptions of Bornu's cavalry and army.

For a fuller account of the treaty signed by Bornu and Britain, see "The British Consulate at Lake Chad," by Kirk-Greene, *African Affairs*, October 1959, pp. 334–39.

The long-standing enmity between Bornu and Wadai included heavy condescension. Islam and its tradition of scholarship reached Bornu 500 years before penetrating Wadai. Consequently the Bornuese, wrote Nachtigal, "were imbued with the arrogance of a civilised people towards barbarians; the latter, on the other hand, . . . despised the decadent conditions and the cowardly camarilla of the neighbouring kingdom." This sounds much like Europe's arrogance toward Africa. Nachtigal illustrates Bornu's attitude toward Wadai with a story then making the rounds in Kukawa: Wadai's king, Ali, during a détente between the kingdoms, requested a fine horse from the stable of Aba Bu Bekr, Sheikh Umar's oldest son. Aba Bu Bekr allegedly replied to Ali that "if he needed an animal to ride, to climb on the back of his mother."

On the other hand, when Bornuese traveled to the Mediterranean or did the haj, it was their turn to endure arrogance. Haj Beshir, the vizier, went to Mecca in 1843, where "he had an opportunity both of showing the Arabs near the coast that the inhabitants of the interior of the continent are superior to the beasts," wrote Barth, "and of getting a glimpse of a higher state of civilization than he had been able to observe in his own country."

Chapter 16: "The Horde of the Welad Sliman"

The modern spelling for the nineteenth-century tribe of mercenary Arabs is variously Walid, Ouled, Oulad, or Uelad, sometimes followed by Soliman or Suliman.

Rodd's comment about waterskins: *People of the Veil*, p. 232.

The Kanuri and some Fulani peoples clean their milk bowls with cow urine, imparting a tang to the milk. They believe this practice keeps the milk from going sour for several days without affecting the taste. Barth disagreed. So do Tuaregs. "The taste of urine is detested by the Tuareg," writes Nicolaisen, "who know this taste all too well as the water drawn from pools and wells is frequently flavored with urine and the excrement of domestic animals."

For the section on the raiding party, I have also drawn on the more melodramatic account given from memory by the youth named Dorugu, at that time a servant of Overweg (and later of Barth). It can be found in *West African Travels and Adventures*, cited in the notes for chap. 12.

Chapter 17: Razzia

I have been unable to locate Ptolemy's "*Mandros oros,*" which seems so familiar to Barth and Haj Beshir.

Denham's account of the razzia parallels Barth's—the capture of women and children, the massacre of the mature males, the burning of villages. Eduard Vogel, who followed Barth into Central Africa, accompanied Sheikh Umar on a slave raid to Musgu in spring of 1854, and sent an account to the Foreign Office in which he says he saw "much useless cruelty towards the prisoners, 36 of whom were on one occasion cut to pieces alive. Of the 4000 slaves carried off, all women and children under twelfe [*sic*] years of age, I regret to state that 3500 died of dysentery and small-pox before the army reached Kouka. The army consisted of about 20,000 horsemen with 10,000 camp-followers, accompanied by about 5000 camels and as many bullocks."

Barth's prediction that the Musgu would be exterminated was wrong. They survive, principally in Cameroon.

Chapter 18: Captive in Bagirmi

For the history of Bagirmi, Denham, Brenner, and Trimingham were helpful additions to Barth.

Barth's close observations of ants may remind some readers of Thoreau's similar inclination. Another link: when Barth's *Travels* was published in the United States in 1859, Thoreau read it carefully, according to *Thoreau as World Traveler*, by John Aldrich Christie (Columbia University Press, 1965).

Chapter 19: Letters From Home

For Palmerston's relationship with Queen Victoria, see *Lord Palmerston*, by Herbert C. F. Bell, 2 vols. (Longmans, Green, 1936). The information about the donations raised by Bunsen comes from von Schubert.

Chapter 20: Resurrection and Death

The vocabularies of twenty-four dialects that Barth collected were enclosed with a letter to William Desborough Cooley from Kukawa in 1852 but were lost for sixty years. They were found in a Foreign Office file in 1910 by a British district officer named P. A. Benton who served in northern Nigeria. Benton became fascinated with Barth and turned into a productive part-time scholar. See *The Languages and Peoples of Bornu: Being a Collection of the Writings of P. A. Benton* (Frank Cass, 1968), with a valuable introduction by Kirk-Greene.

The correspondence between Barth and Cooley is collected in the British Library, "Letters of Barth to William Desborough Cooley," ADD. MSS 32117E. More information about Cooley can be found in Curtin, but the preeminent source is *The Negroland Revisited: Discovery and Invention of the Sudanese Middle Ages*, by Pekka Masonen (Academia Scientiarum Fennica, 2000). Masonen writes that Cooley and Barth represent a brief "golden age in the [European] historiography of Western Africa," before "the ideological turning point" of the 1860s, when the attitudes of colonial imperialism began distorting accounts of Africa and Africans.

Barth sent many examples of African craftsmanship back to Britain, but I could find no trace of them at the British Museum or the British Library.

The section on Overweg's death also draws on the account of his servant Dorugu in *West African Travels and Adventures* (which also appears in von Schubert), and on Kirk-Greene's "The Death and Burial of Adolf Overweg," *West African Review*, no. 378 (March 1959), pp. 227–28. Years after Overweg died, a chief named Maimana, the grandson of Overweg's servant Abbega, was asked by the British to recover the explorer's remains. He went to Maduwari and found an eighty-year-old woman who knew about the gravesite. The British dug, found Overweg's bones, and took them to Maiduguri, the new regional capital of Bornu, where they were reburied in the small European cemetery.

Chapters 21: Westward

Helpful for these chapters: *The Sokoto Caliphate,* by Murray Last (Humanities Press, 1967); *Social History of Timbuktu: The Role of Muslim Scholars and Notables,* by Elias N. Saad (Cambridge University Press, 1983); *The Hidden Treasures of Timbuktu: Rediscovering Africa's Literary Culture,* ed. John O. Hunwick and Alida Jay Boye (Thames & Hudson, 2008); and Albasu.

Dorugu's accounts about his father and the trek through the wilderness of Gundumi can be found in *West African Travels and Adventures.*

Chapter 22: The Prospect of the Niger

Tazyīn al-Waraqāt, edited and translated by M. Hiskett (Ibadan University Press, 1963).

Tarikh al-Sudan is sometimes spelled *Tarikh es Sudani.* The passage quoted from the work is taken from *African Civilization Revisited,* by Basil Davidson (Africa World Press, 1991).

Chapter 23: "Obstructed by Nature and Infested by Man"

The anecdote about Clapperton's couriers comes from Wellard's *The Great Sahara.*

The proverb about hyenas comes from *Hausa Ba Dabo Ba Ne: A Collection of 500 Proverbs,* trans. by A. H. M. Kirk-Greene (Oxford, 1966).

Caillié's book is *Travels Through Central Africa to Timbuctoo* (1830, 2 vols.). A few of the many books that treat him: *The Quest for Timbuctoo,* by Brian Gardner (Harcourt, 1968); *Africa Explored: Europeans in the Dark Continent, 1769–1889,* by Christopher Hibbert (Norton, 1982); *The Slaves of Timbuktu,* by Robin Maugham (Harper & Brothers, 1961); *The Race for Timbuktu,* by Frank T. Kryza (HarperCollins, 2006); *Hearts of Darkness,* by Frank McLynn (Carroll & Graf, 1992).

Chapter 24: Golden City

In addition to the books cited above for Caillié, see also Bovill; Briggs; Saad; Hunwick and Boye; *The Gates of Africa: Death, Discovery and the Search for Timbuktu*, by Anthony Sattin (St. Martin's Press, 2005); *The Primitive City of Timbuktu*, by Horace Miner (Oxford University Press, 1953); and *Imperial Eyes*, by Mary Louise Pratt (Routledge, 1992). The quote from Barrow appears in Sattin. The poem from Baba appears in Hunwick and Boye.

Chapter 25: In Timbuktu

The house where Barth stayed is now marked by a bronze plaque. It is privately owned, but one room is a museum with some posters about Barth's route and accomplishments. The house has been extensively remodeled since Barth's stay and doesn't conform to the floor plan printed in *Travels and Discoveries*, but the Sankore mosque remains visible from the terrace. The sheikh's house, unmarked and shaded by two acacia trees, is still catercornered across a tiny square. Plaques also mark the houses where Laing and Caillié stayed.

Barth's remark that it was better not to know how much time separated him from home was echoed by Nachtigal, who also didn't expect to spend five years wandering Africa:

> If I had known then that my fate would keep me back for more than five years in the unknown regions of the mysterious continent, would I perhaps have had the courage to go forward with my plan? To endure complete intellectual isolation for more than five years in the midst of severe privations, oppressive austerity, pitiless disease and threatening dangers is more than even the most ardent enthusiasm cares to bring upon itself. Later, indeed, far from the feverish haste of European life and its manifold pleasures, one learns to judge time and space differently, and becomes less demanding in one's purposes, more tenacious in carrying out one's plans, more patient in endurance and in suffering.
>
> Bodily resilience, the strength to withstand disease and fatigue, the natural gift for mixing with men of all types in the midst of that strange world, are the indispensible conditions with which the exploring traveler must be endowed. Patience, however, is the virtue which holds the secret of success. To practice it is often not easy and I had to fight my way through many a hard struggle before, to some extent puri-

fied in this respect, I was able to find my way through men's folly and untrustworthiness.

Kunta is sometimes spelled Kounta, and Bakkay is also spelled Bakkai. Helpful sources about this interesting clan: Saad; Boahen; Hunwick and Boye; "The Economics of Islam in the Southern Sahara: The Rise of the Kunta Clan," by E. Ann McDougall, in Levtzion and Fisher; "The Nineteenth-Century Jihads in West Africa," by M. Hiskett in *Cambridge History of Africa*, vol. 5, ed. John E. Flint (1976); and "The Expansion of Islam," by J. Spencer Trimingham in Kritzeck and Lewis.

The quotations from al-Bakkay's reply to Ahmadu Ahmadu are taken from translations in *Travels and Discoveries* (vol. 3, app. VIII), and Boahen.

Attitudes about skin color in Africa go back at least 2,500 years, when lighter-skinned Egyptians reviled darker-skinned Nubians as uncultured savages. Gradations of skin color are part of cultural and racial identity. Northern Africans—Arabs, Berbers, Tuaregs, Moroccans—often have dark skin but call themselves white and may assume themselves racially superior to black Africans. Similarly, black Africans from the Sudan don't consider themselves truly black. My guide in northern Nigeria, a Fulani, remarked that in contrast to the Fulanis and Hausas, the Kanuris were black. In Timbuktu my dark-skinned Songhai guide, while describing the city's many ethnic groups and tribes, said that the Buzus—blacks descended from slaves—"aren't white like me." The Janjaweed, today's murderous raiders in southern Sudan, have black skin but are descended from Islamic Arab tribes, so their war cry as they attack black tribes (now Christian rather than pagan) is "Kill the slaves!" Similarly, the Janjaweed's tactics resemble the vizier's of Bornu during a razzia—shoot, kill, rape, loot, and then burn everything to debilitate survivors.

Chapter 26: Stuck

For Davidson, James Wellard, *The Great Sahara*.
For tobacco, Saad.

Chapter 27: Released, More or Less

The excerpted letters about Vogel appear in Benton.
Hourst's sprightly account was published in English as *French Enterprise in Africa*, trans. by Mrs. Arthur Bell (Dutton, 1899).

Chapter 28: Rumors and Consequences

For the overthrow and restoration of Umar, and the assassination of Haj Beshir, I have drawn on Nachtigal, Brenner, Schultze, and the letters of Vogel in Benton.

Popular accounts of African exploration sometimes get untethered from the facts. In the sparse literature about Barth, one of the most amusing examples occurs in René Lecler's chapter on the explorer in *World Without Mercy* (Werner Laurie, 1954). Once a popular author of books about the Sahara, Lecler inflates the meeting of Barth and Vogel to the level of Stanley's discovery of Livingstone. For his next exaggeration he says Barth sat on the ground and wept when the two met. After Barth dried his eyes, continues Lecler, Vogel treated him to "the best dinner he had eaten in years" (the two men shared Barth's coffee) and then they "sang old German *lieder* together" (not a chance). And finally, concludes Lecler, they spent a week enjoying each other's company in a Chadian village (they parted after two hours and were nowhere near Chad). Lecler's exaggerations stem from admiration: "In terms of exploration no single man ever equaled Henry Barth's magnificent journey."

Sometime after Barth met Vogel, the village of Bundi evidently migrated to a new location, not unusual in Africa. In December 1854, Bundi was about 15 miles northwest of the town of Nguru in Nigeria. Nowadays, Bundi is about 185 miles east of there and 70 miles southwest of Kukawa.

The quote from the German edition of *Travels and Discoveries* comes from *The Great Age of Discovery*, by Paul Herrmann (translated from German by Arnold J. Pomerans; Harper, 1958). Herrmann is often interesting on the methods and motives of explorers but is prone to overstatement. He writes that Barth was "enticed back to Africa time after time," which is true only if that phrase means "twice." To increase drama he says that Richardson died "some days earlier" than Overweg—yes, some 570 days. He describes the ambassador sent from Bornu to Tripoli as a "naked black minister," which is both inaccurate and condescending, and puts this man in Tripoli in 1849, before Barth even arrived there. But then Herrmann also has the expedition leaving Tripoli on March 24, 1848, two years too soon. He also says Barth was probably the first white man to reach Kano, though Clapperton left a famously detailed account of his visit. And he writes that the teenaged servants of Overweg and Barth, Dorugu and Abbega, "settled down in the small Thuringian capital of Gotha," an exaggeration that verges on fabrication—Barth briefly hosted the youths in Germany.

Chapter 29: Getting Out

This account of the bad feelings between Vogel and Church draws on a series of letters in the British National Archives.

The doggerel about the marriage of Victoria and Albert was quoted by Martin Filler in his essay about them, "The Most Happy Couple," in *The New York Review of Books*, August 19, 2010, p. 67. The attitude survives. Princess Diana, notes Filler, "privately referred to her royal in-laws as 'the Germans.'"

Chapter 30: Problems at Home

Shaw's remarks about English geographers and German cheese, and Barth's heated remarks before the Geographical Society of Berlin, appear in Kirk-Greene's biographical essay about Barth. Shaw's dislike of Germans and of Barth in particular must have been well known. Someone named Charles Lewell wrote two letters to Shaw from Berlin in 1859. "I saw Dr. Barth several times," said the first, "he looks more dirty than ever _ entre nous soit dit _." The second letter noted, "I never met with a more disagreeable fellow as that D. Barth. He looks dirtier than ever." Lewell obviously knew that Shaw would enjoy such malicious comments. From the archives of the Royal Geographical Society.

As late as 1930 the Royal Geographical Society was claiming, incorrectly, that it supported Barth financially in Africa. See *The Record of the Royal Geographical Society, 1830–1930*, by Hugh Robert Mill (Royal Geographical Society, 1930).

That other candidates for the RGS Gold Medal felt Barth was most deserving appears in a letter written by Lieutenant General Charles R. Fox, "on the claims of Dr. Barth for a Gold Medal," written May 7, 1856, and found in the RGS archives.

Chapter 31: Last Journeys

For an interesting discussion of the book's illustrations, as well as some biographical tidbits about Barth, see "The Painting and the Pen: Approaches to Heinrich Barth and His African Heritage," by Achim von Oppen, in *Heinrich Barth et l'Afrique*, ed. Mamadou Diawara et al. (Cologne: Köppe, 2006), pp. 105–41. "There is virtually no trace of a cultural landscape," writes von Oppen of Bernatz's illustrations. "This squarely contradicts Barth's account...." Barth was von Oppen's great-great-granduncle. Von Oppen is a professor of African history in Germany.

The section on Livingstone and *Missionary Travels* draws mostly upon Hibbert and upon Louise Henderson's " 'Everyone Will Die Laughing': John Murray and the Publication of David Livingstone's *Missionary Travels*," published by Livingstone Online: http://www.livingstoneonline.ucl.ac.uk/companion.php ?id=HIST2. I am indebted to Henderson for *The Ladies' Repository*.

Rawlinson's comment about Stanley and Livingstone is found in Cairns.

On the racialist theories of Barth's time, Curtin and Masonen are helpful. Curtin is especially cogent on Dr. Robert Knox and his influence, and on the racial underpinnings of British imperialism. Curtin calls Barth "the least prejudiced, least culture bound of all the travelers to Africa."

Masonen suggests that Barth has been marginalized for two main reasons. First, the tendency of British and American scholars to ignore continental Europe as irrelevant (Masonen is Finnish). Second, the difficulty of fitting Barth and his openness to African cultures into the postcolonial theories that have dominated academia since Edward Said's *Orientalism*. See Masonen's review of *Heinrich Barth et l'Afrique* in *Africa*, vol. 81, no. 2 (2011), pp. 342–44.

The section on the delegation from Timbuktu relies on von Schubert, Boahen, and Kirk-Greene in addition to letters from the archives of the Foreign Office.

Hegel's remarks on Africa and history appeared in *The Philosophy of History*, trans. J. Jibree (Dover, 1956), p. 93. More than a century later the Oxford historian Hugh Trevor-Roper repeated Hegel's sentiment: "Perhaps in the future there will be some African history to teach. But at the present there is none; there is only the history of Europeans in Africa. The rest is darkness, and darkness is not the subject of history." *Rise of Christian Europe* (Thames & Hudson, 1964), p. 9.

The account of Barth's death relies primarily on von Schubert and Kirk-Greene. Kirk-Greene, contradicting von Schubert and other sources, says Barth died on November 26.

Epilogue

The quote from Hunwick comes from "Secrets of the Sahara," by Christopher Reardon, *Ford Foundation Report*, Summer 2003.

Selected Bibliography

Ayandele, E. A. *African Historical Studies* (Frank Cass, 1979).

Barth, Heinrich. *Collection of Vocabularies of Central-African Languages* (Justus Perthes, 1862).

———. *Travels and Discoveries in North and Central Africa*. 3 vols. (Frank Cass & Co., 1965, facsimile reprint of the edition published in the United States by Harper & Brothers, 1857 to 1859).

Bell, Herbert C. F. *Lord Palmerston* (Longmans, Green, 1936).

Benton, P. A. *The Languages and Peoples of Bornu* (Frank Cass, 1968).

Boahen, A. Adu. *Britain, the Sahara, and the Western Sudan, 1788–1861* (Oxford University Press, 1964).

Bourne, Kenneth. *Palmerston: The Early Years, 1784–1841* (Free Press, 1982).

Bovill, E. W. *The Golden Trade of the Moors* (Oxford, 1968, reprint of 1958 edition).

———. "Henry Barth." *Journal of the African Society*. Vol. XXV (July 1926), pp. 311–20.

———, ed. *Missions to the Niger*. 4 vols. (Hakluyt Society, 1965).

Brenner, Louis. *The Shehus of Kukawa: A History of the Al-Kanemi Dynasty of Bornu* (Oxford University Press, 1973).

Briggs, Lloyd Cabot. *Tribes of the Sahara* (Harvard University Press, 1967).

British National Archives, Central African Expedition: FO 101/23, FO 101/26, FO 101/30, FO 101/34, FO 101/36, and FO 101/45.

Burton, Richard Francis. *Lake Regions of Central Africa* (Horizon, 1961).

Cairns, H. Alan C. *Prelude to Imperialism: British Reactions to Central African Society, 1840–1890* (Routledge & Kegan Paul, 1965).

Caillié, René. *Travels Through Central Africa to Timbuctoo.* 2 vols. (London, 1830).

Carlyle, Thomas. "Occasional Discourse on the Nigger Question" (T. Bosworth, 1853).

Christie, John Aldrich. *Thoreau as World Traveler* (Columbia University Press, 1965).

Clarke, Peter B. *West Africa and Islam* (Edward Arnold, 1982).

Clarke, Thurston. *The Last Caravan* (Putnam, 1978).

Cohen, Ronald. *The Kanuri of Borno* (Waveland, 1967).

Cooley, Desborough. *The Negroland of the Arabs Examined and Explained* (London, 1841).

Curtin, Philip D. *The Image of Africa: British Ideas and Action, 1780–1850* (University of Wisconsin Press, 1964).

Davidson, Basil. *African Civilization Revisited* (Africa World Press, 1991).

Denham, Dixon, Hugh Clapperton, and Walter Oudney. *Narrative of Travels and Discoveries in Northern and Central Africa: In the Years 1822, 1823, and 1824.* 2 vols. (John Murray, 1826).

Diawara, Mamadou, et al., eds. *Heinrich Barth et l'Afrique* (Cologne: Köppe, 2006).

Dickens, Charles. "The Niger Expedition." *The Examiner,* August 19, 1848, reprinted in *Miscellaneous Papers.*

Earle, Timothy, ed. *Chiefdoms: Power, Economy, and Ideology* (Cambridge University Press, 1991, reprinted 1997).

Fabian, Johannes. *Out of Our Minds: Reason and Madness in the Exploration of Central Africa* (University of California Press, 2000).

Filler, Martin. "The Most Happy Couple." *New York Review of Books,* August 19, 2010.

Flint, John E., ed. *Cambridge History of Africa, c. 1790–c. 1870,* vol. 5 (Cambridge University Press, 1976).

Gardner, Brian. *The Quest for Timbuctoo* (Harcourt, 1968).

Gautier, E. F. *Sahara: The Great Desert* (Octagon, 1970; first published in 1928).

Godlewska, Anne, and Neil Smith, eds. *Geography and Empire* (Blackwell, 1994).

Henderson, Louise. "'Everyone Will Die Laughing': John Murray and the Publication of David Livingstone's *Missionary Travels*," published by Livingstone Online: http://www.livingstoneonline.ucl.ac.uk/companion.php?id=HIST2.

Herodotus. *The Landmark Herodotus: The Histories.* Edited by Robert B. Strassler (Anchor, 2009).

Herrmann, Paul. *The Great Age of Discovery.* Translated by Arnold J. Pomerans (Harper, 1958).

Hibbert, Christopher. *Africa Explored: Europeans in the Dark Continent, 1769–1889* (Norton, 1982).

Hiskett, Mervyn. *The Sword of Truth: The Life and Times of the Shehu Usuman Dan Fodio* (Oxford, 1973).

———, ed. and trans. *Tazyīn al-Waraqāt* (Ibadan University Press, 1963).

Holmes, Richard. *The Age of Wonder* (Pantheon, 2008).

Hornemann, Frederick. *The Journal of Frederick Hornemann's Travels, from Cairo to Mourzouk, the Capital of the Kingdom of Fezzan, in Africa, in the Years 1797–98* (W. Bulmer & Co., 1802).

Hourst, Lieut. *French Enterprise in Africa.* Translated by Mrs. Arthur Bell (Dutton, 1899).

Hunwick, John O., and Eve Troutt Powell. *The African Diaspora in the Mediterranean Lands of Islam* (Markus Wiener, 2002).

Hunwick, John O., and Alida Jay Boye, eds. *The Hidden Treasures of Timbuktu: Rediscovering Africa's Literary Culture* (Thames & Hudson, 2008).

Jeppie, Shamil, and Souleymane Bachir Diagne, eds. *The Meanings of Timbuktu* (HSRC Press, 2008).

Johnston, Hugh Anthony Stevens. *The Fulani Empire of Sokoto* (Oxford University Press, 1970).

Jones, Adam. "Barth and the Study of Africa in Germany," in *Heinrich Barth et l'Afrique.* Edited by Mamadou Diawara et al. (Cologne: Köppe, 2006), pp. 241–49.

Kennedy, Paul. *The Rise of the Anglo-German Antagonism, 1860–1914* (Humanity Books, 1988).

Kirk-Greene, A. H. M., ed. "Barth's Journey to Adamawa." In *Heinrich Barth: Ein Forscher In Afrika, Leben-Werk-Leistung,* ed. Heinrich Schiffers (Franz Steiner Verlag GMBH, 1967).

———, ed. *Barth's Travels in Nigeria* (Oxford University Press, 1962).

———. "The British Consulate at Lake Chad," *African Affairs,* October 1959, pp. 334–39.

———. "The Death and Burial of Adolf Overweg," *West African Review,* no. 378, (March 1959), pp. 227–28.

———. *The Emirates of Northern Nigeria,* with S. J. Hogben (Oxford, 1966).

———, trans. *Hausa Ba Dabo Ba Ne: A Collection of 500 Proverbs* (Oxford, 1966).

———. "Heinrich Barth: An Exercise in Empathy," in Rotberg.

———. "That Indefatigable African Traveler," *West Africa*, December 20 and 27, 1958.

———. *West African Travels and Adventures: Two Autobiographical Narratives from Northern Nigeria*. Translated and annotated by Anthony Kirk-Greene and Paul Newman (Yale, 1971).

———. "What Became of the Boat?" *West Africa*, May 23, 1959, pp. 489–90.

Kritzeck, James, and William H. Lewis, eds. *Islam in Africa* (Van Nostrand-Reinhold, 1969).

Kryza, Frank T. *The Race for Timbuktu* (HarperCollins, 2006).

Last, Murray. *The Sokoto Caliphate* (Humanities Press, 1967).

Lecler, René. *World Without Mercy* (Werner Laurie, 1954).

Levtzion, Nehemia, and Randall L. Pouwels, eds. *The History of Islam in Africa* (Ohio University Press, 2000).

Levtzion, Nehemia, and Humphrey J. Fisher, eds. *Rural and Urban Islam in West Africa* (Lynne Rienner, 1987).

Livingstone, David. *Missionary Travels and Researches in South Africa* (London, 1857).

Low, Victor N. *Three Nigerian Emirates: A Study in Oral History* (Northwestern University Press, 1972).

Lyon, Captain G. F. *A Narrative of Travels in Northern Africa* (London, 1821).

Masonen, Pekka. *The Negroland Revisited: Discovery and Invention of the Sudanese Middle Ages* (Academia Scientiarum Fennica, 2000).

Matar, Nabil. *Turks, Moors, and Englishmen in the Age of Discovery* (Columbia University Press, 2000).

Maugham, Robin. *The Slaves of Timbuktu* (Harper & Brothers, 1961).

McLynn, Frank. *Hearts of Darkness* (Carroll & Graf, 1992).

Mill, Hugh Robert. *The Record of the Royal Geographical Society, 1830–1930* (Royal Geographical Society, 1930).

Miner, Horace. *The Primitive City of Timbuktu* (Oxford University Press, 1953).

Moorehead, Alan. *The Blue Nile* (Harper & Row, 1962).

———. *The White Nile* (Harper & Row, 1960).

Nachtigal, Gustav. *Sahara and Sudan*. 4 vols. Translated by Allan G. B. Fisher and Humphrey J. Fisher (Harper and Row, 1974).

Nast, Heidi J. *Concubines and Power: Five Hundred Years in a Northern Nigerian Palace* (University of Minnesota Press, 2005).

Nicolaisen, Johannes, and Ida Nicolaisen. *The Pastoral Tuareg: Ecology, Culture, and Society*. 2 vols. (Thames & Hudson, 1997).

Oppen, Achim von. "The Painting and the Pen: Approaches to Heinrich Barth and His African Heritage," in *Heinrich Barth et l'Afrique*. Edited by Mamadou Diawara et al. (Cologne: Köppe, 2006), pp. 105–41.

Palmer, Sir Richmond. *The Bornu Sahara and Sudan* (Negro Universities Press, 1970).

Park, Mungo. *Travels in the Interior of Africa*. 2 vols. (Cassell & Co., 1893, reprint edition).

Porch, Douglas. *The Conquest of the Sahara* (Knopf, 1984).

Pratt, Mary Louise. *Imperial Eyes: Travel Writing and Transculturation* (Routledge, 1992).

Prothero, R. Mansell. "Barth and the British." In *Heinrich Barth: Ein Forscher in Afrika, Leben-Werk-Leistung*. Edited by Heinrich Schiffers (Franz Steiner Verlag GMBH, 1967), pp. 164–83.

———. "Heinrich Barth and the Western Sudan." *Geographical Journal*, vol. 124, no. 3, (September 1958), pp. 324–39.

Raby, Peter. *Bright Paradise: Victorian Scientific Travelers* (Princeton University Press, 1997).

Richardson, James. *Narrative of a Mission to Central Africa*. 2 vols. (London, 1853).

———. *Travels in the Great Desert of Sahara, in the Years of 1845 and 1846* (London, 1848).

Robinson, David. *Muslim Societies in African History* (Cambridge University Press, 2004).

Rodd, Francis Rennell (Lord Rennell of Rodd). *People of the Veil* (Anthropological Publications, 1970; first printed in 1926).

Rotberg, Robert I., ed. *Africa and Its Explorers: Motives, Methods, and Impact* (Harvard University Press, 1970).

Royal Geographical Society: Archives.

Saad, Elias N. *Social History of Timbuktu: The Role of Muslim Scholars and Notables* (Cambridge University Press, 1983).

Sattin, Anthony. *The Gates of Africa: Death, Discovery, and the Search for Timbuktu* (St. Martin's Press, 2005).

Schubert, Gustav von. *Heinrich Barth, der Bahnbrecher der deutschen Afrikaforschung* (Berlin: D. Reimer, 1897).

Schultze, Dr. A. *The Sultanate of Bornu*, translated by P. A. Benton (Frank Cass, 1968, reprint of 1913 edition).

Segal, Ronald. *Islam's Black Slaves* (Farrar, Straus & Giroux, 2001).

Skolle, John. *Azalaï* (Harper's, 1956).

Staudinger, Paul. *In the Heart of the Hausa States*. 2 vols. (Ohio University for International Studies, 1990, reprinted from 1889).

Stone, Ruth M., ed. *The Garland Handbook of African Music* (Garland, 2000).

Trimingham, J. Spencer. *A History of Islam in West Africa* (Oxford University Press, 1962).

Tsiga, Ismail Abubakar, and Abdalla Uba Adamu, eds. *Islam and the History of Learning in Katsina* (Ibadan: Spectrum, 1997).

Villiers, Marq de, and Sheila Hirtle. *Sahara: the Extraordinary History* (Walker & Co., 2002).

———. *Timbuktu* (Walker & Co., 2007).

Waldman, Marilyn Robinson. "The Fulani Jihad: A Reassessment." *Journal of African History*, vol. 3 (1965), pp. 333–55.

Wellard, James. *The Great Sahara* (Dutton, 1965).

Index

Page numbers beginning with 371 refer to notes.

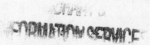